Underground Warfare
1914-1918

Underground Warfare
1914-1918

Simon Jones

Pen & Sword
MILITARY

First published in Great Britain in 2010 by
Pen & Sword Military
an imprint of
Pen & Sword Books Ltd
47 Church Street
Barnsley
South Yorkshire
S70 2AS

Copyright © Simon Jones, 2010

ISBN 978 1 84415 962 8

Printed and bound in the UK by
MPG Books

Pen & Sword Books Ltd incorporates the Imprints of
Pen & Sword Aviation, Pen & Sword Maritime, Pen & Sword Military,
Wharncliffe Local History, Pen and Sword Select, Pen and Sword Military Classics,
Leo Cooper, Remember When, Seaforth Publishing and Frontline Publishing.

For a complete list of Pen & Sword titles please contact
PEN & SWORD BOOKS LIMITED
47 Church Street, Barnsley, South Yorkshire, S70 2AS, England
E-mail: enquiries@pen-and-sword.co.uk
Website: www.pen-and-sword.co.uk

Contents

To Nicola with love

List of Plates

1. The British siege exercise at Chatham in July 1907.
2. A French miner at the face of demi-galerie G5, Beta salient, Carency.
3. German miners in chalk, Somme.
4. German mine gallery, Hooge, Ypres Salient, late 1916 or early 1917.
5. A French officer uses a geophone to detect the sounds of German mining.
6. The opposing lines and mine-riven no man's land of Éparges ridge.
7. The aftermath of a German mine blow viewed from their side of the Éparges ridge.
8. Vauquois, 16 June 1916.
9. Sapper William Hackett of Mexborough, Rotherham.
10. The explosion of 40,600lbs of ammonal by 252 Tunnelling Company beneath Hawthorn Ridge.
11. General Plumer, Major General Harington and Lieutenant General Byng.
12. Lieutenant Colonel Mike Watkins MBE lifts a bag of ammonal explosive from a 6,500lb mine charge.
13. A German electrical boring machine used for dugout construction.
14. Men of the German 148th Infantry Regiment in a tunnel 15m below ground in the Champagne area in 1917.
15. 'To the last penny.' A well-stocked canteen store.
16. The Grange Subway, one of twelve infantry communication tunnels prepared prior to the assault on Vimy Ridge in April 1917.
17. A German dugout.
18. A scene in a German dugout at 9m depth.
19. Bunks in the main gallery of Martha House Dugout, 1996.
20. The shaft to the Vampir dugout excavated by the Association for Battlefield Archaeology and Conservation in 2008.
21. A stepped incline entrance to a British dugout system at Ravine Wood.

Abbreviations

1/Pi 30	1st Company of the 30th Rhineland Pioneers
ANZAC	Australian and New Zealand Army Corps
BEF	British Expeditionary Force
cm	Centimetres (1cm = 0.39in)
CO	Commanding Officer
CRE	Commander Royal Engineers
ft	Feet (1ft = 0.30m)
GHQ	General Headquarters
GS	General Staff
GSO	General Staff Officer
HSS	German Army self-contained breathing apparatus *(Heeres Sauerstoff Schutzgerät)*
in	Inches (1in = 2.54cm)
kg	Kilogramme (2.2lb)
LAC	Library and Archives Canada
lb	Imperial pound (0.45kg)
LLR	Line of least resistance
M	Metres (1m = 3.28ft)
MG	Machine Gun
MGC	Machine Gun Corps
NA	British National Archives, Kew
OC	Officer Commanding
OP	Observation Post
RE	Royal Engineers
REL	Royal Engineers Library
REM	Royal Engineers Museum
RF	Royal Fusiliers
SEM	Service Électromécanique
SHAT	French Army archives, Service Historique de la Défense, Département de l'armée de Terre
t	Metric tonnes (1t = 0.98 imperial long ton)
TOCA	Tunnellers' Old Comrades Association
WD	War Diary
yd	Yards (1yd = 3ft = 0.91m)

Glossary

Ammonal
: Ammonium nitrate-based commercial blasting explosive, safer and more powerful than gunpowder, adopted in 1915 as the standard British mining explosive.

Camouflet
: Explosive charge intended to destroy an enemy tunnel, which is not of sufficient power to cause a crater.

Cheddite
: A blasting explosive adopted by the French for mining.

Chevaux-de-frise
: Crossed pointed iron stakes generally used with barbed wire for defensive purposes.

Clay-kicking
: Method of digging small tunnels quickly and silently through clay, imported into the British Army by sewer tunnellers.

Common mine
: Explosive charge which has just sufficient charge to form a crater on the surface.

Cordeau detonant
: Detonating cord used for simultaneous firing of large charges.

Countermine
: Tunnels dug to defend against enemy mines.

Demi-galerie
: Standard French mine gallery, dimensions 1.30 to 1.50m high by 1m wide

Firestep
: Raised step on the trench wall facing the enemy, which enables the defender to fire out of the trench.

Gaize
: Sandstone which comprises the Vauquois ridge.

Geophone
: Instrument used to magnify underground vibrations as sound waves.

Grafting tool
: Type of spade used for clay-kicking.

Guncotton
: Nitro-cellulose explosive used by the British Army for demolitions.

Gunpowder
: Traditional explosive comprising saltpetre, sulphur and charcoal, used for military mining until 1915.

Incline
: Sloped entrance to a tunnel used as an alternative to a vertical shaft.

Line of least resistance
: The distance of a mine to the surface, used to calculate whether it would form a crater.

Mine
: Explosive charge laid underground, or the tunnel in which that charge is laid.

Overcharged mine
: Explosive charge which has more than sufficient charge to

	form a crater on the surface and which forms in addition lips of debris.
Proto	British self-contained breathing apparatus capable of lasting 45 minutes.
Push pick	Tool used for working in clay.
Radius of rupture	The globe around an explosive charge in which damage will be caused to mine workings.
Rameaux de combat	French attack branch gallery measuring 0.80m by 0.65m.
Russian sap	A shallow underground gallery which could be converted into a trench by breaking down the top cover.
Salvus	British self-contained breathing apparatus capable of lasting 30 minutes.
Sap	A trench dug towards a point to be attacked (sometimes used for a mine gallery).
Sapper	Generic term for a military engineer, also the basic rank of a member of the Royal Engineers.
Seismomicrophone	Electrical version of the geophone.
Spiling	Sheet piling technique used for working in sandy ground.
Stollen	German term for mine gallery or tunnel, also sometimes used for a tunnelled dugout.
Tamping	The backfilling of a mine tunnel to prevent the force of the explosion being directed back down the tunnel in which it was laid.
Tramming	Use of wheeled trolleys to remove spoil and carry forward explosives.
Transversal	Defensive tunnel dug parallel to the front line trench, used for listening and as a starting point for listening and attack galleries, also called a lateral.
Tubbing	Steel cylindrical sections used for sinking shafts in wet ground.
Westfalit	Ammonium nitrate-based commercial blasting explosive and one of several brands adopted by the Germans.

Preface

Trench warfare during 1914 to 1918 was fought as much beneath the ground as above it. Tunnelling offered a means of bypassing the machine guns and field defences, while underground shelters provided a refuge from shells. The deep networks of tunnels were the secret domain of the men who created them and their mystery, and perhaps also the close-knit nature of miners, means that this work has remained little-known.

Only three significant books have appeared since the end of the First World War on the British mining effort, with the exception of technical publications. The Old Comrades Association of the British Tunnelling Companies produced a history, *Tunnellers* (1936), written by one of their officers, the mining engineer William Grant Grieve. Grieve made use of a large number of accounts submitted by his fellow officers, now alas lost, and was given comprehensive access to the records being used by the British Official Historian of the Army. It remains the most comprehensive account of British mining operations during the First World War. The publisher, however, brought in a popular writer, Bernard Newman, to enliven the style and remove some of the technical details. Newman had served as a Staff Sergeant in the Army Service Corps on the Western Front, but had gained a reputation as a military authority on the basis of a novel imagining what would have happened if the war had been fought the right way, as opposed to the way that it was actually conducted. Newman seems to have brought this simplistic perspective to parts of *Tunnellers* and those parts which now feel most dated may be ascribed to his rewriting.

In the late 1950s Alexander Barrie wrote *War Underground*, his first full-length book, using interviews with a number of surviving tunnellers and, like Grieve, access to still secret War Office records (on the condition that he made no reference to having seen them!). Barrie's intended focus was the Battle of Messines, but the remarkable stories that he was told led him to try to tell the whole story. Although unreferenced, his research stands up well to modern scrutiny and the interview transcripts are now in the Royal Engineers Museum.

Beneath Flanders Fields, which appeared in 2004, was the work of three well-qualified authors: a film-maker with a long-term interest in underground warfare, a geologist, and a mining engineer resident in the Ypres Salient who has spent many years exploring surviving tunnels and dugouts. The book is highly recommended for understanding the British mining effort in Flanders, not least for the significance of geology and for British tunnelling methods and dugout construction.

Important as these three works are, however, none examines underground warfare in the context of the rapid evolution of fighting methods on the Western Front. Moreover, almost nothing has been written in English describing the French and German mining efforts, or presenting them alongside those of the British. The purpose of this book is to assess the military effectiveness of this antique means of warfare, which was elevated through mass civilian participation and modern technology to the point where it seemed to offer a solution to the deadlock. The text of this book is dispassionate and detached: the personal testimony of individuals is included to convey that underground warfare was, despite the use of technology, fundamentally dependent on human skill, courage and endurance.

Time and space has prevented me from covering the no less remarkable mine warfare of the Vosges and Italian fronts. I am grateful to Mrs Margaret Heese for permission to quote and use illustrations from the diary of her father, Cyril Lawrence, published as *The Gallipoli Diary of Sergeant Lawrence of the Australian Engineers – 1st A.I.F. 1915*. It has proved impossible to contact copyright holders of other quoted material which may still be in copyright. I would like to extend my thanks to staff at the Royal Engineers Museum and Library, and at Special Collections at the Sydney Jones Library, University of Liverpool and the National Archives, Kew. I am also grateful to Peter Barton, Nick Evans, Peter Lane, Chris McCarthy, Lieutenant Colonel Philip Robinson, Johan Vandewalle and the Amis de Vauquois for their help.

Simon Jones, Liverpool, August 2009

Chapter 1

Military Mining Before 1914

The attack of a fortress by mining is recorded in the ninth century BC. A tunnel was driven beneath the walls and the soil replaced by timber props, which were then destroyed by burning, causing the walls to collapse. Mining was usually resorted to when artillery had failed and was a slower, but ultimately more certain, method of reducing a fortress. In the first century AD the Roman writer Vitruvius described methods of attacking fortress walls. At ground level covered protection, such as a 'testudo', or tortoise, was used against projectiles thrown from above to enable the walls to be attacked with hand tools or a battering ram. Where mining was employed he described the burnt-prop method to bring down walls and also the use of a tunnel to emerge inside the fortress or walled town, from which attacking soldiers issued to surprise the garrison. This technique was used by the Romans to end their nine-year siege of Veii in 396 BC.[1] Sometimes the knowledge that the walls of a fortress were undermined was sufficient for the garrison to capitulate, as at Marqab in 1285 when the Knights of St John surrendered after being shown the extent to which Egyptian miners had tunnelled beneath their great tower.[2] Defences against mining incorporated into fortresses included ready-dug countermines and a deep and wide water-filled ditch. A breach in the walls was so often decisive in breaking a siege that in medieval times it became a convention that the garrison of a castle or fortress might surrender with honour once their walls were breached, whereas if they continued to resist quarter would not be shown and the castle could be sacked.

In fifteenth-century Italy there occurred the only major technological change in military mining from antiquity until 1914, when gunpowder replaced the burning of props to bring down walls. This greatly increased the power and potential of mining, as walls would now not just collapse, but be hurled into the air along with the defenders. Gunpowder also enabled miners to engage in warfare beneath the ground, attacking their opponents' tunnels by exploding charges, called camouflets, to collapse them, which did not break the surface of the ground. The increased danger to the user entailed by gunpowder saw the rise of regulations to cover mining and, during the seventeenth century, highly sophisticated and standardized forms of fortifications and the means of assault were developed. The French emerged as the masters of siege craft, with the engineer Vauban the dominant figure. The usual method of approach by the besieger was to dig a trench, known as the first parallel, 600 to 700m from the fortification. This was at a distance far enough away for the trench not to be enfiladed (i.e. fired along the length of) by the defenders and earthworks were then thrown up in front for siege artillery to begin firing. Under cover of these guns engineers began to dig approach trenches, known as saps (hence the term 'Sapper' for a military engineer), towards the fortress. These were in a zigzag pattern to reduce the effect of enfilade fire. At about 300m from the fortress, a second parallel was dug and new artillery emplacements prepared. From this range the guns could begin to batter a breach in the walls. The defenders might attempt sorties to spike the attackers' guns. If the artillery assault was not successful, the besiegers continued sapping forwards, by now under small-arms fire, to within a few metres of the walls, or a ditch or moat surrounding the fortress, and constructed a third parallel. If the artillery was still unable to smash gaps in the walls, mining would begin.[3]

A well-designed fortress incorporated a system of tunnels surrounding its walls designed to detect the mines of the attackers, known as countermines (the term 'mine' being used for both the explosive charge and the tunnel from which it was laid). Camouflets would be used to destroy the attackers' mines, but the defenders were restricted in the size of charge that they could use, for fear of destroying their own defences. The distance at which a charge was likely to damage an opponent's tunnel was known as the 'radius of rupture'. Mines that were powerful enough to break the surface of the ground to form a crater were known as 'common mines'. The distance of a mine from the surface, used to calculate whether it would break surface, was the line of least resistance (LLR). To prevent the blast of a mine being directed down the tunnel in which it was laid, the tunnel would be extensively backfilled in a process called 'tamping'. In the late seventeenth century formulae for the sizes of charges were developed by Vauban and Mesgrigny, followed by Belidor, who carried out trials in 1725. His calculations were not accepted in France, but were taken up by Prussia and used at the Siege of Schweidnitz in 1762, where the Prussians blew mines of up to 2,500kg. The Russians gained much experience during the Russo-Turkish War in 1828 and at Brailov fired two mines of 4,000kg, although with only partial success, as the huge quantity of debris thrown up buried the junction box, preventing the next set of mines from being blown and also ultimately hampering the Russian advance. It was thus not just size that mattered: mines also had to be coordinated with the attack. The Russians used this experience during the most significant mining of the nineteenth century, in the Crimean War during the Siege of Sebastopol. Against a Franco-British attack the Russian chief engineer, General Todleben, organized a system of countermines and some twenty mines were blown, varying in size from 550kg to 2,000kg. Mines were driven through a layer of clay beneath hard chalk. Todleben discovered a second layer at about 15m depth, which he used for a deep level system of countermines. He laid a charge of 4,000kg, which was discovered after the fall of Sebastopol; at that depth it would not have been great enough to break the surface.[4]

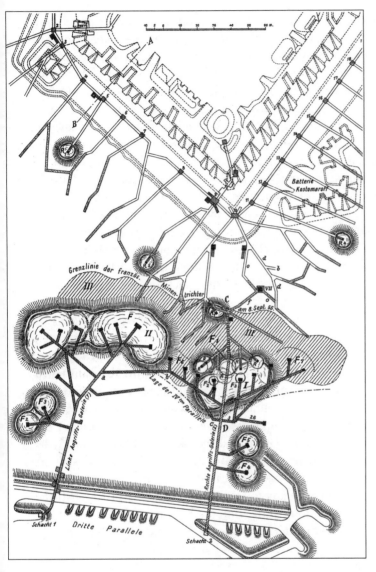

The French mining attack on the Mastbastion at Sebastopol between February and April 1855, launched from the third parallel about 190m from the Russian ditch. Todleben's countermines surround the Mastbastion. (From Zschokke, *Handbuch der militärischen Sprengtechnik* (1911).

The French right attack gallery in the above plan, 0.8m high, has been driven through a clay layer beneath hard chalk at a depth of about 6m but has been broken by heavily overcharged Russian blows.

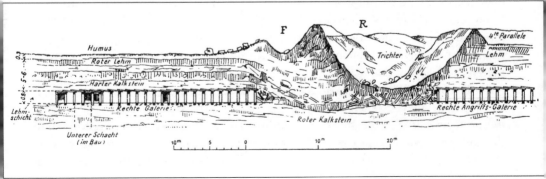

Protracted siege warfare and mining did not, however, play a major part in the Franco-Prussian War of 1870–71, during which the French fortresses were forced to surrender through containment or powerful bombardment. After 1870, the opinion of most artillery and engineer officers in the great military powers was that long-range, large-calibre artillery, especially mortars and howitzers with plunging fire, would always defeat fortresses that previously could be breached only by mining.[5]

By the 1880s it seemed that fortresses had become obsolete, along with the ancient means of assaulting them. There were, however, opposing trends. The Russo-Turkish War had involved a five-month siege of Pleva in 1877, conducted by Todleben. During the American Civil War mining was used against field works rather than a fortress at the siege of Petersburg. A 511ft gallery was driven by the 48th Pennsylvania Infantry, which was both commanded by and composed mainly of coal miners. The unit laid a charge of 3,600kg at 6m depth beneath a Confederate earthwork known as Elliott's Salient, which was blown on 30 July 1864. The mine killed 250 to 350 Confederate soldiers, but in the resulting Battle of the Crater the Union attack was badly coordinated and many of the attackers were trapped in the crater by a counterattack.[6]

There was an unexpected revival of mine warfare during the Russo-Japanese War of 1904–05, especially during the siege by the Japanese of Port Arthur. The position was defended by a ring of concrete forts linked by strong points and entrenchments but, possibly believing that the ground was too hard for mining, the Russians failed to construct an adequate system of countermines. They also lacked tools and only began mining after the Japanese underground attacks had started. By the standards of the Crimean War the mining was unsophisticated and the lack of training of the Russians, who were to suffer defeat, demonstrated that skills could very quickly be lost. The first contact underground demonstrates the Russian lack of skill. A shallow Russian countermine at Fort II (see p17) caved in beneath a shell crater and the tunnel was deepened with a shaft sunk to 4m. From the bottom of the shaft the Russians began a gallery inclined downwards and, on 20 October 1904, they heard noises of Japanese mining. On 26th, after determining the direction of the Japanese attack by listening, the Russians loaded the end of the gallery with 123kg of gunpowder, continuing picking until the last moment to deceive the Japanese. They blew the following day, destroying the Japanese gallery and killing several miners. However, they had miscalculated the weight of the charge, which was probably intended only as a camouflet, and broke surface to form a crater, as well as bringing down part of their own defences and effectively loosening the ground, facilitating the Japanese advance.

By December 1904 charges of 900kg to 1,300kg were used, and on 31 December the Japanese blew 5,000kg of dynamite.[7] High explosives, such as TNT and dynamite, invented in the 1860s, were at least twice as powerful as gunpowder, but did not immediately replace it in mining owing to their high rate of detonation. The war also saw the construction of very strong field fortifications, involving

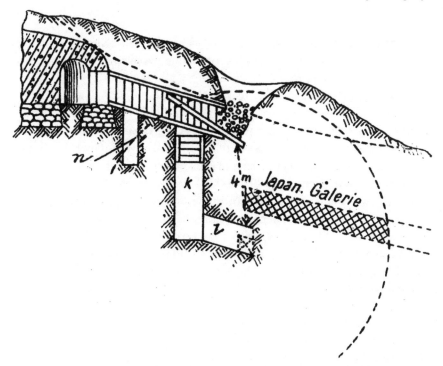

Japanese attack gallery and Russian countermine *k*, October 1904. The dotted line *n* shows the radius of rupture of a Russian charge *l* of 123kg. (From Zschokke, *Handbuch der militärischen Sprengtechnik* (1911).

earthworks, entrenchments and barbed wire, which were so resistant to attack that mining was also used against them. In the winter of 1904-05, when the opponents were facing one another on the banks of the Shaho river 100m apart, the Russians advanced by sapping and mining to capture the Japanese bridgehead. They also attempted this at the village of Li-chia-pu, where the positions were about 300m apart. In the final land action of the war, for three weeks in February to March 1905 until the Russians were forced to fall back, armies of over 300,000 on each side faced each other from entrenchments at Mukden on a forty-mile front.[8]

The Russo-Japanese War led the armies of Europe to pay renewed attention to their ability to conduct a siege. The Germans held extensive siege exercises between 1908 and 1913 and that year issued new regulations. Moreover, the prospect of a war on two fronts against France and Russia led to an extension of the fortress system. Fortress battalions, and pioneer battalions in fortress areas, were given special training in siege operations and in time of war Fortress Pioneer regiments were to be formed. Interest in mining specifically, however, was more lukewarm in Germany. Previously the German mining and fortress warfare regulations contained detailed instructions. These included the use of boring machinery, procedures for listening duties and action on breaking into enemy galleries, where the use of stink balls made of hair, tow and sponge soaked in petrol was advocated.[9] In the years before 1914 an abbreviated form of mining attack was preferred. The German demolition manual of 1911 (*Sprengvorschrift*) and the regulations for fortress warfare of 1913 contained less detailed instructions than previously.[10]

There was a general tendency for technical training to be downplayed in European armies, which was exacerbated by the introduction of conscript armies with short terms of service. In the German pioneers the normal period of service was two years, of which the first was devoted almost entirely to infantry training.[11] Captain Toepfer, a German engineer officer, in assessing the role of technical troops in the Russo-Japanese war, argued in 1906 in the *Kriegstechnische Zeitschrift* that the war showed that it was impossible to assault the field fortifications constructed by the Russians, especially as the artillery preparations were, as a rule, inadequate. Building such extensive field fortifications was an error on the part of the Russians as they became an end in themselves, which imprisoned them: 'they paralyzed action and obscured the view of the objective.' Moreover, such field defences would require the weapons and tactics of siege warfare:

> … it has been demonstrated that a well-fortified position cannot be taken by field-warfare alone. Only a continued fire of heavy artillery and a step-by-step advance of the infantry under the protection of this fire will bring about its fall.

He predicted that there would be a role for the sapper and miner, not only in fortress warfare, but also against such field entrenchments:

> It has been suggested that in fighting against well-fortified field positions a method similar to that of the fight against fortresses is necessary, which will not only bring the artillery, but also the technical troops into action and at the same time bring them recognition.[12]

The Anglo-Boer South African War of 1899-1902 had also shown the difficulty of attacking field fortifications, especially barbed wire. In the years before the First World War, however, responses to the power of such obstacles, entrenchments and the defensive power of the machine gun were countered by doctrines of rapid mobility and moral force. In assessing the German regulations for field fortifications in respect of the experience of the Russo-Japanese war, a commentator in the *Militär Wochenblatt* in 1910 was confident that obstacles used during that war, including wire entanglements and mining, would not feature in a European war. The rapid movement that would characterise a future war would not allow such extensive works to be completed, nor would the adversary display such a passive attitude as the Russians:

> We shall never see a war in Europe like that in Manchuria, still less like that in South Africa. Such extended and strongly fortified positions will never be reproduced in Europe.[13]

This attitude was shared in France, Germany's potential adversary. A French assessment of the German army regulations, revised during 1906–09, contained a brief section on the assault on field fortifications. Heavy fire from howitzers over several days would be joined, at dawn on the day of the assault, by infantry and machine-gun fire, forcing the enemy to burrow in his trenches, during which time the obstacles could be destroyed and the assault delivered. For the author, however, the Germans need not even have considered having to carry out an assault on field or permanent fortifications:

> Such are the principal prescriptions of this very special form of combat, which resembles much more a siege operation than a field operation… In a war between France and Germany we do not anticipate a battle of such nature. The fortified places are already quite numerous, and an army that would shut itself up in a permanent defensive position would be inviting destruction.

The French would never allow themselves to be attacked in such a passive manner: 'Battles in entrenched camps as occurred at Plevna or Mukden will never take place in a war with the French army.'[14]

The French, however, retained, and to some extent updated, their manuals for mining prior to the outbreak of war. These included comprehensive coverage of areas such as shaft sinking, driving of galleries, the construction of charge chambers, the calculation of charges, ventilation, lighting, the use of a range of mechanical boring devices, the preparation and firing of charges and rescue work.[15] The French also included siege warfare practice in their 1913 manoeuvres.[16]

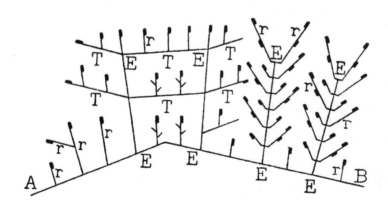

Diagrammatic representation of a scheme of countermines. The listening galleries or écoutes (*E*), 30–40m in length, run from a counterscarp gallery beneath the fortress or from a covering (envelope) gallery (*A–B*). The listening galleries may be linked by transversals (*T*) to improve security and ventilation. Smaller galleries, rameaux de combat, or attack branches (*r*), are run to deal with sounds of the attacker, from which charges may be blown. From the French *Livre de l'officier* of 1908.

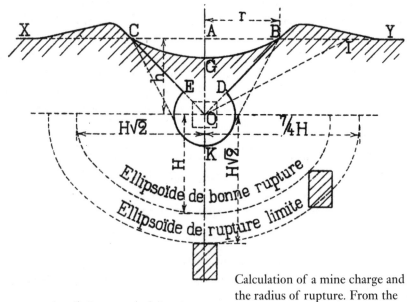

Calculation of a mine charge and the radius of rupture. From the French *Livre de l'officier* of 1908.

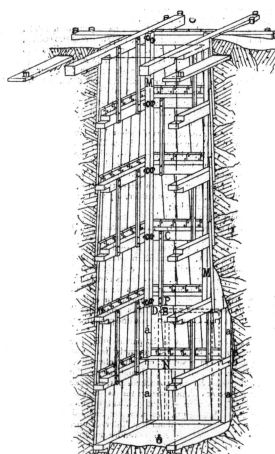

A timbered shaft sunk in easy ground, 1m square, to 6m depth. From the *French Livre de l'officier* of 1908.

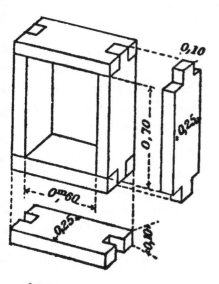

The timbers for the French rameaux de combat, or attack branch gallery, 60cm wide by 70cm high. This was the smallest gallery, designed to be driven quickly towards an enemy mine. From the French *École de Mines* manual of 1909.

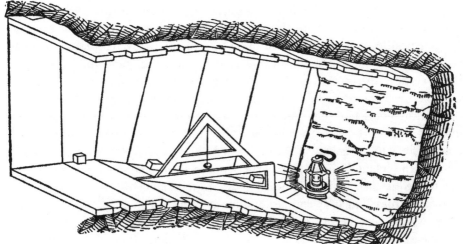

Instruction in change of gradient of a close-timbered mine gallery. From the French *École de Mines* manual of 1909.

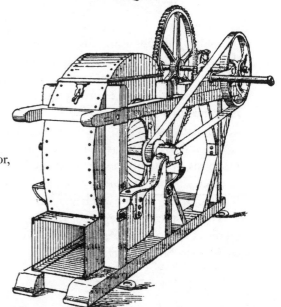

A large French hand-powered mine ventilator, 1879 model. Pre-war equipment proved too noisy for use in trench warfare. From the French *École de Mines* manual of 1909.

In 1907 the British staged their first siege exercise since 1887 at the School of Military Engineering at Chatham. For two months mines were advanced beneath two obsolete forts and a number of charges were fired. These manoeuvres were provoked by the events of the Russo-Japanese war and, in particular:

> ...the want of technical skill shewn by the Japanese troops in their attack on Port Arthur, directed the attention of the English Military Authorities to the great necessity for the instruction of troops in siege warfare, more especially with regard to mining and counter-mining operations, the study of which had been practically neglected for many years. It was thought that the days of mining and of hand grenades were numbered. The recent Russo-Japanese war has, however, clearly demonstrated that this is far from being the case.[17]

The forts around Chatham, though obsolete, were chosen because they possessed many features in common with those around Port Arthur. Following the exercises many practical lessons were reported on. The sappers discovered that in the chalk their galleries could be mainly unsupported by timbering, and that rather than sinking vertical shafts, sloping, inclined galleries started a few yards back were preferable from the point of view of spoil removal and ventilation. Progress was about 2ft an hour, but some men were much more expert than others. It was important to conceal the excavated spoil so that the locations of mine entrances were not given away to the enemy. A former miner who visited the exercise and another serving in the infantry showed that experience enabled men much more clearly to estimate the distances of sounds heard underground. The noise of picking in chalk was distinct from 20m away and just audible at 45m. Footsteps were very clear and the commanding engineer of the defenders recommended the use of rubber or rope-soled shoes, hobnail boots also being dangerous in flinty ground when handling explosives. The small trucks used for removing the spoil were too noisy, and it was recommended that they should have rubber tyres and ball bearings. On several occasions the opposing mine galleries broke into one another, but there was difficulty in deciding who occupied the gallery. It was thought that such cases would not occur in war, as one side or other would probably fire a charge before the galleries actually met. However, the commander of the attacking forces was able, by reference to Vauban's *Traité des Mines* of 1795, to verify that such encounters did occasionally occur and for such eventualities he recommended the use of pistols, knives and grenades, as well as a small shield on wheels.[18] Sophisticated deception measures were employed or suggested, such as the use of work in a shallow tunnel to disguise work at a lower level, and for some men to continue picking to disguise that fact that a gallery was being charged with explosives and tamped.

The most dramatic event of the exercise was the blowing of five charges of 225lbs gunpowder to destroy the sheer counterscarp wall of the defensive ditch, which could then be assaulted. All charges were fired electrically, but there were some

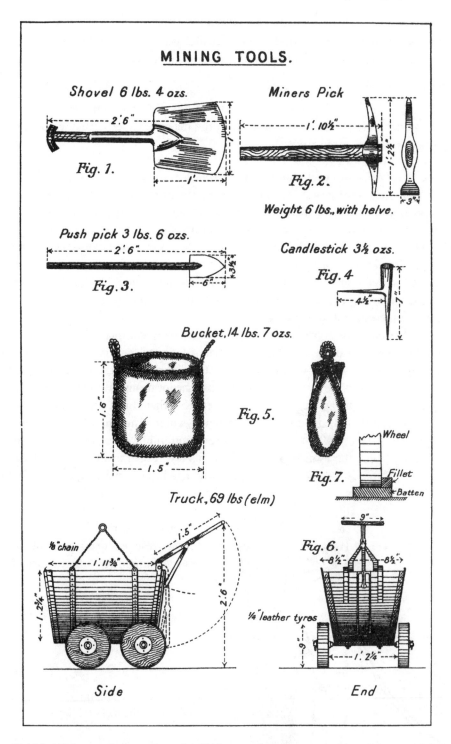

MINING TOOLS.

Shovel 6 lbs. 4 ozs.

2' 6"

1'

Fig. 1.

Miners Pick

1' 10½"

1' 2½"

3"

Fig. 2.

Weight 6 lbs., with helve.

Push pick 3 lbs. 6 ozs.

2' 6"

3½"

6"

Fig. 3.

Candlestick 3½ ozs.

Fig. 4.

4½"

7"

Bucket, 14 lbs. 7 ozs.

1' 6"

1' 5"

Fig. 5.

Wheel

Fillet

Batten

Fig. 7.

Truck, 69 lbs (elm)

⅛" chain

1' 11¾"

1' 2¼"

1' 5"

2' 6"

¼" leather tyres

Fig. 6.

9"

8½"   8½"

9"

1' 2¼"

Side   End

British mining equipment from the 1911 manual, but recognisable to sappers of the Crimean War.

problems with over-sensitive fuses. The largest charge blown was 414lbs, but the gas produced by the explosion hampered the advance of the miners:

> ...it was found that although it was possible to enter the galleries very shortly after the various explosions, yet that directly an attempt was made to go on excavating, the gases confined in the debris escaped, causing nausea, and in one case insensibility.[19]

The standard issue of breathing apparatus for entering the gassy galleries, of which two types were described in the report, was primitive and of no use, and had probably been in store for many years as the rubber was perished. The Denayrouze respirator (see below), designed for entering only a short distance, was a long tube held in the mouth, fitted with a one-way valve which prevented exhaled air being re-inhaled. The air was not pumped, but had to be sucked in by the wearer. The one issued to the defenders was in too poor condition to be tried: '...it does not seem a very efficient arrangement, is most unpleasant to use, and unless each man had his own mouthpiece, most unhygienic.'[20]

The other type, the Applegarth Aérophore (see p25), comprised a copper helmet, resembling that of a diver, to which was attached a water and gas-proof jacket. Air was fed into the helmet with a hand pump. The apparatus was not designed for walking stooped in a mine gallery and the window in the helmet, which also quickly became misted, prevented the wearer from seeing more than a few feet in front: 'Captain Charles, who tried this apparatus, reports that he was very nearly stifled after about two minutes.'[21]

It was recommended that more up-to-date rescue apparatus be obtained. The commander of the attacking

The Denayrouze respirator. From the French *École de Mines* manual of 1909.

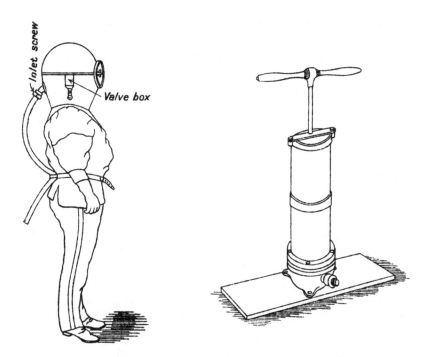

The Applegarth Aérophore, a copper helmet fed by an air pump, already out of date when it was tried at the 1907 siege exercise. When issued in France in 1915 it was mistaken for diving apparatus. From the British 1911 mining manual.

force also recommended that the army again have specialist miners amongst its personnel:

> If, as seems not improbable, mining operations are likely to be frequently undertaken in future wars, I would suggest that the trade of miner should be re-introduced into the Corps of Royal Engineers.[22]

The report of the exercise, printed at Chatham, contained many useful lessons, but as the Chief Instructor in Fortification at the School of Military Engineering on the outbreak of war, R.N. Harvey, recalled: 'Unfortunately the report on these operations was treated as confidential and the lessons derived from the exercise were not generally known.'[23]

Following the exercise the British War Office appointed a committee in 1908 'to consider and report as to the means for maintaining and improving the science of siege warfare.' It recommended that Royal Engineer (RE) units be earmarked as Siege Companies and trained annually in siege exercises.[24] In line with this, the 20th and 42nd Fortress Companies Royal Engineers staged a siege exercise at Lulworth in June 1913, against an earthwork based on part of a fort at Port Arthur. Although not on the scale of the Chatham exercise, practical experience was again gained and a 250lb (113kg) gunpowder charge was blown. The detection of the opposing miners by listening was found to be highly subjective and means were tried to improve the effectiveness: 'One method of listening is to drive a peg in, bite on it and stop your ears.'[25]

A boring tool devised by Captain Rogers was tried, and found to be valuable in soft ground where the mines were within a few feet of one another, but on very stony ground it was said to be hardly worth trying.[26] After blowing a 100lb (45kg) camouflet the danger of carbon monoxide was a nasty revelation:

> As soon as untamping began at the far end of the air space, the officer and men working began to feel giddy and faint; no fumes or smell were observable and a candle burned well; it was probable that carbon monoxide was present, and the Medical Officer and War Office Chemist, who were present confirmed this view. Work had to be stopped, it was resumed next morning, but had to be suspended at once. The Chemist gave it as his opinion that the poisonous gas might remain absorbed in the earth and sandbags for days and even weeks.[27]

The camouflet not forming a crater, there was nowhere for the gas to vent and it remained trapped in the gallery and surrounding strata.

Renewed interest in the problems of siege warfare was reflected by the formation of a siege committee chaired by Major General Hickman, which sat in 1914 to consider the resources needed to attack a German fortress, in particular the heavy artillery requirements. It also considered engineering resources and recommended that gunpowder should remain the standard explosive for mining and that an apparatus for bored mines should be provided. The committee reported in December 1914, by which time events had overtaken it.[28] The war had been in progress four months and trench warfare was established along the Western Front. The impossibility of assailing field fortifications without very high casualties was proven beyond doubt and siege warfare techniques, including sapping and mining, were in progress against them.

The British issued new manuals on Mining and Demolitions and Attack and Defence of Fortresses in 1910. These incorporated some of the lessons of the 1907 exercise, but had not kept up with civilian practice in respect of technology, equipment and explosives. The authors also refused to anticipate that defensive works constructed in the field could be sufficient to stop a determined attack; defences were described as 'storm-proof' where: '...attacking infantry can be destroyed as fast as they can approach, no matter how great their dash and determination.'[29]

Such a work, according to the manual, could 'only be rendered storm-proof by the construction of a deep ditch' a notion later ridiculed by the Royal Engineer Corps History:

> In short: by the methods of the eighteenth century! This too after the South African War, ten years earlier, in which Boer defensive positions consisting of simple trenches and barbed wire had proved themselves over and over again to be storm-proof! The general attitude taken up in regard to instruction in siege works was that operations in a European war would be so mobile that the necessity for siege operations would be most unlikely to arise.[30]

This attitude extended to all the major belligerents. There were, however, some officers, mainly engineers, who recognised the difficulties that trenches and barbed wire could cause and that the attack might be held up to such an extent that mining would be necessary. A French army engineer, Captain Genez, in 1914 concluded in a historical study of underground warfare that the experience of the Russo-Japanese War suggested that mining might in future have to be used in the attack and defence of not only fortresses, but also defensive field works.[31] This view was echoed by Lieutenant Colonel R.N. Harvey RE, the Chief Instructor in Fortification at the School of Military Engineering, who, in a lecture to senior officers in 1914 on the problem of attacking barbed wire, ended with a similar proposal:

> There remains the way under, by which the entanglements may be destroyed by mining. This, I think, will be the way of the future, for it is difficult to imagine any troops again facing the carnage wrought at Port Arthur.[32]

After the war Harvey described the pre-war training of RE units as:

> ...usually limited to 2 or 3 days and by special care this period could be so extended that a gallery of some 30ft could be completed and a mine laid and fired. The mines of course [were] driven in the most favourable soil available.

For the conditions that the British were to meet in 1914 he described this as 'almost useless'.[33]

In 1920 Toepfer, who as a Captain fourteen years before had hoped for more prominence for the technical troops, lamented the lack of preparation for mining on the outbreak of war:

> When in the Russo-Japanese War the Russian Sappers advanced against individual Japanese strongpoints by mining, the fact was not really heeded that, as a development of defensive warfare, trench warfare was born.[34]

In the world war, he said, the arena of combat for the miner shifted from the fortress to no man's land, and mining became a weapon of major importance for commanders. Major deficiencies soon become apparent, however, with the German mining capability. There was a lack of proper principles for underground warfare and the tactical and technical training was inadequate, both at the level of command and among troops. The 'high command frequently didn't know where to start'. The miners were competent at sinking shafts and driving tunnels at shallow depths through easily workable soil, but 'experience was lacking' and the impact of geological strata and water levels were insufficiently studied or considered. Technologically the military had fallen behind the civilian mining industry and so the equipment available was not remotely adequate for a vigorous and intense mining programme: 'It was not easy to find civilians with mining experience involved in the military effort.' Finally, the pioneers alone could not deal with the situation:

> The trained pioneer mining personnel were not numerous enough by far and the engineer field companies were by training and number unable properly to increase mine warfare to the full extent, so that professionally trained and also untrained auxiliary workers had to be called on.[35]

Toepfer's analysis of the shortcomings of German mining on the eve of the war also reflected the ability of the Germans to respond to the shortcomings. The assimilation of civilian mining experience and technology into the armed forces was to be a deciding factor in the coming struggle.

Chapter 2

Mining Operations 1914 – early 1915

The predictions of Toepfer, Genez and Harvey were proved correct in 1914. After a war of movement during August–September, fought according to doctrines of the primacy of the offensive, the German advance was halted at the Battle of the Marne. Both sides dug in along the River Aisne, with trenches and barbed wire in positions which proved extremely costly to capture with artillery and infantry attacks. Within a few weeks siege warfare-style sapping and mining attacks were begun by the German and French forces.

On the Argonne front the French 22/3 Company of the 1st Regiment of Engineers began constructing underground shelters for the infantry on 15 October, and ten days later commenced a system of countermines by driving rameaux de combat in front of its lines. By 7 December this system was complete, providing defence against possible German underground attack.[1] The French 4th Army remedied the shortage of engineers that this warfare engendered in the Argonne with provisional engineer battalions, comprising auxiliary companies formed from the infantry.[2]

South of the River Somme, at Dompierre, in October the general commanding the 28th Division ordered an attack on the village by sapping and mining. The lieutenant commanding the 14/2 Engineer Company pointed out that the distance to be covered, 300m, and the lack of mining material, would make the operation very lengthy, and in this he was backed by the Chief Engineer of the Corps. This was overruled by the Divisional commander and mining was started by two companies. On 11 November the Germans took prisoner some soldiers of the French engineers, who revealed that in their sector major mine workings were in progress. Counter measures were assigned to the 3rd Bavarian Pioneer Company, who took delivery four days later of a consignment of timber mining frames, 'the first of millions and yet more millions' and commenced the construction of underground listening posts the same day. Thus mining escalated and spread along the whole front of the French 28th Division. It continued for ten months, but without significant results for either side.[3]

The Germans provided the necessary pioneer troops for the unfolding trench warfare by expanding eight fortress battalions into regiments, the various companies being split up and allotted to different sectors. These extra companies were particularly useful for sapping and mining and were the only German troops who had practised mining before the war. They were under army command, which meant that potentially they could remain in a sector when divisions were relieved. This advantage for the miners, however, was not always exploited.[4] One of the earliest attacks by sapping and mining, which culminated in the blowing of underground mines, was made in the woods of Argonne on 13 November by one of the fortress units, the 2nd Company of the 30th Rhineland Pioneer Regiment. In early November the Pioneers drove forward saps and used grenades to defend them from French attack. As in a siege, the work of the sappers was particularly dangerous:

> Most sap heads had already approached quite close to the enemy posts. The attempts by the French to prevent our sapping led to violent hand grenade fights. Since these were a novelty, it was recognized as a particularly brave act that Pioneer Weils picked up a French grenade and pulled out the burning fuse. After that use was often made of this method; also French hand grenades with burning fuses were frequently thrown back.
>
> On 13 November in the sector of the 6th Company of the 30th Infantry Regiment, after the tunnel had been driven forward sufficiently, an explosive charge of 40kg was brought in and detonated. Immediately after the explosion a heavy mortar fired into the French main position, which lay 12 metres ahead of the blow. A pioneer troop under Lieutenant Nitsche jumped with infantrymen into the 6.5m diameter crater resulting from the mine and furnished the edge with sand bags and steel screens for defence.
>
> To the left, on the front of the 8th Company of the 173rd Regiment, a tunnel was bored from our foremost position to only a few metres from the French trench. To prepare the way for the assault the Pioneer commander [Witte], here fortuitously, himself threw hand grenades into the enemy position; the tunnel was right up against the enemy position forming a breach. Through this open path, led by the Pioneer commander and an infantry officer, infantrymen and pioneers crept forwards and occupied the trench, which was immediately prepared for defence after overcoming and driving off the enemy garrison. (Major Karl Witte, Commander 3rd Rheinland Pioneer Regiment No.30)[5]

This attack captured the French front line and penetrated several hundred metres.[6]

The French 5/2 Engineer Company begin mining in the Argonne on 18 November, 3km east of the Rhinelanders. Work on two galleries just west of the Haute-Chevauchée road, north of Hill 285, marked for the Company the start of over two years of mine warfare in one of the major active mining areas of the front: 'Underhand fighting filled with danger, demanding of the workers a continuous and punishing effort.'[7]

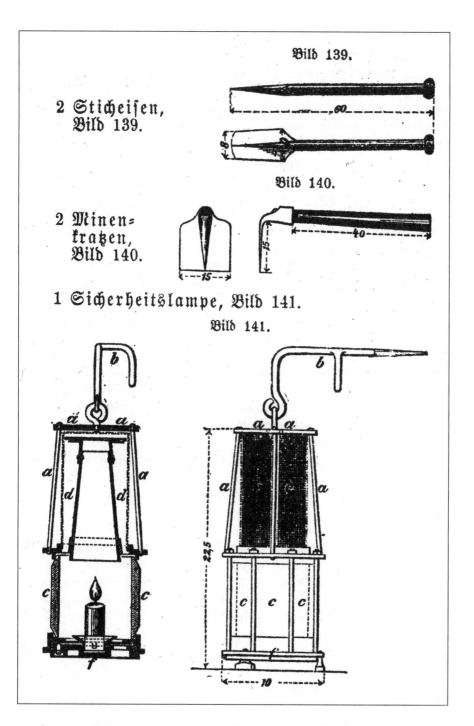

German mining tools and safety lamp. From the 1911 *Sprengvorschrift*.

On 8 December the company fired the first two charges and the following day they began three new tunnels. On the 12th, however, the Germans blew eight or nine charges and attacked, forcing the French out of their front line. A new location for mining was selected to coincide with an attack by the Garibaldi Regiment at the start of January 1915. Nine galleries were worked on night and day: by the New Year they had reached 45 or 50m in length. The company loaded a mine on the night of 4 January with 3,000kg of gunpowder. It was blown at 6.50am the following morning and followed by an infantry attack, which was successful.

A kilometre north-west the 1st Company of the Rhineland Pioneers prepared for a similar attack, which initiated a tit-for-tat series of mine blows. Several saps were pushed to within 2–3m of the French lines ready for charging. However, on 3 December, the day before the assault was due, the French blew a camouflet, trapping Corporal Steil and Pioneer Glöckners at the end of the sap. After several hours digging, Glöckners was found alive, but reaching Steil took longer as a tunnel had to be dug under heavy fire. It was not until 10pm that he was found, trapped but alive. Food was brought to him and at midnight he was finally brought to safety. The 2nd Rhinelanders prepared a larger attack for 17 December, in conjunction with the 2nd Company of the 16th Pioneers, in which they fired six charges, each of 60kg, from tunnels. The blows badly damaged the French front line, killing or wounding a number of the garrison. The remainder were too shaken to put up much resistance and the Germans took and held the ridge west of the Ravin de Mortier. The 1st Rhinelanders retaliated on Christmas Eve, blowing a charge that buried part of the French trench. On the 29th the French fired a charge that formed a crater in no man's land, which the Germans occupied.[8]

In exceptional circumstances the terrain might allow the sap to approach unseen, as in an incident at the Meuse heights, in front of Varnéville, in November, described by a member of the Chasseurs Alpin in the French press:

> As one cannot get close to the enemy in broad daylight, one gets the advantage of him underground. Our Chasseurs continually have shovel and pickaxe in hand. The captain, well-liked by his men, says little; but one morning, he lets slip a remark when, head against one of the loop holes, he studies a German blockhouse which each day is increasingly resembling a real stronghold. This threat is only 100 metres away. 'There,' says the captain, 'a nest which it is imperative to blow.'
>
> 'To blow this nest' becomes an obsession. All brains deliberate and in the evening the solution is found.
>
> At a certain point, undetected, a path will be cut out which will lead towards the blockhouse, which is just 20 metres from the cliff. The mountaintop overhangs there and completely conceals the flank.
>
> The diggers will thus be out of sight. They will not be burdened by the spoil removed by the excavations, which it will suffice to throw into the valley.

One does not sleep this evening in the trench. The plan is discussed and when properly decided, the captain is informed. He is made to understand the minor details of the project, supplements them himself, when it appears to him that some important detail has been missed. Next morning, men are immediately picking, those following behind throw the spoil into the valley. In two hours, the course is determined. The enemy cavern must now be mined.

So far as space allows, the men, who are held in Indian file, on the warpath, dive into the underground hollow and, in turn, gouge out the earth and make it fly.

Then, in a hole dug vertically below the German blockhouse, they insert shrapnel shells and melinite, sticks of dynamite, and bags of powder. An artillery artificer comes to give the last helping hand to the preparations. The chamber evacuated, the fuse is placed, a Chasseur wants to fire it himself. All the Alpins are anxiously in their trenches. A premonition has made them put their noses to the loop holes. Time passes slowly.

Suddenly, the ground rises, an immense fissure unleashes a column of fire. Debris of stones, trees, of earth, of iron, fly in all directions. An infernal noise…

A vast cloud blots out the sky. Then when all is done, the Chasseurs approach: the enemy nest is blown up along with its occupants. (Anonymous French Chasseur Alpin).[9]

From 8 December, the Germans noticed more activity on the part of the French. In the Champagne, sapping and mining towards Hill 200 throughout November reached a critical point at the beginning of December. General de Langle, commanding the 4th Army, obtained permission on 8 December from General Joffre, the French commander in chief, to combine the mining with an infantry and artillery attack. This was limited to Hill 200 and took place that day at 1300 with the blowing of three mines. The 34th Division succeeded in taking the German front line trenches and held them against repeated German counterattacks. The same unit attacked on the 20th after the blowing of two mines.

On 10th December the French blew a mine from a sap attack on La Targette in the Vimy sector. General Pétain, commanding the 33rd Corps, ordered the response after documents were found on the body of a German officer indicating that the 1st Bavarian Division planned a vigorous attack by sapping and mining on the village of Ecurie. The French seized the resulting crater and mine warfare was initiated on either side of the Lille road, which lasted all winter and into the spring of 1915.[10] North of the Somme, mining warfare began at Beaumont when the French blew a German listening gallery on 17 December and the Germans blew their first mine on 3 January 1915 using 110kg of Donarit, a commercial ammonium nitrate blasting explosive.

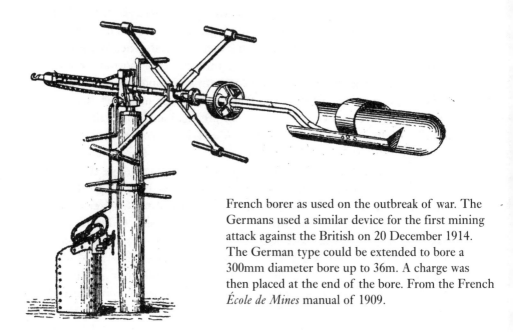

French borer as used on the outbreak of war. The Germans used a similar device for the first mining attack against the British on 20 December 1914. The German type could be extended to bore a 300mm diameter bore up to 36m. A charge was then placed at the end of the bore. From the French *École de Mines* manual of 1909.

In the December the British Expeditionary Force suffered its first attack by mining. The British were themselves attempting mining and the Dehra Dun Brigade of the Indian Corps began a gallery from the cover of an orchard in its front line, in conjunction with a proposed attack. The tunnel was pushed 70ft to a point estimated to be within 13ft of a German sap and charged with 45lbs of guncotton explosive. Before it could be blown, however, heavy German mortar fire forced the position to be abandoned.[11] The Germans were preparing an attack by sapping immediately to the south, at Festubert, which they launched on 20 December. This was to be regarded as the first mining attack made on the British, although it was made by using bored charges placed in the ends of saps. The Germans managed to drive ten saps toward the front line of the Indian Corps. The 3rd Company of the 7th Westphalian Pioneers was responsible for completing saps 5, 6 and 7, which it took over when partly completed on 9 December. Six men under an NCO drove each sap forward and were relieved every 24 hours. The rain was relentless and the work arduous and hazardous. In the high water table in Flanders trenches were constructed half in and half out of the ground in the form of sandbagged 'breastworks'. Work in Sap 6 was particularly hampered by working permanently in water. Some of the pioneers lost their boots in the mud in the communication trench and even took part in the attack with no boots. Ten metres from the British line the work became particularly dangerous, with heavy grenade attacks from the British. The Germans erected wire netting at the sap head to keep the grenades out and covered the last 4–5m with planks, throwing the evacuated spoil over them. Well-aimed fire from British snipers in trees made the work particularly dangerous. The British, however, failed to keep the saps from approaching their lines. In Sap 6 the Germans were so close that at night they stole empty British sandbags. At 3m from the British front line, the Germans used hand-turned earth-borers to cut tubular bores several metres long beneath the British trenches. Through the soft sandy upper soil of Flanders this boring could be carried out silently and undetected by the garrisons of the trenches only a few metres away. They then charged each bore with 50kg of explosives, inserted electrical detonators and tamped. Blowing the charges would also have the effect of extending the sap into the British trench. The British twice got into Sap 6 but were ejected with grenades and seemed unaware of the bored charges. Sap 6 was completed and the mine charged in time, but while testing the circuits it was found that this mine would not function and could not be used in the attack.[12] A British attack on all the saps was prevented by infantry fire. The British got either side of Sap 5, but the two pioneers continued work in the covered sap while the infantry held off the attackers. The attack was made on 20 December. Three white flares were the signal for the pioneers in each sap to blow the charges, which would link the saps to the British front line, after which infantry were to flow right and left and capture the trench. They also placed a charge of 300kg beneath a house in the British front line, but this failed to detonate. Sap 7 first flew into the air, followed by Sap 5, where a perfect connection was formed and the attackers were rapidly into the British position. At Sap 6, where the circuit failed, the sap commander crept forward and pulled down the British sandbag breastworks to gain entry into the British trenches. In Sap 7 the blow did not reach far enough and it took the attackers three attempts before they pushed back the defenders. Nevertheless, 'with the aid of the overpowering effect' of the mines, the British in the first line were taken by surprise and were killed with grenades and bayonets or captured before they could resist. The second line, defended, according to the Pioneer historian, by 'English mercenaries', was also taken after a short fight. After the attack the British trenches were filled with their dead and the Germans 'literally ran over corpses'.[13] The impact of the mines was both moral and physical, the German report stating: 'In the dugouts of the trenches which were destroyed by the mines, a large number of Indian corpses were found still sitting; they had apparently been suffocated.'[14]

Only after taking the second line was the attack halted by British machine-gun fire from the flanks. Repeated British counter-attacks were beaten off and the German report claimed that nineteen officers and 815 men were taken prisoner, while six machine guns and eleven small trench mortars were captured. The claim that 5,000 British dead were left on the battlefield was an exaggeration,[15] but the failure of the British to hold off the methodical sapping attack was very alarming to the command. The British had put out no saps of their own and had not anticipated that the Germans would use bored mines to make the final breakthrough into their trenches. The British shortage of mortars, grenades, engineers and equipment, along with the suffering of Indian troops poorly equipped and suited for the winter conditions in Flanders, all contributed to the success of the German attack.

The day after the British disaster at Festubert General Foch, commanding the French Northern Armies, wrote to Joffre pointing out the severe effect of the fighting on his troops, especially on his units of engineers, and requested that more engineer units be transferred to the front and new units be formed. He pointed to the arduous nature of trench warfare, involving the defence and attack of strongly fortified positions, and said that his 8th Army holding Ypres was carrying out large numbers of sapping attacks as well as having constantly to repair roads damaged by the German artillery ranged around the salient. He also asked that new units be recruited from the class of 1915, which need not be trained in the full range of field engineering, but only in sapping and mining. General de Langle, commanding the 4th Army in Champagne, reported the lack of engineers on 23rd, asking Joffre to double the number available for three corps due to take part in his attack, in view of the increasing importance of sapping and mining.[16] Joffre partly remedied the situation by taking territorial units of engineers from the interior and converting them to units of sappers and miners. In the meantime, on 30 December, he authorized armies to form auxiliary engineer companies from officers and men from other arms: '…who would appear to you to be able to enter this new formation, in consequence of their aptitude or of their occupation.'[17]

These units would not have the full range of equipment of a peacetime unit and would not, he intended, allow them to increase the number of sapping and mining attacks, but would enable them to push more actively those already in progress by providing double or more the existing labour. This led to the formation of specialized mining units in the French army.

The British, relying on a voluntary small Regular Army and Territorial Force, particularly felt the shortage of engineers. In September 1914, British GHQ recommended increasing the number of Field Companies per division from two to three to meet the new situation at the front.[18] The Field Companies were fully engaged in providing accommodation and defence for the Army. Colonel Harvey, former Chief Instructor in Fortification at Chatham, was an assistant to General G.H. Fowke, the Engineer in Chief, and he later recalled the situation:

> …the British army engineers had had no training to fit them for mining in the wet running sandy clay which was the soil they encountered on more than two-thirds of the British front in 1914-15.[19]

Two RE Fortress Companies that had carried out the siege practice at Lulworth in 1913 were in France, but they were even weaker in personnel than the Field Companies. 20th Fortress Company attempted mining 'through the sandy loam into green sand' and had to learn a difficult technique of sheet piling, or 'spiling':

> I think I took part in the earliest mining which was at Rue de Bois… This was in January 1915. The trenches there were only about 30 yards apart. I

was a subaltern in the 20th Fortress Company. Was sent with my section to put in a mine to protect their (infantry) trench against alleged mining. Infantry were up to their necks in water. It was a pretty gloomy business. We started sinking this shaft and it filled with water, so we pumped it out with hand pumps (lift and force). We got down about 10 feet or so. It was heartbreaking – I hated it. Had a job to keep my men going. The Boche saved us. We were making a lot of noise with spiling. The Boche opposite us were Saxons, rather friendly, and they put up a notice on a blackboard, 'No good your mining. We've tried. It can't be done.' The notice was in English. I reported this to my OC and it went up to HQ and they stopped the mining. (Lt. F. Gordon Hyland, 20th Fortress Company, RE)[20]

All RE units lacked the personnel to allow the continuous shifts needed for mining. At the end of December General Rawlinson, commanding the 4th Corps, asked for a special battalion for sapping and mining, which was supported by General Haig, commanding the First Army, who asked for a similar unit to work on the 1st Corps front at Givenchy.[21]

In very late 1914 or early 1915, the newly formed Armies of the BEF 'were instructed to proceed with offensive sapping and mining with such suitable personnel as they could find in the ranks, formed into "Brigade Mining Sections."'[22] In the meantime, a letter had been received at the War Office which, were it not for the influence and reputation of the writer, would have been dismissed with the many other letters received from cranks. A Member of Parliament and engineering contractor, Sir John Norton Griffiths, suggested employing the men that he used for carrying out sewerage contracts on mining at the front:

In thinking over the position that was taken up so early in the war, of opposing trenches being so near together, as an old miner the idea of undermining and blowing up the enemy occurred to me. As early as November, 1914, I sent in a scheme to the War Office and begged permission to be allowed to take out a handful of men, whom I described as 'Moles', and make a start; but although the scheme was listened to sympathetically, and, indeed, was sent out to France for approval, it went no further...[23]

Griffiths's curious memorandum stipulated that the training and equipment of the Moles should be left to the officer commanding, by which he meant himself. He should also 'have as free a hand as possible in advising when and where he considers, as a technical expert in these matters, the "Moles" should be used.' While he made a careful study of the ground to be mined at least 100 of his 'Moles' would be trained 10 or 20 miles from Chatham, although they could be used at the earliest possible moment with little training except in the use of the rifle and bayonet.

The suggestor [sic] of the use of "Moles" who has handled this class of men for many years is convinced that, given a fairly free hand, their use will prove of such importance that a very much larger number than at present anticipated would be asked for by the early spring. Water or adverse weather conditions would not necessarily affect the usefulness of these men.[24]

According to Harvey, his proposal reached GHQ from the War Office on 28 December, but, writing after the war, Harvey recalled details which he may only have learned later, in particular:

…that certain men specially skilful in tunnelling clay – termed clay-kickers – were admirably suited for mining and sapping. As the soil on the British front was all clay of a sort his suggestion was at once agreed to and a demand for 500 of such men… sent to the War Office.[25]

According to Norton Griffiths his proposal got no further until 13 February 1915, when he received a telegram to report immediately to Lord Kitchener at the War Office. He described the meeting at a reunion of British Tunnellers in 1927:

Alone in his room at the War Office he showed me the urgent despatches which had been coming from Lord French, to the effect that unless some means could be found of checking the mining efforts of the Germans, he (Lord French) would probably have to withdraw certain sectors of the line. Lord Kitchener, to whom I had had the honour of being known, both in the South African campaign and in Egypt, asked me to amplify my suggested mining scheme. Just before this interview the Boche, it will be remembered, had given us a nasty blow at Ypres, had lifted, almost *en bloc*, most of the officers of one of the Lancers regiments then in the trenches in the Ypres sector, in a dug-out near Hill 60, and had buried some 22 or more at Givenchy, in addition to several minor mines they had sprung in our front trenches.
    To his demand I replied that the only thing I could suggest, subject to examination of the ground, would be to use 'Moles'. When he said, 'What on earth are "Moles"?' I said, 'Clay Kickers, or workers on the cross', using a North-country expression for this class of small tunnel mining. As his patience showed signs of giving way, I then proceeded to demonstrate, much to the amusement of Major-General Sir George Scott Moncrieff and others of the Army Council with the fire shovel from the War Office grate, and showed him lying on the floor, what a Clay Kicker really was, and what a small hole he could work in, with the result that he turned round and said, 'Get ten thousand immediately.' I replied that I did not think there were ten thousand in the British Isles, and that it would be necessary to examine the ground before one could ascertain whether this form of mining were

possible. The result was I was off that very night to France, with two of my
expert London underground tunnellers who were employed on important
underground works at Manchester for that Corporation.
(Sir John Norton Griffiths MP)[26]

Norton Griffiths was to have a profound impact on British mining capacity.

In the New Year mining over much of the Western Front rapidly escalated. West
of the Argonne lay the Champagne region. The area of Hill 191, between Massiges
on the French side and the hill called by the Germans Kanonenberg, was taken and
retaken and saw the early acceleration of mine warfare. From Hill 191 the French
had observation deep into the Aisne valley in the German rear. After spotting
French spoil heaps, by means of mirrors on the trench parapet, the German
pioneers embarked on countermeasures and sapped to within 20m of the French
trenches. After several attempts to storm the trench failed with heavy casualties, they
continued sapping on the night of 8 December and used mining to get to within 5m
of the French positions. On the following evening they charged a mine and, once
infantry were in place, the pioneer officer lit the fuse 'using a cigar – matches were
inappropriate because of the proximity to the enemy'.[27] The charge blew a path into
the French trench and also by chance detonated a French mine, destroying a
significant part of the position.

On 20-21 December the French Colonial Corps launched a major attack and
took the whole of the Massiges position, leaving the Germans 500 to 600m from the
summit of Hill 191. The side of Hill 191 facing the Germans presented a steep
escarpment and the Germans proceeded to sap up to the foot, from where they
would be able to mine into the side of the hill protected from observation and fire.
As the saps progressed, the French fire on them became heavier, forcing the
Germans to sink their saps more deeply. The French also began to push forward
saps, attempting unsuccessfully to counter the German advance, and, in the words
of Captain Arndts, commanding the 4th Ruhr-Hessian Pioneers, 'on both sides the
saps strained forwards like antenna.' By connecting the sap heads about 50m from
the French a new trench system was formed as a base from which to begin the
mining operations. The French made a determined attack to push back the
Germans on 28 December but, after heavy grenade fights, the Germans regained
control of their positions. The Pioneers used aerial photographs to assist in
forming a survey accurate enough to begin mining and started driving six tunnels
into the chalk at the end of December, four of which were against the escarpment
position of Hill 191. The amount of work was such that a reinforcement company
was placed under Arndts's control. In line with siege practice, Arndts also dug a
transversal defensive gallery running across his position from which listening could
be carried out for French countermines. On 7 January they heard noises from the
tunnel on the right flank, forward 20m, and from other points. Arndts blew a charge
from his tunnel 3 on 9 January and the French occupied the crater until the

Germans drove them out with grenades. On 13th, the French blew charges against tunnels 1 and 2, but without success. As the German tunnels progressed the pioneers could hear the French underground in front and on either side. The chalk conducted sound some distance and the Germans began to deliberately intensify work in the two defensive tunnels to mask the progress of the main attack galleries (1, 2, 5 and 6). On 21st they established by listening that the French had reached very close to the main galleries 5 and 6 and were able to blow one of the defensive galleries without damaging their attack galleries. The French miners still came on and could be heard continuously at work from all the German galleries:

> Those who saw such mine warfare at its peak know what pressure on the nerves this underground struggle costs. Furthermore they know what sense of duty and what contempt for death are demanded foremost of the honest pioneers in the mining section who, in short breaks from work, strained to listen deep underground in bad air which hardly supported breathing... (Regimental historian of Ruhrhessische Pionier Bataillon Nr. 11)[28]

In the early hours of 23rd, the French blew against tunnel 2, destroying the defensive tunnel. They blew again shortly afterwards and a third time at 5pm, reaching close to the shaft of tunnel 2. It was vital that the French were stopped before they could destroy the shaft, as this would seriously set back the work. Throughout the night, in conditions of maximum quiet and care, the Germans loaded a large charge in tunnel 2, tamped and fired it. This was effective in halting French work in the area. On 26th, 27th and 28th there were alternative French and German blows at tunnels 6 and 4, but the main German galleries remained intact. The German deception measures apparently prevented the French from identifying the main threat. On 27th the four main galleries measured between 35 and 45m and the order was issued to enlarge the ends for each to take 5,000kg of gunpowder. Special carrying parties were organized to bring the 20,000kg of gunpowder into the trenches. Carrying the boxes of powder through the long saps exposed to French fire was particularly dangerous, as it was liable to be detonated by impact or naked flames. On the night of 30 January, tunnel 5 had been charged with about 4,000kg when some ignited at the tunnel entrance, but it burnt itself out before reaching the main charge. Charging was completed by the night of 1 February and the charges fused and tamped. The blowing of the mines was scheduled for 3 February and was to be followed immediately by an infantry attack. Heavy French shelling was directed particularly on the jumping-off trenches from which the Germans would attack, and on the morning of the attack this broke the detonator leads in several places, which had to be quickly repaired in time for the attack.

The mines were in two groups of two and the firing, carried out by Lieutenants Kühn and Oehlmann, was described by Arndts:

It was an unforgettable sight of terrible beauty, when on this day - zero 12 midday - four enormous columns of earth, each about 100m high, with a dull crash ascended high into the air, and then collapsed majestically onto themselves. How then the earth from four craters spat out enormous masses of smoke, which veiled the whole area. It was the largest blow which had been carried out up to then on the western front. Over 400 hundredweight of powder was detonated at the same time. Complete portions of the enemy position flew into the air. The stone hail had hardly rained down when the infantry with the pioneers stormed forwards.[29]

An eyewitness description of the assault appeared in the *Frankfurter Nachrichten*:

We had worked feverishly four months long and for the last four days without sleep in order to make all preparations to make the attack. Mountains of small scaling ladders lie ready to be carried forward at night and all the equipment – shields, entrenching tools, flare cartridges, sandbags, ammunition etc. – lies ready brought up overnight. Now morning comes. Ceaselessly man after man trudges forwards with timbers, scaling ladders and equipment. Their boots stick over the ankles in the tough mud and with trouble they climb step by step the stairs, well-worn by hundreds of heavy boots, upwards to the copse. We move forward. The assault columns are already standing at the ready. Still some quietly spoken words and a handshake with the column commander. Watches are synchronized one last time. The slight rifle fire is as normal and betrays nothing of what is approaching. Again we check the time, still five minutes, then from four places in the enemy front line will be detonated the mines which our pioneers previously placed with indescribable troubles over 50m away under the enemy position. Now two minutes to go. We stand crouching in the trench – still ten seconds – then one second – two muffled explosions. I see, like volcanoes, as high as a house – no a steeple – four black fountains of earth. Human body parts, cubic metre-sized lumps of earth fly, turning ponderously, into the air. It grows dark. Masses of earth now come clattering down. Many men are buried up to the waist. They must be dug free.

Nearly in the same instant, without wavering, the assault wave of our column takes the mine craters. Terror has seized the enemy. Already numerous prisoners are appearing who, escaping the explosion, wish to save themselves by promptly surrendering. Right and left, in unison, the storm columns jump forward. With the motto 'on, then through!' the second and third lines of enemy trenches are also taken in a rapid assault.[30]

In fact many attackers were injured by falling debris from their own mines, having been too close to the blows.

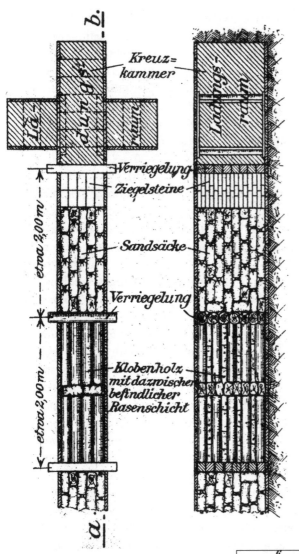

b.

*Kreuz=
kammer*

Verriegelung

Ziegelsteine

Sandsäcke

Verriegelung

*Klobenholz
mit dazwischen
befindlicher
Rasenschicht*

*Ladungs=
raum*

etwa 2,00 m

etwa 2,00 m

a.

Mine charge chamber with tamping in
bricks, sandbags and timber bracing.
From the German demolitions
regulations (*Sprengvorschrift*) of 1911.

The German mining attack on Hill
191 of 3 February 1915. The four
mines are shown as circles at the ends
of the saps. From *Das Ehrenbuch der
Deutschen Pioniere*.

On 17 February the French carried out attacks preceded by mine explosions on the ridges of Éparges and Vauquois. These ridges, providing important observation east and west of Verdun, were to become major centres of underground warfare. The Éparges ridge, 320m in height, allowed the Germans observation across the Woëvre plain towards Verdun. The French Company 14/15, under Captain Jean-Louis-Laurent Gunther, began sapping and mining up the northern and western slopes in mid-November 1914. On 7 February there were signs that the Germans had taken underground countermeasures against the westernmost mines driven from four saps and, so as not to lose four months of work, it was decided to blow these and for the infantry to assault the western part of the ridge on 17 February. The four mines were blown at 1400 but, unlike other mining attacks, this was not the signal for the infantry assault, but for the start of an hour-long artillery preparation, following the methodical procedure of a siege, whereby the artillery and mines together gradually broke down the defences and the artillery bombardment would prevent the Germans from occupying the mine craters. However, it ran the danger of losing the shock value of the mines. The infantry waited at the foot of the slopes at the entrances of the saps until the mines were blown, at which point they entered the saps to be ready to rush the craters as soon as the bombardment lifted at 1500.[32] An infantry officer of one of the assaulting columns described the agony of waiting to attack and the moment that the mines were blown:

> Everything is empty. I can feel or express nothing but this. All that normally makes up the world, the flow of sensations, thoughts and memories which carry each second of time, nothing is left of them, nothing. No consciousness penetrates the suspense; neither anguish, nor the vague desire of what may occur. All is insignificant, it no longer exists: the world is empty.
>
> And it is at first, against our crouching bodies, a heavy shudder of the ground. We are upright when the monstrous, white fumes, specked with fluttering black things, rise up at the edge of the plateau behind the lines near the horizon. They do not shoot up but expand into immense plumes, which separate one from another, more and more, until forming these four smoking monsters, motionless and riddled with dark projectiles. Now the mines thunder, heavily, gruesomely, like vapours. The noise ebbs, rolls over our shoulders; and at once, on the other side, in every valley, on the whole plain and also the sky, the guns release the breaking floodgates of tumult.
>
> 'Forward! Single file; behind me.'
>
> We climb up towards the entrance to the communication trench without seeing it, buffeted by the tremendous uproar, staggered, crushed, dogged and furious.
>
> 'Forward! Quick!'
>
> The sky splits, cracks and crumbles. The hammered ground gasps for breath. We no longer see anything but a reddish-brown dust which flames or

bleeds, and sometimes, through this sooty black and stinking cloud, a fresh stream of adorable sun, a tatter of dying sun.

'Forward! Follow me... Forward... Follow me...'

(Second Lieutenant Maurice Genevoix, 2nd Battalion 106th Infantry Regiment)[33]

Genevoix's battalion moved up the four saps, from the ends of which the mines had been laid, and at 1500 the artillery lengthened its range and infantry and engineers left the saps to capture the craters. The mines and the bombardment were effective in breaking down the defences and the French took and held the western part of the ridge. There unfolded on Éparges a ferocious underground warfare which lasted until the autumn of 1917.[34]

As predicted by some military engineers before the war, mining was indeed reverted to as a means of overcoming field fortifications. When taken up it was carried on as part of an established methodology of siege warfare, a series of well-described procedures tested over centuries. Both the Germans and French used mining to bite off parts of their opponent's defensive systems. Mining, however, required yet more men and trench warfare already drew in large numbers of engineers to maintain and supply defences.

But for a lack of manpower, French and German, and to a lesser extent British, military engineers regarded mining as being well within their technical ability. During 1915 the use of mining would rapidly escalate and in the process many of the practices of siege warfare would be modified or cast off. Ultimately it was the British, starting with the least technical skill, who were to most fully embrace mining.

The western end of the Éparges ridge, showing the saps from which mines were blown. Maurice Genevoix led the second wave at Sap 6. From Feriet, *La Crête des Éparges*.

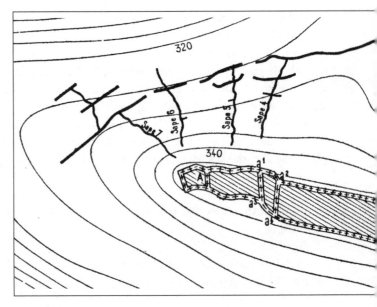

Chapter 3

French Mining Sectors: Carency, Oise, Les Éparges and Vauquois

Carency

Mining operations between the French and Germans reached an intense level in 1915. Initial French success in some sectors was followed in 1916 by German supremacy. An early and celebrated French success was against the German-held village of Carency at the north of Vimy ridge. Sapping and mining preparations towards the defences of Carency were set in motion by the French on 1 January 1915. Three points were identified for attack (designated Alpha, Beta and Gamma salients) and preparations for five saps made by widening the communication trenches and bringing up two trench guns. Continuous rain and vigorous bombing accompanied the sapping, and the French lost a sapper killed and four wounded when a German bomb fell into a sap head. As the saps neared the German lines they were linked to form a new front line. On 6 January, before the new defences were complete, the French began to mine towards Beta salient, and the next day heard the first German countermines. On the 8th the rain rendered progress impossible and the trenches became impassable, as the labour needed for sapping and mining meant that the engineers were unable to build shelters or drain the trenches. From 18 January the French heard more noises, which became so distinct in Gallery 1 that they feared the Germans would break into their gallery. They used a hand borer to drill from the front line towards the noises, which they blew with 10kg of cheddite, a commercial blasting explosive introduced by the French for military use in November 1914. As the mine galleries progressed, the scale of timber and materials required became a problem. The Germans had clear observation over their rear positions and began to shell the dump immediately behind the trenches. The mine timbers had to be carried up 800m of communication trenches to the mines and large fatigue parties were needed for this dangerous and unpleasant duty. By 29 January, however, the French had charged three mines in front of each salient, ready for an attack on Carency. The attack, however, was postponed and the engineers were redeployed onto the defensive works, which had been neglected while mining. Not for the last time were miners to experience the difficulty of coordinating their intensive labour to the timetable of a wider operation with which, to be effective,

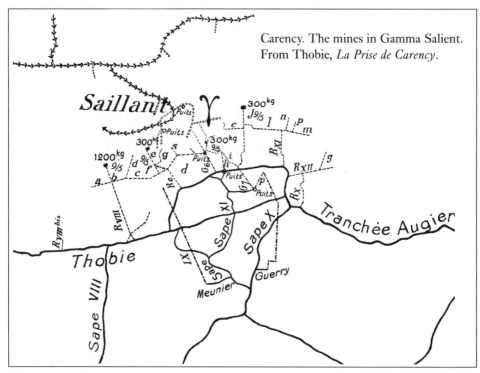

Carency. The mines in Gamma Salient.
From Thobie, *La Prise de Carency*.

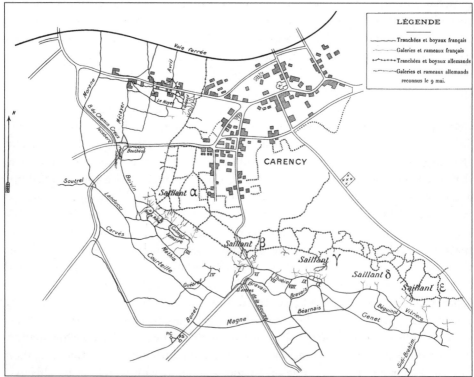

Map of the German-held village of Carency. From Thobie, *La Prise de Carency*.

Diagrammatic
representation of the
French demi-galerie
and rameaux de
combat. From Thobie,
La Prise de Carency.

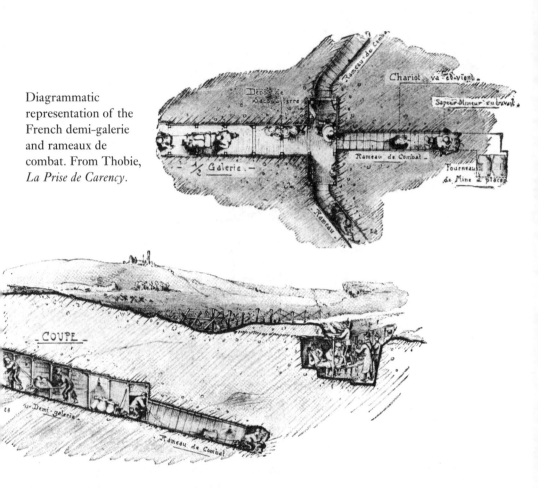

they must be synchronized. Their predicament was now that they did not know how
the charges would fare if left: the gunpowder was susceptible to damp and the
detonating cord was liable to be damaged by mortar fire. In addition, the Germans
now had time to mine themselves. When the French heard them approaching the
charge laid at Gallery 1, they detonated a small bored mine of 10kg of cheddite, the
largest they could blow without affecting the charge already laid. They decided to
use the threatened charge in conjunction with a raid, at 0445 the next morning. As
the debris fell the infantry ran forward, temporarily occupying the resulting crater,
which was about 15m in diameter, and entered the adjacent German trenches. They
did not remain in the crater, but found evidence in the German trenches of
numerous new mine entrances. On the 8th the Germans blew their first mine. They
did not damage the French positions, but the blow served as a warning that mine
warfare was now fully engaged in. The French, having only Gallery 1 to counter the
large number of workings begun from the Alpha salient, soon discovered that they
had lost the initiative. As a rather desperate defensive measure, they drilled a large

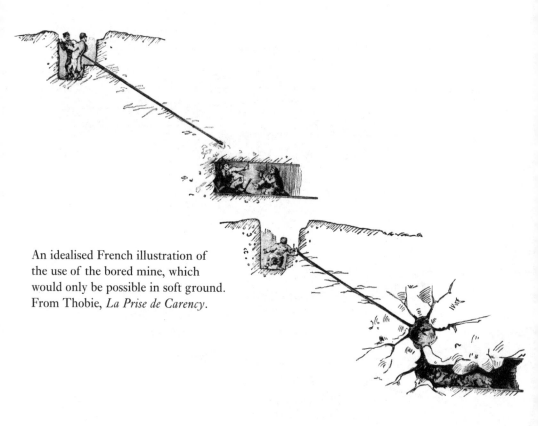

An idealised French illustration of
the use of the bored mine, which
would only be possible in soft ground.
From Thobie, *La Prise de Carency*.

number of boreholes from their front line trench, with which to blow charges. They
hoped that these would impede German progress underground by breaking up the
ground, making it unstable and saturating it with hazardous gas. This did not prove
viable, but they used the bores as a means of listening and deepened two shafts in
the front line to 8m (G2 and G3). They also prepared new tunnels towards Beta and
Gamma from points behind their front line trenches, to begin a new, deeper,
underground attack. Previously the practice had been to begin galleries as close to
the enemy as possible and to drive short, shallow tunnels with the maximum speed
and minimum effort. In order now to drive beneath the German tunnels, they
started further back to get greater depth. Not having to incline the tunnel too steeply
facilitated more rapid removal of spoil.

When the Germans blew (at G1), causing a crater but without damaging their
workings, the French realised that they had reached further than they thought. They
were also growing concerned about the condition of the unused mines at Beta and
Gamma, and on 24 February mounted a raid in which they would be blown at 0430.
At Beta the Germans were on their guard after the previous blow at Alpha, and had
already been alerted by noise caused by the raiders assembling across the very

narrow no man's land. After the explosion, a French patrol was met promptly by German fire and the raid was abandoned. At Gamma the charge failed to detonate; the sappers remade the fuse but it still failed and, as there was not time to untamp the charge, this raid was also abandoned.

The French could now hear noises underground at many places:

> The Germans show a tenacity which worries us and which can be countered only by determination and constant effort. There is not a moment to lose, no time for hesitation.[1]

The Germans blew three mines in the first few days of March, but without seriously damaging the French tunnels, which they drove to meet them. On 6 March, 20/11 Company were reinforced by 14/5 Company, who took over the workings at Alpha (galleries 1-3). Working on the right-hand salients, where Gallery 7 reached 28.6m in length, the miners encountered a large block of sandstone which, being too large to move or cut, caused a detour. At 11pm the following night they met the timbers of a German gallery. The French miners removed the timbers and discovered a charged mine ready to fire. The Germans were apparently waiting for the French to advance further past the charge before blowing, when the unexpected change in direction caused them to discover the ambush tunnel. A sapper volunteered to enter the German gallery and cut the leads to prevent firing. The sapper then placed a charge against the tamping and discovered a second electrical primer which, when he withdrew it, detonated. The French dug the sapper free, but he was dead. They prepared a charge to destroy the German defensive galleries.

On 12 March the Germans struck twice with heavy charges close to the French lines. The first destroyed three galleries, leaving them open to the sky and burying two miners, who were later rescued alive. The second destroyed the end of Gallery 5 from a point 40m from the entrance, burying five miners, part of a detachment of 80 miners from Lens attached to the 6th Territorial Regiment. The French could hear the buried men using a distress call distinctive to the Lens collieries. They charged Gallery 7 with 200kg of cheddite and dug to rescue the miners.

> This day is truly disastrous for the sappers. All our offensive galleries are destroyed completely or in major part and the enemy reaches close to our trenches. Will we have time to regain our balance and hit back? The infantry have a poor view of us and regard our sector as insecure. The garrison which is found close to the heads of our galleries is anxious and at every moment fears being lifted into the air amid a cascade of earth and chalk. At night the agitation grows. The pace of work is slow; listening becomes unreliable and it is necessary constantly to make allowance for imagination.
>
> We will pass through a very difficult period, and, it must be fully admitted, confidence begins to falter.

On 13 March, the rescue operations at Gallery 5 continue with great difficulty. The calls of the miners are still distinguishable but the series of setbacks which we have just suffered leaves us in great distress and at every moment we wonder whether it isn't our enemies who, to draw us into a trap, imitate the calls of the Lens miners…

At 2 am, we find the flattened body of one of the buried soldiers; this discovery increases everyone's dark forebodings. Work, despite everything, continues doggedly; the calls become increasingly distinct. Finally, after much effort and anguish, the four other miners surprised by the explosion are rescued. They are alive and safe but in a pretty poor state; they have spent twenty-five hours in the shattered gallery and, thanks to their coolness and courage, have assisted their rescue by clearing a three to four metre passage through the broken ground. (Lieutenant Hippolyte-Michel Thobie, 20/11 Engineers)[2]

The French now believed that a large number of pioneers were pitted against them and later discovered that there were six German companies. As they staged a fight-back the mining took on an extraordinary intensity. After rescuing the men from Gallery 5 they charged it with 200kg cheddite and very quietly tamped it while the Germans worked vigorously, confident that their two heavy blows had destroyed the French defences. The French tamped very thoroughly, with 9m of backfill and five timber barriers, to minimise the damage from the explosion so that they could immediately resume their offensive. As the last listener left Gallery 5 before the blow he could hear the Germans still hard at work underground. After the blow the commotion and cries from the German front line raised the spirits of the French miners and gave them the feeling that they no longer needed to be pre-empted by the German mines or camouflets.

In response to the two German blows, the French set out to strengthen their underground defences considerably by creating a two-level system with a transversal to form a subterranean front line. At Gamma they began branch galleries at right angles, which connected their tunnels 20–30m from their trenches to form transversals, which were to be a feature of a completely new tunnel system. They realised that they had to go deeper, with new galleries beginning from yet further behind their front line, from the second or even third line. If they remained in the systems started from the front line or just behind, they would be caught by deeper German tunnels passing beneath them. Shafts in the front line were vulnerable to German raids in which they might be destroyed or permanently captured, and with them access to the whole underground system. Two engineer companies, the 4/8 and the 9/2 Territorials (i.e. reservists) began work on nine new galleries, mainly at the two most threatened points, Alpha and Gamma. These galleries were started far behind the front line and passed under it at 15 to 20m depth.

The new tunnels would all be linked by transversals once they were under no man's land, forming an extremely powerful system. From the transversals they could listen at any point along the front and in the chalk could hear the Germans working 20m away. The galleries now had effective natural ventilation, doing away with the need for noisy hand-turned ventilators. The multiple entrances gave the miners greater confidence, as there was more than one means of escape should one entrance be blocked. They increased the size of charges and in mid–March exploded 400kg, while noting that the Germans continued to blow smaller charges and spent longer preparing them.

Four French engineer companies plus attached infantry were now working on the operation, which they talked of as the 'Siege of Carency'. Thobie emphasized the need for decision and confidence. The natural tendency for inaction to avoid criticism was largely compensated for by the energy of all those who took part in the siege. By 26 March they could hear the Germans underground on all sides, working constantly and loudly and blowing frequently, but to no effect:

> We are lodged deeply in the compact chalk in which the sound of the pick is transmitted a long way, there we can wait without fear. Work continues without danger, we are content to keep watch on the enemy who is not threatening for the moment. (Lieutenant Hippolyte-Michel Thobie, 20/11 Engineers)[3]

There followed a curious calm that lasted almost a week. It was broken by a German charge blown near their lines which the French took to be a bluff. On the night of 16 April the French miners encountered the timbers of a damaged German gallery and entering found abandoned clothing, in the pockets of which were tobacco and an envelope dated 12 March. Canvas covering the walls was spattered with blood and they deduced that this was a gallery lost after their blows of either 29 March or 2 April. They believed that they had panicked the Germans, but that they were pausing for breath and would hit back. This counter-offensive came on 22 April when the Germans blew and killed two French sappers. The French prepared and immediately blew charges of 100 and 400kg at 15m depth. In hard chalk neither charge broke surface.

By early May 1915 the French miners had reached points close to the German trenches all along the line in front of Carency. When, on 5 May, an attack was finally ordered on the village for the following day, they were in a position to prepare a major assault with seventeen mines. However they had barely twenty-four hours' notice to carry the explosives into the front line and charge, fuse and tamp seventeen mines, all the work to be carried out in one night, a total of 11.75 tonnes of explosives. To their relief the attack was postponed for 24 hours and all the mines, ranging from 200 to 1,500kg, were completed on time. They then learnt, however, that the attack was to be delayed again, for a further two days, to 9 May. This was a cause of anxiety: the French would have preferred to tamp on the night before the attack, in case of any problem with the firing leads. Moreover, a period of prolonged silence after intense activity would alert the Germans to the fact that they had charged and tamped, and might prompt them to fire their own mines to detonate those of the French. The French therefore resumed work in all galleries that were still open in an attempt to give the impression of normal activity.

The infantry assault, part of the 2nd Battle of Artois, was at 1000 on 9 May and was preceded by a four-hour artillery bombardment that began at 0600. As at Éparges on 17 February, the blowing of the mines was part of the preparatory phase, during which the defences were breached in combination with the artillery. The seventeen mines were blown three and a quarter hours before zero during the bombardment.[4] The mines were blown in batches by salient from 0645, so that blows did not damage adjacent mines, and the process took around twenty minutes. Thobie, in his highly detailed study of the battle, does not specify the time of blowing, which does not seem to have been regarded as critical. It may be surmised that the intensity of the bombardment already strongly indicated to the Germans the imminence of an attack and blowing the mines did not significantly rob it of surprise. Given the strong possibility of a failed circuit, the timing allowed the engineers to repair a broken lead and still blow during the preparatory bombardment:

> Suddenly the ground trembles, an enormous cascade of earth and chalk rises into space and falls with a terrible crash. A white and opaque cloud of smoke floods the trenches. It is the simultaneous detonation of the three mines of Epsilon salient. A few minutes later, another deep tremor, and this time in the shower which rises majestically is clearly seen a German; he will be found a few hours later twitching on the lips of the crater. From moment to moment, the ground is shaken by a powerful shudder which spreads into the distance with diminishing ripples. These are the seventeen charges, prepared by the 20/11 and 14/5 companies of engineers, which detonate in turn. Those of the 20/11, we have seen, are grouped in threes and contain together approximately two tonnes of cheddite. During the artillery preparation, a section was in charge of the firing which was carried out without a snag. For around twenty minutes, the entrails of the ground spout out demoralization, terror and death. And throughout, with method and precision, the hail of shells tears the air and beats down upon the enemy.
> (Lieutenant Hippolyte-Michel Thobie, 20/11 Engineers)[5]

At Alpha salient the German front line and dugouts were either collapsed, partly buried by debris or completely obliterated along a line almost 300m in length. The defences were taken with little resistance; the mines, however, did not lead to the immediate capture of the village of Carency, which was itself converted into an extremely powerful fortress and only fell three days later. The mining attack was successful in the capture of the outlying defences of Carency and had benefitted from a German hesitancy which was not characteristic in other sectors. The French success, however, seemed to indicate the potential of mining in overcoming fortified positions.

In response to the spread of mining Joffre's Chief of Staff, General Belin, issued instructions on mine warfare tactics on 3 March 1915. These served to remind commanders of proper practice and attempted to establish principles for its use. They were wholly derived from pre-war practice, the scenario still being seen as one of siege warfare. Belin emphasized the parallels between underground tactics and those used above ground. He pointed out that mines were used most frequently to attack important parts of the enemy front, such as machine-gun or observation posts, armoured shelters, the exits of communication trenches or any centre of resistance. He advised commanders to use two parallel routes when attacking, 15 to 20m apart, in view of the uncertainty of success that one gallery had, and to use branch galleries from which listeners could protect the flanks. Work was to be pushed as actively as possible to anticipate the work of the enemy in developing countermines. The presence of a tunnel should not be revealed by exploding a charge prematurely and one should seek the most direct attack on the point to be destroyed. If one was attacked by mining, one should adopt either active or passive defence. The active defence required pushing galleries to meet the enemy until the moment had arrived to charge and profitably fire. In the passive defence, one would stop work, load charges and fire when the enemy arrived in range. Usually it was beneficial to advance and vigorously attack the flank of enemy galleries. Belin laid down technical rules: generally mines should be a demi-galerie, i.e. 1.30 to 1.50m high by 1m wide, to allow monitoring and good ventilation. If the length exceeded 40m then the rameau, 0.80m by 0.65m, should be used. Depth was always to be sufficient to be out of reach of shells bursting on the surface. Shafts were to be used only to gain depth more easily through rocky ground (entrances were normally inclines). Spoil should be removed so that the enemy was not alerted to work, either by its presence or by the colour of the extracted material. Against enemy advances, miners should seek to go deeper and use camouflets, which when deeply placed could be large without causing surface craters, the ground being left clear for the attack. Significantly, Belin's instructions did not anticipate that mining would be initiated where it might prove counterproductive. During 1915 this was to be the case in many areas.[6]

At Bois Saint-Mard in the Oise sector, the Germans were able to gain an advantage, owing to the lack of experience of the commander of engineers, by blasting through hard limestone to reach the French front lines.[7] However, the effort required for the gains was highly questionable. The German 9th Pioneers made use of an underground quarry immediately behind their trenches from which to begin mining. The limestone required drilling and blasting and the sound carried for long distances. In early January 1915 the French infantry reported noises and their commander stated that he believed the Germans were advancing a deep tunnel. For the previous month they had also seen the exhaust from an engine coming from the German trenches which, it was surmised, was powering a drill. The commander of the 19/1 Engineers, Captain Gourlat, began listening from a shallow tunnel on 16 January, but three days later his superior, Colonel Prange, the commander of engineers for the 37th Division, ordered this work to stop. Prange denied that mining was possible through the hard rock, a response dictated both by logic and the regulations in the pre-war manuals of military mining. That evening the infantry commander reported that he had been perplexed by two explosions underground, which appeared to come from close to his trenches. When Gourlat listened, however, he heard nothing and concluded that the report was exaggerated. On 20 January Prange dismissed the reports of German mining and maintained that the noises were the sound of work in the underground quarries some distance away, transmitted through the rock. The same day, however, Gourlat heard the sounds for himself. They appeared to be getting closer and the Germans were firing field-gun salvos to mask the noise. On 25th Gourlat actually felt the blasting as vibrations coming through the ground. He then listened virtually continuously from midday until 8.30 the next morning and concluded that there were three German mining attacks, of which the two closest were about 15m from the French front line. He detected a pattern of work from 3am to about 4am during which there was picking or drilling, followed by four or five explosions, which the Germans tried to mask by throwing grenades. He recorded explosions at about midday, 4pm, 8pm and midnight when they ceased, and they then resumed at about 8.30 the next morning and at midday. The Germans were clearly drilling boreholes and blasting and now seemed to be critically close to the French lines. Gourlat ordered drilling down to the hard rock with the intention of firing a large bored charge and inducing the Germans to blow a mine from their gallery before reaching the French lines. However, the drill head became wedged 2m down on account, he reported, of the clumsiness of the sappers, and work had to be resumed by hand with the pick. The noise of this picking, however, seems partly to have had the effect that Gourlat wished for, as that evening the Germans blew two mines, 4 to 5m in front of the French trenches. These formed craters 20 to 25m in diameter, wrecked 50m of trench and killed twenty-five of the trench garrison and wounded twenty-two.

The situation was now critical for the French front line. During the night noises of German boring and blasting continued and Gourlat concluded that they were constructing a chamber to take a mine charge in the third tunnel and that a blow could occur four to five hours after the last blast. He proposed that the infantry should evacuate the front line, leaving only sentries, and increase the barbed wire and *chevaux-de-frise* defences. His sappers should, in the meantime, listen and try to provoke the Germans to blow again by drilling down, although this would be highly dangerous for his men. He also proposed the urgent creation of a new defence line, 30 to 40m behind the first, from which he could set about creating a system of countermines to form a defence underground, which he could not do from the present front line as the

Germans were already too close. He also proposed that a retaliatory mine be blown in the mining system of the division to their west. The divisional commander agreed to these proposals, except that of blowing a mine in a neighbouring sector as a distraction. He also asked for the replacement of Prange as his commander of engineers, blaming him for allowing the German miners to reach his front line despite clear warning signs. The Germans having initiated mining, the French were obliged to take counter-measures, despite the difficulty of driving through the rock.

At the end of 1915 there was a growing view in the French command that too much uncoordinated mining had been carried out, which had been a waste of effort. On 13 December General Joffre sent instructions to his Army Group commanders on the subject. Until then mining had been conducted on the initiative of subordinate units and this had resulted in a dilution of effort, with only partial results. He stated that it was likely that more benefit would be gained by concentrating effort at carefully chosen points. Mining was a means of wearing down the enemy that should not be neglected, and tube mines especially should be used to obtain superiority. Joffre wished to learn from experience so far and called for reports of mining already in progress, wanting details of which units were involved, any special equipment in use and whether equipment and personnel were adequate. He called for reports as to whether there were other parts of the front where mining could be usefully commenced and for officers who had gained experience to report on modifications that could be made to equipment in service.

In responding to Joffre's call for reports, both General Ebener, commanding the 35th Corps, and General Nivelle, commanding 61st Division, made direct reference to a mine blown on 23 December at Bois Saint-Mard, which had given the Germans no advantage whatsoever. The tunnelling in this sector through hard limestone, initiated by the Germans in January, had led to the blowing of 15 German and 25 French mines and camouflets during 1915. This was not a particularly active sector and demonstrates how mining was resorted to because the other side was using it, but with neither side achieving anything. By December the French defensive system was such that they felt confident that they had defeated any German prospect of threatening the security of their lines. Instead of mining, the Germans found it easier to use heavy mortar fire against the French mine shaft heads. The large mine of 3 or 4,000kg blown by the Germans on 23 December was after a French camouflet had also detonated one of their charges. The German blow created a crater 32m in diameter and killed Sergeant Mourdon and Sappers Ballas and Chaumont, buried at a gallery face, whose bodies could not be recovered. On the surface an infantry sentry, Private Fortineau, was killed and his brother was partly buried but rescued alive. The French had taken possession of the crater, bringing their line 15m closer to the Germans. Ebener was dismissive of the amount of effort that the Germans had put in to killing four men: 'Such is the result for the Germans of several months work.'[8]

Nivelle pointed out that it had taken the Germans long months of work to lay the mine blown that day, but that the French now occupied the crater: 'Offensive mine warfare would be pointless without a worthwhile objective. When the only objective is the enemy trench, the effort is not in proportion with the result.'[9]

Ebener was equally forthright about the lack of value of mining and stated that it should only be carried out in those areas most threatened and even there should be reduced to defensive work:

> The result of studies made on the ground and the experience gained by more than ten months of mine warfare is that, on the front of the 35th Army Corps, there is no location where a mine offensive could be advantageously undertaken. At various places where the proximity of the two opposing lines could facilitate the work, the only result which would be obtained by mining would at best be to blow up a salient or a portion of trench. One would then be immediately opposite an intact second line trench and the meagre success thus acquired by months of work and all the consumption of men, material and inevitable effort could be obtained just as easily by a concentrated shooting of the 58 [58mm mortar] and howitzers lasting a few hours.[10]

The Bois Saint-Mard sector did not in itself possess sufficient tactical significance to justify the level of mining effort and here, as in many other sectors, the French were able to reduce the scale of operations. The scepticism of the French as to the value of mining saw a major decline in its use in their sectors during 1916. Only in those areas where the Germans refused to scale back mining in response did it remain active.

Les Éparges was one such sector. After the French mining attack on the western end of the Éparges ridge on 17 February 1915, their attacks continued in March without mines but, during May and June, mine warfare 'darkly, slyly, develops, then predominates.' Within a month the plateau on the summit ceased to exist, obliterated by craters up to 60m in diameter: 'On each side, and month by month, the shafts and the galleries multiply, the explosive charges increase, the craters become more vast.'[11]

In late September and October the Germans exploded a series of mines around Point X at the eastern end of the ridge. In the first, on 26 September, three were killed, four wounded and fifteen were buried or disappeared. Two days later they blew two more mines nearby, killing six. Heavy daily bombardments with mortars and artillery followed and then, on 13 October, a massive mine, blown at 1.30am, wiped out five complete sections of the French 303rd Regiment, whose bodies could not be traced, and threw up high lips. Two more mines followed at 2.15am and a fourth at 4.10am, even larger than the first and burying more of the 303rd. The survivors attempted to defend the positions, but could not establish where their own lines had been: 'The instantaneous and fantastic metamorphosis of things makes it no longer possible either to locate or to recognize anything.'[12]

Gradually the French consolidated their hold on the northern side of the craters, the Germans on the south side. Some men were dug out, but on 14 October an officer and fifty-seven men were still missing. The French replied on 16th with two mines to the west, in no man's land, and seized the craters, which dominated the German trenches. At certain times, during October and November 1915 and in the spring of 1916, the rate of blows at Les Éparges exceeded four in a week. For three years, until mid-1918, mining was carried on continuously by both sides along the 800m ridge top and no man's land comprised an almost continuous furrow of mine craters 700m in length. The German pioneers made use of the steep escarpment along the southern slopes of the ridge to start deeper mines, driving into the side of the ridge, and were able to gain the advantage over the French. The possibility of a German attack on Verdun increased the significance of the ridge as an observation post over the Woëvre plain. General Dubail, commanding French Army Group East, proposed on 11 November 1915 to force the Germans from the ridge with a major mining attack. This was planned from 29 December, but the French handicap in mining, stemming from a shortage of specialist troops and modern equipment as well as the distance between the opposing lines and thus the amount of effort required, led to its abandonment.[13]

The opening of the Verdun offensive in February 1916 ensured the continuing importance of the ridge. In May General Nivelle, recently appointed to command the 2nd Army, gave detailed instructions to the 2nd Corps over the need actively to continue mining at Les Éparges. Nivelle, critical of mining being used where there was no worthwhile objective, ordered mining to be stepped up at Les Éparges. He instructed the 2nd Army to take precautions against German mine charges west of point E, which the Germans could blow before they had the means to counter them. They were to reduce the garrison of the threatened zone and to use methodical listening to establish the extent of the zone. Listening should be done at intervals of not less than 40m, during which time absolute silence should be enforced in their lines. Surface saps and trenches would have to be supplemented in case of disruption by German charges. He specified that the countermines should be begun somewhat behind and with a slope of about 40 per cent and take into account the declivity of the ground so that they reached a depth of at least 20m. If listening indicated that the Germans were deeper then it would be necessary to begin the inclines further back. It was essential that work continue day and night and, once the galleries had sufficient depth, dugouts should be constructed to accommodate the shifts and to conceal spoil until it could be evacuated after dark. Finally Nivelle ordered that spoil should not be allowed to accumulate around the gallery entrances where the enemy could detect it.[14] The struggle at Les Éparges continued throughout 1916 with charges of up to 40 tonnes. In 1917 German galleries reached into the rear of the French position, under and beyond their shafts, although the French held tenaciously on to their side of the ridge. From the autumn of 1917 the blows became less frequent, but they continued into 1918, with a mine blown as late as August 1918. The ridge was captured by a combined Franco-American offensive on 12-13 September in which mining played no part.

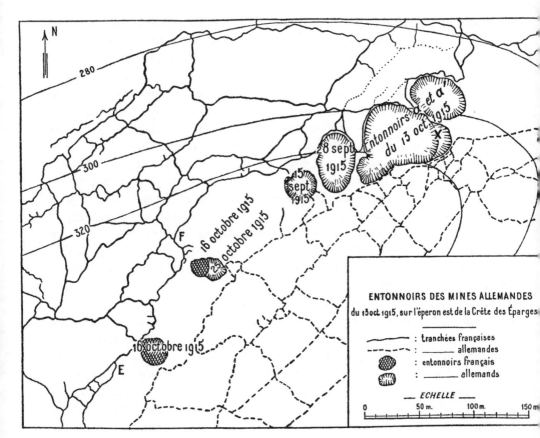

Les Éparges ridge showing the mines blown in September and October 1915. From Feriet, *La Crête des Éparges*.

Vauquois

> You, *the others*, who are not here and who will come later, you will never understand…you will be like strangers and enemies, you will not know what it means, *the mine in the west, at Vauquois, the mine of 14 May 1916*, or how *Death* towers *alive* over mankind. (Lieutenant André Pézard, 46th Infantry Regiment)[15]

In 1914, the village of Vauquois sat on a plateau on a ridge, the Butte de Vauquois, 289m above sea level. The value of the ridge for observation led to fierce fighting over its possession in the winter of 1914. As at Les Éparges, mining began owing to the value of the position and escalated to the extent that it seemed to have become an end in itself, despite attempts by commanders to control it. Between March 1915 and April 1918 there were 519 mines or camouflets blown at Vauquois, within an area of front 464m wide and 340m deep. The French launched an attack on 17 February 1915, corresponding to that of Les Éparges, supported by six mines of 25 to 50kg. Half of these failed to explode, however, and over the following weeks the French slowly pushed on to the summit through the remains of the village. This fighting resulted in a situation which encouraged further mining, as the lines were too close together for the French to use artillery to render the plateau untenable to the Germans. This was possibly a deliberate policy on the part of the Germans, as by allowing the French partial occupation they retained their observation but made it harder for the French to dislodge them.

In March the 1st Company of the 30th Rhineland Pioneers (1/Pi 30), a regiment created from a pre-war fortress battalion, began mining from the house cellars, which the French become aware of and began defensive galleries. Both sides soon reached the sandstone, called gaize, which forms the bulk of the ridge. This was very hard and could only be worked by picking, but had the advantage that in its unblown state it did not require timbering. French engineers of Company 5/1 sank shafts to 3.60 and 4m and began rameaux de combat 0.80m high by 0.60m wide. Initially they advanced these untimbered but, as they neared the Germans, timbered them according to their regulations. By mid-April the French had nine shafts running from their front line, but these were vulnerable to German rifle grenades and even hand grenades and also caused congestion in the trenches. In early May the French attempted another assault, supported by a mine to be fired five minutes before the infantry attack. However, the powder had become damp and failed to break surface. The French gained a foothold in German positions in the west but the main attack in the east failed.[16]

The advance of the German miners led the French to fire two small camouflets of 30kg cheddite on 13 May in an attempt to forestall them. On the same night the Germans broke through the roof of a shallow French gallery after sinking a shaft in no man's land, surprising the miners at work with pistol fire and also, reportedly, asphyxiating grenades. The French were driven from the gallery and Corporal Menges, leading the patrol, jumped in and loaded a charge of 100kg, which destroyed it. The French used their intact galleries over the next few days to blow four mines and a camouflet, destroying German positions in the front line and also those German tunnels approaching their own lines. By doing so, however, they revealed the location of their own galleries. The Germans were able to resume their advance and fired three powerful charges close to the French front line.

The French responded in June by starting work on a stronger system of defences based on shafts every 15 to 20m along the whole 400m front, with the aim of preventing any German tunnels reaching within 15m of their front line. These galleries gave the French a potential advantage, but the Germans responded with new galleries to a depth of 4m, started from their second line and again using house cellars. They achieved rapid progress through the sandstone with electric drills powered by a generator in Varennes mill behind their lines. The Germans also began to link their galleries with transversals, creating more powerful defensive systems, which the French at Vauquois almost never did. The network quickly grew. On 19 June the French broke into a German gallery but found it empty apart from a lantern, picks and shovels. On 22 August they discovered a void, which on investigation turned out to be a natural fault. However, in the light of his electric torch the officer suddenly saw a German in front of him and fired his pistol, seriously wounding him. A German gallery had also broken into the void. The French blew a charge to destroy it and hastily tamped their gallery. The Germans in their turn investigated the following day and blew camouflets of 475kg and 550kg.

Two additional French engineer companies, the 5/3 and 5/51, joined the 5/1 and, during summer 1915, the French appeared to have the advantage, blowing, in four months, 77 charges to 51 German. During 1915, two out of three charges broke surface, creating a mass of craters each of about 10m diameter. The infantry gave up trying to occupy these craters, which caused casualties with negligible advantage and proved impossible to hold. The opposing sides satisfied themselves with 'crowning' the crater lip nearest to their lines and connecting it by saps. The action of the mines rendered occupying the plateau increasingly difficult and the two sides concentrated more on attack underground as a means of destroying the enemy positions. In June 1915 this battle was conducted at 4–6m below ground, but by the end of the year was down to 15–20m. As each side attempted to dig beneath each new crater so the level gradually deepened and, as they worked through ground blown by earlier explosions, timbering became more necessary and pockets of gas a hazard. The Germans were frequently able to resume the underground advance more quickly than the French following a blow and this forced the French to fire their tunnels closer to their own shafts and even to destroy them in the process. From December 1915 explosive charges exceeded one tonne when the French Company 5/1 exploded a 1,300kg charge at E17, forming a crater 20m in diameter. On 22 February Company 5/3 blew a mine of 2,030kg. By this time, the French mine entrances were concealed in dugouts under the trench parapet to protect them from rifle grenades and mortars. Within the dugouts were housed hand-operated centrifugal fans, while at the bottom of each shaft was an area 2–3m in length to store filled sandbags of spoil, ready to tamp a charge laid at short notice.

Both sides also dug accommodation for their troops beneath or immediately behind the front lines. The Germans in particular excavated deep and extensive dugouts into the gaize, which enabled them to squeeze a defence system with first and second lines, and large numbers of infantry, into the narrow band of plateau between their front line and the steep side of the ridge. At the end of 1915 the Germans ceased using vertical shafts from the first or second line and had begun to use the sheer slope on their side of the ridge for a new series of galleries about 15m from the top of the ridge. They installed a 60cm gauge railway line in the galleries to remove spoil, which they tipped directly down the slope. In November 1915 they began deep flanking galleries on the east and west of the plateau at 25m depth. By using the rear slope they could easily pass beneath the craters to reach depths of 40m. The Germans also continued to blow charges from their shallow system on the flanks some way from the French lines, to make them believe that they were making little progress in these sectors. The French believed that sunken lanes on the east and west would enable them to detect German mining in the vicinity, but the new German galleries were far too deep to be heard from the surface.

The opening of the Verdun offensive increased the importance of Vauquois as an observation post and shortly afterward the Germans were to demonstrate their dominance by devastating the French positions above and below ground. On 3 March they detonated a mine on the eastern flank of the plateau of 16,500kg, which they had placed over 35m deep. The French had not detected this mine and three sappers were lost in a gallery and twelve infantry were missing in the posts:

I took the risk of crawling along the length of my first line. All the minor posts of the eastern extremity were blown up along with the communication trench; a whole corner of the Ridge disappeared in the void; the hole is 60 metres wide. It is almost unimaginable; the hill is sliced through, opened, in space... The first German line was blown away, it too; between it and us a crater opens which widens and grows deeper more and more towards the right. The depths of the broken ground are of a yellow and raw colour; an immense odour of mildew floats in the void. Over the whole of the top of the sunken lane and on the site of the minor posts there are accumulations of monstrous rocks, each one the size of a tomb. The lip of the crater is twenty metres wide, eight or ten metres thick. There we have a half-section buried alive, sealed in the ground, that neither the end of the war nor the flow of the centuries will ever convey to the military ossuaries. My men, my poor fellows, are in there crushed and contorted. And I do not yet know their names. And when we know them, no one will dare to make them public, and each family will imagine that a bullet passed, quickly and cleanly, through their dear one's heart. (Lieutenant André Pézard, 46th Infantry Regiment)[17]

Four days afterwards noises of picking were heard near one of the buried posts and on 9 March, after six days underground, three men were rescued alive.

To retaliate, the French engineer command quickly prepared a strongly overcharged mine in the centre of the plateau. They were assisted by a technical section of the engineers from Versailles, the Service Électromécanique (SEM), with an experimental Bornet electric drill (see p62). This had to be carried in pieces more than 20m below ground and was powered by a generator installed in a dugout. The drill was capable of 15cm diameter bores of up to 50m in length, drilling at about 8 to 10m per hour. The principle was the same as the pre-war borers, but this device was capable of cutting through rock. At the end of the bore a small charge was

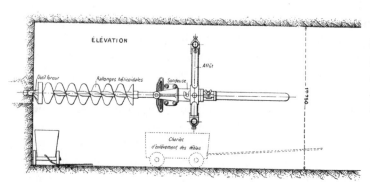

Bornet electric drill used at Vauquois. From *École de Mines Supplément au Livre de l'Officier*, 1917.

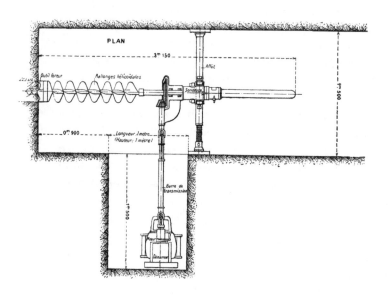

exploded, disguised by blowing a charge in a neighbouring gallery or a bombardment on the surface, to create a cavity capable of holding a larger charge (see p63). This process was repeated several times until the cavity could hold 10 tonnes of explosive, which was inserted along the borehole. The French passed the bags by hand along the gallery so that the German listeners were not alerted by the sounds of explosives being dragged along the ground. The French were alone in continuing to use gunpowder for mining operations, which was both less powerful than ammonium nitrate explosives and also far more liable to explode accidentally. After 5 or 6 tonnes had been charged the atmosphere was laden with a highly dangerous mixture of explosive dust and, in the confined space of the gallery, probably set off by a candle, there was a violent explosion. The main charge, however, did not detonate and remarkably the French seem to have suffered no casualties. Listeners detected German activity in the vicinity and the French halted charging, immediately tamped and blew on 23 March. Most of the remains of Vauquois church were hurled into the air, about 60m of the German front line was destroyed and about 30m of the second line was damaged. Thirty German infantry disappeared. The French infantry occupied the southern lip of the crater, nearest their own line, but were forced back over the crater lip by German fire and counterattacks, which continued for the rest of the day. The lips were higher on the German side and the blow left them with improved observation over the French positions.

The German western flanking tunnel (Stollen 1b), in progress since November 1915, was pushed ahead in difficult conditions in a gallery 80cm in height and 150cm wide. Former Pioneer Herman Hoppe recalled in 1969 that they worked without shirts and had to use oxygen cylinders at the face because the air was so bad. By mid-February the gallery was 86m in length and the Germans prepared a chamber 5m long, 4.5m wide and 2.7m in height to take a massive 50 tonne charge. Five railway trucks were needed to bring up the explosives. It was the largest mine charge of the entire war, larger than the 43.2 tonne St Eloi mine blown by the British at the Battle of Messines in June 1917. Charging began on 25 February and, with tamping, took thirty men three and a half weeks. Hoppe described how the yellow powder of the Westfalit and Astralit explosive came in packages about 25cm long, which they stacked like bricks. Five hundred detonators were used, with three separate sets of leads. The tamping included a 6m barrier of concrete and extended for 80m in total, almost the entire length of the tunnel, requiring 25,000 sandbags with wooden barriers every 5m.[18]

The Germans fired the mine on 14 May 1916. Hoppe remembered the moment of detonation:

> ... the whole mountain rocked. One could feel it at Varennes and beyond - like an earthquake. With the debris a leg with the buttocks came over us flying through the air. In my diary it says that four Frenchmen were thrown over which I am not sure about now. But I definitely saw the leg.[19]

The crater was almost 60m in diameter, destroying the French lines for 35m right back to the third line and pulverising the French underground shelters and their occupants. One hundred and eight men were missing, mostly from the 9th Company of the 46th Infantry Regiment. Three mine shafts and galleries disappeared and with them nine miners.

> It is an upheaval so beyond measure, such a complete eradication, such an absolute transformation, as to seem at first too powerful to enter familiar eyes. I do not comprehend, I cannot. This emptiness crushes me. (Lieutenant André Pézard)[20]

Despite the massive destruction that the mine had wrought on the French positions, the Germans did not coordinate this mine with any attempt to force the French from the ridge. The only explanation for this is that the Germans wished to secure their hold on the ridge, but it nevertheless suited them to allow the French a small foothold. Two days after the blow General Halloin, commanding the French 5th Corps, issued orders that it was essential to give more power and energy to mining at Vauquois, to catch up with, or even overtake, the Germans and that it should be possible to blow 100 tonnes at the same time with combined charges. The commander of Company 5/1 studied a project to open a breach of 130m in the German lines in the centre of the ridge, to gain observation over the northern slope and to destroy the deep German underground shelters. He planned four charges laid in galleries dug using compressed air-powered drills: two 30 tonne charges would be placed at 25 and 23m depths in two branches from the E4 gallery. Two others of 10 tonnes and 20 tonnes would be at 25m depth at the head of E18. The plan was supported by General Valdant, commanding 10th Division, but would require 250 workers, who were not available. The scheme was abandoned.

French High Command, on the contrary, prescribed a purely defensive attitude to mining, while acknowledging that energetic action was needed to combat the deeper German galleries. Therefore the creation of a second system at a lower level was ordered and the engineers began six new attack galleries from shafts about 30m behind the front line. These had to be inclined downwards at 45 degrees to reach a depth of 30m by the time they passed the French front line. The engineers had to rely on less skilled infantry pioneers to carry this out, whose work was slower. They also had to keep the shafts in the front line in operation, where the fight with the Germans continued unabated. Daily bombardments by well-observed German mortar fire impeded progress by frequently blowing in the entrances of galleries. In May the French tackled this problem by constructing new concealed entrances linked to the front line workings some 15m back.

From April 1916 the Germans deepened their mine system yet further by driving three tunnels, Ost, Mittel and West, at 42m depth into the steep northern slope. They blew a large mine on 20 July, increasing the crater of 14 May in size and further threatening the French galleries in the west. In the east, on 7 June, the French infantry had felt three jolts which they suspected were due to German underground blasting. Lieutenant Pézard described their desperate desire to leave Vauquois; it was a wish that was fulfilled fifteen days later when the 46th Regiment left the ridge for good. The Germans blew another large mine in the east on 26 July, creating a 50m-wide crater which overlapped that of 3 March.

In August 1916 the three French engineer Companies were relieved after over a year at Vauquois, during which time they had lost 215 men killed, and were replaced by Companies 27/51, 16/3 and 27/1. Company 27/51 blew a charge of 10 tonnes gunpowder and 1 tonne dynamite on 19 August, creating a 40m wide crater, although the Germans had detected the work and evacuated their front line and

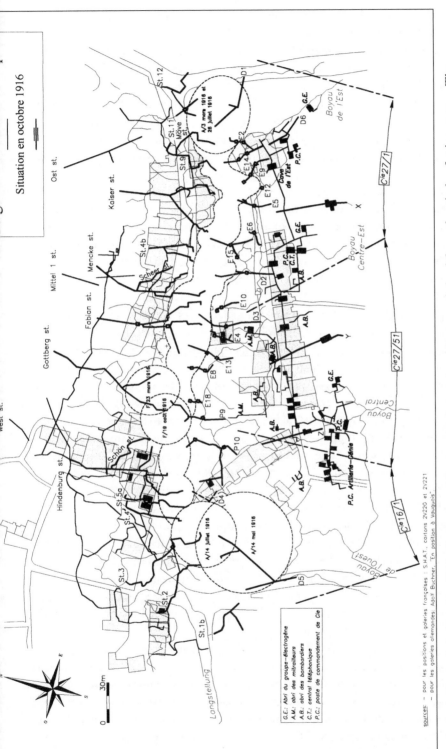

Situation en octobre 1916

G.E.: *Abri du groupe–Électrogène*
A.M.: *abri des mitrailleurs*
A.B.: *abri des bombardiers*
C.T.: *central téléphonique*
P.C.: *poste de commandement de Cie*

sources: – pour les positions et galeries françaises : S.H.A.T. cartons 2V220 et 2V221
– pour les galeries allemandes Adolf Buchner. 'En position à Vauquois'

Mines at Vauquois in October 1916. German positions are in the north, with no man's land formed entirely of mine craters. The Germans have abandoned their front line shafts and are driving deep galleries from their rear slope. The French were still reliant on their front line shafts for defence. A/ indicates a German blown mine, F/ a French blown mine. From Amis de Vauquois, *La Butte Meurtrie*. (Collection Amis de Vauquois) shelters. Over the following three days 1/Pi 30 blew five charges in return. In September Captain Mathey, commanding the 27/1, proposed creating a third system of galleries, which started on the French rear slope, in imitation of the Germans. Three inclined galleries, X, Y and Z, were begun which would pass beneath the French front line at 38m depth. At the end of September the French got electric power and compressed air to these three galleries, allowing the use of pneumatic picks and electric winches. A 40cm rail line was installed on 19 November. These measures went some way towards compensating for the French lack of labour, but the power supply was insufficient for all winches and they had to be used alternately.

On 16 November the French D3 deep incline, underway since June, entered service and the French believed that they could take on the Germans. However, despite daily listening and a strong camouflet of 3.5 tonnes, the Germans responded with a charge ten times greater from the end of Kaiser Stollen on 10 December, forming a 70m crater and destroying four of the E shafts and much of the French front line and underground shelters. Fifty men were rescued but twenty-one were not found.

In September the Germans completed a gallery, Gotteberg, to protect the sector where the French had blown on 23 March. At the end of 1916, the Germans still had the advantage, gained through superior equipment, personnel and mortars, to systematically put shaft entrances out of action. Poor weather prevented aircraft observation, which would have alerted the French to the increase in spoil on the northern slope. The new German galleries were 10m beneath the deepest French workings and the French were unable to surprise the Germans. When they heard the French the Germans stopped work and used activity in the upper galleries to disguise the lower work. They could blow to a range of 30m without fear of retaliation from the French systems at 20 and 30m depth (see cross section p69). The French were forced to abandon the last seven shafts put into service, or to destroy them when blowing camouflets, owing to the short distance from the shafts to the ends of their galleries. Their radius of rupture was only 20 to 25m and caused very little damage to the German galleries. The French system of D shafts, intended to fight at 35ft depth, was barely in service before it was outclassed by the German galleries. The shafts were either abandoned or rendered unusable by German camouflets. To make matters worse the new X, Y and Z attack galleries passed beneath the French front lines at only 25, 20 and 30m instead of the planned 38m, owing to a levelling error by Captain Mathey.

At the end of 1916 the French began work on a series of new galleries, only one of which was started from the rear slope. This was a new deep gallery (V) on the eastern flank, driven on a steep gradient of 70 per cent and equipped with an electric winch and fan. In addition four major listening galleries were started from in, or near, the front line and a 22-tonne camouflet was to be blown from D1 to destroy a deep German gallery between D1 and D6. The camouflet was to be 11 tonnes gunpowder and 11 tonnes cheddite, but on 31 December, during charging, the powder went off and the blast killed thirty-six men at work in the gallery.

In January the French engineers were again relieved when there was a change of corps. Company 8/14 took over mines in the west, 8/64 in the centre and the mining company M5, afterwards M5/T, of which the commander had only moderate experience, in the east. In order to preserve some continuity Mathey remained in command. The French made efforts to regain the advantage and the driving of galleries took on an increasingly mechanized character to compensate for a permanent lack of labour. The Service Électromécanique operated generators, compressors, ventilators, pumps, winches, drills and borers, but electrical output remained inadequate. There was 1,800m of compressed air piping from the French rear position at the Mamelon Blanc feeding the pneumatic picks and pumps in the galleries. During the winter these were affected by freezing weather and rising water also flooded some of the galleries.

The V gallery in the extreme east was quickly begun, but only after the work was established was it found that the entrance was subject to flanking fire from the Bois de Cheppy, by which time it was too late to change the location. The lack of labour and delay in installing the 40cm railway hampered the removal of spoil. Work on the new listening galleries was hardly begun before one was halted by a German camouflet. Nevertheless the French planned new galleries, S and T, from their rear slope and began a 'revenge gallery' branched from X in reply to the German 35-tonne mine of 10 December, creating a diversion by drilling from another branch. Despite a German camouflet on 5 February, the French were able to charge with 5.7 tonnes to destroy two German workings to the north-east and north-west.

On 24 February the Germans blew a mine in the mid-west of the ridge, destroying a French shaft, damaging two others and confirming French fears of major German deep workings. On 9 March, the French urgently considered a plan to lay three enormous mines to destroy the German galleries and surface positions and to give up the Vauquois position in favour of the Mamelon Blanc position. This involved placing three charges 60m apart, each of either 144 tonnes at 40m depth or 280 tonnes at 50m. This was not adopted, as it was estimated that the mines would only partly destroy the German surface and underground positions and the craters could then be used by the Germans as cover for maintaining their occupation of the ridge. To be effective the charges would have to be placed behind the northern lip of the craters which formed no man's land, which was impossible to achieve, and if the French had that degree of freedom underground there would be no need for them to give up the ridge. On 9 March they decided to dig a fourth and final deep gallery, W, between X and V to reach 50m depth. The Germans blew a mine on 19 March, making a 60m crater and destroying two French shafts as well as the infantry and engineers' shelters. It was to be the last of the large German mines. The French, however, were making some progress with their deep galleries. In February their X gallery came into service, in April Y, Z and T, and in June V and S. On 30 June the

French blew what was to be their last mine to break surface, which destroyed a German machine-gun dugout. At these deep levels even massive charges no longer broke surface to form craters and mine warfare became an almost entirely underground affair. Its immediate purpose was no longer to attack surface positions, but purely to destroy the enemy galleries and kill the mining personnel. Using sensitive listening apparatus both sides tried to blow camouflets to cause maximum casualties to the miners of the opposing sides. When charges did not break surface or find enemy galleries there was frequently nowhere for the gas generated by the explosion to vent, in which case spherical voids were formed which the miners might then break into. In February the French discovered one 10m in diameter; the Germans used a 6m cavity as a listening chamber for several days before destroying it. By this time the Germans did not attempt to recover the bodies of their men killed by camouflets. Pioneer Tschörtner, posted to 1/Pi 30 at the beginning of 1917, explained the reasoning in an interview in 1970:

> Pioneer Damman was buried by a French blow. We walled him up. We always did it that way because we no longer recovered people. Once we unearthed one. He had been surprised in a squatting position by a French blow not during the usual time for blows. The head sat in the right upper corner, the trunk was beneath and the legs were gone. We always closed the galleries after that.[21]

In the summer of 1917 the Germans worked on driving three new galleries deeper than any previously used. Rader Stollen in the east, Mittel II Stollen in the centre and Treppen Stollen to the west were to pass beneath the level of the sandstone gaize, through layers of clay and green sand, to reach limestone at over 100m depth. After driving horizontally into the hillside 42m beneath the level of the summit, they were steeply inclined to reach about 60m depth before doubling back and by March 1918 reached 95m.

In June 1917, the French decided to discontinue active mining on the west end of Vauquois ridge. The chief engineer of the 31st Corps recommended the adoption of a purely passive attitude, reacting only if the German miners became too threatening. The commander of the 64th Division, holding the line above ground, also approved a report by his commander of engineers to 'put to sleep' mine warfare in the whole Vauquois sector. From that date the French proposed to carry out only maintenance work and monitoring. There remained the problem of German threats. If the French were to blow a German gallery approaching their workings it would reawaken mine warfare, which the French could not then counter, as their system was insufficiently developed and had been allowed to flood. It thus proved extremely difficult for the French to disengage from mine warfare at Vauquois. Their attack galleries were within a few metres of the German lines and were inevitably met by German miners. On 26 June a German borer broke into the head of the French T

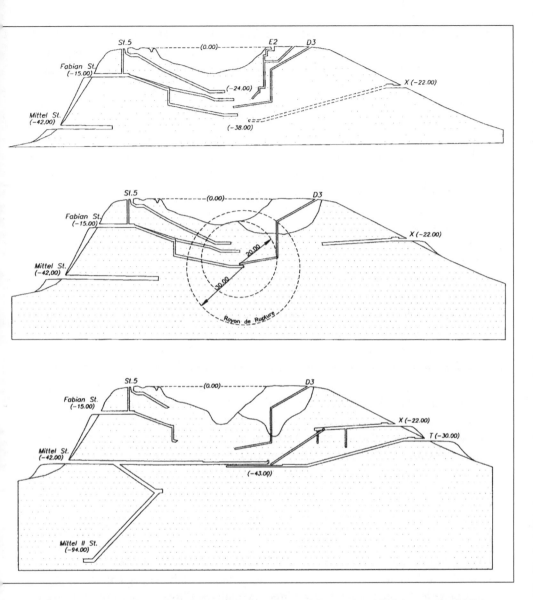

Cross sections of the Butte de Vauquois, September and December 1916 (top and middle) and April 1918 (bottom). The village stood on the plateau, which was deeply cratered by September 1916. Depths in metres below the summit are shown. The sheer side of the German position (left) can clearly be seen, and the spoil dumped at the tunnel entrances. On the French side E2 vertical shaft was sunk from the French front line in March 1915, while on the German side Stollen 5 was begun from further in the rear. The Germans began Fabian Stollen at the end of 1915, making use of the rear slope, and began Mittel in May or June 1916. The French began D3 incline in June 1916 and X gallery from their rear slope in September 1916, but with insufficient incline. They started T in January 1917. The Germans began Mittel II Stollen in spring 1917. From Amis de Vauquois, *La Butte Meurtrie*. (Collection Amis de Vauquois)

gallery. The French constructed a barricade and brought in dynamite, but the Germans blew as they were doing this, burying a corporal and wounding, gassing and concussing an officer. The French attempted to continue laying a charge but the Germans blew again, killing a corporal and a sapper, and then blew a third time the following day.

The Germans blew a camouflet on 27 July from Paul Stollen, which caused the sympathetic detonation of a French charge of 6.9 tonnes of dynamite and cheddite and injured eleven of their miners. On the night of 13 August the French completed a charge chamber just one metre from Paul Stollen, in which voices were audible with the naked ear. The Germans, however, used a borer to place a 50kg charge, which broke through into the chamber at about 4am. No French were in the chamber at the time, but the shift arriving for work at 7am discovered the debris from the charge and set about clearing it, unaware that an opening had been created between the German and French systems. As they cleared the opening they facilitated the release into their gallery of the poisonous gases produced by the explosion. At this time the French generator broke down, depriving them of both ventilation and lighting and forcing them to withdraw. The Germans noticed the lack of French activity and, fearing a camouflet, also withdrew. However, Staff Sergeant Menges, picking his way in darkness over sandbags brought up for tamping, climbed through the partially blown in opening. At 1pm a shift of four French miners under Sergeant Charbonnier resumed work. The man in front, Sapper Rubbefat, shouted back to Charbonnier that the air was clear. He was then seized by Menges who, firing a shot in the direction of the others, dragged him back to the Paul Stollen. Charbonnier had a pistol but panicked and went back up the gallery, pushing ahead of him the other two. Menges continued his exploration of the French system. Others began to bring in cases of explosives to prepare a charge to seal off the two branches of the D6 gallery from the shaft entrance to prevent the French entering. A French infantry bomber stationed at the entrance of D6 saw down below a man carrying an acetylene light, but took him for a French sapper still in the gallery. A French engineer officer, Lieutenant Pech, descended into the gallery, followed by several men including a bomber. He could not see or hear any sign of the Germans but smelt a strong odour, which he recognized as a slow burning fuse. He immediately evacuated the gallery. Three or four minutes later the German charge blew, hurling sandbags and pieces of wood towards the entrance and blocking the gallery. After the blow, the Germans were able to visit the whole of the system undisturbed, discovering tools and rescue and listening equipment. The French set about bracing adjacent galleries in their X and V systems against an expected German charge, which they could hear being prepared at midnight. The Germans blew a charge of 5 tonnes at 4.30am, which formed a crater above ground.

The French were left without defence between their V and X galleries. The final deep gallery W in this area had been stopped in June owing to lack of labour and bad ground and it would take a month and half to recover the lost ground. They therefore drove a branch from X gallery to the right to extend 50m, and also blew a 6-tonne camouflet on 20 August, which cut the German gallery. The Germans replied on 28 August. The struggle with camouflets continued, particularly in the centre and east sectors, and between February and August 38 German and 47 French charges were blown. The quantity of gas trapped in the workings required an increase in the number of ventilators, which the French reversed to suck rather than blow in order not to force the gas further into the system. In the west, after a heavy German camouflet on 1 September, the French blocked D5 gallery with barbed wire and abandoned it. In October and December 1917 the French engineer companies were again changed, with only M5/T remaining in the east.

During autumn and winter 1917 the French continued to attempt to stabilize the situation without actually giving up the ridge. This was not solely in order to avoid creating a gap in the French line, but also for purposes of morale and, according to a French report, for the sake of the 'dignity of the French miner'.[22] The French pushed their galleries to reach the centre of the craters, but did not go beyond that line so as not to attract German attention. They planned to use a new drilling machine to drive a transversal between Y and Z in the centre-west sector to cover an undefended area. This was one of the few uses by the French at Vauquois of lateral tunnels to link their attack galleries.

At Christmas a remarkable incidence of fraternisation deep underground occurred, which was indicative of the desire by the French to introduce a degree of 'live and let live', and also probably war-weariness on the part of miners on both sides. On 17 December French listeners heard working beneath their D3 gallery and began a shaft to meet it. The two galleries reached within a metre of one another and the French heard the Germans addressing them in their own language: 'If you do not advance any more, we will not advance any more.' The French listeners were forbidden to reply. A little later, when the French were clearing spoil, they heard 'Tu travaille?'. The French put a 200kg camouflet and a microphone in place in the gallery face, with which they could hear the Germans speaking and also singing. Corporal Feikert recalled how the Germans broke the truce:

It was around Christmas time. We advanced straight forward, until one day we heard the French speaking in the gallery. We succeeded in making contact and it was genuinely cordial with them. Since we couldn't understand each other, the French sang the Marseillaise and we the German national anthem. When the French were quiet, we also left the gallery, attaching however listening apparatus at the tunnel entrance for security.

This didn't please our second lieutenant and he told us to do something. No one volunteered. We were all cowards in his eyes. A pioneer corporal however then came forward with one of my mates (a Saarlander). The pair put in two 25kg boxes of explosive. It was tamped and blown. (Corporal Ludwig Feikert, 399 Pioneer Mining Company)[23]

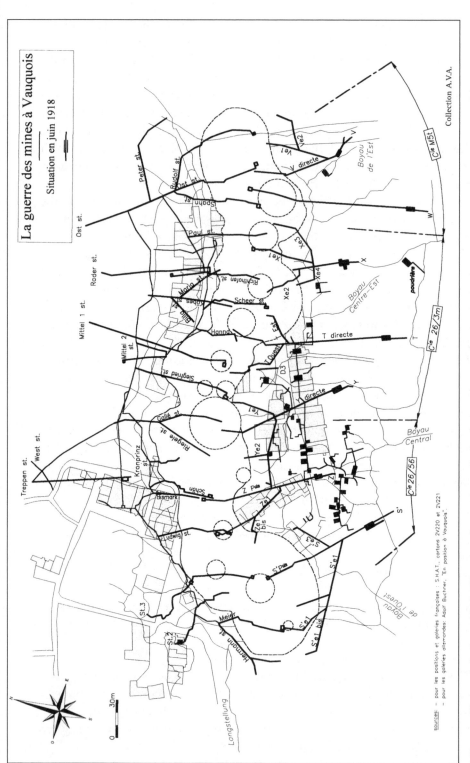

Mines at Vauquois in June 1918. The situation at the end of mine warfare. Only the deep active galleries are shown. The French have belatedly driven long galleries from their rear slope on the south of the ridge, but the Germans have a deep network already established. From Amis de Vauquois, *La Butte Meurtrie*. (Collection Amis de Vauquois)

The Germans blew the charge on 29 December, gassing two French sappers.

At the end of February 1918, in the expectation of a German offensive on the western front, preparations were put in hand by the French engineers to destroy the underground workings should the ridge be abandoned by their forces. The Germans continued to advance underground and, at the beginning of 1918, their three deepest galleries had reached 95, 94 and 92m depth and remained undiscovered by the French. They began a chamber at the end of Mittel Stollen capable of taking a charge of 200 tonnes. The French, however, believed that there were signs that the Germans were also becoming less aggressive and looking to stabilize the situation. When the Germans blew a camouflet in February they then halted their gallery, timbered the face and installed a listening post. In the month of March 1918 they blew just one camouflet. After the launch of the German offensive on 21 March an attack on Vauquois seemed unlikely. On that day the French blew 3 tonnes of cheddite, which was to be their last camouflet at Vauquois. At the end of March the German pioneers were ordered to cease work in the deep galleries, but to blow on 9 April against the French Y attack gallery and to answer the French blow of 21 March. This camouflet, which destroyed two French galleries, was to be the last at Vauquois. The 1/Pi 30 left Vauquois on 18 April after three years and four months on the ridge and its place was taken by 399 and 412 Pioneer Mining Companies. The French recovered their galleries and continued maintenance. Their listening revealed almost no German activity in the east and west. They put seismo-microphones in the ends of their galleries, with charges of 100kg for contingencies. On 16 May Italian troops relieved the French on Vauquois, who left some engineer units. On 2 June the French began to remove their mining plant from the galleries, which they blocked with barbed wire and sandbag barricades. The deeper galleries quickly flooded after the pumps were removed. The listening devices were left in place, with the last report recorded on 22 June. Some galleries were left with charges in place, several of which remain to this day.

The German Vauquois position, where previously infantry were packed densely into the forward positions in underground shelters, was superseded by changes in defensive tactics in which the main forces were held further back. By 1 January 1918 the main line of resistance in the sector was through Varennes and Cheppy 1.5 miles in the rear. Vauquois was in the outpost zone, which would normally be expected to delay an advance while counterattack forces were mustered. The ridge, however, was not to be abandoned if attacked but held as a 'closed work', and the garrison was reported to have been equipped to hold it even though it was completely isolated. When Vauquois fell to the Allies on 26 September 1918, in the first phase of the Meuse-Argonne offensive, the garrison had been greatly reduced. The US 35th Division was supported by massive quantities of artillery and tanks and was aided by fog and smoke. Its troops bypassed and surrounded the ridge, which fell after some fierce but brief resistance. Mining played no part in the assault and little part in the defence.

The Germans maintained the initiative and supremacy underground at Vauquois during 1915-1918. Their position was potentially difficult as they held just 50m width of the plateau, which then fell steeply away in the northern slope. All their defences had to be squeezed into this small area and they dug extensive accommodation for an infantry garrison. They also turned the rear slope to their advantage, for it enabled them to drive only slightly inclined or even straight tunnels into the side of the hill, which were already beneath those shafts sunk by the French from their front lines. They could also easily evacuate the spoil by tipping it over the side. These mine entrances were impossible for the French to observe, except by aircraft, or to bombard. The more gentle slope behind the French position was less useful in this respect and it took the French longer to make use of this method of driving inclined galleries, which on their side had to be longer and more steeply sloped. The Germans also benefited from keeping the same pioneer unit in place at Vauquois for the whole of the active mining period, so that experience was gained in working the particular geology of the ridge and an intimate knowledge of the location and working habits of the French miners was acquired. The 1/Pi 30 was supplemented at Vauquois by infantry mining companies, for example Stollenbaukompanie (Tunnelling Company) 1, formed from the 98th Infantry Regiment, and Stollenbaukompanie 2 from the 130th. In April 1917 these were converted into 398 and 399 Pioneer Mining Companies.[24] The Germans were less hampered by a shortage of personnel, but seem to have more quickly mechanized their mining at Vauquois.

Both Vauquois and Les Éparges were active mining areas owing to their value as important observation posts. They also were heavily fought over for doctrinal reasons. The Germans, until 1916, defended their front lines tenaciously and held large numbers of men in or immediately behind it for that purpose. The French made extremely costly attacks to recover the smallest villages from German hands. Both sides, however, considered withdrawal from Vauquois. The French wished to disengage from mining as not worth the effort and a war that they were not winning, but found it difficult to do so without wholly giving up the position. Ultimately it was the change in German defensive doctrine which was the deciding factor in mining coming to an end at Vauquois. By the time of the capture of Vauquois by the US 35th Division the ridge was, in effect, an outpost of the main defence line and was enveloped by a tank advance.

Chapter 4

British Mining Operations 1915- early 1916

The year 1915 saw the spread of mining, usually directed at very local targets with little or no central coordination. The British started mining without the experience of the French or German military engineers of continental siege warfare. The vacuum was, of necessity, filled by civilian experts, who were given far more freedom and in time incorporated into the army structure far more effectively than in the German or French armies. This was to a great extent brought about by the forceful personality of Norton Griffiths, and it is hard to imagine a civilian exerting such influence in the German or French armies in the field in wartime. Ultimately this meant that the British in 1915-1916 developed a very powerful mining potential. Unfortunately, although they had the technique, they knew less about how best to use it.

Norton Griffiths reached France late on 13 February and the next morning was taken by Colonel Harvey to the front line at Givenchy. Griffiths established that the ground was suitable for the clay-kickers, whose technique he had demonstrated to Kitchener with the fire shovel.

The clay-kicker, with grafting tool, and the timber brace which was propped between the mining frames and gave it the name 'working on the cross'. From Grieve and Newman, *Tunnellers*.

At GHQ Griffiths, Harvey and Fowke, the Chief Engineer, discussed the use and organisation of the units. They rejected an initial idea of forming sections that would be attached to the existing Field Companies and instead proposed complete units of five officers and 269 men. This strength was calculated on the basis of working 12 galleries continuously, each of which had three working faces.[1] They wished to form eight such companies, using a mixture of skilled men transferred from units already in France and men specially enlisted from the United Kingdom. The units were to be known as Tunnelling Companies, and the men called tunnellers rather than the existing term miner, presumably because the men recruited were not trained sappers, in which there had previously been the trade of miner, but were specially enlisted civilians. Norton Griffiths persisted in referring to the troops and units as 'Moles'; he said for security purposes. On 17th Norton Griffiths reported back to Kitchener at the War Office:

> …laying before him what I thought was possible, and saying that the position was more than serious for the poor devils doing the dirty work in the trenches, for you could not expect Tommy to be shot at from the surface, boofed at from above and blown to hell from below.
> (Sir John Norton Griffiths MP)[2]

He wired his manager, James Leeming, to bring down to London the next day the first batch of clay-kickers, who were engaged on a major sewerage contract in Manchester. Eighteen were passed fit for service, including Norton Griffiths's foreman Richard Miles, who was made a Sergeant, attested into the Army and sent to the Royal Engineers depot at Chatham. On 19th the War Office approved the GHQ proposal for the formation of Tunnelling Companies and Norton Griffiths and the 18 men crossed to France.

On 17 February British sappers blew a small mine taken over from the French south of Ypres at Hill 60, but without great effect. The Germans retaliated with a small mine nearby at Zwarteleen, but were driven out of the British positions. On 21st, however, they blew a large mine nearby killing forty-seven men and ten officers of the 16th Lancers (the attack referred to by Norton Griffiths). In mid-March the Germans blew another large mine at Zwarteleen, creating a 30ft deep crater but damaging their own lines in the process.[3] In April Hill 60 was to be the scene of the first British mining success of the war. The position was formed from railway cutting spoil and named after its height in metres. It was an important observation point in the southern part of the Ypres Salient and was destined to be severely contested both above and below ground. The British took over a French rameau de combat (M3 on illustration, see p77), which had been used for a few blows, and began two new tunnels. The work was carried out by Territorials of the 1st Northumberland Field Company, RE, and the 1st and 3rd Monmouthshire Regiment. Before the Tunnelling Companies were in operation and for many months afterwards, mining in the British sectors was carried out by Brigade Mining Sections and ad hoc units formed from miners and mining engineers in units already at the front. Two important sources of experienced miners were available for these units. The first was the British Army Reserve. Officers on the Reserve included civil engineers, who were to be given command of some Tunnelling Companies later in 1915. In early 1915 men in the ranks who had served in the British Army and remained on the Reserve, but who had subsequently taken up mining, were a source of miner-soldiers. The second source was the part-time Territorial Force units that recruited in mining areas, such as those at Hill 60, which provided officers and men with important experience and skills. The Territorials at Hill 60 were under the command of a regular Sapper officer and were joined latterly by the first men of the newly formed 171 Tunnelling Company. They charged six mines beneath and immediately in front of the German front line, which they blew on 17 April as part of a coordinated attack on the Hill. The larger pair of charges (M1 and M2, see below) were 2,700lbs and the total of the five mines was 9,900lbs. Norton Griffiths, visiting one week before the blow, advised the Engineer-in-Chief that the mines should be blown at the same time that the infantry advanced to assault the hill:

> This will prove the biggest mine yet exploded. If advantage is taken of the dust! (Bricks, mortar & G.'s) by sending forward attacking party the same time the button is pressed. Not waiting for air to clear it should give ample cover for attacking party. Wiser to get a few men hit with falling bricks or G's than to get a larger number hit by Machine Guns.[5]

Rough plan of the Hill 60 mines blown by the British on 17 April 1915. From *Military Mining*, 1922.

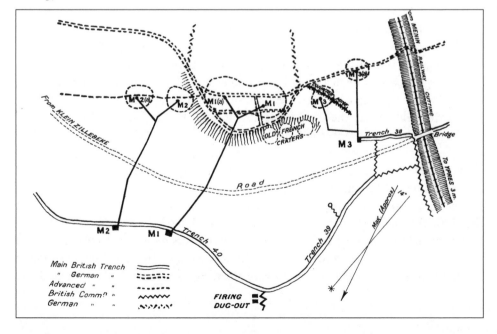

Full surprise was achieved with the mines, which were blown at ten-second intervals, with the artillery only opening fire on the detonation of the first pair. The troops were warned to take cover from the debris, which was thrown 200–300ft high and scattered over 250yds, although a man who looked over the parapet to see the explosions was killed. Those Germans who survived the mines were overwhelmed by the attackers, who took the craters in minutes, and the actual assault cost the British just seven casualties, although the Germans brought very heavy fire onto the captured positions.[6]

It was realized that Hill 60 alone would be difficult to hold, as the Germans were still in possession of the Caterpillar on the opposite side of the railway cutting. Two days after the capture, Norton Griffiths visited Major William Johnston VC, commanding 172 Tunnelling Company, which had just taken over the Hill 60 sector. Norton Griffiths was constantly looking for opportunities for his Moles and recommended that General Glubb should now attack the Caterpillar:

> It is important for the Chief Engineer to know that some 450 feet from the position we now hold there is another Hill which is strongly fortified. It would be easy to mine this from the position we now hold running the Mole along the side of this Hill & then run under them. A good blow & happy results could be obtained here. Johnston keen on this & no time should be lost to get busy at once.[7]

Norton Griffiths was also becoming aware of the larger potential of mining and the danger of using it merely to deal with positions which were a local annoyance. An officer on Glubb's staff later described the problem of attempting to hold Hill 60 in isolation:

> Probably, as events turned out, it would have been wiser to have raided the defences and retired as originally proposed, forcing the enemy to keep a large garrison on the hill exposed to fire if he wished to retain it. For Hill 60 when recaptured would form a small but pronounced salient, exposed to attack on both sides: officers who knew the ground were of [the] opinion that it could not be held unless the Caterpillar also was taken. (Col. James Edmonds, Staff Officer to Engineer in Chief, GHQ)[8]

Indeed, the Germans retook Hill 60 using chlorine gas just nineteen days later on 5 May and held it for almost two years.

The mine blows of 17 April apparently came as a surprise to the Germans[9] and the difficulty of pushing forward tunnels at Hill 60 led to an attempt by the Experimental Company of the Prussian Guard Pioneers to use an electric tunnelling machine, without success (see Chapter 8). In early October the company was ordered to the sector on either side of the Menin Road to take over mine workings there, including at Hooge. The company took over the Divisional Mining unit and addressed the technical problem of sinking mines in this area, which led to successful blows in June 1916.

On 14 March the Bavarians fired two mines at St Eloi, south of Ypres, capturing the village, trenches including a mine shaft and a 30ft high heap of earth called the Mound by the British and the Lehmhugel by the Germans. After severe fighting the British retook the village, but the Mound remained in German hands.[10]

British mining was carried out by a Field Company, which ran out two galleries and was relieved on 25 March by 172 Tunnelling Company. Both sides frequently blew small charges against one another and then, exactly a month after taking the Mound, the Germans again fired a mine, creating a very large crater 70ft in diameter. It did not, however, damage a 172 Company shaft sunk from the cellar of a ruined house 50ft away.[11] The regular Sapper OC of 172 Company, Johnston VC, disliked mining and obtained a posting in early May, leaving in command a Territorial Captain in the Monmouthshire Regiment, William Clay Hepburn. Hepburn was an experienced mining engineer and colliery agent and the first non-regular Sapper to command a Tunnelling Company.[12] Norton Griffiths worked to persuade GHQ that mining engineers should be allowed to command Tunnelling Companies and by the autumn of 1915 this became accepted.

Hepburn placed Lieutenant Hickling in charge at St Eloi and by early July he and Second Lieutenant Gard'ner had charged two large mines of 1,400 and 1,500lbs and a series of smaller charges. The explosive was ammonal, a commercial blasting explosive safer and more powerful than gunpowder, which was to become the standard British mining explosive. Both of the two large charges were just short of the German front line and when blown would damage the parapets and bury the Germans with debris. Hepburn recalled forty-five years afterwards that he had gone to General Glubb, Chief Engineer of the 2nd Army, to ask for artillery support, but was told that there was insufficient ammunition for an attack and that he would have to blow the mines without an accompanying attempt to seize the craters. They blew the charges on 10 July:

William Clay Hepburn, the first professional mining engineer to command a Tunnelling Company. From *Just a Small One*, a magazine produced by 172 Tunnelling Company, Christmas 1915. (RE Museum)

Hickling fired the right-hand charges and Gard'ner the left, which he described in a letter two days later:

> We have just fired some very successful mines. We had two main mines and four smaller ones. The net result of it was to destroy an obnoxious 'snipers' house', blow up a section of trench and swamp a lot more of it with earth, and utterly wreck a lot of German attempts at mining. Altogether we fired off about 4,000lb. of explosive. The Germans were scared to death and ran as if the Devil was behind them, so that our machine-guns were able to get in a lot of useful work. We did not attempt to take the trench, though it could have been done without difficulty – the trouble would have been to hold it afterwards.
>
> The sight was magnificent. With our main charges the explosion was terrific. The earth heaved up like a big pimple, broke with a tremendous flame bursting through, and then the earth shot up in the air for 200 feet like an enormous fountain. In one instance one of our smaller charges exploded a counter-charge in a German gallery which we knew to be alongside of us. We knew we had to take prompt action, and were putting forth every effort to get our main charges completed and ready for firing. The débris was scattered over a tremendous area, and we had to crouch behind parapets to protect ourselves. As the craters were about 100 yards away, you may imagine what it was like in the German trenches. The earth rocked like a ship at sea, and it is reported that one man was actually sick!
>
> The men in our trenches were in great glee, all up on the firing-step of the parapet and blazing away at the panic-stricken enemy.
>
> All the authorities are highly delighted, and the Commander of the 2nd Army Corps sent H. [Hickling] and myself a special telegram of congratulations, so we may yet figure as 'mentioned in dispatches'. (2Lt Walter Gard'ner, 172 Tunnelling Company).[13]

With superiority in ammunition, the Germans were able to retake their abandoned front line and the Mound.[14] At this stage the tunnels were at about 30ft and into the loam, but Hepburn and Hickling were keen to go deeper.[15]

There was undoubtedly frustration amongst the Tunnellers that the BEF was unable to make better use of their growing ability to place mines under the Germans. After another blow on 24 July, Gard'ner expressed disappointment that the Army did not have the capability to occupy even temporarily the craters that they were blowing in the vicinity of the German lines:

> It would have been advantageous if the infantry could have occupied this crater. As it was, being close to the enemy line, it was occupied by the Germans, who found it a very useful starting point for further mining

operations. They were driving piles, &c., without any attempt at avoiding noise, and could be heard most distinctly. Later on, after the system of raiding developed, a party would no doubt have been detailed to rush the crater and destroy the enemy works. (2Lt Walter Gard'ner)[16]

At Hooge, however, on 19 July, the British succeeded in blowing and occupying a large crater. The 175 Company managed to sink a shaft about 35ft through green sand to blue clay and ran a tunnel 190ft and charged it with 4,900lbs, mainly ammonal.[17] The British seized the crater after the blow; there was no preliminary bombardment, owing no doubt to lack of shells, but this gave the British complete surprise, and the Germans had not suspected mining in the area, having abandoned their own attempts owing to the extreme difficulties caused by water.[18] The British were able to consolidate the crater and captured trenches. Eleven days later, however, in an operation with parallels to their recapture of Hill 60 using chlorine gas, the Germans retook Hooge with flame throwers in their first use against British troops.

Another early success by a Tunnelling Company was achieved by Preedy's 170 Company at a position known as the Brickstacks, which was dominated by piles of bricks at a former brickworks. Some of the stacks were in British hands, some German. The company sank three shafts, 4ft square, from the front line to a depth of 16ft, and drove tunnels beneath no man's land in order to check German mining work. At 65ft from the shafts they joined the three tunnels with a transversal. On 13th March Norton Griffiths reported that Preedy's instructions limited him to defensive work, and that his No.3 drive had 150ft to go before it would reach the German lines. Subsequently, however, he was authorized to drive an attack with two of the tunnels. The soil was a softish sandstone mixed with loam, which was not suitable for clay-kicking and gave off a lot of water. These galleries were 3ft 6in high by 2ft 9in at the bottom and 2ft 6in at the top. As the tunnels grew longer, however, conditions became extremely difficult as water pumps and air blowers proved inadequate. They stopped work 25ft short of the German lines as the risk of detection became serious and Preedy had to give three days notice that he was ready to fire a mine. Permission being given, he continued driving until just short of the German trench: No.2 gallery was 170ft and No.3 158ft. The drive had taken 15 days. They charged No.2, in front of one of the brickstacks, with 1,000lbs gunpowder and No.3 with 650lbs guncotton. When blown on 3 April, No.2 was claimed to have brought down the face of the brickstack, while No.3 destroyed 90ft of trench.[19]

The first operation by a Tunnelling Company was to accompany the British attack at Aubers Ridge on 9 May to coincide with the Second Battle of Artois. With difficulty, 173 Tunnelling Company and Norton Griffiths's manager Leeming drove two long tunnels, of 285 and 330ft, beneath the German lines and charged each with 2,000lbs of explosive. They had to abandon four galleries further to the south owing to flooding, but discovered that at Cordonnerie Farm, 15ft beneath the waterlogged running green sand, was stiff blue clay. Leeming was to pioneer the sinking of shafts through the running sands to the clay levels. The clay-kickers could drive tunnels though this layer, although at times they accidentally broke into the sand above. The distinctive blue clay had to be concealed during the digging of the galleries as an indicator of mining activity. The Germans were aware of the blue clay layer but probably lacked the skill to sink a shaft to it and to work through it:

> ...the British offensive came as a surprise on our front. No special preparations had been noticed, and even the presence of the mines driven under the front trenches of the regiment next to us had not been perceived. Our own efforts at mining up to now had failed owing to the amount of surface water, nevertheless the enemy had dug a gallery through a belt of loam that underlay the thin clay stratum which held the surface water. He thereby prepared a way for his initial success. (History of the Bavarian Reserve Regiment No.17)[20]

The two mines, 70ft apart, were, like the Hill 60 mines, blown at zero. They assisted the attacking infantry of the 1/13th London Regiment (Kensingtons) in this particular sector, who took the craters, and supporting troops continued beyond the German's third trench.

The blows by Preedy's 170 Company at the Brickstacks in early April against the German 14th Westphalian Division caused it immediately to set about forming specialized mining companies. Very probably due to a realisation that the British must have used specialist miners to have driven quickly through difficult ground, miners and reserve officers who were mining engineers or mine surveyors in civil life were found from the infantry and formed into two mining companies. They were placed under the commander of the 3rd Company of the 7th Westphalian Pioneers, which had carried out the first attack against the British on 20 December 1914. The actual construction of tunnels in the Division was placed entirely in the hands of the mining companies, while the charging and blowing of explosives was the responsibility of a 'Sprengkommando' under an NCO from the 3rd Company of the 7th Pioneers. The miners set about pushing forward defensive galleries and blowing mines to destroy the British tunnels reaching close to their lines. Two large craters, called Monokel and Brille (monocle and spectacles), were blown, seized and consolidated and then used as the starting points for new attack tunnels, in the manner traditional in siege operations, as they moved from the defensive to the offensive. Soon the German miners neared the British line and were both above and below British galleries. They worked with great care and in silence, using neither drills nor mine trucks. They went without boots in stockinged feet and placed each cut spit of sandy clay into sandbags, which they carried up the incline. In conditions of silent working, there were break-ins in which Rothe, commanding the Sprengkommando, particularly distinguished himself in the ensuing underground fights, and:

...who penetrated into an enemy tunnel and whose personnel settled the matter partly with the pistol, partly by taking prisoners, whereupon the tunnel was speedily charged with explosives and blown. The Iron Cross First Class formed the wages for his courageous act.[21]

They constructed defensive transversals and placed microphones in the listening galleries to detect the British at work. The inclined mine galleries begun from the front lines did not allow them to descend quickly enough to the required depth and they began to set them back either between the first and second trenches or behind the second trench. They sank beneath and behind the piles of bricks, and quickly reached down 5–6m before reaching a thick water-bearing chalk layer. The removal of this water required electric pumps and a special troop of fitters to pipe away the water into the canal. Eventually it was found that the labour and difficulties of dewatering rendered working below the water table impractical. The German tunnel system at the Brickstacks lay at most 6–7m deep and the water level did not permit going any deeper. According to the regimental historian, miners were frequently cut off by British camouflets, but at that comparatively shallow depth they were able to dig themselves free. The miners adopted their own faster system of timbering, using frames only every 50cm unless the ground was badly shaken by blows. Apart from defensive blows to destroy enemy mining, in principle they only blew if they heard British work with the naked ear. The Germans claimed that their mining companies prevented the British from approaching or blowing under their positions. They also managed to drive a gallery 200m, working knee-deep in water, to the British second trench and blow a charge of 7,500kg beneath a brickstack which they believed to conceal a headquarters dugout.[22]

South of the Brickstacks, the quiet working in sandy clay also led to incidents where the opponents broke into one another's galleries. On 6 September, 173 Company experienced two instances of contact. The first occurred when a heading came up against German timbers, behind which the Germans could be heard talking. They placed a charge and tamped it, leaving a length of armoured hose running through the tamping to the German tunnel. Through this a German-speaking intelligence officer listened for nineteen days, hoping to find some information of value. In the second contact, the floor of the British tunnel suddenly gave way and collapsed into a German gallery. The Germans were lying in wait and opened fire on the British miners. In the darkness, the British managed to place and fire a 25lb charge of blastine. Lt Fred Bell then entered the gallery and used his revolver to clear the Germans out and keep them at bay while a sandbag barricade was built. The British then placed a 200lb charge against it, tamped and blew the charge.[23]

Some of the mine blows resulted in fierce fights above ground and troops in an active mining area lived in an atmosphere of continual fear and uncertainty, robbed of any security that the trenches and dugouts might have given them. All noises became suspect. As early as June 1915 the Brickstacks sector was a mass of craters along the length of no man's land for a distance of 1,000yds.[24]

An attack was carried out on 15 June at Givenchy to support a French attack scheduled but then postponed. The Tunnelling Company, 176, was commanded by a civil engineer on the RE Reserve, Captain Edward Momber. It blew a mine of 3,000lbs of ammonal, plus 30lbs of guncotton, at the Duck's Bill near the junction of the British 7th and the Canadian Divisions. The artillery had been carrying out a slow bombardment for 48 hours before the attack, which did not come as a surprise to the Germans. The mine was fired at 5.58am, two minutes before the infantry attacked. Some Canadians who had not heeded warnings from 176 Company to leave the danger area were injured by falling debris. The German infantry, however, manned the trench firesteps and were ready to repel the attack at 6am. The British lacked artillery owing to a serious shell shortage and any impact that the blowing of the mine had was lost to German superiority in artillery.[25]

The British fired several mines on 25 September 1915, either directly as part of the British offensive at Loos or for diversionary attacks on other parts of the front. The most extensive subsidiary attack was at Ypres on the Menin Road, preceded by the firing of two pairs of mines under the German front line, prepared by 175 Company with assistance from the 9th Brigade Mining Company. At the same time as the mine explosion, sappers from a Field Company rushed forward to blow gaps in the German wire and the German trench was taken in the first rush. Further progress could not be made, however, and in the afternoon the Germans forced the British out of their trenches with shelling and grenades. North of the road a mine was blown just before the attack, and although British troops managed to keep possession of it, they also could not retain any German trenches.[26] On either side of the La Bassée Canal, where the 2nd Division attacked on the northern flank of the actual British offensive, four mines were fired as part of the attack. Prior to 25 September, however, the extent of mining in this area caused the Germans to modify their defensive tactics. They evacuated their front trench, levelling the parapet so that it offered no cover for attackers, and converted the trench 100yds behind into their main defence. Although the pre-war doctrine of holding the front line in strength was to remain official German practice until late 1916, pulling back from the front line was a simple means of increasing the width of no man's land and negating the danger of mine galleries that had taken the British many months to construct. The high lips of the craters in no man's land also left the front lines vulnerable to parties of attackers assembling close by under their cover. In particular, south of the La Bassée Road, the two largest craters, known as Vesuvius and Etna, had lips over 8ft high which concealed the trench lines. Such withdrawal was not an option easily available to the Allies: for the French every piece of ground was liberated territory and in the northern area around La Bassée contained valuable coal mines.[27] The British were unaware of the German withdrawal and on 25 September the 2nd Division attack was made against the evacuated front line. Four mines were blown on the 2nd Division: at the Brickstacks 170 Company blew two mines to support the 2nd South Staffords, while to their right 173 Company also blew two (each 1,000lbs of gunpowder) to support the 19th Brigade. These, however, were ordered to be fired at two minutes before zero which, in the words of the official historian, 'put the enemy thoroughly on the alert.' The infantry crossing no man's land (already hampered by their own drifting chlorine gas) were forced to bunch into the gaps between existing and new craters, which served to disorganize the attack and helped the Germans to concentrate their fire. Furthermore, the prior evacuation of their front line by the Germans wholly negated the effect of these mines.[28] North of the La Bassée Canal a major diversion was staged commencing at 6.00am, half an hour before the main attack. At Givenchy 176 Company was ordered to blow a mine which they had laid under the German front trench, again at two minutes before zero. Again, owing to the German withdrawal, the attacking infantry found the German front trench empty and, continuing to the support trench, came under heavy fire.[29]

An exaggerated claim for the possibilities of mining at Loos was put forward by Grieve and Newman in 1936, who appeared unaware of the four mines on the 2nd Division front and asserted that the Tunnellers were required to do no mining for the attack:

> ...why were the possibilities of mine warfare so completely ignored? ... Suppose a dozen large mines had been fired at the moment of battle? It would not have been impossible, and the results might have been far-reaching?[30]

To place a dozen mines on the Loos front would have required perhaps a four-month delay to the offensive, which was not an option as the date as well as the location of the British attack was dictated by the French. Placing mines under the German lines of a determined and skilful enemy was especially difficult in the Loos area, which would require going deep into the chalk, in which it was almost impossible to work silently. The use of mines at the Battle of Loos exhibited problems of mine warfare that were to appear again. Firstly, a legacy of active mine warfare was the deeply cratered no man's land which, while it might offer cover for advancing troops, could also impede and confuse the attackers. Secondly, by ordering the mines to be blown at two minutes before zero, rather than precisely at zero, there was confusion on the staff over the danger of casualties amongst the infantry from falling debris, which it was believed might cause the attack to waver. As will be seen, this confusion remained unresolved into 1916, despite a growing body of experience in the BEF.

Away from the developing experience on the Western Front, mining was actively pursued following the landings in Turkey on the Gallipoli peninsula by British and Anzac troops in April 1915. Fighting was deadlocked in trench warfare and mining was initiated in May by the Turks at the Anzac front and by the British at Helles. Mining units were formed in both sectors. At Helles the 8th Corps Mining Company operated under Captain H.W. Laws, a temporarily commissioned mining engineer in the Royal Naval Division. Not everyone, however, regarded mining as beneficial:

> Personally I could never appreciate what material advantage we gained from our labours, nor did I ever meet any one who was particularly enthusiastic over the work, with the very notable exception of the O.C. Mines, 8th Corps ... (Surgeons Geoffrey Sparrow RN and J.N. MacBean RN, Royal Naval Division).[31]

After the British advance in June and July, 8th Corps resumed mining near the Vineyard and Fusilier Bluff, attacking local objectives using small charges from shallow tunnels. At Fusilier Bluff, galleries were driven through the sandstone to create positions looking over the Turkish positions, in the manner of mining at Gibraltar during the siege of the 1780s. In softer ground there were numerous contacts underground, especially in the clay at the Gridiron and the Vineyard. From the comparatively shallow tunnels, miners buried alive were sometimes able to dig themselves out. Joseph Murray, a Durham miner attached to the 8th Corps Mining Company, described regaining consciousness after a Turkish blow to find that he and a comrade were trapped in a collapsed tunnel beneath no man's land:

> Alec and I groped about in the dark, looking for our candles and matches. We found neither so decided to explore the gallery to ascertain where the explosion had occurred. The level part was reasonably clear. Several minor falls of roof had taken place but we had no difficulty in climbing over these obstructions to reach the rising part. From here we should have been able to see daylight, but we couldn't.
>
> We knew now that we were entombed but the gallery was still open. We groped our way up the rising gallery and at once realized we should not be able to go much further. Everywhere was broken up. Timber—not broken but dislodged—prevented any further movement up the slope and we did not know if this blockage was the seat of the explosion or only another fall. We tugged at the timber until we got it free. Quite a lot of earth came away with it which told us we had no more gallery left and our only hope of survival would be to claw our way upwards through the broken earth, knowing full well that if it was too loose it would suffocate us. We estimated that we were at least twenty-five feet below the surface... and decided that if we endeavoured to burrow slantwise, making steps as we went, we would have further to go but would be able to get rid of some of the earth and, at the same time, have more room for air.

I began to burrow, with Alec behind me heaving the lumps of clay down the eight feet or so of the sloping gallery. We changed over repeatedly and, as time passed, found it increasingly difficult to clear the earth away. The burrow behind us had closed in and the roof kept caving in. We were unable to extricate ourselves from the earth we had clawed away and the constant falling of the roof altered our direction.

We burrowed where the earth was loose, clawing side by side now, with only our arms free. Inching our way upwards, we clawed with our hands and pushed with our legs to keep us moving. We had very little room but the air seemed better. The earth felt more lumpy and we found it difficult to move. Lumps of earth were wedged between us and were most uncomfortable.

Twisting and turning in an effort to free my legs, I fancied I saw daylight for a fraction of a second. Alec did not see it, but believed me. With new hope we struggled on; our time was running out and we both knew it. Again and again we were completely buried but, in time, managed to clear ourselves. After one fall of earth I could feel what I believed to be clothing. It certainly was not earth—and I was violently sick.

Alec was delighted though; in his super-human effort to free his legs so that he might also feel the body, he brought down more earth and shouted that he, too, had seen daylight. This time I did not see it—I was too sick and my eyes were closed, but... was satisfied that we were near the surface... This body we could feel must have been in the line; if only we could manage a few more feet!

With renewed strength we clawed but the daylight—if it was daylight— remained out of sight.

We had burrowed a long way and the hope of a while ago had long since gone. I think we slept from exhaustion. We had lost all sense of time and it seemed that we had been entombed all our lives.

I was awakened by Alec shouting that he could see daylight again. The air was certainly fresher. I had lots of energy now and, after another fall of earth, we had our heads above the surface. My arms were pinned with the rest of my body and the glare of the light, even though it was almost dark, compelled me to keep my eyes closed... Strangely enough, neither of us made any attempt to free ourselves. We were satisfied to have our heads above ground. We were on the Turkish side of a huge crater, about five feet below the rim. (Able Seaman Joseph Murray, 15 September 1915)[32]

At Anzac tunnels became a major feature of the fighting on 'Second Ridge' both, as at Helles, for shallow level mine warfare, but also in the use of underground saps by which the front line was pushed forward (described in Chapter 9). Cyril Lawrence worked on an underground sap driven from the Pimple towards Lone Pine, which was extended to make a mine gallery:

Last night I arrived at our sap mouth B5 about 1.30a.m. instead of midnight due to my having been hunting for the damn thing in the dark. As I said before, the trenches are just full of sleeping men and one cannot walk about very freely; consequently it took some time to get round and find the thing. Before I went up, it had been decided to continue our operations underground instead of breaking through the surface. This will give us more protection and will be better in many ways. With our tunnel which is called B5 we are in about 120 feet. The tunnels are about five feet six inches high and three feet wide. All the earth is carted out in sand bags and then shovelled on to a dump in some convenient spot. It is jolly hard work picking and shovelling by candlelight and after working for a while you are wringing wet and then you spell and immediately get cold, because down here in these burrows it is both cold and damp. I was not sorry when we knocked off this morning at 8 o'clock and got back to camp. (Lance Corporal Cyril Lawrence, 2nd Field Company, Australian Engineers, 6 June 1915)[33]

The intense mining activity resulted in numerous break-ins and underground fights, especially at Anzac. However, perhaps as a result of the debility caused by the conditions on the Peninsula, there were also instances of 'live and let live' above and below ground. An example of this occurred at Lone Pine when 2nd Australian Field Company blew a charge of 30lbs guncotton on 11 September after sounds of Turkish working. After the tamping was removed an opening was discovered into the Turkish tunnel and both sides built barricades and posted sentries within yards of one another.[34] Cyril Lawrence described, and drew, the situation in his diary five days later:

Near one of our tunnels, old Johnno had been working against us for some days and it was decided to blow him. The mine was laid and fired in due time, poor Johnno working away right up to the last moment. What happened to him we never found out, but as the trenches were so close we could not place a large charge for fear of damaging our own lines. Consequently all we did was to blow a hole into their tunnel. Immediately both sides erected barricades something after this style [see p89], and for some days firing went on from both sides, no one being hit. During this time we started further back in our tunnel and burrowed in and down eight feet-odd and then along as shown dotted. We eventually blew the whole concern up – Turk and all. (Lance Corporal Cyril Lawrence, 2nd Field Company, Australian Engineers, 16 September 1915).[35]

The strength of the defences above ground at Anzac meant that from September offensive work moved underground and the corps commander, Birdwood, ordered a comprehensive scheme along much of the sector. The plans

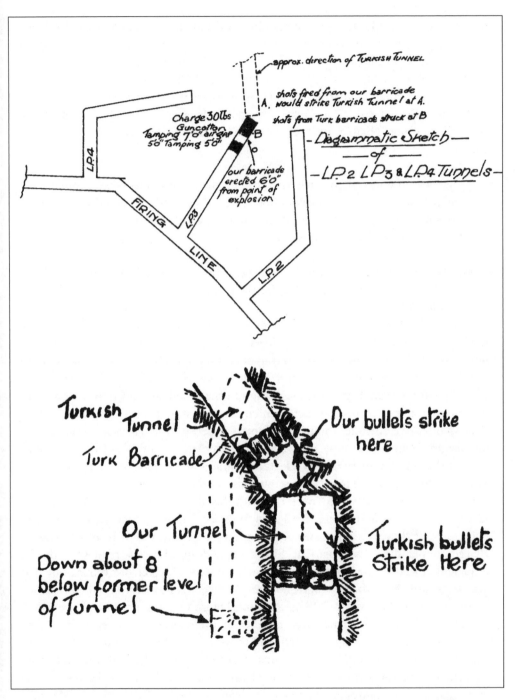

Drawings by Cyril Lawrence of the break in on the southern flank of Lone Pine, September 1915. From *The Gallipoli Diary of Sergeant Lawrence*.

of Major General J.G. Legge, commanding the 2nd Australian Division, for Lone Pine were the most ambitious, with a low-level system at 60ft commenced on 20 October and a yet deeper pair of tunnels ('Arnall's Folly' – described in Chapter 9) intended to enable infantry to emerge behind the Turkish lines.[36] By mid-November the mines along the Anzac position were either approaching, or in many places actually beneath, the Turkish trenches. Charles Bean speculated in the Australian Official History about the possible impact of these mine galleries on the Turks:

> The position was then such that, if all the mines had been exploded simultaneously, there could undoubtedly have been administered to him a shock only comparable to that inflicted upon the Germans two years later by the firing of the mines at Messines.[37]

He claimed that a general attack launched at the moment of the explosion might have met with important success, but for the fact that reserves were no longer to be allocated to Gallipoli.

When the decision was taken to evacuate the Anzac and Suvla positions, Birdwood, in overall command at Gallipoli since 23 November, wished to use the mines to cover the hazardous withdrawal operation, for which he anticipated up to 2,000 casualties. In addition General Monro, commanding in the Mediterranean while he left the planning of the evacuation to Birdwood, asked firstly for a system of defensive mines to be considered to cover the withdrawal. Secondly he asked that 'an offensive attitude' should be adopted to deceive the Turks as to the British intentions. General Godley, now commanding Anzac, and his Chief of Staff replied that in certain carefully selected positions the explosion of mines might assist by forcing the Turks to be cautious. However, overall Godley strongly objected to the offensive to cover the withdrawal and had already started on a reverse tactic of conditioning the Turks to expect periods of quiet, especially at night, so that they would not suspect the ultimate withdrawal of troops.[38] General Byng, commanding IX Corps at Suvla, replied to Monro's request with the information that he was already organising a system of defensive mines, but that attack would be difficult and costly. Birdwood, however, wished serious consideration to be given to offensive action before the evacuation and the use of mines. The result was that a large number of mines were prepared prior to the evacuation and in the event not used, and they lie today beneath the Peninsula. At Anzac sixteen mines containing 14.5 tons of explosive were charged ready for firing in case of emergency (see table). General Godley instructed that, with the exception of three mines at the Nek, they were only to be fired on the order of a senior officer if the Turks were actually to attack. Those at the Nek were to be fired on the discretion of the Rearguard Commander at the very end of the evacuation, to prevent the Turks from following up the retirement. This was done at 3.30am on

20 December, completely destroying the Turkish front line, killing seventy men and forming two large craters. It served to alert the Turks to the evacuation of Anzac, but by this time the garrison was clear of the hills and almost entirely embarked.

Location	No. of Gallery	Charge
Russell's Top (the Nek)	L11	3/4 ton (1680lbs)
	L8	3/4 ton (1680lbs)
	Arnall's	2 tons (4480lbs)
Pope's	8	1/4 ton (560lbs)
Quinn's	18	1/2 ton (1120lbs)
	36A	1/2 ton (1120lbs)
Courtney's	D25B	1 ton (2240lbs)
	D9A4	1/4 ton (560lbs)
	D26E	1/4 ton (560lbs)
	D3	2 tons (4480lbs)
Opposite Johnston's Jolly	C7	2 tons (4480lbs)
	C38	3 tons (6720lbs)
	C2	1 ton (1120lbs)
	C5	1/4 ton (560lbs)
Lone Pine	Two mines	1/4 ton (560lbs) each

Evacuation Mines at Anzac. Only those at Russell's Top were blown, the remainder were left intact. Total 14.5 tons of which 11 tons were left undetonated.[39]

The British blew a large number of mines at Helles on 19 December during operations to divert Turkish attention from the evacuations at Suvla and Anzac.[40]

A similar number of mines were left at Helles as at Anzac. For over a week before evacuation at Helles on 9 January 1916, Joseph Murray recorded that the miners were filling 'all existing galleries' with explosives: 'Every gallery had to have its quota of explosive and most of them were ready for firing.'[41]

As at Anzac, the mines were for use in case of Turkish discovery of the evacuation and to forestall an attempt by them to advance while it was in progress. Of the large number charged, only six mines on the front of the Royal Naval Division seem to have been blown.[42]

The large number of mines blown during the Gallipoli campaign from May 1915 to January 1916, as on the Western Front during the same period, arose from intense but extremely local struggles and what were usually small and costly attacks. As such they were a symptom of the deadlock rather than the key to unlock it. There was to be no large set-piece use of mines, as Bean hoped might be made at Anzac, but which might only have achieved the securing of Second Ridge, that is, the objective of the first day.

In Flanders, Norton Griffiths was constantly trying to interest Fowke, the Engineer-in-Chief, in large-scale mining schemes, seemingly unaware that throughout 1915 British attacks were severely limited by the requirement for the BEF to conform to the French command on where and when they should attack, as well as a severe shortage of artillery ammunition. In May 1915 he suggested a means of taking the villages of Wytschaete and Messines, which stood on the rising ground south of Ypres called by the British the Messines Ridge (the Germans called it the Wytschaete Bogen or Bow). He included a crude drawing in his daily report to Fowke, but the suggestion was not taken up. In July Harvey and Norton Griffiths sketched the idea out but, according to Harvey, Fowke rejected it with derision.[43]

What particularly engaged Norton Griffiths were the possibilities of driving along the blue clay level as a means of getting beneath the German positions. The blue clay was closer to the surface on the low-lying ground, so by starting further back they would not have to sink through a deep expanse of running sand. They would, however, have to drive very long tunnels. In geological terms, therefore, holding the high ground was to be a disadvantage for the Germans. At the Spanbroekmolen, Peckham and Maedelstede Farm positions the Germans would have to sink shafts through up to 81ft depth of running sand to counter the British miners. By December 1915, the tunnellers facing the Ridge were exploring the possibilities independently of Norton Griffiths's lobbying. The commander of 250 Company, Cecil Cropper, had already begun sinking shafts with the sanction of the Canadian Corps and 2nd Army:

> The crux of the whole matter… was that we should be able to get down into the Ypresian Clay Bed, blue clay formation, in which we could carry on tunnelling operations. It became clear to me that this could not be done by trying to sink shafts in the front or support trenches. I discovered that by choosing a contour further down the slope of the hill or ridge the clay bed lay at a depth we could expect to reach. I chose a site situated in the cover of a wood where work could be concealed from the enemy. We were successful in getting the shaft down on to the blue clay beds. But this opened other questions, was it of any value now we could get to the blue clay? We were some distance from the enemy's position and a good depth below it. The enemy at this point were holding a strong point on high ground known as Spanbrukmolen [sic]. It would mean a tunnel of about 250 to 300 yards to get under it and it would be a question of a very large amount of explosive in a deep charge.

Along the sector facing the Messines Ridge for which my Company were responsible and in a North or North Westerly direction from Spanbrukmolen the enemy was very strongly situated at places known as Peckham (Farmhouse), Maedelsted Farm, Petit Bois & Hollandschur Farm.

I thought it would be possible to destroy all these positions by deep mining attack so I submitted my proposals for this to the Chief Engineer, Canadian Corps, who put them forward to the 2nd Army High Command. On receiving orders to proceed with the scheme we began work on shaft sinking about the middle of December 1915. (Captain Cecil Cropper, 250 Tunnelling Company).[44]

On 20 December, Norton Griffiths visited 250 Company and reported that Cropper was 'getting well into his stride & has got the big idea', with three shafts underway and a fourth site located. He further reported that a gallery that 175 Company was driving in the clay towards Hill 60 had advanced 600ft and that the commanders of 172 and 171 Companies also appreciated the importance of, as he put it, 'earthquaking' the ridge. He warned, however, that secrecy was vital: '…if no Company be allowed to blow the deep level game until the whole is completed the enemy, it is very unlikely, will tumble to it.' [45]

Harvey summed up the state of British mining at the close of 1915 as a defensive success but in need of greater coordination and direction:

By the end of the year in spite of the fact that mining had been in progress for nearly 12 months there was little to show for it, but a number of isolated mine shafts from each of which ran a multitude of galleries the whole representing on a plan a curiously misshapen tree. In spite of this the progress of the enemy miner had been checked and in many sectors of the front the fact that our miners were underground had done much to relieve the minds of the men in the trenches.[46]

He expressed this more light-heartedly in a lecture ten years later:

Most of the offensive mining of 1915 was devoted to what I call ornamental destruction, which is the demolition of individual snipers' nests, O.P. and M.G. outfits. These were frequently fired to celebrate some day of public rejoicing, Brigadiers' birthdays, and so on, but in no connection with any infantry operation. This sort of mining is perfectly useless for ending a war, it is very unsettling for the occupants of the posts blown up, certainly, but the *straf* which always followed made our trenches most unhealthy.[47]

As early as 3 March 1915, General Fowke had written to the General Staff concerning the need to coordinate mining operations so that they were on a definite plan:

> The first parties of miners have been thrown in somewhat hurriedly and while no doubt they are doing good work there is the possibility that the location of points of attack has been based on very local considerations.[48]

On 19 December 1915 Sir John French was replaced as Commander in Chief of the BEF by Sir Douglas Haig. At the beginning of 1916, Haig reformed the way that mining was controlled in his Armies and, after the formation of the Tunnelling Companies, this was to be the second essential step in achieving the effectiveness of British mining.

At the end of 1915 both the French and the British realized that mining had to be controlled centrally to prevent wasted effort on small-scale, uncoordinated schemes. British technical ability gave them the potential to gain an advantage over the Germans, but they were often unable to make use of it owing to lack of artillery and lack of tactical skill. Amongst the British command there was not yet the ability to use the potential that mines gave the attack; the problems of coordination would take another year to resolve. The BEF was not an instrument that could be used to carry out complex operations. Amongst the civilians there was an unrealistic understanding of what mines linked to infantry attacks could achieve. This was displayed by Norton Griffiths to some extent and was reflected post-war by Bean and Newman.

Chapter 5

Hohenzollern and St Eloi 1916

The year 1916 was to see the British succeed in placing large charges beneath the German trenches, which were detonated as part of major coordinated attacks of growing importance at the Hohenzollern Redoubt, St Eloi and the opening of the Battle of the Somme. This coordination was made possible by an important reorganisation of British mining on the Western Front, enacted on 4 January. The faults recognized with British mining – the lack of coordination of effort – were augmented at the end of 1915 by a complaint from the War Office that, despite the large numbers of miners that had been recruited, there was an apparent absence of any tangible result. It suggested that the appointment of an Inspector of Mines at GHQ to coordinate work would result in a more effective use of personnel. A similar suggestion having been made by GHQ, Harvey was instructed to draw up the duties of the Inspector of Mines:

> Knowing well the difficulties we had had in getting up-to-date information from the front, I drew up a charter for the I. of M. which would enable him to visit any mine, anywhere, and at any time, without any reference to the Headquarters of any formation, except to tell them he was going into their areas, and added the ordinary duties of an inspector. To my surprise, the G.S. at G.H.Q. accepted it, for it gave the I. of M. more freedom of movement than anyone else in France, except the C.-in-C. himself.[1]

Fowke offered the position of Inspector of Mines to Brigadier General H.F. Thuillier RE, who declined it. Harvey himself then asked to be considered and was given the post, which he held until 1917.[2] He was generally regarded as well-suited to dealing with the mining engineers and miners under his command. Although a regular, he was not from a military family and his father was a Bristol vintner who invented a cream sherry which today still bears his name. Harvey's experience in the business world perhaps prepared him for dealing with civilians.

The second element was the appointment to each Army of a Controller of Mines, who would be responsible for all the Tunnelling Companies and mining schemes in his Army, answerable to the Inspector of Mines at GHQ and the Chief Engineer of his Army. This move was in recognition of the tunnellers' potential being wasted on shallow defensive galleries or offensive schemes against minor targets chosen by the brigade, divisional or corps commanders. Norton Griffiths urged this to be hastened on 12 December 1915:

> To get the best possible results from any aggressive work may the controller of mines to each army – particularly the 2nd A be appointed as quickly as possible please! The time before us is, as it is, now very short.[3]

Control of the tunnellers was effectively taken from the control of these lower formations and placed at Army level. The Controllers were selected from those Regular RE officers who had commanded tunnelling companies since spring 1915.

The strategic situation seemed to suggest that Norton Griffiths's scheme to 'earthquake' the Messines Ridge might come to fruition in 1916. Haig planned an attack in Flanders and the first phase would be the capture of the Ridge. In early January he convened the first of weekly meetings of his Army commanders and Norton Griffiths gave a typically flamboyant and overstated explanation of the plan:

> …my old chief, that great man, General George Fowke, took me, with the then Colonel Harvey for an interview with the five Army commanders, upon which interview we considered so many lives depended. At that interview the scheme was unfolded to them, and I do not think it would ever have been undertaken had I not then said we could guarantee that if our mining system were completed – and we saw no reason why it should not be – it would save the lives of at least ten thousand men, and that when the day of the attack came the Army could walk to the top, smoking their pipes. I well remember these words being used, for we all knew, from the attacks which had already been made, the impossibility of a frontal attack on the Ridge being successful unless we were permitted to co-operate by undertaking this work. It was explained that the intention was, not to 'blow out', but to earthquake the whole of the Ridge, which, owing to the fact that the sandhills were virtually one big hill of sand, sitting on blue clay, gave us a splendid opportunity of achieving success in this direction and we guaranteed that not a single German machine gun, of the thousands that existed on the Ridge at the time, would bark on the day of the attack, if that attack were preceded by our little earthquake.
>
> The answer was still in the negative, but late that night my chief, General Fowke, informed me that authority had been given and we could proceed with the laying out of this work.[4]

During the next six months, from Hill 60 south seven miles to Le Gheer, all work was to be devoted to this operation and by June six mines were prepared for the attack. In March 1916, however, Norton Griffiths asked to be relieved of his duties in order, he said, to attend to his business affairs. This was probably correct, but he must also have realized that his role at GHQ was increasingly anomalous. The British tunnelling effort was established with excellent personnel and a structure for command and control that rendered his liaison work extraneous. His contribution had been through his force of personality and wide knowledge of civil and mining engineering, which injected vital civilian expertise into the BEF.

The British mining attack on the Hohenzollern Redoubt, 2 March 1916. From Edmonds, *Military Operations, France and Belgium, 1916*.

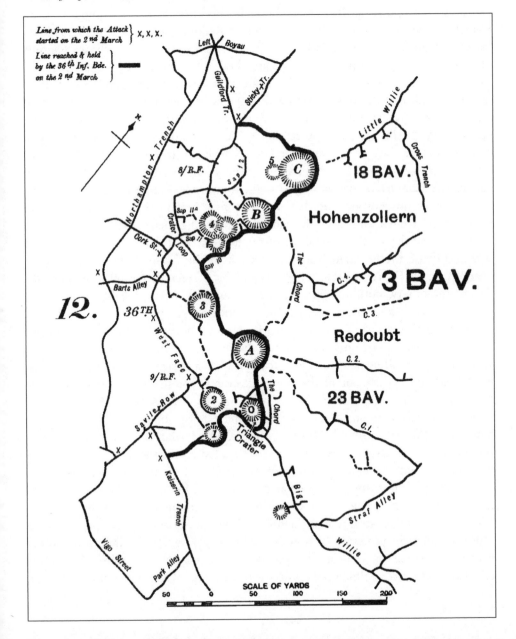

In the meantime, in March 1916 the British used mines in two operations involving infantry attacks at Hohenzollern Redoubt and St Eloi. At the end of the Battle of Loos on 13 October 1915 the British had attacked a complex of German trenches known as the Hohenzollern Redoubt and occupied half of the position. With the opposing lines very close to one another, tunnelling was carried out through a clay layer which was about 20ft deep. Below the clay was chalk of increasing hardness. Norton Griffiths suggested on 24 October that Preedy's 170 Company be moved so as to be opposite this position and that 'a big offensive work' should be carried out over the winter by two tunnelling companies using compressors to power drills to make bores for blasting.[5] Preedy's Company began work for a mining attack on the Hohenzollern Redoubt on 14 December 1915. By the end of the month he was in the process of sinking six shafts, with two sections of 180 Tunnelling Company due to be attached to his unit to begin another three. Preedy carried out mining in the clay to distract the Germans from their drilling into the chalk and the mine fighting during the winter resulted in a number of craters with high lips. The Germans were repeatedly more successful in occupying craters very quickly after they were blown, even when the British blew them. The reasons for this lay in the superior overall level of training of the Germans, especially the ability of NCOs to show initiative and leadership, combined with superiority in mortars, grenades and night illumination. The Germans used the advantageous observation afforded by these new craters to capture the British front line, a trench known as the Chord. By late February 1916, however, 170 Company had driven three galleries through the chalk between 161 and 200ft to within 30ft of the German front-line trench in the Chord. The galleries were charged on 29 February: the largest, 10,055lbs (Crater B, see p97), was at 30ft depth, the others, both 7,000lbs (Craters A and C), were probably at a similar depth. An additional mine of 1,000lbs, beneath the lip of crater No.2, was designed to throw debris into a network of German saps.[6] The decision to use these mines was taken only 'after much discussion' by the I Corps commander, General Gough.[7] Blowing the mines would lead to a fierce fight and the Germans might end up in possession of the new large craters and in a yet stronger position. Delay, however, would lead to the discovery of the charges by the Germans and Gough decided that an attack to retake the Chord should go ahead by two battalions, the 8th and 9th Royal Fusiliers, on 2 March. The attack orders prepared by 36th Brigade were extremely detailed and embodied a great deal of experience from the crater fighting of the previous months. In particular, the actual firing of the mines was used as the signal for both the infantry attack and the opening of the artillery: there was to be no preliminary bombardment. This acknowledged the central role of the mines. There was a desire to use surprise and rapidity rather than the step-by-step procedures of a siege, and a determination to beat the Germans in the race to take the beneficial position afforded by mine craters. There was no time interval between the firing of the mines and zero hour, when the troops were to leave their trenches to cross no man's land, but troops were warned to avoid falling debris:

> The assault must be delivered immediately the danger of injury from the falling earth is over, and before the dust and smoke have cleared away. Everything depends on taking the enemy by surprise.[8]

It was hoped that the German wire in front of the 9th Royal Fusiliers' attack, which was known to be formidable, would in the south be buried by debris from Crater A. The attackers were warned not to enter the bottom of the crater for ten minutes owing to the danger of gas, or 15 minutes if there was no wind. Trench mortars were to fire smoke bombs to screen the southern flank, with orders that it was 'essential that these bombs should be fired while the debris from the mine is still in the air.'[9] To gain entry and exit from the craters, which would have steep and unstable sides, the attackers were equipped with 15ft ladders, and as part of consolidation pathways were immediately to be cut.

The three main mines formed craters with diameters between 100 and 130ft and thus destroyed large portions of the Chord. The infantry at once assaulted and in the south, between and around the new Crater A and the enlarged Crater No.2, the 9th Royal Fusiliers reached the German trenches with hardly any casualties, as the Germans were still emerging from their dugouts, and took 80 prisoners. To the north, however, the 8th Royal Fusiliers, between and around craters B and C, were not so successful. The Germans were manning the parapet as the attackers attempted to cross no man's land and shot down all except a few on the right. In the following days, the Germans captured a crater (Triangle Crater) on the southern end of the Chord and made strenuous efforts to take Crater A. The 36th Brigade had to be relieved by the 37th. On 18 March, the Germans blew five shallow mines laid short of the British line in a counterattack; the Bavarian attackers were immediately behind the mines as they blew and, although this caused the attackers alarm, they were able to force the British back to their old front line. The British held only the near lips of the craters; the forward lip closest to the Germans proved impossible to defend 'as its breadth, and the great masses of clay, twelve to twenty feet high, lying about, prevented a field of fire being obtained.'[10] Attempts by the British to hold the interior of the craters also proved too costly in men. The Germans poured artillery and mortar projectiles into the crater and the bottom became a morass of liquid chalk and black mud, while the crumbling sides were too unstable to consolidate. The Germans occupied their side of the lips and the British abandoned further attempts to hold the Chord. The commander of the 37th Brigade, Brigadier General Cator, reported that trying to make the far lip of the crater the front line was not practicable and that the best options were either a trench line in front of the crater or the lip nearest the British lines. At Hohenzollern both sides held the near lips, leaving the interiors of the craters unoccupied, which they filled with barbed wire and iron *chevaux de frise*. The resulting line of craters along no man's land, with each side occupying the opposing lips of the same crater, was the characteristic surface form of an active mining sector on the Western Front.

The Hohenzollern Redoubt attack showed that even with the advantage of destroying the German front line by surprise mining attack, the British could not always capture and hold the ground gained. They might not win the race across no man's land before the defenders were alerted to the attack. It also demonstrated that holding a crater against concentrated fire and determined German counterattack was extremely difficult. The question of the right time to fire mines, and the perceived danger of falling debris, was to recur during 1916.

While the Hohenzollern fighting was still in progress, the British 2nd Army was planning another larger attack with mines at St Eloi. These mines were to come as a profound shock to the Germans, and for the first time they really realized the nature of the British achievement in forming their Tunnelling Companies. But the attack was to prove again that the British lacked the operational art to exploit the potential of mining.

In the autumn of 1915, Hickling and the sappers of 172 Company managed to sink shafts through the sandy clay, called Paniselien or 'bastard' clay, to the dry Ypresian or blue clay below. These shafts were to offer the potential of a mining attack combined with infantry, which had not been available when they had blown

The British attack on St Eloi, 27 March 1916, with British mines numbered 1–6. From Edmonds, *Military Operations, France and Belgium, 1916.*

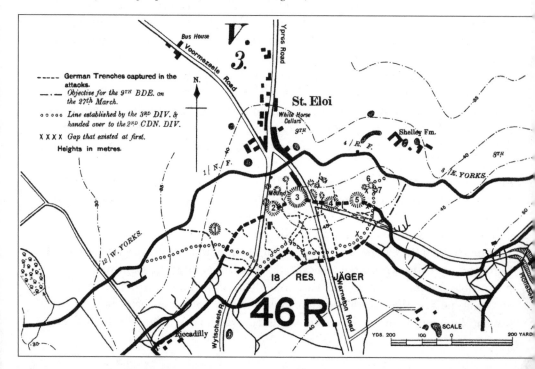

their mines at St Eloi in July 1915. The shafts had to be strong enough to hold back a very heavy pressure of water and wet sand. At 23ft they were into the bastard clay and at 43ft they reached the blue clay.[11] It was wettest at the junction between the bastard and the blue clay. Working with Hickling was Lieutenant Frederick Mulqueen, who took over when Hickling was promoted in early in 1916. He recalled that they placed a pumping station just below the start of the blue clay and continued down to about 64ft. The first deep gallery through the blue clay, D1, was towards the Mound. Miners preferred the tunnels to the trenches and Mulqueen recalled fondly that the blue clay layer was a refuge from both the pervading shelling and the sodden conditions of St Eloi:

Autumn [1915] arrived and with it came the inevitable rain. Mud was the order of the day. Even in billets at Dickebusch one could not get away from it. Rubber hip boots became standard dress. One's clothing became saturated with moisture. 'D1' heading progressed steadily. It was deep. The blue clay was clean. It was hard. It was dry. It was a place of escape. (Lieutenant F.J. Mulqueen, 172 Tunnelling Company)[12]

The Germans, however, had an extensive defensive system and were aggressively mining at the intermediate levels. Mulqueen was in the D1 gallery when the Germans blew a camouflet:

It is true strange noises were heard there, but that was no cause to worry. Rather the surroundings were a pleasant place in which to listen to them. And then the shock came. It was possibly 3.00 AM. Five of us were in the heading. The gallery heaved first to one side and then to the other. It shuddered. It regained its equilibrium. It shuddered again. It was intact. We picked ourselves up.
   A mine had been fired close by. But where? As we neared the top of the shaft we could feel the earth shake under the impact of heavy bombardment. The noise too became deafening.

He discovered that the Germans had blown against the F heading on the far east of the position:

Bewildered members of the infantry working party were standing at the shafthead not knowing quite what to do. They were put to work on the blower. Almost immediately the Corporal arrived with a canary. Together we went below. A sapper followed and was stationed at the foot of the shaft.
   As we approached the face we heard shouting and knew that at least one man was alive. The forward part of the gallery was badly smashed. The mine had been fired from the right and [the gallery] assumed the form of an "X".

There was insufficient oxygen in the air to burn a candle. We were forced to fall back on our flashlights. The canary was O.K. and for the moment at least there was no fear of gas.

It was the practice in this heading to move the sandbags from the face to the shaft on a small rubber-wheeled truck. The first obstacle encountered was the truck. It was jammed in a lower section of the "X" and had evidently kept the timbers from completely crushing the man who was pushing it. He was wedged on its far side between the splintered timbers, but could talk to us. Further down the heading the shouting continued and then came a most reassuring instruction. "For God's sake shut your bloody mouth". Unfortunately the instructions were not followed.

The Corporal left to get a rope, a jack and some assistance. I surveyed the situation. Care would be necessary. If we pulled the truck out and any of the timbers, the whole gallery might collapse and bury the men who were forward. The man at the truck was cool. He reported there were in all four men in the heading.

The Corporal returned. The rope was tied to the truck and it was pulled gently and slowly out without bringing down any dirt. The man on the far side helped considerably by giving directions and he was released little the worse for wear. But the following step was not so simple. The next two men were badly squeezed between the timbers. The jack was brought into action. It was difficult to get a good bearing for it. Gradually the splintered timbers were removed. Two hours passed. Our flashlights started to give out. Fortunately the air improved. One man was released. Then the other. The fourth was at the face. The mine had been fired behind him and he was not badly jammed. The man who had done all the shouting was not badly hurt. All four were sent back to headquarters for medical observation and rest.[13]

The men in F gallery had a lucky escape. Mulqueen concluded that the Germans had blown prematurely because the noise of the truck had caused them to misjudge the distance. On 2 November, Norton Griffiths reported that Mulqueen was working well at 60ft and proposed that they sink twenty or thirty shafts into the blue clay, about 50–70yds apart, from St Eloi east to the Bluff. On 9 November General Fanshawe, commanding 5th Corps, informed General Plumer that with the assistance of the mines being prepared they might capture the trenches around the Mound. He gave Plumer the option of carrying out the attack when the mines were ready, but put forward the view that it would be better to preserve the mines for a larger attack.[14] In November, apprehension was felt for the St Eloi sector after the Germans blew at the Bluff and Fanshawe ordered 172 Company to construct a continuous line of shallow galleries.[15] Norton Griffiths, however, was convinced that local commanders, including at Corps level, were not using mining on a large enough scale. On 7 December he reported that 172 Company had three deep shafts at St Eloi, but that their work was held up because instead they had to improve the shallow defensive galleries: 'the usual 5th Corps attitude'. He continued to press his scheme and encouraged Syme, now commanding in place of Hepburn who had been sent home sick, to put forward a proposal for six more shafts between St Eloi and the Bluff.[16] The shaft at F, where the Germans had blown the camouflet, was constructed of timber only, and on 8 February failed under the pressure of wet sand. They enlarged the shaft to take a steel caisson, but the ground behind the timber became so unstable that both the shaft and the dugout housing it began to cave in and the deep gallery had to be abandoned.[17]

Operations at the Bluff, for which 172 Company was also responsible, affected those at St Eloi. On 21 January the Germans blew several large mines, which caused work on the shallow mines at St Eloi to be stopped in order to complete the deep scheme as soon as possible.[18] Then, on 14 February, the Germans succeeded in capturing the Bluff from the British, also taking prisoner an officer and a number of miners and attached personnel from 172 Company. On 18th Syme was ordered to have two deep offensive mines each from shafts D and H ready by 10 March. He was also to lay defensive charges in the trenches and shafts in case the Germans should attack at St Eloi as they had at the Bluff.[19] Norton Griffith learned from Syme that the loss of the Bluff meant that the operation using the mines was now a priority, and also the reason why it was urgent:

...the St Eloi effort was to be rushed with a view to blowing the deep series in three weeks. It is feared that the 50 [sic] or so miners taken prisoners will be forced to give this deep level scheme away hence the hurry. The intention is to attack after blowing & occupy enemy position round about the Mound.[20]

The mines were therefore used in a smaller operation than originally intended because of the danger that the Germans would discover the presence of the deep mines. They were used not simply, as stated in the British Official History, because of General Plumer's desire to retaliate for the loss of the Bluff, but because of the real danger of the advantage of the deep mines being lost. Plumer ordered that the operation take place as soon as the mines were ready under the Mound and the German front line. Initially set for 10 March, the attack date was put back several times as the miners were hindered by the presence of the Germans as they neared their front line. Mulqueen was posted to command another company on 24 January, after which the St Eloi mines were in the charge of Lieutenant James Douglas:

Work progressed rapidly and we were nearly half way across before we had our first set back. Enemy noises were reported from the central drive, and listening patrols were able to prove the existence of a German gallery almost immediately overhead, along which footsteps could be followed at various time intervals as far back as our front-line trenches. Lack of active mining

noises suggested that a mine had been already laid. It was therefore decided
to stop work here and push ahead with the remaining four galleries as fast as
possible. (Lieutenant James A. Douglas, 172 Tunnelling Company)[21]

The delays with the mines put back the date of the attack and on 24 February
Plumer revised it to 15 March. Ultimately six mines were to be used in the
operation, of which four from the two deep shafts would be the largest. The first of
the mines (H1 or mine No.5) reached its objective on 24 February. Charging with
12,000lbs of ammonal and tamping took another twelve days and it looked unlikely
that they would meet the revised date. On 3 March Norton Griffiths complained to
the Inspector of Mines that he was concerned that the charging was being carried
out too soon, given the danger of the Germans discovering the mines:

> Capt Hill told me the 15th was the date fixed for St. Eloi but they now
> thought the end of the month instead. Then why charge mine heads so close
> to front line? Please Sir![22]

On 4th the mine under the Mound reached its objective (D1 or No.3) and
charging began, to be completed by 15th. On 18th charging was complete for No.4
(H4). On 25th the four large mines (Nos 2–5) were being tamped:

> Cases were carried up at night, lowered down the shafts and then carried
> along and stacked by picked men during the day shift. I was personally
> responsible for laying, priming and subsequently testing the 60 detonators,
> each of which was inserted into a guncotton primer and then in a waterproof
> bag of 25lb of Ammonal.[23]

There were four central mines, two laid from the shaft D and two from H. The
largest (D1), beneath the Mound, contained 31,000lbs of ammonal (Crater 2 on
illustration, p100). The other three mines were charged with between 12,000 and
15,000lbs (Craters 2–5). In addition, two smaller mines were laid on the flanks,
Plumer having ordered on 24 February that the mine (designated 'I' or No.1) on the
far west was to be fired with the others. On 10 March, however, the Germans blew
a camouflet in this gallery, 330ft from the shaft, killing three men and collapsing the
last 20ft. On 24th the Germans were heard so close that 172 Company blew a 100lb
camouflet from a borehole 50ft from the face, which badly damaged their own
gallery for 20ft. It was impossible to work through the section of damaged tunnel in
time for the attack and so a small charge of just 1,800lbs had to be laid 240ft from
the shaft, even though this was about 150ft short of the German front line. At a late
stage, a shallow 38ft-deep gallery was run out on the opposite flank from the failed
deep shaft F. After 200ft, and still 100ft from the German line, this gallery came
close to the German defensive gallery and was halted and charged with 600lbs to

form mine No.6.[24] Thus the two flanking mines (Nos 1 and 6), owing to German defensive mining, were both small charges laid short of the German front line. On 26 March the tamping was completed and GHQ notified 5th Corps that the attack was to take place the next morning at 4.15am.

The mines were expected to give the attackers, 9th Brigade of the 3rd Division, a great advantage of surprise and shock, but they also complicated the operation. The report of the Hohenzollern attack of 3 March was not yet available, but General Haldane, commanding the 3rd Division, had realized after the loss of the Hooge crater in July 1915, eleven days after his troops had captured it, the difficulty of holding craters. He knew that because the troops would be very heavily bombarded by mortars and howitzers, the craters themselves could not be held.[25] As a preliminary study, Haldane and Brigadier General Douglas Smith, commanding the 9th Brigade, went on 4 March to the active mining area at Bray-sur-Somme 'to assist them in the solution of their problem of occupying ground gained by an explosion of mines'.[26] Before the operation, however, Douglas Smith was promoted and his place taken by Lieutenant Colonel H.C. Potter, who had not previously commanded a brigade. The plan was devised by Haldane and the detailed orders drawn up by Potter. Potter issued his preliminary order on 18 March, instructing that parts of the front line should be strutted to prevent them collapsing when the mines were blown, and that parts would need to be evacuated. No advance would be possible for 30 seconds after the explosion of the mines, owing to falling debris. The attackers therefore assembled lying on the ground behind their front line. On 12 March the 2nd Army Controller of Mines, Colonel A.G. Stevenson, had produced a map showing the location and likely size of the craters and the extent to which debris would fall. He estimated that large lumps of clay would fall 500ft from the largest mine and that the danger area might be 700ft.

Potter issued the Operation Orders on 24th. These were not as detailed or careful as those for the Hohenzollern operation. However, a practice area of trenches was marked out and troops were instructed to rehearse every detail of the attack on this ground.

The six mines were to be fired simultaneously and watches were to be synchronized to time given by the Brigade Signal office. Two battalions were to attack, the 2nd Royal Fusiliers from the east and the 1st Northumberland Fusiliers from the west. Owing to the four mines blowing in the centre of the position Haldane, with the approval of Plumer, ordered that the two units were to advance on either side and converge in the German third line trenches, about 600ft beyond the craters. There was to be no preliminary bombardment and the attack was to rely on the shock and surprise caused by the mines. The signal for the firing of the mines was to be the first salvo of heavy shells. The two battalions would then assault 30 seconds after the explosion of the mines to achieve the optimum balance between avoiding the falling debris and gaining maximum advantage from the initial chaos caused by the blows. The orders also emphasized the need to defend the captured trenches against German counterattack: 'Consolidation on both lines must be commenced at once and continued with unceasing energy.'[27]

Occupation of the craters themselves was regarded as impossible, as so much German fire would be poured into them, and the line to be captured and defended was to be in front of them.

A series of communication trenches were to be dug to link the captured positions to the old front line, to enable them to be reinforced and supplied during the heavy German bombardment, which would follow the attack. On the western flank a trench to the small No.1 crater in no man's land was to be made by blowing a long pipe charge, which had been forced beneath the surface by a hydraulic Barrett jack. This promised to create a trench at the moment of attack.

At 4.15am, Syme and Lieutenant Birtles pressed the plungers of the exploders (Douglas was in hospital injured). They did not blow the mines simultaneously, but in sequence: first 2 and 3, (D2 and D1), followed by 4 and 5 (H4 and H1), then 1 (I) and finally 6 (F).

Harvey described the result:

> On firing the mines a mushroom shaped mound appeared over each charge which rose to a height of 40 to 60 feet and then fell outwards releasing a volume of gas and flame and cloud which rushed skywards to a height of 200 to 300ft. There was an earth shake but no roar of explosion.[28]

To witnesses 'it appeared as if a long village was being lifted through flames into the air' and two miles away, at Hill 60, the trenches rocked and heaved.[29]

The Northumberland Fusiliers attacked through a gap with the group of four mines to their left, and the small mine No.1 to their right. The commanding officer reported that the mine blew at 30 seconds after 4.15 and that his men did not wait the 30 seconds but moved off 'in quick time', crossing their own parapet with ladders forty seconds before the German barrage landed on it. The first obstacle was the German wire, which was strong and unaffected by the mine explosions, although it did not stop the advance and they were through it before the German artillery began bombarding no man's land.

The CO reported that the mines 'had a great moral effect upon the enemy' and that they saw the Germans fleeing their trenches 400yds from the westernmost mine.[30]

In the east, however, the Royal Fusiliers' attack fared badly. The intervals between the blows, which appeared to the commanding officer as three distinct explosions, caused the attackers confusion. Unlike the Northumberlands, the Royal Fusiliers did not have an obvious gap between craters to pass through, facing instead Nos 4 and 5, the two eastern of the large mines, which formed an impassable barrier. When mine No.6 exploded on their front left, they mistook it for mine No.5, which caused them to lose direction:

My instructions were to wait 30 seconds after the explosion before advancing as I understood that there would be practically only one and that all six mines would be fired simultaneously. The officers and men, however, appear to have [been] too eager [and] apparently moved directly after the first explosion with the result that quite a large number of Y Company were over our parapet when No 5 mine [sic] exploded in front of them. Directly the mines went up an enemy machine gun somewhat near point 85 opened on the parapet where W, X and Y companies were crossing. The fire from this gun was very accurate and caused a large number of casualties amongst the three companies. (Lieutenant Colonel G.G. Ottley, commanding 4th Battalion, Royal Fusiliers)[31]

The Royal Fusiliers were not able to move so swiftly, probably because of the mines directly in front of them, and this delay proved fatal. Whereas the Northumberlands avoided the German fire on their trenches and no man's land by seconds, the Royal Fusiliers were caught by it. The battalion lost forty per cent of its strength almost immediately from machine-gun fire and a shrapnel barrage in no man's land:

I regret to have to confess that my battalion failed to take the objective allotted to it. I knew well before I started that if I was to be successful I should have to take the enemy completely by surprise and was counting on reaching the enemy first line unobserved. That the enemy were very much on the alert and expecting an attack was proved by the quickness with which he opened on my parapet with a M.G. and swept the ground over which my companies had to advance with shrapnel before many men had time to even get over my own parapets. (Lieutenant Colonel G.G. Ottley)[32]

The new mine craters had so altered the landscape and removed familiar landmarks that the Royal Fusiliers, attacking before dawn, found it impossible to orientate themselves. Mine No.6, as well as causing confusion, was too small and too far from the German trenches to assist them in their advance. They succeeded in occupying the crater made by mine No.6 and an old crater adjacent, mistaking them for the two large mines 4 and 5.

The British, therefore, were holding craters 2 and 3, and crater 6 and the adjacent crater (called 7), although it was reported that they held all four central mine craters. The point after the attack was the most vulnerable to German counterattack – before the attackers had time to construct defences and bring up ammunition they could be cut off by a barrage. The charge supposed to blow a trench to mine No.1 failed to explode and other efforts to dig communication trenches to the positions held proved unsuccessful under the heavy German fire and in the sticky and loose debris thrown up by the mines. Consolidation proved very difficult: the mines had destroyed the drainage installed in the German trenches and they began steadily to fill with water, and rain became heavier.

Over the following week, British attempts to gain a line beyond the craters were unsuccessful. Finally, in an attack in the early morning of 3 April, they took the four central craters. General Haldane confirmed this for himself by going round the whole front that morning, but consolidation had hardly begun. The 2nd Canadian Division was due to relieve the British 3rd Division during the night and the Canadians could barely find a front line distinguishable as such. There was no wire in front of the trenches, which were collapsed and just a series of shallow ditches. The four large craters formed a continuous and almost impassable obstacle and the only route was around the flanks; carrying parties had to be roped together to rescue men from shell-holes, wounded and dead lay half-buried in the mud and the line was held by a series of detached posts.[33] Brigadier General Ketchen, commanding the 6th Canadian Brigade, fully expected a German counterattack. He concluded that the line beyond the craters was untenable, as it was observed by the Germans on the Ypres ridge. It was impossible to drain the trenches and German shelling prevented work to strengthen the position. He wished therefore to hold only the rear lips of the craters. However, the German attack came on the night of 5 April: they took all four central craters and secured the area with an intense barrage while they consolidated. Attempts to retake the craters were foiled by broken communications and confusion as to finding objectives. A Canadian bombing party reported itself in Craters 4 and 5 when they were holding Craters 6 and 7 (making the same error as the Royal Fusiliers):

> In a broken sea of old and new craters, shell holes and damaged trenches, where if men even dared to raise their heads above the surface by daylight they were shot, orientation was practically impossible. There were seventeen mine craters in the area, and although Nos. 2, 3, 4 and 5 were the largest, the troops did not know this, and any one pair of craters might only too easily be mistaken for another.[34]

When it transpired that the Germans held the four large craters, it was accepted that the only option was to withdraw from the craters and attempt to render them untenable to the Germans, just as they had to the British. The British in fact lacked the heavy artillery ammunition they needed and the Germans proceeded skilfully to drain and fortify the craters. On 19 April the Germans succeeded in driving the Canadians from craters 6 and 7, failing against Crater 1. The Canadians held the original front line and the Germans held and had consolidated the four large craters.

The operation had been a failure and the advantage of the mines was lost. Douglas summed up the results for 172 Company: '…our work had been more or less useless except as a great blow to German morale and the killing of several hundred of their troops.'[35]

The reasons for the failure of the attack lay in the problem of integrating mines into the attack and the inability to hold the position once captured. The reports and enquiries into the loss of the craters drew a number of lessons. Major General Haldane reported that the psychological impact of the mines was very great, not only on the Germans but also on the attackers: 'The explosion of the mines had a curious paralysing effect on our men for a few seconds only.'[36]

The Royal Fusiliers were not prepared for the fact that the six mines would not fire simultaneously. This was inevitable with multiple blows, but it had a crucial effect on their attack. Despite their earth-shaking power, the effects of the mines were also very local. There was barely a need to delay the infantry advance after the detonation of the mines as the debris fell much faster than expected. Brigadier General Potter stated: '60 yards is about the limit of debris of a dangerous size even from very large mines and Infantry can safely advance 15 seconds after the explosion.'[37]

No attacking troops were injured by falling debris. Haldane reported that no heavy fragments fell further than 50yds beyond the crater lips and 'very little of any kind but dust beyond about 80 yards'. No one had experience of the effects of very large mine charges and Stevenson, the 2nd Army Controller of Mines, had estimated three times these figures. Although reports were contradictory as to whether the British front line trenches were damaged by the blows, the infantry could possibly have laid out closer to the mines before attacking, that is, in front of their trenches rather than behind. Haldane criticized the location of the mines as being too close together. In the wet ground, the mixture of clay and sand slurry scattered by the explosions was particularly sticky and treacherous. It made moving anywhere near the craters extremely difficult and meant that it was impossible to pass between the four central craters: '... on a front of 700 yards, 500 yards was rendered practically impassable to Infantry and the attack was narrowed down to a front of 100 yards on either flank.'[38]

The attack could only be launched at the shoulders of the salient and this worsened the problem of the two battalions making contact and thus consolidating. The attempt to consolidate and hold the position was also made particularly difficult by the very bad state of the ground, which prevented both movement and digging. Communication trenches to the captured positions, not started beforehand because of German observation, were almost impossible to construct after capture for the same reason and were under heavy German artillery fire. The charge placed by a forcing jack, which was supposed to blow a communication trench to crater No.1 failed, for reasons that are unclear. Reports state that it either failed to go off, or did but only resulted in wrecking the existing British trench.

The confused landscape proved disastrous when it came to relieving the attacking troops. Efforts were made to prepare the attackers for the changes in the landscape that the mines would bring; for example the craters were marked on the taped training ground. The mines, nevertheless, had a fatal effect on the British and Canadians' orientation in the position. The 3rd Division was already weakened and tired by operations at the Bluff and the attacking troops had to be relieved immediately after the attack. The whole Division was then relieved by the 2nd Canadian Division before the position was properly consolidated or fully understood by the troops in occupation, with the consequence that the Canadians made the same mistakes as the British in the confused mass of mine craters.

Haldane put forward another reason why his two battalions did not link up, despite his impressing beforehand on the two commanders the need to push along adjoining trenches to assist one another: 'But for this most unfortunate error... which I can only attribute to the inexperience of the present junior infantry officers, this would have been done...'[39]

In fact, of the 14 Royal Fusiliers officers in the attack, eleven were casualties. There was nevertheless a contrast between the ability of junior officers and NCOs in the British and German armies to act on their own initiative: the superior German ability to take and hold mine craters was just one manifestation of this.

General Plumer placed blame further up the chain of command:

> Major General Haldane attributes the failure in a great measure to the inexperience and lack of military knowledge of the subordinate commanders, but I consider the onus of responsibility lay in the first instance with the Officer Commanding the left battalion – Lieut. Colonel G.C. Ottley of the 4th Royal Fusiliers and Brig-General H.C. Potter commanding 9th Infantry Brigade.[40]

Plumer commented to GHQ that whilst Haldane's attack was 'well planned and most carefully worked out', he had not sufficiently taken into account the difficulty of holding the position:

> I do not think Major General Haldane impressed on his subordinate Commanders sufficiently the importance of taking steps to ensure that the mine craters should not fall into the enemy's hands. Whatever opinion he may hold as to the best means to take to defend them and good as the original objective line was the possibility of its being rendered untenable by heavy artillery fire was not sufficiently taken into account.[41]

Ultimately, the St Eloi attack was on too small a front, a failing which was beyond Haldane's control, but which was the Corps and Army commanders' responsibility. Plumer felt obliged to use the St Eloi mines for fear of losing them before he was ready to make real use of them. The Germans had very good observation over the position at St Eloi and so could concentrate artillery fire and render it untenable. An attack on a wider front, as was under preparation on the Somme, might have seemed to be a means of preventing this. The British were struggling with the problems of coordinated attacks, in particular the artillery barrages which were being developed, whereby troops could advance behind their protection. Timing was critical to the success of this method, as shown at St Eloi by the success of the Northumberlands and the failure of the Royal Fusiliers. Adding mines to this equation served to complicate the problem further.

The method of consolidating the near lip of a mine crater, which has been incorporated into the front line. Note the use of observation tunnels to monitor activity inside and on the far lip. Issued by British GHQ, May 1916. From *Notes on Trench Warfare for Infantry Officers*.

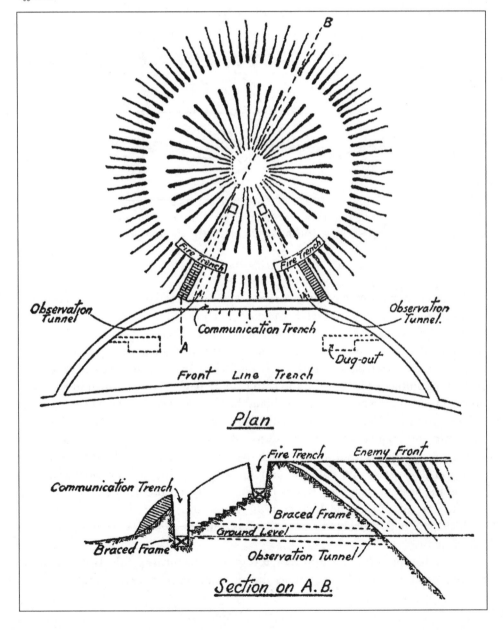

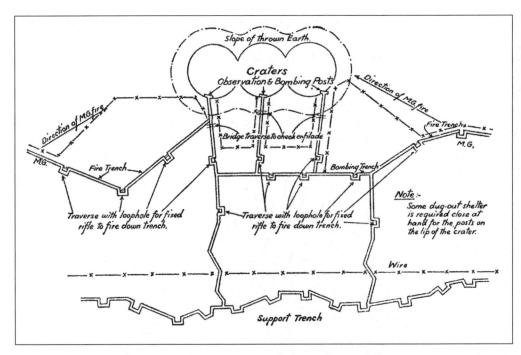

The method of converting the area behind occupied craters into a strong post. The British usually found it too dangerous to occupy the interior of a crater owing to German mortar and rifle grenade fire. Issued by British GHQ, May 1916. From *Notes on Trench Warfare for Infantry Officers.*

To improve the British performance at taking mine craters and consolidating and holding captured positions, GHQ issued a set of printed instructions in May 1916. These emphasized that: 'success will only result if there is also an absolute determination on the part of all ranks to get the work done promptly at all costs.'[42]

When mines were blown, whether by the British or Germans, parties were to be rushed out immediately to seize the crater lip. If blown by the British in an attack on the German trenches, the object should be to seize and hold the whole crater, or a line in front of the crater. It was usually better to hold a line in front and to turn the crater or craters into strong points. When the craters were blown by the Germans, either as a result of an attack overland or fighting underground, troops were usually to seize and hold the near lip only. The British blew practice mines behind the lines to train their troops in capture and consolidation, two in May and one in June of 1916. The Inspector of Mines also made efforts to have these explosions filmed, probably because this was a means of observing and timing the fall of debris.[43]

Given their performance at St Eloi, it is perhaps fortunate for the British that the mining attack on the Messines ridge did not take place in 1916. Haig's Flanders attack was to fall victim to the requirements of coalition warfare, as he was obliged to cooperate with General Joffre in his proposed attack on the Somme. In contrast to the Flanders position, in which Haig saw real strategic possibilities, the Somme was chosen by Joffre solely because it formed a junction of the French and British forces and so was convenient for a joint attack. At the beginning of 1916, however, it seemed that the Flanders attack could still be the main British offensive of the summer, and throughout the first half of 1916 Haig kept the attack under preparation. The major German attack on the French at Verdun, which began on 21 February 1916, at first made it seem that the Flanders attack would take precedence over the Somme, as the French would not now be able to cooperate in the Somme attack. On 10 April British GHQ instructed Plumer to submit promptly his plan for capturing the Messines Ridge and its northern continuation, the Pilckem Ridge, with an attack to start on 15 July.[44] On 27 May he was ordered to press his preparations with all speed. The ferocious battle at Verdun had the effect of severely reducing the French contribution to the Somme offensive, but the British were obliged to mount their part of the attack regardless. By 4 June the Flanders attack was scaled back to include just the Messines element, because Rawlinson's 4th Army was to be too far committed to the Somme offensive to attack in Flanders. Haig clung to the possibility that if the Somme attack was not a success, Gough's Reserve Army could still be sent to Messines. However, after the decision to continue the Somme attack in early July despite the disastrous first day, the Messines attack was further reduced in scale and the date altered to 31 July. It was then postponed again, and by mid-August it was apparent that it would not take place in 1916.

Mining, however, came to dominate day-to-day trench warfare on the Western Front. In 1916 the British blew 750 mines and camouflets, while the Germans blew 696 against the British. The most active month was June and the most active sector was the front of the British First Army, which centred on the area Givenchy-lez-La Bassée, Hulluch and Loos.[45] The value of mines blown which were not part of a wider offensive plan was questionable given the labour which each required. On the Somme front, however, the British were attempting to use mining for the breakthrough offensive of 1916.

Chapter 6

The Somme 1916

The Somme, and not Haig's Flanders operation, became the major British operation of 1916. The BEF took over the northern Somme sector from the French in July and August 1915. Although the front of fourteen miles was largely quiet, there were parts which had seen very fierce but local fighting in the winter of 1914 and the spring of 1915. In a number of places mine warfare had broken out, in particular at Carnoy, Bois Français, Fricourt and La Boisselle. General Fowke moved 174 and 183 Tunnelling Companies south, but the British did not have enough miners to take over the large number of French shafts and they agreed to leave their engineers at work for several weeks. To provide the tunnellers needed the British formed 178 and 179 Companies in August, followed by 185 and 252 Companies in October. These units were created partly by recruiting men from units in the sectors and partly from enlistment at home. Good recruits were still found from units such as the 51st Highland Division, which included many Territorials who were professional coal miners from the Fife coalfields. Those miners coming from home were increasingly unfit and many were sent home soon after arrival in France, or within a few weeks, especially during the winter of 1915-16.

The British found shafts of 20–30ft depth, mainly sunk from the front line or close behind. The Germans had the advantage in all of the sectors and in many places were very close to or actually below the front line taken over by the British. During the autumn and winter these companies fought a hard battle. They had first to secure the British lines, in places having to abandon the front line and beginning a new series of shafts further back. The British tunnellers regarded their French counterparts as unproductive, using tunnels which were too cramped for effective working and with excessive timbering, which further slowed their progress. Close below the surface was chalk and inclined entrances were largely used, as the chalk would support them and they facilitated the removal of spoil by tramming. As they sank deeper the chalk became extremely hard and both sides used blasting, especially when closer to their own lines, but it was a method which alerted the other side to activity. The Germans did not feel much threatened until the early months of 1916, by which time the British had created defensive systems at around 40ft depth, including transversals to protect their front lines and deep attack tunnels just above the water level, which they encountered at about 100ft. As the British were achieving this, however, they also relieved more of the French front, at Arras and Vimy Ridge, which contained active mining areas, and in February 184 and 185 Companies were withdrawn from the Somme and sent north. At the beginning of March 1916, Haig formed the 4th Army, which took over the Somme front in order to carry out the Franco-British attack due to begin in June. He placed General Rawlinson in command and Rawlinson obtained Preedy, whose 170 Company had just carried out the Hohenzollern mining attack, as his Controller of Mines. The five remaining Tunnelling companies on the Somme front were to play a major part in the Somme offensive, especially the first day of the infantry attack.

The Somme was to be characterized by yet larger mines, laid deep in the chalk and often overcharged to throw up high lips for screening and to give advantage to the attackers when, or if, they captured them. The tunnellers were to make two major contributions to the opening attack. Firstly they placed a number of mines beneath or close to the German front lines. Secondly they prepared a series of shallow Russian saps from the British front line into no man's land (see Chapter 9). Rawlinson's original attack plan was for a limited advance such as he had evolved during spring and summer 1915, concentrating on taking the first line of German trenches in a tactic that he called 'bite and hold'. This was a safer method of proceeding, but was extremely slow and politically unacceptable, as the Government believed that the BEF now had both the manpower and munitions to beat the Germans. Haig therefore required Rawlinson to redraw his plan to capture all of the German in-depth defences in his initial attack, to allow a general advance. Rawlinson acquiesced, even though he knew that his artillery was insufficient to destroy either the defences or the defenders to such a depth. Haig likewise complied with the desire of the British government for a quick victory, despite reservations that he had about the ability of his forces to fight effectively. The infantry attack was preceded by a six-day bombardment, prolonged so that the British artillery could shell all of the German defences.

The northernmost corps carrying out the main attack (there was also a diversion further north at Gommecourt) was VIII Corps, commanded by Lieutenant General Hunter-Weston, a Sapper whose recent experience of mine warfare was at Helles. Controversially and disastrously, a mine beneath the Hawthorn Redoubt was to be mishandled by VIII Corps. This particularly powerful position, on the crest of a hill dominating the valley in front of the village of Beaumont Hamel, was selected for mine attack. A gallery (H3) to destroy the Redoubt was started at 80ft depth by 252 Company, commanded by Captain Rex Trower, on about 4 April and at the end of the month he reported good progress:

> This Company has every record for the Army beaten by the driving in the Hawthorne Mine. In this we made 35 feet in 24 hrs 200 feet in one week of 7 days – 322 feet in fourteen days, and 565 feet in 26 days. This is one tunnel with one face only and the length to destroy the enemy trench will be 1055 feet.[1]

As they neared the German lines, however, work slowed: the air was bad at the end of the long tunnel and it was extremely difficult to work without alerting the Germans:

> Extraordinary difficulty is being encountered with mine H3. The length is now 900ft and work is being carried on silently by wetting the face and working the chalk out with bayonets. This face is now entirely flint and progress is very slow.[2]

On 22 June, however, a charge of 40,600lbs of ammonal was in place beneath the Hawthorn Redoubt. On 25th Trower was informed that the infantry attack was to begin at 7.30am on 29 June, but the following day the date was postponed to 1 July. He was also told that he was to detonate the mine at 7.20am, ten minutes before zero. This contradicted the recent experience of St Eloi, where only a few seconds were regarded as necessary for debris to fall. The 29th Division plan required the 2nd Royal Fusiliers to rush the crater before the main attack at 7.30. Therefore, the heavy artillery was ordered to 'lift' onto the next target from the front trenches at 7.20am instead of lifting at zero hour (7.30am). However, it was ordered to lift not only from the Hawthorn Redoubt and the surrounding trenches, but also from the whole of the German front line on the 8th Corps front.[3]

The Hawthorn mine gallery H3. Hawthorn Redoubt was situated in the German lines on the right (not in the British lines as implied by the map). The twin circles indicate the crater and fall of debris of the 40,000lb mine. The crater was calculated to bury the front trench with debris. From NA WO153/905.

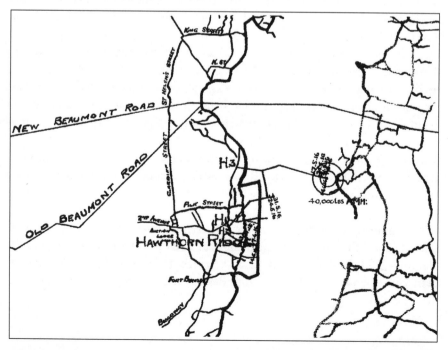

An official cameraman was on hand to film the Hawthorn mine, who began filming thirty seconds before he expected the mine to go up, then became convinced that his film spool would run out before the explosion:

> Then it happened. The ground where I stood gave a mighty convulsion. It rocked and swayed. I gripped hold of my tripod to steady myself. Then, for all the world like a gigantic sponge, the earth rose in the air to the height of hundreds of feet. Higher and higher it rose, and with a horrible, grinding roar the earth fell back upon itself, leaving in its place a mountain of smoke. (Lieutenant Geoffrey Malins)[4]

The mine completely destroyed the Hawthorn Redoubt, garrisoned by Wurttembergers of the 119th Reserve Infantry Regiment:

> During the intense bombardment there was a terrific explosion which for the moment completely drowned the thunder of the artillery. A great cloud of smoke rose up from the trenches of No. 9 Company followed by a tremendous shower of stones which seemed to fall from the sky over all our position. More than three sections of No. 9 Company were blown into the air and the neighbouring dug-outs were broken in and blocked. The ground all round was white with the debris of chalk as if it had been snowing and a gigantic crater, over fifty yards in diameter and some sixty feet deep, gaped like an open wound in the side of the hill. This explosion was a signal for the infantry attack and everyone got ready and stood on the lower steps of the dug-outs, rifles in hand, waiting for the bombardment to lift. In a few minutes the shelling ceased and we rushed up the steps and out into the crater positions. Ahead of us wave after wave of British troops were crawling out of their trenches and coming forward towards us at a walk, their bayonets glistening in the sun. (*History of Reserve Regiment 119*)[5]

Many Germans were entombed in a large dugout, all four entrances of which were blocked, but they were rescued later in the day. Others were crushed or blown to pieces. Despite the shock and disorientation caused by the detonation, German troops immediately occupied the rear lip of the crater. The Germans also immediately brought down a heavy artillery barrage onto the British trenches. The British heavy artillery having already lifted from the German trenches, they emerged from their shelters and opened fire on the British. The 2nd Royal Fusiliers, crossing no man's land to occupy the crater, came under heavy German rifle and machine-gun fire from either flank and the rear lip. A Fusiliers officer had no doubt about the fatal effect of the ten-minute interval between the blowing of the mine and the main infantry assault:

…had this been timed for firing almost simultaneously with the attack we should in the general confusion have been able to over-run the Redoubt with little or no opposition and thus stop the intense direct machine-gun fire and permit the following waves to get across No Mans Land, subject only to indirect machine-gun fire and artillery barrage.

The notice, however, given by the mine was such as to permit the enemy's lines being manned and for the crater to be defended, with the result that the major portion of the first wave of the three Companies of the 2nd R.F. were placed out of action almost immediately, with no one getting into the enemy's trenches.

My own Company which followed shortly afterwards as second wave was also put out of action, after which no more troops could leave our trenches, mainly owing to the constant machine-gun barrage on our parapet from the Redoubt. (Lieutenant Albert Walter Whitlock, 2nd Royal Fusiliers)[6]

A few of the Royal Fusiliers actually managed to reach the closest lip of the crater and held on until noon when they were forced out. The failure to take the Redoubt had a serious effect on the attack north of the Ancre, which was the least successful of the day.

VIII Corps and 29th Division failed to integrate the blowing of the mine with the artillery programme and infantry attack. Unable to find an explanation in the surviving records for the decision to blow the mine at 7.20am Edmonds, the official historian, wrote to everyone involved with the decision from corps commander down. The replies were highly contradictory and no one could recall who wanted the mine blown early, although General Hunter Weston, commanding VIII Corps, accepted the ultimate responsibility. Edmonds first asked Harvey, who revealed that VIII Corps had wished to blow the mine at 6.00pm the day before the attack. Harvey had fought this 'tooth and nail' on the grounds that the British 'never had made a good show at occupying a crater whereas the Germans were extremely proficient.'[7] He had managed to get the General Staff at GHQ to forbid it, but they compromised at ten minutes before zero. The recollection of Hunter-Weston was that in the original orders the mine was to be blown at zero, but that at the request of the commanders of 29th Division and 86th Brigade it was brought forward ten minutes: 'their strongly urged view being that the falling debris would do as much damage to the assaulting troops as to the Germans.'[8]

Hunter-Weston's Chief of Staff, Brigadier General Walter Hore-Ruthven, concurred in this view. The commander of the 29th Division, Major General de Lisle, however, told Edmonds that he had 'highly disapproved' of the mine being blown ten minutes before zero and that he had raised it with Rawlinson, along with his concerns over the prolonged artillery bombardment. He repeated his objections to Haig when he visited a few days later with Rawlinson.[9] De Lisle's senior staff officer, Colonel C.G. Fuller, stated that the delay was at the request of Trower, who required ten minutes grace in case there was a problem with firing the mine.[10] Harvey told Edmonds that he suspected that it might have originated with the Tunnelling Company commander:

> My own impression of Trower is that he probably had something to do with the firing of the mine early, and that when the result was a fearful massacre of our own troops, he denied all responsibility for it.[11]

Trower pointed out that he would not have asked for this grace period as, if the mine failed to fire, there would be nothing that he could do about it in ten minutes, an explanation with which Harvey concurred. In a letter to Harvey, Trower placed responsibility on VIII Corps:

> I remember distinctly VIII Corps HQ wishing to fire the mine the night before and you stopping that. I also remember the keen disappointment amongst the company when we understood that the mine was not to be the signal for going over.
>
> The VIII Corps were of the opinion that the falling debris would kill a great many of our own men, and not having fired a mine as big, I was not willing to swear that some of our men might not be hit by falling stuff. That is, I think, the point that made the VIII Corps insist on 0-10 as the hour.[12]

Harvey could not recall the issue of the debris being raised, and said that if it had been he would have used the example of the attack of 27 March to show that ten minutes was excessive: 'at that date I had the experience of the worries at St Eloi and could have said that 2 minutes was ample.'[13]

Preedy, the Controller of Mines, was also consulted. He recalled that he had seen Trower two days before the attack and discovered that VIII Corps had arranged to blow the mine the evening before it. He went to see VIII Corps to stop this without result (perhaps unsurprisingly, as at age 29 Preedy was a very junior temporary Lieutenant Colonel) and so saw General Buckland, the Chief Engineer of 4th Army. When he saw Trower again on 30 June he learned that the time had been altered to ten minutes before zero because the infantry were afraid of the danger to their men and that 29th Division would not agree to blowing it nearer to zero. Preedy again saw Buckland, who took it up, but later told him that it had been decided to stick to the arrangements as VIII Corps did not wish to force 29th Division against their will:

> I have always imagined that the reason for the early firing of this mine was the fear that too many of the attacking infantry might be knocked out if it was fired at zero, and am quite certain that this was the reason given to me by Trower. Otherwise I should certainly have tried again to have it altered.[14]

The evidence, though highly contradictory, points to the 29th Division fearing injury through falling debris. The problem remains that some elements of the Royal Fusiliers left the trenches to attack the crater before zero, negating any purpose in blowing the mine early. The commander of 29th Division put forward another reason for blowing the mine early, whether the evening prior or ten minutes before, of which he was not aware until after the attack. This was that the northern attack was designed to divert attention, and draw troops from, that to the south:

> Until after the attack we were in ignorance of the fact that the main attack was south of the Ancre, and that ours was only subsidiary. I then realized that the hour of the mine explosion was intended to draw the enemy's attention to the northern flank, and this appears to have been successful as they expected ours to be the main attack.[15]

This was tentatively accepted by Edmonds, who in the official history states:

> It seems to have been in the minds of both Sir Douglas Haig and General Rawlinson that, even if the mine – the only one North of the Ancre – did give the alarm, it might be to the advantage of the attacks of the XIII and XV Corps on the right. There success was all-important, and it might be helpful if the attention of the enemy could be drawn to this situation north of the Ancre before they were launched.[16]

Given that the deaths of thousands of men resulted from the failure of the VIII Corps attack, it is not surprising that memories were unclear. As de Lisle pointed out: 'The terrible losses in the VIII Corps would not have occurred to the same extent but for the mine, which enabled defenders to leave their deep dug-outs and to man their trenches.'[17]

What is apparent is that there was a limited understanding of the way to use mines in the attack amongst the commanders and staff despite, or perhaps because of, the fact that Hunter-Weston and Fuller were both Sappers and Fuller had been a member of the Committee on Siege and Fortress Warfare of 1908. Furthermore the experience of VIII Corps and 29th Division at Gallipoli had been with mines of a much smaller size, and they had not experienced the latest fighting in France during 1915 and early 1916. Nobody, Preedy and Trower included, really knew how a mine of 40,000lbs would behave, as no one had seen one blown. The episode, however, showed a lack of clearly enforced policy on attacking with mines, which was the role of the General Staff through the Inspector of Mines. Harvey called the blowing of the mine at 7.20am 'Hunter Bunter's folly', but only later in the year did he issue a Mining Note stating clearly that mines should not be blown early on account of the danger of falling debris.[18]

Five miles to the south of Hawthorn, 179 Tunnelling Company placed two large mines immediately either side of the Albert to Bapaume road in front of the German lines at the village of La Boisselle. The road was a key axis of the attack and the Germans had incorporated La Boisselle into their defensive position and fortified the ruined houses and cellars. La Boisselle was an area of fierce underground fighting from the beginning of 1915 and when the British took over the sector no man's land was already a mass of chalk craters on the western edge of the village, which the troops named the 'Glory Hole'. From August 1915 until June 1916, 179 Company, and for four months 185 Tunnelling Company, secured the British front line with defensive systems and aggressive blows:

> We fought the Boche on the 30 foot level, then we went down to 60ft and then 90ft, and then down to about 120ft, which was our final deep level and nothing could get past us there. We fought him right back all along the front – blew big, about 10,000lb series. Shoved the Boche right back – he knew we were going much faster than he was. (Captain Hugh Kerr, 179 Tunnelling Company)[19]

The Germans fought hard and the worst of many incidents occurred on 4 February 1916 when two officers, including the OC of 185 Company and 16 men, were burnt or gassed to death after a German camouflet. The Germans developed at least four systems. During 1915 they worked at about 30ft depth, but in the autumn of 1915 went down to 50–60ft in response to the British going deeper. By early 1916 they had a main defensive transversal at 80ft covering almost the whole of the area in front of La Boisselle. In the spring the Germans started a deeper system of inclines, driven from their reserve lines, to 100ft.[20] Owing to the powerful German mining system in front of La Boisselle and the difficulty of working in silence in chalk, it was impossible for 179 Company to drive tunnels beneath the village itself and instead they bypassed it. On the southern (right) side of the Glory Hole, a long drive was begun from Lochnagar Street communication trench by 185 Company in November 1915. This was directed towards a German position known as the Schwaben Höhe, which dominated the shoulder of a low-lying area to the south called Sausage Valley.

The tunnel began 300ft behind the British front line and over 900ft from the German lines. When 185 Company was withdrawn from La Boisselle in February 1916, they had driven it 799ft at a depth of 45–50ft. 179 Company resumed work on the tunnel in March, which was now close enough to the German lines to require very careful silent working. This meant very slow progress, with the floor of the tunnel carpeted with sandbags, tunnellers working without boots, always with an officer present and no talking above a whisper. The miner at the face prised out a lump of chalk with a bayonet attached to a wooden haft held in one hand and caught it with the other, then another man placed the chalk in a sandbag, which was carried back along the tunnel. Air had to be pumped to the face and a candle would only burn directly at the point that it issued from the hose. During this work they could hear the Germans with the naked ear, stumping down an inclined tunnel, and established from listening that they had a transversal defensive gallery just below them, but took comfort as there was no work being driven in their direction. By mid-April they had driven the tunnel a total of 820ft and were about 135ft away from the right edge of Schwaben Höhe. They then branched the tunnel, driving one gallery ahead and slightly to the right and a second about 45 degrees left towards the middle of the redoubt. In about mid-June they stopped driving, with the left branch at just under 70ft and the right at 45ft, because of the need to begin chambering so that they could begin the long and dangerous process of charging before the preparatory bombardment began. Neither chamber was beneath the German position and the blows could only hope to destroy the right end of the Schwaben Höhe. To compensate, the mines were to be 'overcharged' with explosive in order to throw the maximum amount of debris over the German trenches and bury the defenders alive.

The Y Sap and Lochnagar Mines at La Boisselle. The right angle tunnel of the Y Sap mine, called S4, can clearly be seen to the north-west of the village. The Lochnagar tunnel ran from the British support trench and was just short of the Schwaben Höhe position. The tunnel captioned H3 Kirriemuir St was a Russian sap which was connected to the north-western end of the Schwaben Höhe. From NA WO153/905.

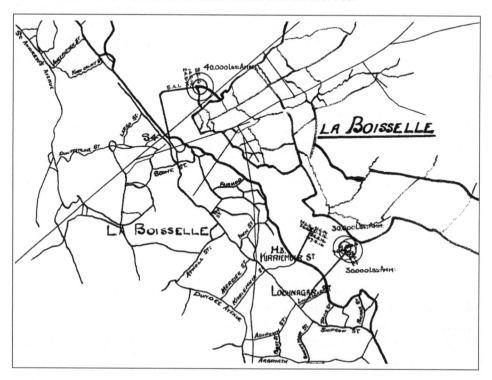

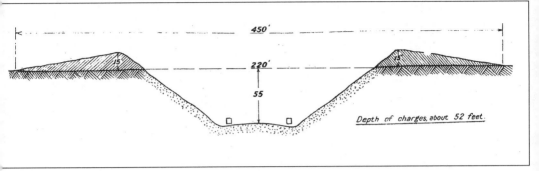

The Lochnagar Crater, formed by two charges which formed a single crater. From *The Work of the Royal Engineers in the European War, 1914–19. Military Mining*, 1922.

Each of the two branches was allocated 30,000lbs of ammonal, which filled the chambers and extended down the tunnels. In fact the longer left-hand branch was charged with 36,000lbs and the right with 24,000lbs. The detonation of the two charges would create one massive crater and the combination of the two charges made it the largest British mine blown up to that point.

Between the two large mines, they charged two chambers in the Glory Hole with 8,000lb each to destroy the German mining system, and dug a communication tunnel for use immediately after the first assault. On the northern flank, Captain Henry Hance, commanding 179 Tunnelling Company, obtained permission to place a mine under a position known as Y Sap, which enfiladed the German line in front of Ovillers. He could not drive directly towards it, owing to the German underground defences, and therefore drove a tunnel diagonally across no man's land for almost 500ft before making a sharp right turn for another 500ft back to the German lines. Hance later claimed that this was the longest offensive drive made in chalk in the war.[21] Work, however, was running late and they completed chambering only on 28 June, an estimated 30ft from the nose of the Y Sap and 75ft beneath it. They could hear the Germans in their mine system above them but took fewer precautions over silence, apparently using hand picks throughout. This would have been partly because of the need for speed, but also because they were confident that the Germans could only reach them with a charge that would also destroy the Y Sap. They charged Y Sap with 40,000lbs of ammonal.

The two large mines were heavily overcharged and were designed to throw debris over the adjacent German positions, as well as create lips 15ft high. At the moment of detonation, the dust thrown up by these mines would screen the village from observation and prevent mutual support. The lips would then serve the same purpose, provided the British reached them first.

The Division attacking La Boisselle was the 34th, while to the north the 8th attacked Ovillers. The mines were blown two minutes before zero hour rather than

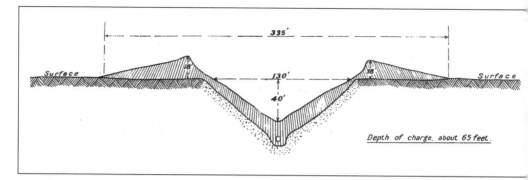

The Y Sap Mine crater. This overcharged mine at La Boisselle threw up high lips supposed to prevent enfilade fire. This drawing appears in *The Work of the Royal Engineers in the European War, 1914–19, Military Mining*, 1922, wrongly captioned as the Hawthorn Crater.

the ten-minute delay of the Hawthorn mine. The initial operation orders issued on 21 June by 34th Division indicated that both La Boisselle mines were to be blown at zero hour. These were subsequently amended so that the Lochnagar mine was to be blown at two minutes before zero and the Y Sap mine at zero, then that both should be blown at two minutes before.[22] The timing of the mines was not only concerned with the danger of falling debris, but also with the requirement by 34th Division that the first waves of attackers should rise to the attack no more than 200yds from the German front line, to obtain maximum benefit from the British barrage before it lifted to the next target.

Hance, however, believed that the Y Sap mine should have been blown before the attack and an attempt be made to narrow the very wide no man's land north of La Boisselle, which was up to 650yds wide. This attack, by 34th and 8th Divisions, was across the wide marshy expanse of Mash Valley towards the village of Ovillers. He thought that destroying the Y Sap would enable the British to advance their front line prior to the attack. He was convinced that the attacking infantry would never get across no man's land:

No doubt it was hoped that the barrage then coming down would enable them to do this, but I never had any faith in it. For hours, if not days, before zero I could have blown up the Y sap any time I liked, and I, accordingly, saw the Corps Commander, asking for permission to do so. Sir William Pulteney, whilst agreeing that the destruction of the Y sap would save life locally, was of opinion that the explosion of such a great mine would have warned the Germans for five miles North and South that the attack was imminent, and caused every German machine gunner for 10 miles to be on the qui vive. In my humble opinion they would be in any case, and what if the mine had been blown two days before? However, having put forward my view, and having been overruled by the Corps Commander, with all his infinitely wider knowledge of the issues at stake, and the possibilities of success on the Front involved, I could only abide by his decision, but, personally, I have never ceased to regret it. (Captain Henry M. Hance, OC 179 Tunnelling Company)[23]

In fact the Germans knew that the Y Sap was undermined and were forced to evacuate the position: nevertheless, their whole front line north of La Boiselle still effectively enfiladed the British advance.

The infantry attacking at the Y Sap mine were led by the 20th and 23rd Northumberland Fusiliers. The mine dealt only with the sap projecting into no man's land: the German front line to their front right, running parallel to the Albert to Bapaume road and backed by the defended village, was untouched by it. They were also subject to fire from the village of Ovillers to their left. Immediately they left their trenches, machine-gun fire came from both these positions and the two leading battalions were almost annihilated before they reached the German front line.[24] The 8th Division suffered equally badly, although Hance claimed that his mine created a screen from fire from the north:

> Such loss as was incurred by fire from this point was suffered before the mine was fired. Thereafter the infantry were able to approach his trenches on the south of the crater protected from fire by the lips formed.[25]

The 34th Division did not attack across the crater field of the Glory Hole owing to the impassable nature of the terrain, comprising wholly of craters filled with barbed wire and steel stakes. There was a great danger, however, from flanking fire from the village against the infantry attacking either side.

Battalions were to attack either side of the vast Lochnagar mine. Harvey described the impact of the mine on the Germans:

> We reckoned we closed in 9 deep dug-outs, each with an officer and 35 men – for prisoners were taken from the next dug-out, they were all marched out and the officer said there were 9 other dug-outs with the same numbers of inhabitants as his, i.e. 9 x 1 officer and 35 men – 9 officers and 315 men.[26]

He claimed that as a result of the mine, 'our troops went over with few casualties.' This was true only of the 102nd Brigade on the left, the 21st Northumberland Fusiliers followed by the 22nd, who succeeded in overrunning the trenches of the Schwaben Höhe. They then continued across the next two lines of trenches before being halted by the failure of the 101st Brigade to the right of the mine.[27] The task of this Brigade was more difficult. They had to advance up Sausage Valley, where the German line was drawn back so that they were overlooked on both sides by German trenches. No man's land was up to 500yds wide and so, on the morning of 1 July, the attacking battalions assembled in no man's land ready to advance. On the right of the crater, however, the 10th Lincolns were ordered to assemble further back to avoid debris from the mine, evacuating a small salient called the Nose. This caused them to begin their attack some way behind the 15th Royal Scots on their right. When the plan of 101st Brigade was presented to the battalion commanders on about 27 June, the commander of 15th Royal Scots, Lieutenant Colonel A.G.B Urmston, argued strongly that the two battalions should advance in line, otherwise the German fire would be concentrated on each battalion in turn. He offered to change places with the Lincolns and take the risk of his battalion being hit by debris, which he believed was preferable to the damage caused by German machine guns firing from the village of La Boisselle to their left and Sausage Valley in front. The Brigade commander, however, told him that the plan could not be changed.

Hance reported the impact of the Lochnagar mine:

> The mine was fired at -2 minutes on Z day, and was wholly successful. An enormous crater was formed, extending considerably behind the enemy trench, which, with its occupants and machine guns etc, was entirely destroyed for a considerable length, as well as all his dug-outs for a considerable distance beyond the actual crater being entirely closed, and large portions of his trench being buried. There can be no doubt that the mine generally caused him considerable loss, and by the violence of the shock to his garrison, and the shelter afforded by the lips of the crater itself, enabled our attacking infantry to reach his trenches here, and to pass over them in the first assault, with comparatively light loss. Such loss as was incurred must have been caused by fire from his flank.[28]

Devastating as it was, the effects of the mine were, as ever, very local and dealt only with the left shoulder of the Schwaben Höhe position. It also possibly hindered the attackers by disrupting the rapid advance that was vital to stay behind the barrage. The 10th Lincolns were to advance at 7.30 like the other battalions but, because of having to withdraw from the mine danger area, they had further to advance. Within two minutes of zero, before they had crossed their own front line, machine-gun fire raked them and the 10th Suffolks following. Colonel Urmston witnessed the leading companies going forward:

> I could see the blowing up of the mine in front of 10th Lincolns had no effect whatsoever on the German defenders, but utterly ruined our advance, and also re-acted by leaving right flank of 102nd Brigade 'in the air' as well.[29]

La Boisselle was only captured by the British on 4 July. The attack failed on 1 July because the artillery preparation had been inadequate to deal with the fire that the Germans could bring on the attacking troops from this very powerful position. The failure to capture the village of La Boisselle early in the attack meant that fire from this position had a very bad effect on troops both north and south of the village. The two mines eliminated only a very small part of this fire.

The Germans held the village of Fricourt with, to the east, the mining sector of the Tambour, worked by 178 Tunnelling Company, and to the south Bois Français, worked by 174. The British 18th Division held this front in the autumn and winter of 1915. Its commander was impressed by the skill and bravery of the tunnellers, but sceptical of the real value of the mining activity. He wrote to his wife in early September after the first two weeks in the trenches:

> The most awkward and nasty job has undoubtedly been the German underground mining. The Berkshires, Queens and Buffs have each had one or more mines blown up in front of their trenches, and the Buffs had one platoon with about 15 casualties from the explosion. They behaved wonderfully well and when I went to see the company concerned that evening (1st Sept) they were all as cheerful as possible, in spite of the fact that in front of the Buffs two craters were formed which blew up over 50 yards of their front parapets.
>
> The 'craters' are 30 feet deep & some parts of their sides are perpendicular. The bottoms, in this weather, are a jumble of soft mud and destroyed wire entanglements. They form a row of formidable obstacles between our own and the German parapets (which are in places only 15 to 25 yards apart). We also have blown up three mines from a depth of 50 feet below the surface, but I honestly do not see how either we or the Germans have bettered our situations after months of mining effort!!
>
> The Germans of course started first. We inherited the situation from the French who had allowed the Germans to get the upper hand, or rather lower-hand of them: and we are consequently, from a mining point of view, somewhat handicapped. Digging down shafts 50 feet deep and running horizontal 'galleries' for 100 to 300 feet from them is no light labour, and I grudge the useless but inevitable work. It's very exciting for the miners underground who are often only 10 feet apart – when the question arises which shall blow 100,000 tons of earth first into the air? On the face of it the amusement seems senseless, but those concerned (500 men one way or another, here) are very keen indeed on their job – so are the R.E. officers of the mining companies. (Major General F.I. Maxse)[30]

At the beginning of October Norton Griffiths advocated the use of poison gas to deal with the Bois Français sector (referring to the head of the British gas warfare troops Colonel C.H. Foulkes):

Apparently the real bad position is Bois Francais - & the best remedy ... some of 'Foulkes Cough mixture' in small doses just to push the Gs back & blow in their shafts – taken once at night time – a Divisional dose.[31]

The proposal was not taken up. On 21 December the Germans fired two camouflets within ten minutes of each other at the Tambour. Captain Wellesley, commanding 178 Company, expected the blows and had arranged for the infantry to evacuate the front line. His miners were still working below and those at the face were buried alive while two rescuers were killed by mine gas when they mistakenly took off their breathing apparatus. Immediately after their first mine the Germans heard another explosion and observed a column of flame shoot from the surface, which they assumed was caused by their camouflet detonating a British charge. Altogether 19 were killed and 22 injured and it was probably the worst loss of life suffered by a British tunnelling company in a single incident. Thirty yards of the British front line collapsed and a new line was dug immediately behind it. As retaliation, Wellesley blew two camouflets the following day, using the explosive used for shot blasting, 'blastine', perhaps because it was immediately available, which produced far more carbon monoxide than ammonal. The Germans suffered one pioneer gassed or crushed and commented on the great quantities of gas which flooded their system, although Wellesley could not know this at the time. On 26th Wellesley held a conference with the senior staff officer of the 18th Division and Major Danford, who had commanded 174 Company but was now a staff officer for mining with 3rd Army. They decided on a more radical policy, which Danford had already introduced at La Boisselle in October:

It was felt that this 'pin pricking' policy of frequent camouflets did the German galleries and his transversals very little damage and the best method to adopt to force the Germans back was to 'Blow large' all round the front face of the Tambour du Clos.[32]

This would result in the destruction of the 40ft-deep system taken over from the French and they would need to push forward vigorously the deep level shafts, some of which were already at 100ft and would go still deeper. Wellesley would explode four large mines, which would destroy parts of the British front line. The British would join the lips of the craters to form the new British front line. On 28 and 30 December Wellesley fired four mines of between 8,000 and 10,000lbs, the shake from which was felt three miles away. German galleries were destroyed by the first pair of blows and the men at the face were crushed to death. The second two mines were less successful, with no casualties recorded and a few slightly crushed mining frames. The German mining diary records that the British were heard in all their working faces until ten minutes before the blow, indicating both the energy of the

British counterattack and also the deception tactics employed to prevent the Germans suspecting that a blow was imminent.[33]

The German miners at the Tambour, the 104th Pioneers, responded when the British blows destroyed their shallow galleries by developing a new deeper system. They dug six chambers behind the front line 20-30ft down, from which they drove inclined shafts running to 100ft. They linked these with a transversal along the whole of their front line and every 80 to 90ft ran out attack galleries towards the British. This was taken over in April by the Bavarian Pioneers and by June 1916 was a powerful underground complex. The system was provided throughout with electric light, powered by a generating station in Fricourt village. Ventilation was provided by centrifugal fans, two of which were electrical, the remainder hand powered. They placed electrical microphones in all the chambers at the ends of the galleries, which were monitored in a central listening station.[34] The British were not able to defeat this powerful system. Wellesley had electrical power for pumping water and hoisting spoil and an Ingersoll Rand compressor, which could be used for ventilation as well as for powering drills. His galleries were deeper than the Germans' but suffered from water because, it was thought, the water more readily percolated down from surface craters and through shattered ground.

At the end of April the Germans blew two mines at the north end of the Tambour and used incessant mortar bombardment to destroy two of the British shaft entrances and greatly hinder the work underground. They then raided the British trenches in an unsuccessful attempt to destroy the British shafts.

A Bavarian mine gallery, Stollen 1a, at Bois Français south-east of Fricourt. In this case a vertical shaft sunk from a mined dugout was used to get to the necessary depth, although inclines were favoured by both sides as haulage of spoil was simplified. The gallery ends in a chamber 36m beneath the crater field in no man's land. Started 68m from the German front line, very large charges could be blown from the end of the gallery without damage to the shaft. From Lehmann, *Das K B Pionier=Regiment*.

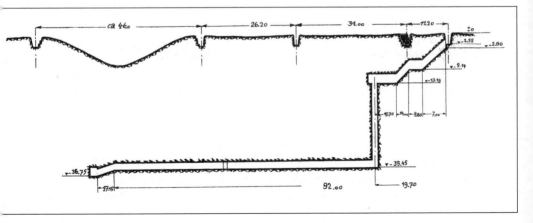

For the British offensive on 1 July no attacks were made across the crater fields of the Tambour or Bois Français. The German positions on the surface around Fricourt were extremely strong and the village itself was like a fortress. As with 179 Company at La Boisselle, 178 Company was unable to place mines under the village itself. Instead, 178 placed three mines 90ft beneath the Tambour position, increasing in size from north to south, of 9,000, 15,000 and 25,000lbs. These were to form overlapping craters along the whole position, burying the German front line, collapsing dugouts and blocking enfilade fire against the 21st Division attacking north of the Tambour. The mines were also detonated two minutes before zero, at 7.28am, but the larger mine failed to explode and was found to have become damp.[35] The shock effect of the mines may have protected the first two companies of the 10th West Yorkshire Regiment, which attacked immediately to the north of the Tambour, but when the second two crossed no man's land German machine gunners opened a devastating fire. The worst machine-gun fire came from the northern edge of the Tambour and continued in action for most of the morning. The machine gunners had survived the mines and may well have used the lips to gain a better field of fire. The two companies were 'practically annihilated and lay shot down in their waves',[36] the battalion suffering 710 casualties, the worst of any on 1 July 1916. The failure of the largest and most southerly mine to detonate will have had some impact on the ability of the Germans to defend, and meant that the 7th Division to the south also suffered from enfilade fire.

Two gaps in the British 7th Division attack were left south of Fricourt owing to the mine craters in no man's land, at Bois Français and Kiel Trench. A series of 500lb mines were blown in the latter area but the gaps in the attack increased losses to the attacker. Despite the very heavy casualties of the assaulting troops, advances on either side of the village rendered the German hold untenable and they withdrew during the night. Mining cannot be said to have made a major contribution to the fall of Fricourt and its legacy in the form of bands of cratered and impassable no man's land favoured the defenders.

The village of Mametz, assaulted by the right battalions of the 7th Division, although attended by heavy losses, was markedly more successful than the attacks to the north. Furthermore, the attacks of the 18th and 30th Divisions and the French to their right achieved all of their objectives on 1 July. A series of mines of between 200 and 2,000lbs were placed under strong points or at the end of Russian saps (see Chapter 9). The sector of the eastern part of the 7th Division and the 18th Division was that of 183 Company, commanded by Hickling since his posting from 172 Company at St Eloi in early 1915. He was asked to prepare a series of Russian saps for the attack, to be used to reinforce the captured positions and from the ends of which small mines were blown. In view of the work required, he would have to drop defensive mining, which guaranteed the underground safety of the British front-line trenches at Carnoy and Fricourt only up to 1 July. He halted all deep mining except what he called 'camouflage work' to give the impression of continuing activity. He seems not to have had deep drives ready beneath key points in the German lines. Instead he drove shallow tunnels across, the ends of which were filled with small charges except for two larger mines, at Bulgar Point (2,000lbs) and Casino Point (5,000lbs). At Casino Point it was necessary to incline the tunnel down as it neared the German lines, to gain the necessary depth to lay the charge. As the chalk grew harder the method of softening involved drilling holes with a carpenter's auger, into which they poured vinegar. The heading was only just completed and charged in time for the attack.[37]

The mine at Bulgar Point failed to explode, owing to a British mortar projectile cutting the leads shortly before zero.[38] The Casino Point mine, designed to destroy flanking machine guns and dugouts, was fired a few seconds before 7.27am and produced a crater with lips 97ft in diameter and 30ft deep. Hickling reported that three dugouts and four sniper's posts were buried and he suspected a machine-gun emplacement.[39] The infantry of the 6th Royal Berkshires attacked from 200yds away and suffered casualties from the mine debris, but also seem to have derived benefit from it.

Hickling took a calculated risk by abandoning deep mining prior to the 1 July attack. His men surveyed the German mining systems in the captured areas and discovered an inclined gallery running beneath the Kiel Trench crater field, which reached 200ft in depth. They estimated that to form a crater it would require a charge of 450,000lbs and the resulting crater would have had a diameter of 460ft.[40]

Following the 1 July attack there were few mines blown during the Somme fighting. In the south, the front moved on from the mine systems. At High Wood, 178 Company drove a mine at just 25ft depth, 320ft long, which they charged with 3,000lbs. It was blown thirty seconds before zero on 3 September 1916. British infantry occupied the crater, but lost it to counterattacks. The gallery was reopened by 178 Company, charged again with the same quantity and blown on 9 September, and this time it was held.[41] In the north of the Somme battlefield, the Beaumont Hamel mine gallery was reopened by 252 Company four days after 1 July in preparation for a repeat mining attack on Hawthorn Ridge. The tunnel had to be re-driven and they completed charging with 30,000lbs of ammonal on 30 October. The attack of the Battle of the Ancre was launched on 13 November. This time there was no delay between the launch of the infantry attack and the blowing of the mine. The infantry moved forward to get clear of their own wire six minutes before zero, which was at 5.45am. The mine itself was used to signal zero and coincided with the opening crash of the British barrage. Infantry of the 51st Highland Division overran the crater and 252 Company found 58 Germans alive in a dugout adjacent to the crater. They told them that six other dugouts holding a similar number of men were destroyed by the explosion.[42] The Battle of the Somme closed later in November.

The second blowing of the Hawthorn mine was the point at which the British learnt how to use mines correctly in the attack. Mines were not part of a step-by-step process, but a valuable shock weapon, which was nevertheless local and short-lived. Assault had to follow immediately, while the lighter debris was still falling, and before enemy troops on the flanks could gain the crater lips for their own advantage. Casualties from falling debris were minimal and were preferable to losing the race to the lips. The lessons of the Hohenzollern and St Eloi mining attacks of March 1916 were not incorporated into the attack plans of the opening of the Battle of the Somme. For Harvey the key lesson was to blow at zero. Other lessons concerned the location of mines, which were not always well-placed, in great part due to the virtual impossibility of silent working in chalk. The reforms in mining command and control introduced at the beginning of 1916 had only some bearing on the Somme, where local commanders were able to overrule the advice of the Inspector of Mines' staff. In particular Preedy, the Controller of Mines of the 4th Army, lacked the authority to overrule senior officers commanding or on the staffs, especially Hunter-Weston and Fuller, who were both also Sappers. The Somme was the arena in which the British learnt the tactical methods of using the potential advantage offered by offensive mining. Mines could not, however, solve the tactical problems of the Somme, where the objectives were too deep for the capacity of the artillery. British attack tactics concentrated increasingly on coordinating artillery with the infantry advance, and on turning German defensive tactics against themselves. Mining, however, was still to play a major role in British offensives in the first half of 1917.

Chapter 7

Vimy, Arras and Messines 1917

1917 saw the culmination of British mining potential and the establishment of a partial supremacy by British miners on some fronts. In the set piece and limited British victories of April and June mining played a role, although at Vimy and Arras a very limited one. At the Battle of Arras and the assault on Vimy Ridge, launched on 9 April 1917, the British could have placed a large number of mines beneath or near the German lines, but chose not to do so. The Vimy Ridge and Arras positions were taken over by the British from the French in March 1916. Extremely heavy fighting had taken place between the French and Germans during 1915. Following the capture of Carency the French had pushed the Germans to the crest of the ridge but, as at Vauquois, the Germans still retained observation over the Allied rear areas.

The British took over a mining situation similar to that in the active area of the Somme the previous summer, with the Germans dominant and in many places beneath their front lines. Five British Tunnelling Companies were deployed along the ridge and seventy mines were fired in the first two months of the British occupation, mostly by the Germans. The Germans also used trench mortar fire on the shaft heads and this was the cause of high casualties amongst the tunnellers at Vimy. A German overland attack in May 1916, which forced the British back 700yds, was aimed at neutralising British mining activity by capturing the shaft entrances above ground. From June 1916, however, the Germans withdrew many miners to work on the preparation for the new defence system known collectively as the Hindenburg Line, and also, subsequently, for work in the mining industry at home. German activity tailed off and in the second half of 1916 the British established strong defensive underground positions incorporating transversal galleries. From August the British tunnelling companies were able to develop schemes for laying mines to support an attack on the Ridge proposed for autumn 1916, although this was subsequently postponed. The Canadian Corps was posted to the northern part of the Ridge in October 1916 and preparations for an attack were revived in February 1917.

The commander of 182 Company, Mulqueen, described an encounter with General Currie, commanding the 1st Canadian Division, which took over the Carency and Berthonval sectors. Mulqueen explained that his men had obtained supremacy, but still needed to engage in offensive mining in places.

General Currie was very interested in the offensive mines which had been, and were being built. He asked many questions regarding their depth, the weight of explosive in them, or intended, the size of the craters which would result, etc., etc. Nothing further was said and I was asked to keep in close touch with his G.S.O. 1, Colonel Radcliffe.[1]

Mulqueen was a frequent visitor to the Divisional headquarters, but only later did Currie fully explain to him his views on mines for the offensive. Commanders in the Canadian Corps were very likely to have been influenced by the Canadians' experience at St Eloi in April 1916, where the mines that Mulqueen had pioneered had so altered and damaged the landscape as to render occupation of the craters by the infantry all but impossible. Mulqueen's 182 Company, however, and the other tunnellers on Vimy Ridge, were looking forward to playing their part in the coming attack:

Above ground there were persistent rumours of a British attack on the 'Ridge' and underground we drove eagerly forward with our offensive mines, all the while congratulating ourselves on our unquestioned superiority of position. We lived and dreamed mines and the effect which they would have on the Hun. All of this was reported to the G.S.O.1, and he accepted it with patient reserve. When and by whom the meeting was called I have forgotten. All I can remember is the shock which I received at it. The purpose of the meeting was to consider preliminary arrangements for the assault on the 'Ridge'. The meeting was not a large one, but it is probable a representative of the Corps was on hand. I was with Colonel Williams [1st Army Controller of Mines], but I do not remember representatives of any of the other Tunnelling Companies and it may be it was purely a First Division affair. General Currie spoke and stated that he had come to the conclusion that the large mines which were charged would be more of a hindrance than a help and, that they were not to be fired. He was so definite and his reasons were so sound that even had I had the authority to do so, I had no grounds on which to advance counter arguments. He pointed out that should a line of craters be thrown up under the German lines, they would undoubtedly disrupt the German front line position, but they would also hinder the advancing troops and force them to move forward over extremely difficult terrain. The chasms would be at least fifty feet deep and the attackers would be forced to move around their rims and would be sitting targets for enemy machine guns stationed in his support trenches. He considered these alone were sufficient reasons to drop the offensive mining operations, but he advanced the further argument that the Tunnelling Companies would be much better employed building subways. At that time we had several mines charged with some 120,000 pounds of explosive. Our plans called for charging several more, but these were all dropped. The mines which were charged were left undisturbed and while we rounded out one or two headings which were then well advanced, we did not embark on any new offensive operations.[2]

Officers from the Canadian Corps studied the problems of advancing across heavily mine cratered ground and visited La Boisselle and Fricourt on the old Somme battlefield for this purpose. They were impressed by the fact that the decision not to assault across the crater areas had left troops on either side heavily exposed to fire from these areas, but concluded that the craters only rarely caused an obstacle. Parties could infiltrate around the lips of the craters with machine guns (the lighter Lewis gun was by then far more plentiful than in July 1916):

> The general conclusion arrived at is that, with the exception of the big ones of recent formation, such as Montreal and Patricia, the Craters do not present an insurmountable obstacle. This opinion is confirmed by the experience of several raids which have been carried out. They must be negotiated by small parties who can take advantage of the causeways formed by the lips, skirting the actual bottoms, which are likely to be wet and holding [sic]. The advance of these parties will be covered by a barrage of Stokes Mortars and Rifle Grenades.
>
> Special means of ingress into the Craters will be prepared by a trench or Russian Sap, each individual crater being treated differently.[3]

Despite this report, offensive mines were removed from the entire central portion of the Canadian Corps attack opposite Hill 145, which was the highest part of the ridge and amongst the hardest fought over. Further mines were vetoed following the blowing by the Germans on 23 March of nine craters, named the Longfellow group, along no man's land. These craters effectively closed a gap between a large crater to the north, Broadmarsh, and others to the south, leaving just 100yds of no man's land clear. It is probable that the Germans were aiming to restrict the passage of attackers to predictable points as well as blowing craters as tank obstacles. It was therefore decided that three mines laid by 172 Company should not be blown, although the largest was designed to prevent the Germans firing across the Broadmarsh crater. These mines were left in place after the assault and only removed in the 1990s. Of a large number of British mines under preparation on Vimy Ridge, probably eleven were charged in preparation for the attack, but on the day just three were blown, including those forming a northern defensive flank.[4] The 1st Army Controller of Mines, Lieutenant Colonel G.C. Williams, strongly implied after the attack that the Broadmarsh crater was too powerful a position to have been left intact:

The position of Broadmarsh Crater is very commanding, and situated as it is at the commencement of a re-entrant in the enemy lines, it completely enfiladed our position behind the main group of craters to the south. It is a question whether the abandonment of this mine was wise, for our troops suffered heavily in traversing the gap. An inspection of Broadmarsh Crater has shown that the enemy dug-outs at the bottom were practically untouched by the bombardment. There is every reason to believe that the enemy machine gunners accommodated in them were ready on the lip when the assault came over.[5]

In the north of the attack on Vimy Ridge a mine was prepared by 176 Tunnelling Company against the strongpoint position known as the Pimple, which was not completed in time for the attack. This was notable for the use that it made of the geological formation of that part of the ridge, where sand and clay lay over the chalk. The gallery was pushed silently through the clay, but by 9 April was still 70ft short of its target. The Pimple was not captured until 12 April but, despite this delay, the mine would not have reached under the strongpoint.[6]

Owing to the German withdrawal from their front line south-east of Arras, the only mine that was used on the Arras front on 9 April was to the north-east, at Blagny. This was apparently a 2,200lb charge and was blown at zero, 5.30am, and, according to Lieutenant J.C. Neill of the New Zealand Tunnelling Company,

The mine aimed at the Pimple, Vimy Ridge. From *The Work of the Royal Engineers in the European War, Geological Work* (1922).

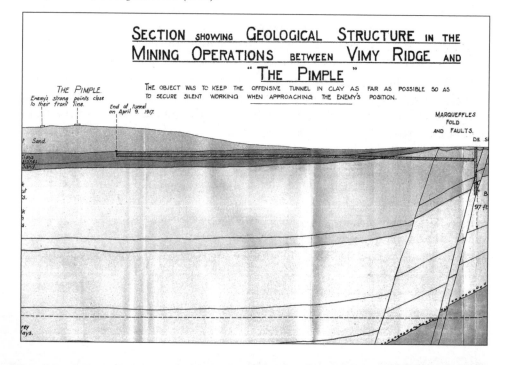

destroyed two dugouts, 50yds of trench and a concrete pillbox. However, it also stunned and apparently buried some members of the 13th Royal Scots and checked their assault temporarily.[7]

Flanders and Messines 1916–1917

It was an eternal struggle both with the enemy and with the water and mud. Working forward, listening, loading and tamping required perseverance, great physical effort, willingness to sacrifice and courage. The deeper one went, the greater the struggle on the wet, narrow steps, the worse the air, the greater also the danger, from direct hits from above, from enemy mines, from inrush of mud and water to be cut off and suffocated. Endlessly the miners vied with one another, officers and men in long lines in smashed galleries lying one behind the other to save trapped mates. It was the same picture while charging in a race against the enemy; everyone wanted to be forward and to help. (Lieutenant Colonel Otto Füsslein, Commander of Miners, German 4th Army)[8]

Although the British were unable to exploit the mining attack at St Eloi on 27 March 1916, the detonation of the mines, as well as killing or burying some 300 men of the 18th Reserve Jäger Battalion, had profound repercussions in the German command, especially the Pioneer service. Within three weeks the Germans formed Pioneer Mining Companies, apparently modelled on the British Tunnelling Companies, and issued new instructions on mine warfare. An officer with experience of mining at La Bassée, Captain Bindernagel, was ordered to the Wytschaete front, south of Ypres, as an advisor to the commander of Pioneers of the XIII Reserve Corps. Investigations by a geologist, Dr Siegfried Passarge, of Hamburg University, concluded that the British had succeeded in getting through the wet sand at 5 or 10m depth.[9]

Subsequently, the commander of Pioneers of the XIII Reserve Corps was replaced by an officer who himself was a civilian mining engineer and experienced in mine warfare.[10] Lieutenant Colonel Otto Füsslein commanded the 25th Pioneer Regiment, one of the units created from fortress battalions, and was brought from the Les Éparges sector, regarded by the German pioneers as the 'school of mines'.[11] Füsslein instigated further geological research and he blamed ignorance of the underground conditions as having caused misinformed and wasted mining work.

Füsslein and Bindernagel recruited five new mining companies, which included the new Pioneer Mining Companies, which were authorized on 7 April 1916.[12] It is possible that the Germans gained a knowledge of the composition of the British tunnelling companies from the prisoners taken at the Bluff in February. According to Füsslein, officers who in civilian life were miners or engineers were gathered from the whole of the German army to form a corps of officers with a technical and mining education. Usually these were formed from existing infantry mining units: for example 352 Pioneer Mining Company was created in November 1916 from an Infantry Mining Company named after its commander, Lieutenant Kurt Schmölling.[13] However, the Germans were unable simply to create tunnelling companies in the same way that the British had. It was thought necessary to transfer qualified pioneer officers to the units, as very few of the mining officers knew field engineering duties. This, however, was opposed by the General of Pioneers at German GHQ, owing to the need to officer a large number of newly formed trench mortar units, for which the pioneers were also responsible, on the grounds that it was part of the pre-war siege capability of the pioneer service. It is questionable whether the mining or the mortar companies needed trained field engineers, and the impression is that the German Pioneer service was unable to accept the same level of civilianisation as the British. It took much urging from Füsslein to obtain authority to form new units and he claimed that the companies comprised transferred infantry without experienced officers and so required training from scratch. In August 1916 the Germans transferred a large number of coal miners out of the army back to Germany for industrial production, and those remaining were regarded as of poor quality.

The new instructions on mine warfare were issued on 19 April 1916 as part of a series of instructional pamphlets, *All Arms Instructions for Trench Warfare*, issued by the German War Ministry. This appears to have been written with the immediate experience of St Eloi in mind, as it emphasized the need to investigate the geology of a mining sector using bores and illustrated the means of using clay levels to drive a gallery.[14]

In June 1916 the Germans had two local mining successes against British and Canadian troops. In the first, at Hooge on 6 June 1916, the Experimental Company

Geological profile from the German 1916 mining instructions, showing a shaft sunk through loam and sandy loam into clay. The gallery is driven through clay to avoid the sandy loam and wet running sand. The Germans did not, however, have the same success as the British in sinking shafts through the running sand in Flanders. From *Vorschriften für den Stellungskrieg für alle Waffen. Teil 2. Minenkrieg.*

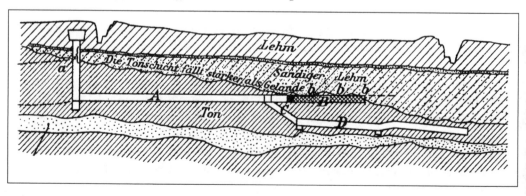

of the Prussian Guard Pioneers succeeded in blowing four large mines under the British front line held by 28th Canadian Battalion. The Germans drove under the British at only 6m depth and later found part of the British system: cramped tunnels only 4–5m deep, which they used to drain their new crater position.[15] The Experimental Company began work either side of the Menin Road in the Hooge sector on 7 October 1915 and took over a divisional mining unit (Mineurzug) formed from infantry miners. They began a new shaft between two existing ones, although in the middle of the work the officer commanding was posted to a mortar unit. The work was laborious and difficult. South of the Menin Road there was frequent contact underground with British miners. One night in early December voices were heard in the workings from Calais shaft and a draught was felt, indicating a break in. A patrol entered and 40m along the gallery a British soldier emerged from a branch. A fire fight broke out, followed by the blowing of charges, during which a pioneer was killed by suffocation. Again there was fighting underground on 9 January 1916. The Germans attempted to fire a 20kg charge kept in readiness, but were forestalled by a

Sketch map of the attack galleries used by the Prussian Experimental Pioneer Company for the four Hooge mines blown on 6 June 1916 beneath the trenches of the 28th Canadian Battalion. The galleries were driven from Schloss, Ypern and Preussen shafts. The four craters remain today, forming ponds in the grounds of the rebuilt chateau. From Held, *Das Königlich Preussische Garde=Pionier=Bataillon und seine Kriegsverbände 1914/18.*

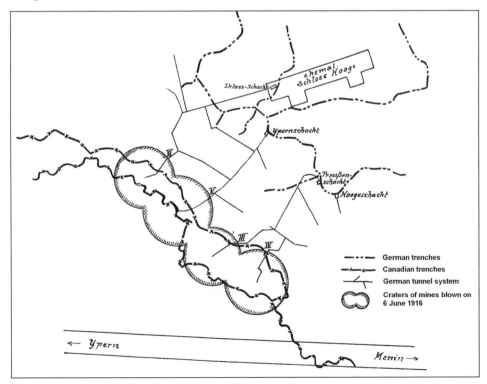

British camouflet blown first. The company was ordered to push forward attack tunnels, which were met with British camouflets in February.

Immediately north of the Menin Road, despite the difficult ground and water, the Germans succeeded in driving four attack tunnels under the British front line. These were at 6–7m depth and not into the deep clay levels, but problems with wet ground from Preussen shaft necessitated a diversion on 20 February 1916. At the beginning of March charges were ready in the four tunnels, but the British abandoned holding their front line, occupying just forward posts and creating a new line 20m behind. The work had to be resumed, therefore, on 24 March to push the galleries forward between the posts and the main front line held by the 3rd Canadian Division. This was reached on 19 April and charging of the four galleries, with a total of 10,830kg, was complete on 1 June. The following day the Germans launched a large local attack on the area immediately to the south against the Canadians and captured Sanctuary Wood and Mount Sorrel. Like other German attacks in the first half of 1916, the Germans were motivated wholly or in part by the desire to capture the British front line, in order to render their mining system unusable. The four mine charges were blown on 6 June, accompanied by an infantry attack. There was debate as to the time of the firing of the mines, which paralleled that occurring on the Somme over the 1 July mines. The mines were blown three minutes before the attack was launched but, according to the Prussian Guard Pioneer historian, the General of Pioneers of the 4th Army criticized the timing, stating that ten to fifteen minutes should be left in case of delay in firing the mines, to avoid casualties. 'Only by good fortune did the eager and impulsive attacking troops, their blood up, not suffer any loss from the punctually fired charges.'[16]

The firing was carried out from the dugout of the Schloss shaft in the remains of the Hooge chateau. The blows practically wiped out two companies of Canadians and formed a continuous crater 120m long, 25m wide and 10m deep, somewhat larger than the Pioneers had expected. A new Canadian line had to be formed further down the Menin Road. To the south the Canadians retook the lost areas of Sanctuary Wood and Mount Sorrel, but the Hooge position remained in German hands until the opening of the Third Battle of Ypres. From their new position, however, the Germans only created a system of galleries 2-6m deep, which was too shallow either to listen effectively for British deep mining, or to blow against it.[17]

Another German mining success occurred at Givenchy-lez-la-Bassée. In this sector, just north of where the chalk of Vimy and the Somme rises from the ground, the shafts and galleries were driven through sandy clay and were very troubled by wet. At 2.50am on 22 June, 295 Pioneer Mining Company blew a large mine, which destroyed two saps and three lines of trenches and wiped out nearly two-thirds of B Company of the 2nd Royal Welch Fusiliers. The blow was followed up by a strong raiding party of Jägers. The British named the result the Red Dragon Crater. The blow also badly damaged the workings of 254 Tunnelling Company, which had taken over the sector on its return from Gallipoli. Five men were cut off at the face by the collapse of a gallery from Shaftesbury shaft, but after twenty hours rescuers managed to make a small opening through which three men could be pulled. A further fall of earth at the face, however, had badly injured Private Thomas Collins, who was too big to be brought through the small gap. There was an immediate danger of a further roof fall, but the last man with him, Sapper William Hackett, refused all instructions to leave the gallery, saying: 'I am a Tunneller. I must look after my mate.' Almost immediately there was another fall of clay and the gallery was completely filled, burying them both alive. The rescuers worked for another four days attempting to rescue them, but it was impossible to recover the gallery and the entire shaft later collapsed. The bodies of the two men were never recovered and Hackett became the only Tunneller to be awarded the Victoria Cross.[18] Following the blow of the Red Dragon crater, however, the British were able to develop their position at Givenchy in the sector without much hindrance from the Germans.

Throughout 1916 and right up until the opening of the Battle of Messines on 7 June 1917, the British and Germans were engaged in an underground struggle along the six miles of the ridge and up to the Ypres Salient. Afterwards Füsslein was blamed for the failure to halt the British mining offensive and he wrote a detailed report in which he justified his interpretation of the situation underground, although he was to some extent exonerated by the German official history published in 1939. Füsslein and Bindernagel remained in Flanders when the XXIII Reserve Corps moved to the Somme at the beginning of September 1916 and Füsslein was promoted to Commander of Miners in the 4th Army. Crucially, however, he did not have tactical control over the use of the miners, which remained under divisional commanders. When Füsslein arrived in Flanders in 1916 the Germans had already started new mine systems in response to fears that the British were making a deep mining attack on the Messines–Wytschaete ridge. These were all, however, from shafts sunk in their front lines and the older galleries were, to a large extent, flooded or lost. Up to that time the Germans had worked in shafts no deeper than 20m, from which they drove galleries forward and connected them with a transversal from which the listening and fighting tunnels were pushed out:

> Here in the Ypres Salient, and throughout the Wytschaete salient, before the summer of 1916 there was the same picture: the old form of mine warfare, which had remained almost unchanged in armies from the time of Frederick the Great until the 1890s, was repeated without thought.[19]

Füsslein says that it was not appreciated then that such a system was only effective where it was possible easily to detect the sounds of the advancing enemy. If the attacker got close then blowing charges to stop him would also destroy the German system. The Germans still believed that because they could not get deep, neither could the British. In most places the Germans expended much energy on the old shallow shafts. In only four places – Railway Wood, Hooge, the Bluff and Hill 60

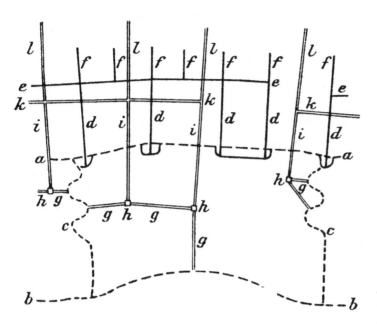

German plan of a mine system from the 1916 instructions, showing a shallow system (single lines) and a deep system (double lines). Key: a = front line trench, b = second line trench, c = communication trenches, d = main galleries, e = galleries, f = listening galleries, g = entrance tunnels, h = deep galleries and mine access, i = deep main galleries, k = deep galleries, l = deep attack tunnels. From *Vorschriften für den Stellungskrieg für alle Waffen. Teil 2. Minenkrieg.*

– did they try after the St Eloi blows to sink shafts through the water-bearing sands. They still tried using the old methods, sinking in the front line with close-timbered or sometimes sheet metal-lined shafts, from cramped dugouts and using old galleries of the smallest dimensions. The Germans had to assume that the British would be going deep, as they had at St Eloi, but they had little reliable intelligence to go on. Füsslein pointed to a major failure at St Eloi that had occurred when the divisions actively mining in the sector until two weeks before the attack (117th and 123rd) were relieved by the XXIII Corps and the knowledge of the British workings was not passed on, 'so that they groped completely in the dark.' In 1916, Füsslein claimed, the Germans considered the Messines–Wytschaete ridge too important to give up and still followed a doctrine of strongly defending their front line. Only later did they adopt a policy of defensiveness in depth:

> It was only recognized later in the enormous defensive battles that, in the 'war of material', such inflexible holding on to high ground which seemed in isolation to be tactically significant was an absurdity.[20]

There was a realisation, however, that they either had to give up attempting to sink shafts in their front lines, or lose the front line itself. The Germans, therefore, began to follow the British practice of sinking deeper shafts from behind the front line, which were of a larger diameter, although unlike the British when timber was inadequate they attempted to use concrete-lined shafts. They aimed to sink at least two shafts in each sector and to link them in case of one shaft head becoming blocked. According to Füsslein, his miners succeeded in spite of the advice of civilian specialists:

> Hydraulic engineering experts from Germany explained that it was impossible with the means available in the field (a lack of drilling rigs and a means of securing the shafts, a lack of powerful heavy pumps with mechanical power), to get through the swimming sand of the east slopes. However, for the miner, the word 'impossible' did not exist. And he succeeded...

This is again in contrast with the British experience, where the whole engineering process became a civilian one and where possible the miners got the equipment that they demanded.

At the Bluff the 1st Company of the 24th Pioneers drove 'infinitely long, cramped galleries' which they blew on 25 July 1916, creating an enormous crater,

German concrete-lined shaft through loam and running sand. The shaft head is protected by a concrete bunker. The Germans were skilled at concrete construction but placed too much reliance on its use for shafts, whereas the British achieved success only by the use of steel tubbing. From Kranz, 'Minierkampf und Kriegsgeologie im Wytschaetebogen'.

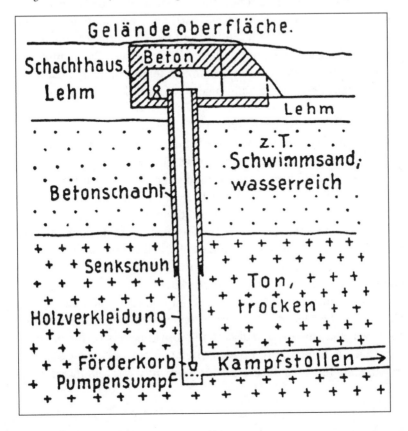

although the 1st Canadian Tunnelling Company had anticipated the blow and casualties were minimized. Füsslein found the situation in the Ypres salient, when he took over in September 1916, was as it had been at Wytschaete:

> …effort dissipated in countless shallow and wet galleries in the front line, paltry beginnings of deep tunnelling, again in the front line, with little imminent prospect of getting deep. Therefore defence against deep attack was nowhere possible.[21]

The 352 Pioneer Mining Company under Lieutenant Schmölling at Railway Wood, the Experimental Pioneer Company at Hooge and Hill 60, and the 1st Reserve Company of Füsslein's 24th Pioneers at the Bluff all struggled. The shafts, sunk with tremendous difficulty, which were stopped at 20m should have gone deeper to get to the dry clay. Instead they were 'just glorified sumps'[22] and they were blowing their charges in the level of the waterlogged strata. In the autumn of 1916 the Germans were unable to advance galleries much distance from these shafts and so each time they blew they damaged their own laboriously sunk shafts. Tactical control of mining remaining with divisions, however, made it difficult to change the practice of shallow mining from the front line. Moreover, the shallow levels had to be kept for defensive purposes, but they had insufficient manpower to push forward new deep workings while maintaining the old shallow systems. In reality the old systems were becoming 'pure death traps', partly because the single shafts had only one exit and partly because British artillery and trench mortar bombs were far more effective at destroying shallow mine galleries. This induced the infantry to agree to give them up. It was also difficult for the miners to give up their existing shafts: 'It was a constant struggle with the traditional ways until the new mine warfare tactics established themselves.'[23]

The new deep levels, begun in June 1916, were sunk 100 to 300m behind the German front and were gradually extended along the whole line. There were delays caused in particular by a shortage of manpower and, of four new companies which Füsslein requested, only two were granted: 'The enemy meanwhile continued working quietly and steadily. The English, being tough and energetic, only blew when we threatened to get extremely close to them.'[24]

The lack of deep systems prevented the Germans from detecting the advance of the British galleries, but from aerial photographs, and the frequent accumulations of bluish grey sandbags, Füsslein concluded that on the whole of the Wytschaete salient and further north the British were working in the clay level.

Füsslein complained of difficulties with supplies to maintain the larger and deeper shafts, of a shortage of miners, of increased British shelling of shafts causing the death of valuable miners, and also of the unwillingness of the infantry to help and materials being thrown away. Füsslein tried to increase awareness of the miners' work through conferences and lectures, but frequently was told that miners were to be kept away as their presence only caused the British to mine. Often he encountered the belief that his miners should prevent every enemy blow, which he likened to expecting the artillery to stop every enemy shell. The divisional commanders could not accept that the British had gained a year's head start over the German miners: '...amongst our troops there was a general lack not just of understanding but also of a desire to understand.'[25]

The opening of the Battle of Messines on 7 June 1917 saw the largest mining attack in the history of warfare. It was the largest quantity of explosives deliberately detonated at one time and the most effective integration of mines with an attack. The history of the British mining operations and the German attempts to defeat them shows that many more than the nineteen mines blown were planned and laid. Many of the mines were laid in mid-1916 and had to be defended against German attack and protected against deterioration. In some cases this was for more than a year. Other mines, by contrast, were ready only days or hours before the attack began. Northernmost were two mines at Hill 60, where in the spring of 1916 the 3rd Canadian Company had relieved 175 Tunnelling Company. The Canadians took over the 'Berlin tunnel', which was in the Paniselien or 'bastard' clay at 90ft, and drove a branch beneath the hill, which in three months had passed under the German mining system before running into bad ground. As it was close enough to destroy the German front line they began a charge chamber, but as they enlarged the gallery it caved in with an inrush of sand and water with yellow clay, indicating that they were almost out of the clay bed. The leak was sealed and a series of small chambers had to be prepared to take a charge, into which they loaded 53,500lbs of ammonal, with an additional 7,800lbs of priming slabs of guncotton packed into the spaces. They completed this on 1 August 1916. The Canadians then dug an intermediate level system at 50ft to form a protective screen above their deep tunnels. They also drove towards the German-held Caterpillar, the spoil heap north of the railway line opposite Hill 60, and again ran into bad ground. They plugged the gallery, side-stepped to the right and descended 15ft into the clay. The gallery was continued to under the German second line and a charge chamber completed by 20 September. While they were loading the explosives, however, gas and water from a captured German gallery flooded the whole of the Berlin tunnel and cut off the charge. When they eventually regained access they discovered that the secure waterproofing meant that the charge was undamaged. Three independent sets of firing leads were installed, allowing nine circuits and sixty detonators. The charge was 70,000lbs. To improve access to the Berlin tunnel the Canadians began to sink a shaft to form a watertight entry past the running sand layer, which would enable a more effective seal than the inclined entrance from the railway cutting. At the beginning of November the 1st Australian Tunnelling Company relieved the 3rd Canadian Company and continued this shaft to 94ft to connect with the Berlin tunnel. They constructed a deeper level defensive gallery to further protect the mines, which

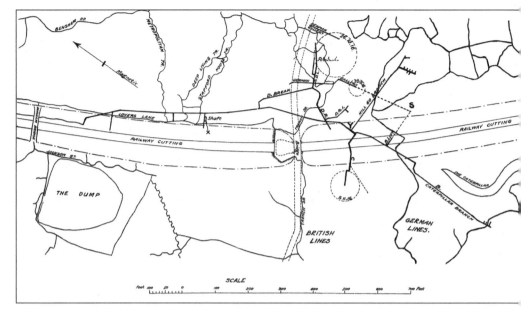

The Berlin tunnel to Hill 60 and the Caterpillar. From *Military Mining* (1922).

were to be kept ready to fire when the offensive was rescheduled. There were clear signs that the Germans were sinking a shaft almost directly above the Caterpillar mine and the Australians blew a camouflet from a branch gallery, causing smoke to rise from two points in the German lines, but also damaging the leads to the charge. The Germans then fired a charge which broke the leads of the Hill 60 mine and cut off miners for two days. Aggressive underground fighting to defend the charges would have alerted the Germans to their presence, so the tactic used by the Australians was to engage the Germans from their upper level galleries to keep them occupied and to hide any sounds from the deep galleries. The Germans carried out a surface raid, which the miners took part in, and thirteen British mine shafts were located and destroyed. The entrances to the deep British systems, however, were beyond the reach of the raiders and Füsslein himself reported that although they had detected the British system at 20m there was no guarantee that they were not also deeper. He later claimed that he realized that the shallow level work was being used to disguise the deep work.[26]

At St Eloi, 172 Company was relieved by the 1st Canadian Company in spring 1916. The shelling and mortar fire made work extremely difficult and in August 1916 the Canadians began a new shaft, named Queen Victoria, well back from the front line. In less than three weeks they had sunk it below 100ft (30.5m). Progress was slowed by continuous cavings, but the Canadians were able to locate and reconnect the old 172 galleries dug for the 27 March 1916 attack. The gallery was driven beyond the Nos 2 and 3 craters and prepared for charging. The charge of 95,600lbs was thought by the British to be the largest of the war (the German charge

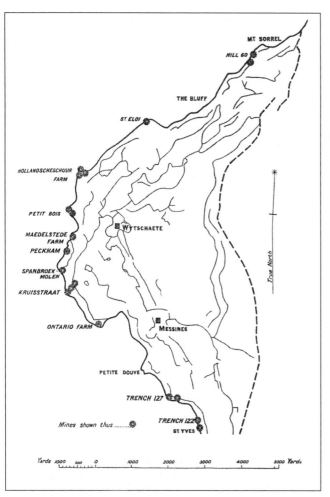

The Messines mines blown simultaneously at zero on 7 June 1917. Mines were placed beneath the key German salients, which could enfilade no man's land. The exception was Petit Douve where the British mine was lost to German action. From *Military Mining* (1922).

at Vauquois of 14 May 1916 exceeded it by 5,500kg). Tamping was completed on 28 May 1917, only nine days before firing. A second drive was begun towards craters 2 and 3, but could not be completed in time.[27]

The German mining system at St Eloi was their most successful, but it still failed to detect the Canadian mine. The Germans had skilfully drained and consolidated the craters and found that they could sink inclined shafts from them owing to the clay being compacted by the force of the explosion. They succeeded in places in getting to 30m depth, which Füsslein likened to a torpedo net around a warship. In the spring of 1917 the Germans felt secure at St Eloi and in places had reached 40m depth and had galleries partly under the British positions. They had not, however, been able to sink shafts outside of the crater area and the Canadian gallery had bypassed much of their defensive system. Information from prisoners suggested to them that their blows had destroyed the British mining system. In fact, as in many

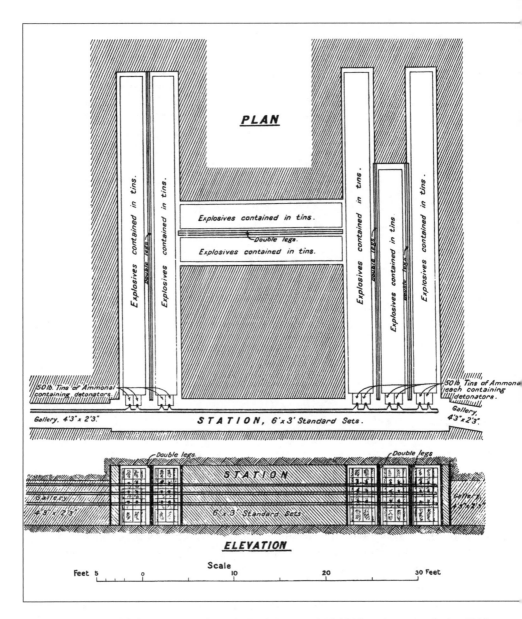

The loading and firing circuits of the St Eloi charge of 95,300lbs of ammonal plus 300lbs of gelignite, which was the largest British mine of the war. Three complete firing circuits were used, each having ten detonators connected in series. Each detonator was placed in a stick of gelignite with twelve other sticks bound to it, which were then each embedded in a 50lb tin of ammonal. The charge was fired at 3.10am on 7 June 1917 by the three circuits, each circuit having an individual exploder. From *Military Mining* (1922).

places along the ridge, the British had already driven their deep mine before the Germans had themselves gone deep.[28]

The British did not blow at the Bluff itself, but maps survive for two extremely ambitious schemes to the south, which bear the signs of being inspired by Norton Griffiths. The first was to lay four large mines around Eikhof Farm and the Dam Strasse, from a tunnel which would have measured about 4,320ft, including 1,500ft behind the German lines.[29] This was attempted with a tunnelling machine, one of two tried by the British, but it was not a success and the scheme was abandoned. An even more ambitious scheme was planned just south of this. A plan from late 1915 shows a long drive of about 4,700ft from Bois Carré behind the British lines to Grand Bois 2,300ft behind the German front line, from which seven charges totalling 240 tons were to be laid. It is probable that this was also planned using a machine, as the labour required would have been considerable.[30] South of this area were the schemes conceived by Cecil Cropper. On the left of the sector of 250 Tunnelling Company, the gallery that he obtained permission from the Canadian Corps to drive went under the Hollandscheschuur salient, or Nag's Nose, where the German line enclosed a piece of high ground. German shelling of the shaft head caused flooding to the tunnel and the objective had to be reduced to three charges laid within the salient. The British drove a gallery 825ft into the rear of the salient. The St Eloi blows caused the Germans to be considerably more alert to any indications of British mining and in June 1916 they heard sounds beneath their lines at both Petit Bois (known to them as Alfweg Cabaret) and Hollandscheshuur. They hurriedly sank timber-lined shafts to meet the noises and managed, despite the wet conditions, to get them to 5m. As the British were completing their gallery the Germans fired charges from shafts Cöln and Cassel in their own lines at the shoulders of the salient. The British managed to repair the damage and laid three charges in June, July and August 1916 of 34,200lbs, 14,900lbs and 17,500lbs at between 55 and 60ft. The Germans blew a very heavy camouflet on 10 February 1917, but the British were able to repair the damage.[31]

Cropper began the Petit Bois tunnel in late 1915 from the ruins of Van Damme Farm 500yds behind the lines, and sank a shaft 97ft into the clay. In February 1916 he sank a second shaft for a tunnelling machine that was to be unsuccessful. From the first shaft, however, he made good progress by clay-kicking of 100 to 150ft per week and the tunnel passed beneath the German front line and was branched into a 'Y'. From the bottoms of shallow shafts at Petit Bois the Germans could hear the voices of the British miners and they blew two heavy charges on the morning of 10 June at the shoulders of the salient just in front of their front line. These produced deep craters, but the Germans noticed that very little debris was thrown up by the northernmost charge. In fact the charge was almost directly above the British main gallery and the wet sand had poured down into it, completely blocking it beyond the 1,250ft point. It also trapped twelve men at the face. A rescue was immediately embarked on to dig around the collapsed portion to reach the cut-off miners. The rescuers worked continuous shifts, digging 40ft a day, but the tunnel was collapsed for 250ft and it took six and half days before they re-established contact with the lost portion. Graves had already been prepared for the miners when they broke into the gallery. They found eleven bodies – the twelfth was assumed buried under the debris – and they left the gallery to allow the air to clear. When they returned they found a man at the opening, alive, who said to them: 'For God's sake give me a drink! It's been a damned long shift!' The man's name was Sapper William Bedson. When the explosion had occurred, the trapped men had gathered at the end of the gallery nearest the collapse, where a tiny amount of air was coming through a pipe, and took it in turns to try to dig themselves out. The next day at 3.00am they gave up and spread themselves out along the gallery. One man died that afternoon and by 8.00pm on the third day only one was left alive. Bedson, 36 years old, was an experienced miner who before the war worked at Cadeby Main Colliery. On 9 July 1912 an explosion had killed thirty-five men and a second about eight hours later had killed fifty-three rescuers. Bedson's role in these events is not known, but his experience led him to remain at the far end of the face, which was a little higher, where the air might be better. He had two ration biscuits, which he did not eat, and a water bottle which he used to rinse his mouth before returning the water to the bottle. To keep warm he made a suit of sandbags and slept at night on a bed of sandbags on a spoil truck, winding his watch before going to sleep. Each day he crawled to the collapse to listen for sounds of rescuers, but when they finally broke in he did not hear them. He was taken to the shaft bottom on a mine stretcher placed on a spoil truck by the medical officer and rested for two hours before climbing the shaft. Bedson was sent home and spent ten days in hospital and one month convalescing and was later discharged. The gallery was repaired and branched and mines of 41,150lbs and 32,850lbs were placed beneath the German salient at the end of July and mid-August 1916.[32] When the Germans reflected on the behaviour of the debris after their blows at Petit Bois on 10 June they concluded that the British must be in the clay levels and that their charges had broken the clay over the British galleries, allowing the wet running sand to pour down into their galleries. They further concluded from the evidence of British deep mining at Petit Bois that if they had broken the covering of clay over their galleries then the British might go even deeper to prevent this occurring again. Therefore it was essential that they forestall the British before they could reclaim their galleries.

To the right of Petit Bois, two shafts were sunk by 250 Company late in 1916 from Maedelstede Farm. They ran two long drives parallel for about 670ft then branched: one to place a mine 2,600ft away in the Bois de Wytschaete, the other beneath the front line. The Germans blew several heavy camouflets in the area and work was delayed as the miners were withdrawn from the face for about three hours each day, presumably the Germans' favoured times for blowing. The first gallery was driven 1,600ft but was halted when it became clear that it would not reach its objective. The second gallery was charged with 94,000lbs and only completed on 6 June 1917, one day before the attack.[33] Bad ground gave particular trouble to a drive towards Peckham Farm, started in December 1915, with one shaft sunk to 65ft and a second to 70ft. At 1,145ft it was beneath the objective and was charged with 87,000lbs. A branch was run off to a second objective but collapsed with an inrush of sand and water, which almost buried the men at the face. A second drive broken out to the right also had to be abandoned, but a third found good clay and was driven to a point just before the German support line until the ground again gave way. Several small chambers were constructed with difficulty and a carefully waterproofed charge of 20,000lbs laid. The electric pumps broke down and the main gallery collapsed, cutting off both charges. The gallery had to be completely redug about 10ft above the old gallery for almost 1,000ft before rejoining the old tunnel. The detonator leads were reconnected in March 1917, but the smaller charge was too difficult to recover and was abandoned.[34]

Spanbroekmolen was the first of the mines that Cropper started behind the British lines in December 1915 to get to the clay level. It took several attempts to sink a shaft to 60ft and 250 Company had run a gallery 90ft when it was taken over by 3rd Canadian Company in late January 1916. The Canadians advanced it 790ft and it was then taken over by 171 Tunnelling Company, who completed a 1,717ft run until it was beneath the powerful German position at Spanbroekmolen. At the end of June 1916 the charge of 91,000lbs of ammonal in 1,820 tins was complete, the largest yet laid by the British. With the postponement of the attack the British selected the additional objectives of two German strong points, Rag Point and Hop Point, 2,700ft and 3,500ft from the shaft. A branch from the Spanbroekmolen gallery was started and inclined down to 120ft depth. By mid-February 1917 the branch was driven 1,140ft and had passed beneath the German lines. The Germans had been attempting to sink but found that all their efforts with timber-lined shafts at Spanbroekmolen proved futile. They lined the shaft with concrete but even this came to a dead halt in the sand. Eventually, by February 1917, they had managed to sink two shafts in the salient and five to the south, where the British branch gallery crossed the German line. The Germans blew two camouflets, the first of which did little damage, but a second a week later smashed 500ft of the branch incline and some of the main gallery. The British decided to abandon the branch because an aggressive attempt to destroy the German shafts would further alert them to the presence of deep British mines in the area. On 3 March the Germans blew the British main gallery, probably with a 13,000kg camouflet laid from their Ewald shaft, leaving it beyond repair and resulting in it being cut off for three months. The British had to drive a new gallery alongside, which was cut in at 1,429ft. They placed a new priming charge of 1,000lbs of dynamite in contact with the original charge and the tamping was completed just a few hours before zero on 7 June:

One of the most dramatic incidents of the Battle of Messines was the receipt by the headquarters of the 36th Division of a pencilled note from Major

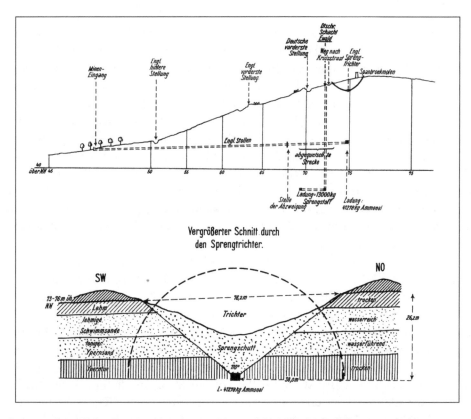

German plan of the Spanbroekmolen position, with the British gallery and the German Ewald counter shaft with a camouflet of 13,000kg. The plan does not show the levels accurately, incorrectly showing the British gallery as driven via a drift rather than a shaft, which exaggerates the advantage of the geographical and geological terrain to the British and suggests that the British did not even need to sink shafts through the running sand layer. From *Der Weltkrieg 1914 bis 1918*, Vol.12, (1939).

H.M. Hudspeth, commanding 171 Coy, to the effect that it was 'almost certain' that the Spanbroekmolen mine would go up next morning.[35]

The Germans often believed that their countermeasures were successful, but they could never know whether the British had already laid mines. Because they had to blow from the bottom or very close to the bottom of their shafts they destroyed them in the process and so had only one attempt at stopping a British gallery before having to sink another shaft. At Kruisstraat, as at Spanbroekmolen, Cropper aimed at a salient which had the potential to enfilade strongly the British line and no man's land. This was also part of Cropper's original scheme, but was worked on by several companies, in particular the 3rd Canadian Company, who sank the shaft to 66ft. By the time it was taken over by 171 Company the gallery was run out 1,051ft. In July 1916, 171 Company placed two charges of 30,000lbs beneath the German front and support lines. It was then decided to place a third charge beneath the next German line, at which point difficulties were encountered with the ground, first with hard clay and then a fissure which leaked water into the tunnel floor. On 25 August the third charge, also 30,000lb, was laid at the end of what, at 2,160ft, was the longest of the Messines operation tunnels. Henry Hudspeth, who commanded 171 Company from July 1916, arranged a water detector to sound an alarm when the level rose to a point to affect the charge. Another further objective, a German redoubt at Bone Point, 1,160ft from the last mine, which would have required a tunnel in total 3,320ft, was dropped. In February 1917 the Germans heard British maintenance work and blew a charge from a 40m shaft. When they saw flames issue from the British lines they knew for certain that they had found the mine galleries and that the blast had been directed back up the shafts. The camouflet damaged and flooded the first of the charges, requiring a new chamber to be cut adjacent, which was charged with an additional 19,000lbs on 11 April. The four mines were ready by 9 May 1917.[36] Füsslein still suspected that the British had mines laid at Kruisstraat, but had no shafts in the immediate area of the British gallery. South of Kruistraat the geology became particularly difficult for sinking shafts as the blue clay lay deep beneath 93ft of water-laden sand and sandy clay. This also meant that the Germans often made little headway with defensive shafts. Ontario Farm in the German lines faced south, covering the whole front towards Ploegsteert, but after abandoning two shafts to attack the position, 171 Company identified a location through test borings. Steel tubbing was used, which decreased in diameter as the shaft descended and during February 1917 the shaft was sunk 95ft to the level of the Ypresian blue clay. The gallery had to be sunk deeper after having been driven about 100ft owing to the depth of sand increasing. Even so, after about 500ft, a third of the way across no man's land, the clay overhead suddenly gave way. Water and quicksand poured in within minutes, filling 100ft of the gallery, which was promptly sealed. Belgian geological records were studied which suggested that they had encountered an ancient river channel. This was confirmed by large blocks of shingle which had been swept into the gallery. The gallery was branched to the left and inclined down, but with the delay and damage to the shaft head from shelling it appeared impossible that the objective would be reached. There was no German interference below ground as a single shaft had failed to get deep. However, German suspicions were aroused by the British response to the blowing of some craters as anti-tank ditches at Ontario Farm by very heavy and uncharacteristic artillery shelling. In addition the change in the water level after the craters were blown suggested that they might have broken through to the British gallery and drained into them. Füsslein wished to blow a heavy mine from the shaft (Gerhard) but the divisional commander refused on the grounds that it would destroy the German concrete defences in the locality. The British were therefore able to continue unmolested and connected the detonator leads just two hours before zero.[37]

At Petit Douve the Germans achieved their one defensive success. A shaft begun by the 3rd Canadian Company was taken over by 171 Company and sunk to 80ft. Despite problems with water it was driven 865ft to beneath a German salient built around the ruins of Petit Douve farm. In mid-July 1916 the British placed 50,000lbs of ammonal directly beneath the farm and then ran a branch tunnel to the left for 134ft and prepared a second charge chamber. The Germans had sunk two wood-lined shafts with great difficulty to 30m, which were in constant danger of flooding. The pumps were inadequate and the water poured between the timbers. On 24 August the British heard the Germans so close that they appeared to be about to break into the gallery. Rather than blow the 50,000lb charge, they placed a small charge in the branch gallery nearest to where the Germans had been heard, which was to be blown only if the Germans actually broke into the gallery. The small charge was designed to rupture the clay membrane above the workings, causing the running sand to pour in and flood them, leaving them inaccessible to the Germans but the British charge intact. The British did not wish to reveal the existence of the large charge beneath the German position for fear that it would alert them to the British deep mining all along the Messines front. They could hear the Germans clearly talking and laughing. In due course the Germans discovered the tamping for the smaller British charge and the duty officer and eight men set about removing the charge and found a detonator enclosed in a glass tube or bottle. The British were listening with geophones and, hearing the Germans break into the chamber, blew the charge just as the officer was about to cut the leads, killing all nine men. The force of the explosion drove up the German shaft and the British observed a large cloud of grey smoke rising from the German lines. The British discovered their main charge intact and placed another small 1,000lb charge in the branch. Harvey was extremely concerned that the blowing of this camouflet would escalate mine warfare in the sector and jeopardize the British operation and he refused Hudspeth permission to blow again. The Germans now knew beyond doubt that the British were beneath the farm and, extending a second shaft to 30m, they located the British main gallery from the noise of the recovery work. They blew a heavy charge on 28 August, which shattered about 400ft of the main gallery and killed four men engaged in repairs. This camouflet wrecked the British gallery completely and the charge was lost. Further activity would have been fruitless and the British were forced to abandon the gallery. Instead they drained surface water into the shaft to deny the Germans access.[38]

South of Petit Douve the British also had trouble with the deep layer of running sand and this may have been the reason for abandoning a drive at Seaforth Farm after about 550ft.[39] Another drive, known as Trench 127, begun in December 1915 towards the Black Shed salient, suffered from a sudden inrush when 700ft in length, which in less than five minutes completely filled a 35ft section. The officer on duty, Lieutenant Brian Frayling, immediately had a barricade of sandbags built until a dam of expanded metal and concrete could be put in place. Again the cause, identified by Professor Edgeworth David, was a pre-glacial river channel. Behind the dam a 30ft sandbag wall was placed and behind this another concrete dam. They broke a new drive out, which they inclined down to 90ft. When the gallery reached 761ft and was just short of the German front line, they branched to the left and placed a charge of 36,000lbs. The main gallery was continued beneath the salient and charged with 50,000lbs by 9 May 1916.[40] Two mines were also ready for the proposed June 1916 attack around Factory Farm. The shaft was sunk from Trench 123 in the British front line and the Ypresian clay was reached at about 30ft. The gallery was driven at 78ft depth, following the course of a road until branching after 450ft. The clay-kickers of 171 Company achieved record speeds, or footage, of 27.8ft and 31.4ft during the eight-hour shifts, the average in clay being 15-20ft. The first charge of 20,000lbs was ready on 14 May 1916, the second, beneath Factory

Mining plan of the four mines laid at the Birdcage but not used in the Messines battle. One detonated during a thunderstorm in 1955. The remaining three are still intact. National Archives, WO153/909.

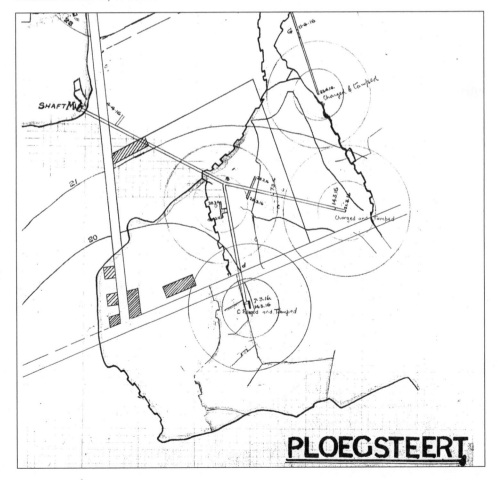

Farm, of 40,000lbs, was ready on 11 June. The Factory Farm mine was to be the southernmost mine blown at the Battle of Messines, but it was not the most southerly laid. In February 1916 171 Company had driven a tunnel 300ft in length towards a large German salient opposite Ploegsteert Wood known as the Birdcage. This had been the scene of active mining in 1915 and extensive workings were at the shallow level. When German activity was heard above work was suspended and very careful listening carried out, after which they resumed work as silently as possible. An additional drive was branched to the right and inclined upwards to provide intermediate level flanking protection and the drives were served by three shafts. A cluster of four mines was completed in March and April 1916. Charges of 20,000, 26,000, 32,000 and 34,000lbs were designed to completely remove the Birdcage.[41]

The Germans pushed the first of their deep systems in front of their lines at the beginning of 1917 during the wettest season. However, in the very wet spring of 1917, the Germans decided to pull back from Petit Bois, Hollandscheshuur and Bois Quarante, as British shelling had rendered the positions untenable and used heavy blows to destroy, they hoped, the British mine workings. They had already begun to prepare new defensive shafts further back. Noises were seldom heard from the British and Füsslein concluded, retrospectively, that they had laid their charges and were just carrying out maintenance on their galleries. Only later did he realize the extent to which the British had placed mines and protected them against wet. When the Germans blew against the galleries containing the charges the British could often repair the breaks to the firing circuits and if necessary place another charge adjacent to detonate it. On Christmas Day 1916, Füsslein reported that in only two places had deep British tunnels been detected, although in others it was suspected. However, British deep mining activity indicated that they were preparing a mining attack and this could only be intended to accompany an attack above ground. He had insufficient men to carry out defence work at the upper levels and also to drive new tunnels at the deep level and asked for four more mining companies, of which three were provided to him in January 1917.[42]

At the beginning of February 1917 Füsslein drew up an instructional leaflet to commands and divisions for distribution to the infantry. In it he pointed out that the British were likely to precede an attack with numerous mine explosions in front of and in the German front line. Therefore the front trenches should be held thinly to minimize the effects and they should treat the mine blows as the prelude to an attack. Füsslein stated after the attack that at the end of February the signs of a British attack became more clear. However, on 8 March he reported that, as a result of several defensive blows, a full tunnelling attack on the Wytschaete salient was no longer possible. On 15th he reported that the situation was unchanged and that all areas were either safeguarded or no deep mining had been detected. On 28 April, however, Füsslein reported that the silence of the British underground, combined with the digging of jumping-off trenches in several places, pointed to the likelihood of a major attack.[43] Füsslein claimed that in March or April General Ludendorff gave the XIX Corps authority to withdraw from the forward positions in the Wytschaete salient if there was a danger that they could not be held. This option, Füsslein says, was rejected by the corps commander. The evacuation of the Wytschaete ridge was considered at a conference of Army and corps commanders convened by the Army Group Commander, Crown Prince Rupprecht. None of the corps commanders considered the evacuation necessary and according to the German Official History, the situation below ground was not mentioned, so far as is indicated by the notes and reports of the conference. On 10 May Füsslein reported that, although the British were working at the deep levels in all sectors, his efforts to oppose them had been successful and they were only doing so where they hoped to pass unnoticed. He went on to admit, however, that a British attack in great depth was still to be expected at those points where he had not been able to counter the British mining. These were at the Caterpillar, Hill 60, the Bluff, between the Bluff and St Eloi, Spanbroekmolen and Kruistraat, and he repeated his warning: 'If a great British attack takes place it will be preceded by large blows at some of these places in front of or in our front line.'[44]

On 24 May Füsslein reported signs of underground work in these areas, but Spanbroekmolen, where the British gallery was blown by a German mine, was no longer considered immediately threatened. Füsslein believed that the danger of a British mine attack against the Wytschaete ridge had been averted by German countermeasures. However, he was convinced that his defences underground were not secure everywhere and that at many places deep blows were not only possible but very probable as a prelude to a major British attack. After the battle, the commander of XIX Corps, General von Laffert, stated that apart from some places, the miners were of the opinion that no sort of danger existed. If there had been any doubt the natural consequence would have been the early evacuation of the whole forward position. He claimed to have left only small garrisons in the forward lines of the places still thought to be threatened, but there is no indication of this in the German regimental histories. The 4th Army reports made no reference to mining after 12 May.[45]

Although the Germans achieved some successes in halting the British mining offensive, it was geological conditions which were the most powerful limiting factor. Far fewer than the projected number of mines were actually ready or used in the attack. On 16 April Harvey reported that of twenty-nine mines, eighteen were ready for use, and another three or possibly four would be ready by 15 May. For three mines the gallery had been destroyed, for two their completion or recovery was doubtful and the remaining two had been abandoned and were 'not required'.[46] In addition, the four mines charged for the June 1916 attack on the far south of the front at the Birdcage were not in the area of Plumer's new attack. He decided to keep these in readiness for use, but they were not required on 7 June.[47]

As the month of June approached, the British artillery fire became steadily heavier. Communications to the front line became more difficult, hampering the work of the German miners and breaking power cables from generating stations. Füsslein ordered his miners to blow their systems, even if it meant destroying them, if there was a possibility of destroying British mines. However, the Germans could not then interfere with the British work to recover their charges as they had destroyed their own shafts and galleries. They buried their own shaft entrances so that the attackers would not find them. German intelligence suggested that the attack would take place on 10 June. On the British side, doubts arose on the eve of battle that the mines would detonate, having been in place for so long and subject to disruption from enemy action and the wet. Haig's concern was made known by the Chief of the General Staff on 24 May:

> There appear to be many instances in the IX and X Corps of a disbelief as to whether the mines can be effectively exploded. This should be rectified. Expert miners and electricians have tested the mines and expressed their satisfaction with the arrangements.[48]

Just over a week before the battle was to begin the possibility arose, however, of all the mines being rendered useless. At the end of May the British obtained a German document giving clear information about new German defensive tactics, which appeared to jeopardize the whole Messines mining attack. In the event of a British attack, the Germans appeared likely to adopt the tactic of abandoning their front line and placing a heavy artillery barrage there, as well as on no man's land and the British front line. The pressing need for the British was to force the Germans to disclose the locations of as many of their carefully concealed gun batteries as possible so that British artillery could destroy them before the attack was launched. The British Chief of Staff, General Kiggell, wrote to Plumer on 29 May in the light of this information. He informed him that Haig wished him to meet the following day so that the decision could be taken as to whether to explode the mines prematurely, before the Germans had withdrawn and as a means of fooling them into believing that the attack was being launched and thus bringing their guns into action and revealing their location. Haig wished to discuss whether the mines should be blown before the attack, i.e. on 'W' day, four days before, followed by immediately seizing the craters with patrols and plenty of Lewis guns, but keeping the mass of troops back. The reports that Plumer had indicated that in places the Germans were holding their front line in strength, in others by posts only, but there was no definite evidence of anything in the nature of a general withdrawal from the front line. His response at first was to use the mines prior to zero day and to endeavour to occupy the German front line. He summoned his corps commanders and found two in favour, one not. He told them to consult their divisional commanders and report to him the next morning. After this none favoured the prior occupation of the front line and all thought that the original plan should be adhered to. At the meeting with Haig, Plumer proposed to deal with the situation by bringing forward his destruction fire by two days and devoting the last two days before the attack entirely to counter-battery fire. Haig concurred with and supported this decision and the use of premature blowing of the mines was ruled out as a means of forcing the Germans to disclose their artillery batteries.[49]

The Messines mines were placed directly beneath the positions that the British wished to destroy. In contrast to the Somme in 1916, where the extreme difficulty of working quietly in chalk meant that it was all but impossible to get beneath German positions, so the mines were often halted in no man's land and relied on shock and the fougasse effect of throwing debris over the position, at Messines the ability to work deeply and silently through the clay level gave the British the ability to position mines exactly for maximum effect. The time of the blowing of the mines was now accepted as being on zero. At Kruistraat, where Hudspeth had laid three mines each beyond the other, he attempted unsuccessfully to persuade the commander of the 36th Division, General Nugent, that he should blow the farthest mine later to catch the Germans as they fled:

> The mines were so laid and the firing arrangements so made that the second line mine could be blown at a time interval after the first mine, of a few seconds, by putting in a time fuse between the two wires. ... This had never been done before. The General in charge of the Infantry was too worried about it, the possibility of the second mine not going off at the right time or being too long delayed, to catch our own infantry he wouldn't risk it, even though I showed him at the camp exactly how it could be done. I gave a demonstration with actual explosives but Nugent wouldn't have it and so they all went up together.[50]

Harvey and Stevenson drew up orders for the safety of the British infantry:

> Prior to the firing of the mines it was necessary to frame such instructions to the assaulting troops as would obviate casualties resulting from the effect of the enormous concentration of high explosive at the depth of 70-100 feet below the surface. There was no information to be obtained from history as no military mining had ever dealt with so many large charges from one operation.[51]

No man was to be within 200yds of a charge until twenty seconds after it had been blown. All trench and surface dugouts within 300yds of a charge were to be evacuated and men were to be clear of any trenches or structures which might collapse when the mines blew. All tunnelled dugouts and subways were to be cleared within 400yds. Old brick buildings were to be avoided. The assaulting troops were not to enter the bottoms of the craters owing to the danger of explosive gas.

Nine Divisions made the initial assault. It is often said that the British Prime

Minister, Lloyd George, heard the detonation of the mines in 10 Downing Street. In fact it was the opening salvo of the synchronized artillery which was heard as the British artillery was timed to open fire simultaneously with the blowing of the mines.[52] At Hill 60 an artillery officer witnessed the mines under the Hill and the Caterpillar:

> At exactly 3.10 a.m. Armageddon began. The timing of all batteries in the area was so wonderful, and to a second every gun roared in one awful salvo. At the same moment the two greatest mines in history were blown up - Hill 60 and one immediately to the south of it. I cleared everyone out of the dug-outs and was watching for it. Never could I have imagined such a sight. First, there was a double shock that shook the earth here 15,000 yards away like a gigantic earthquake. I was nearly flung off my feet. Then an immense wall of fire that seemed to go half-way up to heaven. The whole country was lit with a red light like in a photographic dark-room. At the same moment all the guns spoke and the battle began on this part of the line. The noise surpasses even the Somme; it is terrific, magnificent, overwhelming. It makes one almost drunk with exhilaration, and one simply does not care that we are under all the concentrated fire of all the Hun batteries.[53]

The history of the German 204th Division described the Hill 60 blows in these terms:

> The ground trembled as in a natural earthquake, heavy concrete shelters rocked, a hurricane of hot air from the explosion swept back for many kilometres, dropping fragments of wood, iron and earth, and gigantic black clouds of smoke and dust spread over the country. The effect on the troops was overpowering and crushing ... the trenches were now the graves of our infantry.[54]

The mine at the Caterpillar, placed behind the German front line, slammed the trench shut and buried the garrison alive. The 204th Division claimed to have lost 10 officers and 677 men killed by the explosions at Hill 60 and the Caterpillar. However, German reports and histories tended to ascribe their defeat and losses almost entirely to the mines, whereas the artillery and infantry attack had a devastating impact.[55] Füsslein dismissed these reports, claiming that he could prove that at most thirty-five were lost from a single blow and that the remainder were lost in the ensuing fighting. At St Eloi British infantry converged around the salient, as they had attempted on 27 March 1916. The new mine crater was 50ft deep and 270ft in diameter and made the existing craters appear like shell holes. As before, the broken ground made progress very difficult, but they met little opposition from defenders.[56] At Petit Bois the two mines caused a wide obstruction

(Top) The British siege exercise at Chatham in July 1907. Mines of 200lbs and 250lbs of gunpowder have been blown by the attackers against Fort Bridgewoods, viewed from within the defences. The mines caused craters of 26 and 32ft diameter, but no damage to the defenders' countermines. (From *Report of the Siege Operations held at Chatham July and August 1907*).

(Bottom) A French miner at the face of demi-galerie G5, Beta salient, Carency, prepares for the mining attack of 9 May 1915. British miners would probably not have used such close-timbering in chalk unless the strata was shaken by previous explosions. (From Thobie, *La Prise de Carency*).

(Left) German miners in chalk, Somme. The mate places the chalk into a sandbag by hand. Working quietly in chalk was extremely difficult and meant that there were fewer unexpected break-ins in chalk compared to clay areas. The scene is identical to British working practice except the British miners used less timbering in chalk and larger tools. (From *Das Ehrenbuch der Deutschen Pioniere*). (Right) German mine gallery, Hooge, Ypres Salient, late 1916 or early 1917. Heavy and close timbering was required for the wet Flanders sands and these German miners are wearing waterproof clothing to protect against dripping and flooded galleries. The smaller pipe, bottom right, was connected to a water pump, the larger pipe, top left, was for ventilation. The man in front is descending a shaft to a deeper system. Behind him is Lieutenant Kurt Schmölling, commanding 352 Pioneer Mining Company, who was killed at Langemarck on 7 August 1917. (From *Mineur in Flandern*).

A French officer uses a geophone to detect the sounds of German mining. This invention enabled both the distance and direction of underground sounds to be identified, but required training and aptitude. The nerves and concentration necessary to remain alone and motionless for long periods underground in close proximity to the enemy may be deduced. (Imperial War Museum Q69984).

The opposing lines and mine-riven no man's land of Éparges ridge, called by the Germans Combres Höhe, April 1917. The Germans held the summit with a deep and comprehensive trench system, which was mirrored below ground by a powerful mine network. They have driven through the summit of the ridge to blow the less complete French trenches on the left. Point X, where the French initiated mining in November 1914, is farthest from the camera. (Author).

The aftermath of a German mine blow viewed from their side of the Éparges ridge in a photograph dated 15 August 1918, which makes it amongst the last mine blows of the war. As at Vauquois, the Germans used a steep reverse slope to begin deep mine galleries and about 17 entrances are visible, betrayed by the light-coloured mining spoil. (Author).

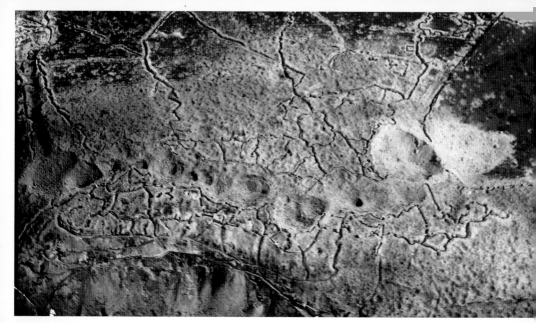

Vauquois, 16 June 1916. No trace of the village remains and the crest is a continuous line of craters. The German positions are along the lower part of the photograph and the German mine entrances and spoil tipped down the slope are just visible. The crater from the largest mine blown in the war, the German 50-tonne charge of 14 May 1916, is at the west end of the ridge on the right. (Author).

(Left) Sapper William Hackett of Mexborough, Rotherham, who served with 254 Tunnelling Company and was the only Tunneller to be awarded the Victoria Cross. Forty-three years old, in age and physique he was typical of the highly experienced miners who were recruited direct from British collieries into the Tunnelling Companies. (Author). (Right) The explosion of 40,600lbs of ammonal by 252 Tunnelling Company beneath Hawthorn Ridge at 7.20am at the opening of the Battle of the Somme on 1 July 1916. The blowing of the mine ten minutes before zero was indicative of British inexperience in integrating mines with a complex attack by infantry and artillery. (Imperial War Museum Q754).

General Plumer, with white moustache, GOC British 2nd Army with, behind him, Major General Harington, his Chief of Staff, and, holding coat, Lieutenant General Byng, GOC Canadian Corps, standing on the lip of an 8,000lb mine exploded at a British training school at Wisques, France, 28 August 1916. Coordination of mines with attacks was a British weakness during 1915–1916 and Byng scaled down the use of mines at Vimy Ridge in April 1917. (Imperial War Museum Q4169).

Lieutenant Colonel Mike Watkins MBE lifts a bag of ammonal explosive from a 6,500lb mine charge, 65ft beneath the surface at Vimy Ridge, in early 1998 prior to removing the detonators and primers. It was one of three mines laid by 172 Tunnelling Company to support the Canadian Corps attack on 9 April 1917, but was not used because the Germans had blown a series of craters in the vicinity two weeks before. Mike Watkins was one of the most experienced explosives experts in the British army, but was tragically killed later in 1998 by a collapse that occured while attempting to access another of the many tunnelling systems under the Ridge. He is commemorated on a plaque near the entrance to the Grange subway. (The Durand Group).

A German electrical boring machine used for dugout construction. Large tunnelling machines were tried by the Germans and British but were not successful for long drives or deep mining. Both hand and mechanised drills and borers were used, however, especially in dugout construction. A lack of spoil removal in this photograph suggests that testing or training is in progress. The man on the right is controlling the speed of the motor. (Imperial War Museum Q55394).

Men of the German 148th Infantry Regiment in a tunnel 15m below ground in the Champagne area in 1917. It is a typical German accommodation and communication tunnel and is reminiscent of the Cornillet tunnel, in which over 300 Germans were trapped and poisoned on 19–20 May 1917 during the Third Battle of Champagne. Like the Cornillet system, these tunnels were electrically lit, with signals cables running along the roof, and a light railway truck. (Author).

'To the last penny.' A well-stocked canteen store, probably in the same tunnel system as the previous photograph. As well as such luxuries, tunnel systems might contain water, food and ammunition to enable survival for ten days. (Author).

The Grange Subway, one of twelve infantry communication tunnels prepared prior to the assault on Vimy Ridge in April 1917. Constructed by 172 Tunnelling Company, the subway was 6ft 6in high by 3ft 6in wide, enough for two men in full equipment to pass, 1,343yds long with 25ft of head cover. It was used by Princess Patricia's Canadian Light Infantry to reach their jumping off trenches before zero on 9 April 1917 and also housed mortar emplacements, headquarters dugouts and a dressing station. It is seen here after restoration for opening to the public in 1936, when obscene graffiti was removed, and it remains open to the public today. (Author).

A German dugout, a posed and peaceful almost domestic scene on a postcard sent home by a soldier in 1917 and typical of the deep dugouts which became a major feature of German defences in the front line in the first half of 1916. (Author).

By contrast, a scene in a German dugout at 9m depth representing the mental and physical exhaustion after enemy bombardment had prevented sleep, rations or relief. By 1917 deep accommodation in the German front line was prohibited owing to the Allies' ability to trap the garrisons underground using creeping barrages and mopping-up troops. (Author).

Tunnel and dugout excavations carried out by the Association for Battlefield Archaeology and Conservation (ABAC) in the Ypres Salient are shown in these three photographs. The flooded conditions ensure remarkable preservation of timber and other organic materials underground. Under the direction of local mining engineer Johan Vandewalle and historian Peter Barton, for over 15 years ABAC has built up considerable expertise in this potentially extremely hazardous activity and has a detailed database of over 350 First World War underground structures. Excavations are now closely controlled by the authorities.

Bunks in the main gallery of Martha House Dugout, 1996. The wire netting shows the impressions of sleeping British soldiers, although the dugout was still under construction when the area was recaptured by the Germans in April 1918. (Copyright Johan Vandewalle ABAC).

(Left) The 37ft timber-lined shaft to the Vampir dugout excavated by ABAC in 2008. The shafthead was double-timbered for protection against shell-fire. (Copyright Johan Vandewalle ABAC). (Right) A stepped incline entrance to a British dugout system at Ravine Wood. Inclined entrances were vital for infantry accommodation and subways but were difficult to sink through the wet Flanders sand. Running into the dugout is the piping with which the dugout was pumped out by ABAC. (Copyright Johan Vandewalle ABAC).

for the attackers, but also destroyed the German opposition. Lieutenant Wallace Lyon, of the 7th Leinster Regiment, faced:

> ...the possibility that we might be blown sky high in the event of any delay of the mine explosion ... the orders were to go on the first shoot of the artillery barrage whether the mine went up or not... But soon we were confronted by a vast crater full of smoke and gas which extended the complete length of our front, so without loss of time I took half the Company round one side and [Lieutenant] Hamilton the remainder round the other flank... We found [the Germans] with few exceptions well shaken with the explosion and we bombed all the dugouts beyond the crater. Although we must have collected and sent back between two and three hundred prisoners, the whole operation as far as I was concerned was a cakewalk.[57]

Press and VIPs were assembled on specially built platforms on Kemmel Hill and from here Lieutenant Brian Frayling observed the detonation of Spanbroekmolen two miles away: '...a white incandescent light darting high in the air. We had calculated the enemy here would go up as gas at over 3,000 degrees Centigrade.'[58] This mine was fifteen seconds late, but the infantry did not wait before advancing and some men of the 14th Royal Irish Rifles were already in no man's land when they were thrown off their feet by the blow:

> But there were no casualties, and the men quickly closed in to the barrage. The size of the craters to be skirted and the darkness made the keeping of direction a matter of difficulty. It would have been impossible but for the use of compasses by the platoon commanders. (Captain Cyril Falls)[59]

Frayling visited the site after the ridge was taken: 'It left a deep crater and the largest piece of the enemy I could locate there in daylight was a foot in a boot.'[60]

Plumer's Chief of Staff, General Harington, also went over the ridge the day after the attack:

> I shall never forget the sight. I remember well going into a concrete dug-out near Spanbroekmolen ... and finding four German Officers sitting round a table – all dead – killed by shock. They might have been playing bridge. It was an uncanny sight – not a mark on any of them. I can see their ghastly white faces as I write. In the wallet of one of them was found a copy of a message sent at 2.40a.m. – 30 minutes before zero – saying 'Situation comparatively quiet.'[61]

The mine at Ontario Farm, placed beneath 90ft of running sand, threw up hardly any lips and for a long time after the blow gas from the explosion continued to rise to the surface: '...the crater resembled a seething cauldron, the semi-liquid mud bubbling like some gigantic porridge pot on the boil.'[62]

The explosion was understood to have caught two battalions of the 17th Bavarian Infantry Regiment during a relief, half of which were 'as good as annihilated.'[63]

The Ontario Farm, Trench 127 and Trench 122 (Factory Farm) mines were on the front of the II Anzac Corps. The splitting of the advance, and the difficulties of visibility, added to those caused by the barrage, caused some Australian commanders to question whether 'the difficulties created by the mines outweighed the advantages.'[64] Where there was no mine at the Petit Douve salient, New Zealand troops still captured the German front line trench. On the southern flank of the attack, the Factory Farm crater lay just outside the attack area and 150yds within German territory, but Australian snipers succeeded in keeping the Germans from occupying it.

Harvey reflected the reservations held by infantry commanders in an even-handed assessment of the value of the Messines mines. He pointed out that many of the objectives had been chosen fifteen months before June 1917 and many were completed for the postponed 1916 offensive:

> The mines of an offensive system after being charged cannot be moved to suit altered surface conditions. They must be abandoned or fired for moral effect. In this case the moral effect is undoubted and is confirmed from many enemy sources.[65]

In the intervening period between the idea of the ridge first being mined in 1915 and June 1917 the British had acquired the technology and skill to capture such a powerful defensive position from the Germans. Harvey acknowledged that, by 1917, mining was being overtaken by other fighting methods:

> Some consider that the destruction of enemy personnel and damage to his morale was worth the effort, while others, admitting the moral effect, consider that the objectives had not been selected with due regard to the tactical situation above ground, and that the casualties inflicted on the enemy, as he was holding his organization so lightly were not in proportion to the amount of labour and material expended in the construction of the mines. Most commanders think that with the introduction of gas, aeroplanes, tanks and all the other innovations of modern warfare, mining only adds a further complication to the operations without corresponding benefit.[66]

Messines was a limited objective battle and mining assisted with the first stage. Mines were particularly suited to dealing with concrete bunkers, which were hurled upside down by the explosions. The succeeding phases of the battle, however, relied on artillery and infantry and it is possible that the British could have taken the ridge without the mines. In combination the Germans were clearly unable to withstand the attack. Füsslein claimed unconvincingly that the German 2nd Division, by following the measures in his leaflet, held their ground better than the others, which could have withstood the mining attack had they done the same.

Whilst on the Messines–Wytschaete ridge, the Germans failed to anticipate the scale of the British mining offensive. To the north in the Ypres Salient they over-estimated British intentions, both before and after the Battle of Messines. The British dug tunnels at the Yser canal north of Ypres to conceal bridging equipment for the coming attack, which were taken by the Germans to be offensive mining. The Germans formed two new mining companies, which set about sinking defensive systems at Boezinghe and Het Sas, both in their front line, to 10–25m depth and from 100–300m behind, which they managed to sink to 30–40m. At both locations they ran tunnels with great difficulty under the canal, but they found no evidence of British mining as there was none taking place. At Railway Wood, just north of the Menin Road at Hooge, where the British 177 Tunnelling Company had been since late 1915, the fight became intense and the Germans brought in another Company alongside 352 Pioneer Mining Company. Füsslein believed that they forestalled the British at Railway Wood after the Battle of Messines with a series of mines blown in their own lines on 13 and 14 June 1917. The British had never planned a mining attack there and the German blows were nowhere near their galleries. This contradicts Füsslein's claim that, after Messines, he resisted attempts to panic blow their systems in the Ypres Salient and was backed by the Army commander. He implied that the British did not begin the Third Battle of Ypres with mine blows because their tunnellers could not get close enough. In fact the British had not prepared mining attacks and the German efforts had been misplaced.[67]

Füsslein stated that the judgement of the German 4th Army and Headquarters vindicated the miners, and summed up his account of the Battle of Messines by blaming ignorance of mine warfare amongst infantry commanders:

> It was astounding, after all the experience of mine warfare in Flanders, La Bassée, Champagne and the Argonne, the disregard and lack of awareness of this ancient and yet modern weapon. This ignorance came to light everywhere, where lack of historical knowledge, expertise and experience was combined with arrogance. Divisional commanders rejected mine warfare because they did not understand it; others made it the scapegoat, although they knew secretly that they had insufficiently valued this weapon. The miner in Flanders stands nevertheless upright and proudly there in the knowledge of having done his duty, recognized only by the few who know of his deeds.[68]

For the Commander of Miners of the German 4th Army, the battle was also a personal tragedy. On 7 June 1917, with the words: 'A Prussian Ensign does not surrender', his son, eighteen-year-old Hans Georg Füsslein, serving with the 25th Pioneers, died defending the village of Messines.[69]

Messines was the greatest and last mining attack of the war. Afterwards, the scale of mining reduced on the British as it had on the French fronts, although the British desire for dominance prolonged it in their sectors. The number of mine blows, 117 British and 106 German, was reduced in 1917 by six-sevenths compared to 1916, owing mainly to the Germans withdrawing or being driven from the active mining fronts.[70] On the remaining mining front, at Givenchy-lez-la-Bassée–Loos, the opposing systems were so well developed that further progress by either side was virtually impossible.

Chapter 8

Miners and Technology

One of the results of the recruitment of civilian experts into mining and tunnelling units was the application of modern technology and mechanisation to the underground war. The side which was able to make the most effective use of civilian skills and technologies gained the advantage. In some cases technology had to be developed, but in most it was already available. In terms of basic mining, the sinking of shafts and driving of galleries, the French had far more detailed instructional manuals than the British or Germans in 1914. The Germans reissued their old mining regulations and these manuals were used to carry out mining during 1914–15.[1] From the start, the British were reliant on civilian specialists and this was to become the major strength of their tunnelling operations. This is not to say that the French and Germans did not make use of civilian expertise. For example, the German 4th Division, part of the 7th Army Corps which was recruited in Westphalia, included many miners in the ranks. During 1915, the mining operations in the La Bassée sector were carried out by mining battalions formed from each infantry regiment:

> The working practices followed those of conventional mining very closely. Three to five men work in a tunnel. A foreman oversees the work; he is responsible for the proper working and keeping the correct direction. Three to four tunnels are each under a foreman-NCO, who leads the personnel from their quarters to the workings, and is responsible for the necessary supply of materials. Several workings, usually twenty to twenty-five tunnels, are brought together under the command of a head foreman-NCO; he reports to a Duty Mining Officer, but can make urgent decisions himself; he gives a daily report to the Duty Mining Officer, who enters these into the Mine Book. The company commander receives a copy of the entries. The working hours in a three-shift system are twelve hours; this long shift was chosen so that the traffic on the roads leading to the workings could be kept to a minimum. Drill takes place at the quarters, where the miners are organized in twenty to thirty man sections, according to which company they belonged. Head foremen and mining officers are on duty for forty-eight hours. Each shift has a three-man pumping-squad; this is responsible for the necessary hoses. Two explosives squads, trained by the pioneers, report to

the Duty Mining Officer for duty in the front line. The measurements are made by a mine surveyor. (Reserve Lieutenant von Klingspor of the 2nd Mining Company, Infantry Regiment No.56)[2]

We have already heard, however, Colonel Füsslein's complaints about the difficulties of forming specialized German mining units. The extreme shortage of engineers in the British Expeditionary Force forced commanders to allow civilian experts freedom to employ their own methods. Much of the skill amongst British officers was derived from mining engineers returned from mineral mines in North and South America, Canada, Africa, Australasia, Malaya and elsewhere. This brought not only a range of skills, but also a tough and adventurous temperament. The first question that a newly arrived officer would be asked in a tunnelling company was 'coal or metal'? It was held by the overseas mineral miners that they were more cosmopolitan and imaginative than the mining engineers from the collieries in Britain, although the many examples of bravery and audacity from this source suggest that there was a strong degree of prejudice. Commanders will have distrusted and feared the militancy of miners, but the British discovered, perhaps to their surprise, that miners already possessed qualities that armies tried to instil into recruits: mutual dependence, personal bravery and remarkable powers of physical strength and endurance.

By the end of 1915 the British had learned that the Tunnelling Companies could function effectively with the right civilian mining engineer in command. The best company commanders possessed not only technical skill and powers of leadership, but also both mental and physical stamina. Norton Griffiths rejected men in whom he did not see the necessary degree of 'go get'. This process was enhanced enormously by the arrival of Tunnelling Companies from Canada, Australia and New Zealand. A Canadian Tunnelling Company was created in France in December 1915 from personnel in the 1st and 2nd Canadian Divisions, and this was joined in France in March 1916 by two more companies recruited in Canada. A New Zealand Tunnelling Company and an Australian Mining Corps arrived in France in spring 1916 and from the personnel of the latter three Tunnelling Companies and an Australian Electrical and Mechanical Mining and Boring Company were created. The best qualities of the mineral miners were found amongst all ranks of these units and the immediate result was the relief of companies, such as 172, which had been engaged for over a year in the worst conditions of the Ypres Salient.

The British often commented on the difference between their work and that of the French and Germans. When the British took over French workings on the Somme in 1915 and Vimy in 1916, they regarded their galleries, especially the rameaux de combat, as too small for effective working. The British adopted a standard size of 4ft 10in high by 2ft 9in wide in chalk. For infantry subways the dimension was 6ft 4in high by 2ft 9in.[3] The New Zealand Tunnelling Company historian claimed that the former size was too small for the size of their men and that

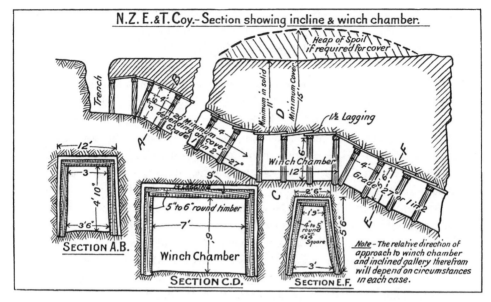

A typical mine entrance of the design constructed by New Zealand tunnellers. From *The New Zealand Tunnelling Company 1915-1919.*

they adopted a much larger size of 6ft 3in by 3ft 6in.[4] This would seem to be accounted for by the fact that the New Zealanders were withdrawn from front-line mining after a few months to work in Arras on infantry communication tunnels, where the larger size was standard. In fact all companies adopted their own methods and tools and claimed that they were superior. An officer of 250 Company described the methods needed for the deep mines in the clay levels at Messines:

> The galleries were first constructed 5 feet high by 3 feet wide, as anything smaller would not allow a man to swing a pick properly. It was found, however, that the clay was so hard and tough that a pick could not be driven into it more than a couple of inches, and this would only dislodge a small piece on the end of the pick. Progress was painfully slow, until the sewer men came to the rescue and taught us clay kicking. In this, an instrument shaped like a small spade – very strong, with a razor edge and heavy shoulders – known as a push pick was used. In operation, the miner sat on the floor with a pile of sand bags behind him to give him purchase. By putting both feet on to the shoulders, he would work the blade into the face and then, by pushing the handle upwards, bring out the clay in chunks. The bottom cut was awkward, but after that the rest of the face was brought out with ease and rapidity. This method, besides being quicker, was much more silent and allowed us to reduce the size of the gallery to 3ft 10ins x 2ft 4 ins. When our men became expert in this method an average day's drive was 25

to 30ft. It was in this respect we were far ahead of the enemy. His galleries were far cleaner and better timbered than ours, but his best speed was 6 feet per day. (Anon. Officer, 250 Tunnelling Company)[5]

The British regarded the German and French close-timbering of galleries as excessive, and accused the Germans of working by the book and lining all their galleries with timber regardless of whether the ground required it. Timbering had the advantage of lessening the damage caused by camouflets, but slowed progress and required a lot of wood. The German officer quoted above stated that, for the system opposite Givenchy-lès-la Bassée, where they were indeed necessary, 12,000 to 15,000 mining frames were used for close-timbering (as well as 500,000 sandbags for removing the spoil).[6] Again the New Zealanders claimed superiority in their lack of timbering, but this was nothing special when set alongside the British, Australian and Canadian tunnellers, who all knew what the ground required for particular conditions. In the most extreme conditions of the deep Messines mines, where the galleries had to support perhaps 100ft of wet sand, and the clay expanded on exposure to moisture, 250 Company found that the standard 9in by 3in timbers shattered, and they replaced them with 6in to 8in pit props with 6in by 4in timbers, and eventually spaces were left between the mining sets to allow for the expansion. At this depth 5in by 3in steel girders were also used to support the galleries.[7]

The British and Commonwealth units regarded their speed as superior to the French and Germans, and there is no doubt that speed was one means by which they were able to obtain an advantage over the Germans. There was also a strong rivalry for footage between Tunnelling Companies, with frequent claims of record speeds through clay or chalk. The fact that the expertise resided in the companies rather than the command in respect of tunnelling practice was acknowledged by the leeway that the British gave units. Information was distributed in 'Mining Notes', which described practice as carried out by companies so that experience might be shared. Any pre-war information about military mining was quickly discarded by the British, even to the extent that the trade of 'miner' was replaced by that of 'tunneller' and the units were known as Tunnelling Companies. In the French and German armies, the pre-war instructions were still used as the basis for underground warfare. The extracts from the old mining regulations, which the Germans reissued in 1915, having excluded them from those issued in 1911 and 1913, contained some practices which were still relevant, but caused the Germans to be hidebound. Likewise, in 1915 the French thought too much in terms of traditional siege warfare methods of classical sapping and shallow mining attacks as a response to trench warfare. The British were willing to allocate very large numbers of men to mining and a tunnelling company might exceed 900 men, including the attached infantry for carrying spoil. By the middle of 1916 the British had 25,000 men employed on underground work.[8] Yet the workings in the most active area in 1916, on the 1st Army front around Loos, were never used in a major offensive and resulted in underground stalemate.

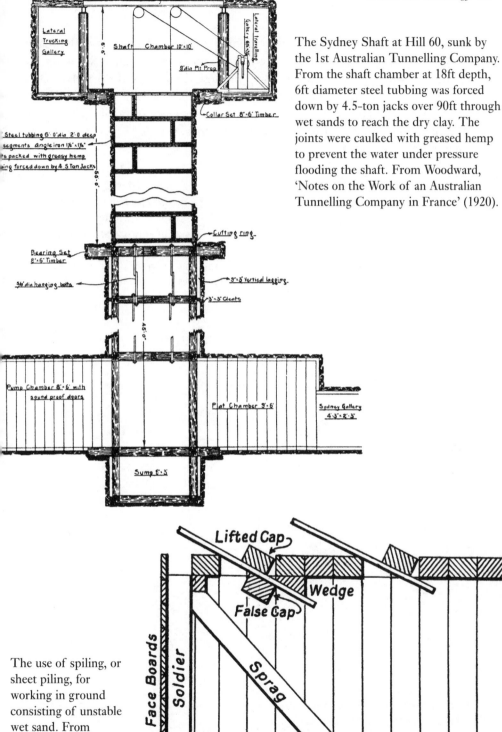

The Sydney Shaft at Hill 60, sunk by the 1st Australian Tunnelling Company. From the shaft chamber at 18ft depth, 6ft diameter steel tubbing was forced down by 4.5-ton jacks over 90ft through wet sands to reach the dry clay. The joints were caulked with greased hemp to prevent the water under pressure flooding the shaft. From Woodward, 'Notes on the Work of an Australian Tunnelling Company in France' (1920).

The use of spiling, or sheet piling, for working in ground consisting of unstable wet sand. From Tatham, 'Tunnelling in the Sand Dunes of the Belgian Coast'.

The ability to work through the wet running sand of Flanders was the major achievement of the civilian miners in the British tunnelling companies. Firstly the sinking of shafts to depths of 100ft or more through the sand to the dry clay below stole the march on the German pioneers, and the Germans lagged behind in the use of steel tubbing to line the large shafts. Secondly, the very difficult technique of sheet piling, or spiling, through sand was mastered by the British and Commonwealth units.

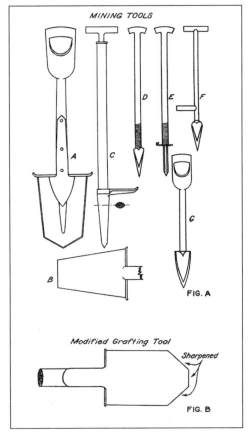

British mining tools used in clay and sand. In Fig. A, D, E, and F are all push picks used by 176 Company for different activities. G is a cut-down grafting tool. Fig. B shows a modified grafting tool used by 171 Tunnelling Company for work in clay. From Trounce, *Notes on Military Mining*.

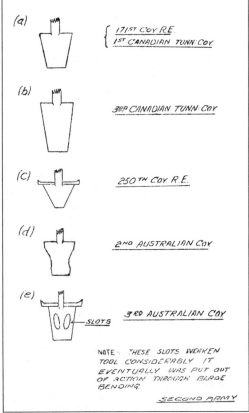

Grafting tools used in the Ypres Salient in October 1916, for a clay-kicking competition held between the Tunnelling Companies. From Mining Note No.66, 5 October 1916.

One very prominent way in which civilian practice improved military mining was the introduction of commercial blasting explosive for mining, which increased the power of charges. The French adopted cheddite, the Germans Westphalite and the British ammonal. These explosives also had the advantage of being safer to use, although accidents still occurred. The Germans also carried out successful trials with compressed air as an explosive. The new explosives and the unprecedented size of charges required new formulae to calculate the amount needed for the desired effect of each mine or camouflet. The fusing and circuits for the large mines were extremely complex and the British adopted the use of detonating cord (cordeau detonant) from the French for such charges.

Mechanisation was a response to the shortage of manpower and the desire to drive faster, deeper and longer than the opponent. Power in the form of electricity or compressed air could be used for drilling, ventilation and pumping. Air blowers in particularly needed to be quiet and the British often commented on the noise made by German rotary blowers. The British found large hand-operated blacksmith bellows often the most satisfactory and these were able to supply air up to 1,000ft. The British often also used compressors to provide air to the working face. The Germans and French were equipped with hand-operated boring equipment before the war and the British had commented on the need for it at exercises. The French found much equipment inadequate in hard ground, but adopted a variety of mechanized types. Their best equipment came into use after they had largely given up offensive mining and was used more for dugout construction.

French sappers using a Guillat-Génie hand borer to create a hole which could be used for ventilation or to house a periscope. From *École de Mines, Supplément au Livre de l'Officier*, 1917.

French Ingersoll
screw drill, used
from 1917. From
École de Mines,
Supplément au
Livre de l'Officier,
1917.

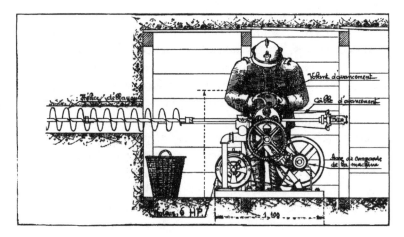

Specialist officers knew the latest equipment. Norton Griffiths spent much of his prodigious energy sourcing the best pumps, boring equipment and much else and making sure that they were provided without delay. Füsslein complained that the British had superior equipment, for example pumps to dewater the deep levels, and that he could not obtain similar equipment from Germany. Trower, who was appointed in command of 252 Company, was the Paris representative of the Ingersoll Rand Company and quickly obtained compressors, which for use in hard chalk. All adopted drills powered by generator or compressor, which were used especially when working some distance away from the enemy and in conjunction with borehole blasting. Blasting was disliked by some British officers because it was inevitably heard by the other side and alerted them to the work. The French and British also experimented with types of forcing jacks, whereby pipes were driven along beneath the surface of the ground, which were used to blow charges. These appeared to offer a means of placing explosive charges against the enemy front line, to blow a breach into a trench and also to blow a communication trench across no man's land. The British did not have success with them at St Eloi on 27 March 1916, where a Barrett Forcing Jack was supposed to blow a ready-made communication trench to the British Crater No.1, but succeeded only in blowing up a section of the British front line.[9] The main problem with forcing jacks was that they could only be used effectively through soft ground. The Sentinel Pipe Pusher was developed for the same purpose by the British but attempts to use it on the Somme, where flints would deflect the head of the head of the pipe and drive it off course, met with little success. It was found that borers were more reliable than jacks and the most effective British, equipment was brought by the Australian Mining Corps. The invention of Captain Stanley Hunter of the Victorian State Mines Department, the 'Wombat', could drill a hole of up to $6^{1}/_{2}$in in diameter up to 200ft at about 3–4ft an hour through chalk. Communication trenches blown using the Wombat were used at Vimy on 9 April 1917.

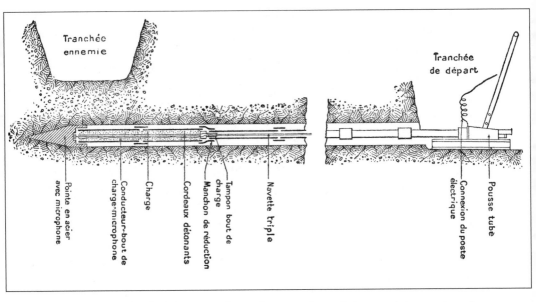

French manual forcing jack incorporating a charge and a steel tip containing a microphone. From *École de Mines, Supplément au Livre de l'Officier*, 1917.

Larger tunnel boring machines were also tried by the Germans and the British.[10] The Germans investigated the use of an electrical machine following the British mine blows at Hill 60 in April 1915, to overcome the difficulty that they experienced in pushing forward tunnels in the sector. On 4 June a detachment of three officers, 12 NCOs and 96 pioneers of the Experimental Pioneer Company (Pionier=Versuchs=Kompagnie) travelled to Erkelenz in the Rhineland, where they trained for two weeks at the works of the Internationale Bohrgesellschaft. A second detachment followed on 21 June. They were trained to operate a machine which seems to have measured about 1.20 x 3.50m and at the beginning of August the detachment began preparation of a dugout to house the machine on the eastern edge of Hill 60. The intention was to drive a tunnel of about 82m length to blow up the British position in front of the 143rd Infantry Regiment. Preparation of the dugout was long and difficult, as all of the spoil had to be removed in sandbags, presumably for the sake of secrecy. By 9 August it was at a depth of 2.20m and a dugout was also begun for transformers. Both were completed by 14 August. At the same time the high-voltage cable was laid from a farm on the Kortewilde–Zandvoorde road towards Klein Zillebeke. The cables suffered continuous damage from shellfire, and the bringing forward of the pipes, machinery and equipment was 'infinitely laborious'.[11] On 19 August the machine and cable were in place and two transformers were then installed. The machine was ready to begin cutting on 22 August at a depth of 4.20m with a gradient of one in twenty. Progress forward, however, was very slow and the machine had to be halted frequently for long periods in order to remove the build up of mud. Although a British camouflet at 2am on 26th did not delay work, two days later the machine had to be stopped owing, it appears, to unevenness of the soil causing the cutting head to race and become damaged. A second boring, parallel to the first, was begun on 5 September and advanced 56m in four days. The effect of the local conditions, however, meant that it had to be halted for maintenance and to lay new cables underground. Strong artillery fire also caused a halt, although it was unaffected by a powerful British camouflet on 11 September. Another drilling was set up for the 15th, 80cm beneath the first, on a gradient of one in fifty, but after only two days it had to be extracted because of ground water and running sand and a new foundation of reinforced concrete 1.20 x 3.50 by 0.25m was constructed. Heavy artillery meanwhile made transport more difficult and caused casualties. Large portions of the cables were buried and were frequently cut by shells. On 19th a new tunnel was begun and after about two days around 71m was excavated. After 55m power from the low tension cables from the transformers to the machine became very feeble. The power consumption rose metre by metre and this boring also had to be abandoned. Repair work had become necessary. Another British camouflet in the path of the tunnel did not affect the work, but it seems to have been accepted that the machine was not a success and on 2 October the company was ordered to the sector of the 39th Division to take over mine workings on either side of the Menin Road. The machine was taken from Hill 60 back to Hollebeke and the bringing back of the power cables was only completed on 28 October. The machine seems not to have been tried again.

The British tried two tunnelling machines with no more success than the Germans. The first, tried at Petit Bois in a second shaft sunk at Van Damme Farm, operated at a far greater depth than the German machine, through the clay at 100ft depth. The compressed air-driven Stanley Heading Machine was lowered in parts down the shaft and first tried on 4 March 1916 . It cut a 5ft diameter tunnel, moving forward at 2ft per hour. The machine, however, had a tendency to dive and each time it was stopped the newly exposed clay swelled and gripped it tightly, requiring it to be dug out by hand. The power output was insufficient and the fuses of the generator powering the compressor repeatedly blew. After 200ft had been managed Harvey ordered it to be abandoned in the tunnel.[12] A second British machine, a Whittaker, was installed exactly a year later by the 1st Canadian Tunnelling Company at a similar depth, from a shaft in the embankment of the Ypres Canal opposite the Bluff, to carry out a 4,320ft projected drive towards the Dam Strasse. This machine was no more successful than the first at coping with difficult ground and was subsequently dismantled and removed.[13]

Military mining before 1914 was not practised at any great depth and did not anticipate detailed geological knowledge. Traditionally, the object in siege works was to drive tunnels which were as shallow as possible, and knowledge of the underlying strata was rarely needed. For the first time, tunnels were being driven at depths which would pass through several different layers and the location in Flanders of the

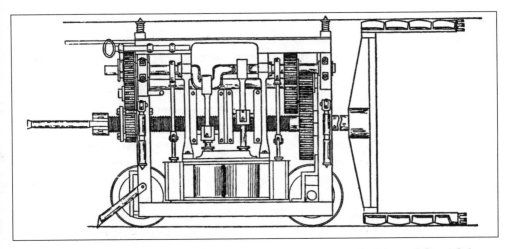

The Stanley Heading Machine. The machine was anchored to the sides and floor of the tunnel and the cutter arms rotated. Once the machine had cut the length of the cutter arms, the debris was removed and the machine was advanced forward. Designed to remove a 5ft diameter circular core of coal, it was less successful in clay. The machine used by 250 Tunnelling Company remains to this day 200ft below ground near Van Damme Farm. From Kerr, *Practical Coal Mining* (1905).

Paniselien and Ypresian clay levels was crucial to the British Messines plan. Such geological knowledge was also required for constructing deep dugouts and detailed maps were drawn up by both sides to indicate where in Flanders their construction was feasible. Geological knowledge was also vital for the fundamental requirement of water supply. The British Army did not have geologists on its staff, which necessitated the co-opting of civilian experts. Once again the Territorial Force provided the bridge by which expertise was brought into the BEF, when Lieutenant W.B.R. King, formerly of the British Geological Survey and serving in the Royal Welch Fusiliers, was attached to the Engineer in Chief at GHQ from June 1915. The head start that the British had in reaching the clay levels at Messines was due in large part to shortcomings in geological knowledge in the German Army. A German geological investigation of the Messines–Wytschaete ridge prior to the British success in March 1916 would, in the view of one German military geologist, have enabled the Germans to take countermeasures in time to stop the British mining offensive.[14] Serving as a temporary Major with the Australian Mining Corps was an eminent Professor of Geology from Sydney University, T.W. Edgeworth David. David made many important contributions to the geological knowledge of the British sectors of the Western Front. In particular he established the seasonal fluctuation of water levels in the chalk areas, which prevented the British systems being driven below the level at which they would be flooded by the rise in early spring.[15]

Detecting the noises made by the enemy underground was a crucial form of intelligence and miners spent long periods attempting to discern the location and activities of their opponents. Listening became the most important means of gaining information on the activities of the opponent underground. It was also the most nerve-wracking activity of underground warfare, requiring a man to crouch in a tunnel for long periods, often alone, and in close proximity to the enemy. Graffiti surviving deep in the Vimy Ridge system of 172 Tunnelling Company indicates only a small number of men employed on listening, working in pairs, and on duty for many consecutive days in the same chamber. As well as good hearing, only a small number of men possessed the temperament to make effective listeners. The hearing and interpretation of sounds was highly subjective and Capitaine Thobie ranked his listeners according to how reliable they were. He placed the best in galleries where the tangle of surrounding tunnels was most complex, as they had to distinguish between noises from their own adjacent galleries and those of the enemy. In the most dangerous places:

> ...a kind of fever of anxiety and fear reigned permanently. The listener's attention was constantly drawn by the workers, to listen to the slightest movement indicating the presence of the enemy miners. At the start of day, all went well; but, as the hours passed, the constant reminder of the burden of responsibility by all those who carried out their task with the greatest possible activity acted on the listeners. Any routine incident of this terrible existence in the trenches 30 or 35 metres from the enemy: a mortar bomb or rifle grenade bursting in the vicinity, all contributed to tightening the nerves and wore down the resolve of the listener towards his task which was to report the slightest noise heard. The result, especially at night where the danger of raids increased, was to excite the listener to the point where he imagined that he heard noises. He warned the workers and the foreman NCO, and as obviously each felt relieved of the individual burden of responsibility of claiming to hear something, there arose a strong conviction of the certainty that noises had been heard which had no basis in reality. These misapprehensions had to be combated in order not to fall into the same error oneself, because a charge, placed without reason at a point where the enemy had not yet reached, led to waste of time and a partial destruction of our own system without any profit.[16]

Listening records had to be carefully kept, so that patterns could be detected, and it was important that they were handed on to relieving units. Where there was anxiety over mining, engineers would frequently be asked to investigate sounds by the infantry, who believed that they were being undermined. Often these would be discovered to be harmless activity in an adjacent dugout, or on occasion a nest of rats. Where miners did discover signs of activity, however, they might not reveal to the infantry that the enemy was beneath their trenches, for fear of inducing panic.

The geophone in use to establish the relative depth of enemy workings. It was more usually placed on the tunnel floor. From *École de Mines, Supplément au Livre de l'Officier*, 1917.

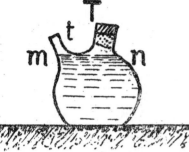

The French listening device improvised from a water bottle. From *École de Mines, Supplément au Livre de l'Officier*, 1917.

Mine listening was greatly improved by technological development. At first the ear was simply placed flat against the wall or floor or in a basin of water. The first French listening aid was a water bottle filled with water, to which were attached stethoscope ear pieces.

A French device which greatly improved Allied listening ability was invented by Jean Perrin, Professor of Physical Chemistry at the Sorbonne, in 1915. The geophone enclosed mercury between two mica membranes linked to stethoscope earpieces to magnify sound waves by about two and a half times.[17] By using two such discs, a listener with training and aptitude could detect both distance and direction and, by taking compass bearings on the same sounds from adjacent galleries, listeners could pin-point the direction of the sound with far more accuracy. In practice this required very powerful self-control from the listener. Lying alone in a gallery which was known to be in danger from enemy mining, the listener first had to become used to the instrument detecting his own heartbeat or any creaking of his clothing or a leather belt. An electrical version of the geophone, the seismomicrophone, was not as sensitive and lacked the benefit of stereo listening, but could be placed in galleries in which it was unsafe for a listener to remain, either because of the proximity of the enemy or dangerous levels of gas. These detectors were connected to a central listening station and would activate an alarm when noises were detected in the gallery. The Germans used a version developed by Dr Erich Waetzmann of Breslau University, the Horchgerät Waetzmann, manufactured by Siemens and Halske, and were using central listening stations by the end of 1915.[18]

The seismomicrophone, invented by the French and also used by the British. The vibration of a lead mass (M) held in rubber rings was recorded by a microphone formed of two carbon discs (P) which was transmitted to a receiver. From *École de Mines, Supplément au Livre de l'Officier*, 1917.

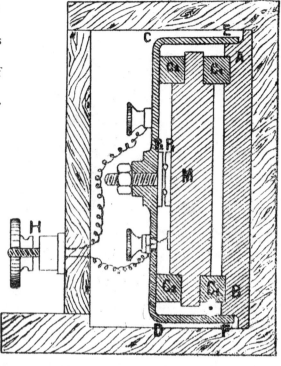

The British drew up guidance on the range of noises in chalk or clay. Picking in chalk travelled the furthest: it could be heard 150ft away with the naked ear and 300ft away with a geophone. Shovelling was audible at 70ft or 120ft with the geophone. Talking was perceptible at 12ft or 50ft with the geophone.[19] In sandy clay the distances were about two and a half times less[20] and work in clay was always more liable to break into the galleries of the opposing side. In the chalk areas it was far more difficult to place a mine directly beneath the enemy trenches and most blows tended to be in no man's land.

Effective listening was usually only possible if work stopped on the listener's side. This would be done either between shifts or during specified listening periods, when an officer would enter the gallery alone for a period of perhaps half an hour. At Givenchy in 1915, for example, the Germans stopped all work for twenty-five minutes every two hours.[21] Listeners, especially when using the geophone, had to learn to recognize the sounds of a range of underground activities. Picking and shovelling were the most common sounds heard, along with the knocking in of timbers, the dragging of bags of spoil along the tunnel, or the pushing of a wheeled trolley. Two men picking at once could indicate that a gallery was being enlarged to form a charge chamber. The dragging or tramming of bags up the gallery to the face would indicate explosives, followed by the further bringing up of bags of spoil for tamping, possibly accompanied by the knocking out of timbers being salvaged from a gallery to be blown. Most ominous and threatening for a listener, after a period of such activity, was silence. This indicated that a charge was laid and tamped and that the enemy was waiting to blow. To disguise this tell-tale silence, miners would continue with false picking in an adjacent gallery until the last minute before blowing, to persuade the enemy that it was safe to remain below. Both sides used dummy picks, operated with a long rope, and the British captured one in the German mining store in Fricourt. It is unlikely, however, that these subterfuges fooled experienced listeners. Another means of deception was the use of work on two levels, used, most famously, by the Australians at Hill 60 to disguise any sounds from the deep Berlin Tunnel. Occasionally, when miners came up against the timbers of an enemy gallery, they were able to carry on protracted listening in an effort to gain some useful intelligence. In June 1916, after they broke into a German shaft head, the British recorded the conversation of German miners for four days, but little of interest was learned.[22]

The danger of poisonous or flammable gas released by explosions was seriously underestimated by both sides in 1915. As charges grew larger in size, so the quantities of gas, in particular carbon monoxide and methane, that were released by explosions underground increased. Carbon monoxide is colourless and odourless and as well as flooding mining systems could also flow up a shaft to gas men on the surface, even causing them to collapse and fall down the shaft. Many succumbed before they were aware, while others might suffer a headache and drowsiness or giddiness. It also caused temporary or permanent mental aberration. Often men became argumentative or violent, physically attacking their rescuers, or hysterical

The use of shallow mining to mask the sound of deep mining, US adaption from a French manual. From Trounce, *Notes on Military Mining*.

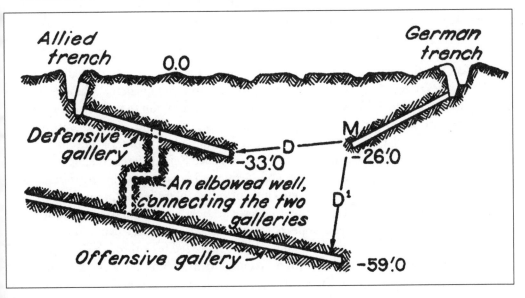

and childish. The mental confusion might last for many weeks. A British officer who was rescued unconscious came round after several hours and was quarrelsome, shrieking and swearing. Later he had no recollection of his accident and was oblivious to his surroundings. After six months his mother told doctors how she had to help him on his bad days and remind him how to carry out simple tasks such as tying his shoelaces.[23]

During the second half of 1915 there were frequent occurrences of men descending to rescue comrades and themselves succumbing to carbon monoxide. Such rescue attempts in tunnels filled with carbon monoxide by men unprotected by breathing apparatus frequently led to more deaths. An example of many such incidents occurred at La Boisselle on 9 December 1915, when the British blew a charge against the 1st Reserve Company of the 13th Wurttemberg Pioneers. What followed was a nightmarish scene of frantic confusion. Georg Maier, a Pioneer on duty at the central listening post, had, immediately before the blow, descended a 15m shaft, a microphone apparently having detected British activity. His orders were to go to the tunnel face, where the particular microphone was located, to establish the direction of the sounds. He had only got about a metre along the tunnel when the explosion occurred, pinning him to the ground and collapsing the last 3m of the shaft behind him. Immediately after the explosion, Tunnel-Corporal Rubensdörfer arrived to ascertain the damage and, hearing Maier's groans and cries for help, alerted men in the mine dugout at the tunnel entrance. Lance-Sergeant Dimmler took command and brought breathing apparatus and rescue equipment to the shaft and with the available men began to clear the damage to reach Maier. After a short time Lieutenant Stolze, the duty officer, took over and, while Dimmler continued in the shaft, divided all men between the shaft, operating the fans to clear the gas and as reliefs. With great difficulty they managed to get an air hose close to Georg Maier and, using a bellows, supply some fresh air to him. By 6.45pm, three and three-quarter hours after the blow, Lance-Sergeant Hämmerle and Corporal Jacob Maier squeezed through a hole to the injured man and found him trapped by the feet but alive. However, the gas soon forced the two men to leave the gallery and they were relieved by Pioneers Zimmermann and Schmiederer. Zimmerman worked at the face to free Georg Maier, but the gas forced him to leave after just ten minutes. Schmiederer continued enlarging the opening and, despite warnings, stayed in the gallery. Lieutenant Stolze was also forced to withdraw and his place was taken by Corporal Koch. Pioneer Fegert reached Schmiederer and managed to give the trapped man some alcohol, and he showed signs of life by groaning and catching his breath. Suddenly a white cloud of powerful fumes swept up the gallery and brought such an intense heat that Fegert and Schmiederer were forced to leave the injured Maier. The cause appears to have been a secondary explosion of gas, probably methane, released by the blow. Fegert squeezed back through the gap into the shaft and tried to pull Schmiederer through behind him, but Fegert collapsed and had to be pulled up the shaft, leaving Schmiederer unconscious at the opening.

Corporal Koch also had to be pulled up, overcome with gas. Pioneers Kastler, Kieninger and Schulze descended the shaft, but Kastler and Kieninger immediately collapsed unconscious. Schulze called on Corporal Sieber to throw him down a harness as he had the unconscious Schmiederer in his arms. Sieber brought it down himself and placed it around Schmiederer, but by this time Schulze was also unconscious. Sieber was now himself on the verge of collapse and called for help, at which point Corporal Rehm descended and brought him to the surface. Rehm returned down with Pioneer Mohr, who tied a rope around one of the men and then ascended to pull him up. Rehm had now collapsed and Mohr went down again and brought him back up. Mohr returned with Pioneer Mauch, who brought the unconscious Schulze halfway up the shaft, from where Mohr helped. Mohr then collapsed, and Mauch had to let Schulze fall in order to save Mohr. He tied Mohr by the feet to the shaft rope and succeeded with the help of some other pioneers in hauling him out. Pioneers Blattner and Kakuschte now tried to rescue the men at the bottom of the shaft, but the fumes, coming more strongly from the gallery, showed that the tunnels were on fire. At 8am Lieutenant Stolze ordered that no one was to descend the shaft. As well as Georg Maier, Schmiederer, Kastler, Kieninger and Schulze perished.[24]

The proper equipping and training of rescue teams went some way to preventing such unnecessary casualties. Mine gas was a recognized hazard in military mining well before 1914, but the apparatus used by the military had been superseded by civilian developments. The helmets fed by air-pumps such as the Applegarth Aérophore sent to France by the British in 1915 were found to be of little use. The demand was for self-contained re-breathing apparatus, in which the wearer carried on his person a cylinder of compressed air and a cartridge of sodium carbonate, which 'scrubbed' the carbon dioxide from exhaled air, which was saved in a rubberized bag. The wearer added air from the cylinder into the bag according to need. The Germans issued large numbers of the Dräger set, which lasted for half an hour, as they were also used to protect key infantry against poison gas employed on the surface, and in 1916 they introduced a military version, the Army Foul Air Breathing Apparatus (HSS).

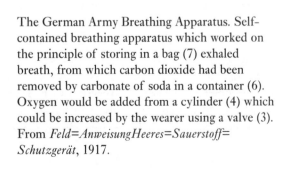

The German Army Breathing Apparatus. Self-contained breathing apparatus which worked on the principle of storing in a bag (7) exhaled breath, from which carbon dioxide had been removed by carbonate of soda in a container (6). Oxygen would be added from a cylinder (4) which could be increased by the wearer using a valve (3). From *Feld=AnweisungHeeres=Sauerstoff= Schutzgerät*, 1917.

The French issued their own version of the Dräger, worn here by a Sapper. From *École de Mines et d'Explosifs*, 1925.

The British equivalent was the Salvus set, although the Tunnelling Companies favoured a larger version, the Proto set, which could last for forty-five minutes. In each mining sector rescue stations were established, similar to those found in civilian mines. The British appear to have been the most thorough in their rescue preparations, establishing schools in each of the Armies of the BEF at the beginning of 1916 to train officers and men in the use of the apparatus and rescue procedures. The instructors were often civilian mine rescue specialists, such as Lieutenant Rex Smart at the 1st Army School, formerly of the Dudley Mine Rescue Station.

The British in particular used animals for detecting carbon monoxide. In 1915 rabbits were most readily available and one would be lowered down a shaft to test the air before descending. Later the British used mice and canaries and each tunnelling company bred its own stocks, under the charge of an older miner. The 2nd Army instructor, G.F.F. Eagar, favoured mice, which men were trained to keep in their pockets and bring out to climb over their hands so they could more easily detect the changes in their behaviour.[25] Smart preferred canaries as they more readily displayed symptoms of a lack of chirpiness, panting and falling off the perch. The claws were kept clipped, otherwise the reaction to bad air was for the bird to grip the perch tightly. The clipped claws ensured that it fell to the bottom of the cage as a clear warning. However, on being brought into the fresh air the birds usually revived quickly. Mulqueen recalled an incident in 1915 which was immortalized as a cartoon in the 172 Company magazine (see below):

> I remember on one occasion I was making a tour during the night shift and in one heading I found the men working, although the canary was flat on its back with its feet in the air. I wanted to know what they meant by continuing to work under such conditions and the sapper in charge expressed the view of the shift when he said 'That bloody bird ain't got no guts, sir'. Needless to say the shift was quickly chased out.[26]

Men were fond of the mice and canaries, but a story was often told of the escaped canary whose presence in no man's land threatened to warn the Germans of the presence of miners in the sector. When snipers failed to remove the bird a trench

Cartoon illustrating Mulqueen's experience with tunnellers continuing to work after the canary had died, which appeared in the Christmas 1915 edition of the 172 Tunnelling Company magazine, *Just a Small One* (RE Museum).

mortar was successfully employed. In exceptional cases miners would use the breathing apparatus to carry out mining tasks. The most extended use of Proto apparatus was for charging a mine at Hill 70 in September 1916, where Smart took over a mine-charging operation in order to halt a German drive that threatened to undermine the British front line. Two shifts spent a total of forty-three hours underground, each man wearing breathing apparatus for about ten hours, during which time they charged and tamped 5,000lbs of ammonal.[27] The most difficult rescue attempted by the British was at the Béthune collieries in September 1917. At the Fosse 8 pit the mine system extended beneath both front lines and part was still worked by French coal miners. The Germans attempted to deny the mine to the French by releasing chlorine and chloropicrin gas, which killed a number of miners and a guard from 170 Tunnelling Company. Tunneller rescue squads had to turn back 1,600yds into the mine because the gas was so concentrated that it penetrated their respirators. The medical officer to the Tunnelling Companies, Colonel D. Dale Logan, improvised gas masks from the facepieces of German masks and two British box filters.[28]

Technology, especially explosives, the geophone and modern rescue equipment, had a major impact on the effectiveness of the miners and contributed to elevating military mining in 1916–17 to a scale and devastating power not reached before or since. The technology went hand in hand with the employment by both sides of many thousands of skilled men. Significantly, attempts at mechanisation largely failed and could not replace the skill and muscle of the experienced miner, working by hand at the face using methods identical to those of his medieval counterpart.

Chapter 9

Tunnels and the Infantry Attack

As well as being a means of placing explosives beneath the enemy, mining could also potentially provide a concealed and protected means of attacking troops crossing no man's land. In pre-war practice, saps dug towards the enemy positions during a siege might need to be covered or 'blinded' by a covering of timber and earth. Where the soil allowed it, the sap might be dug forward wholly underground, at a depth of 25 or 30cm, without timber support. In the French Army these were known as 'sape russe' and the name was adopted by the British as the Russian sap. The saps were shallow enough for the top cover to be quickly broken down so that it could be used as a communication trench.[1]

In the spring and summer of 1915, the French used Russian saps as a means of getting close to the German positions undetected. After the capture of Carency and Neuville St Vaast during the Second Battle of Artois in May 1915, a third attack was made by the French on 25 September 1915 in combination with their attack at Champagne and the British attack at Loos. An attack on the forward slope of Vimy Ridge was to be the Third Battle of Artois. In front of Neuville St Vaast, French

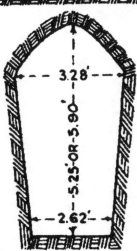

The shallow 'Russian sap' as originally employed by the French (measurements in feet). From 'Sapping Operations' by Captain A. Gay.

attempts to take German positions at Hill 123 and the Cinq-Chemins, where the German front line occupied a sunken road (adjacent to the route of the present A26), had failed. The 3rd Corps commander, General Hache, proposed in August 'a new and very special process' involving attack using sapping above and below ground.[2] The problem, as identified by Hache, was that if the French succeeded in capturing the sunken lane, the Germans would still be able to launch counterattacks from the rear and flanks owing to the large number of communication trenches to the position. They would cut off the French using an artillery barrage on the captured ground and through lack of their own communication trenches to the sunken lane the French would not be able to reinforce them. The novelty of Hache's scheme lay in the wide front in which the sapping attack was applied and the large number of saps which he proposed to dig. The proposal called for a sap about every 40m, or seventy saps on the whole front of the 3rd Corps. The attack was to be made in a 'sure and methodical way'. First a starting parallel was to be pushed to within 50m of the sunken road and then a large number of Russian saps were to be pushed forward to within a few metres of the sunken lane, which troops could capture with grenades. The multiple saps would then provide the means of maintaining supply to the captured position across the German artillery barrage. The rate of advance was to be initially 10m per 24 hours, increasing to 15m. Therefore fifteen to twenty days would be required to prepare for the attack.

Work had started on all parts of the 3rd Corps front by 8 August, on average 130m from the German lines. The French plan was to advance the front line an average of 80m and create a new trench, scheduled to be established on about 18

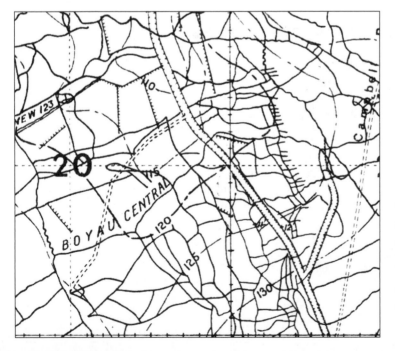

The saps prepared for the attack of 25 September 1915 on the eastern slope of Vimy Ridge, visible on a trench map of May 1918.

August. This line, designated in siege parlance the 'parallèle de départ', was to be the starting point of the Russian saps, which were then advanced to the sunken road. Six hundred men were to work day and night on the saps. It was anticipated that the work would attract the attention of the Germans, who would bombard and possibly also raid it. Hache asked that the heavy artillery of the 10th Army be available for counter-battery work to reduce the artillery fire on the sapping, which it was anticipated might be costly. The sappers were to be protected by covering troops with grenades against German raiders.[3]

Hache's plan was adopted, to be prepared for the attack ultimately made on 25 September 1915. The saps were dug by parties from the infantry, including men who were to make the attack. Vincent Martin, of the 119th Regiment, described the saps:

> Initially underground saps starting from the first line trench about twenty to twenty-five metres apart beneath a thickness of 50cm of earth and driven to emerge in front of the enemy roughly within twenty-five metres of him; from each sap we could only emerge one man at a time. In advance of the excavation work, the enemy is warned by the spoil heaps and is wary of our intentions...[4]

As the saps got closer to the German lines, several men were killed or wounded each day by hand grenades, rifle grenades and mortars. During the sapping underground sounds were heard, but the Germans do not seem to have mined against the saps. By mid-September there were frequent grenade fights between the sap heads and the German trenches. It is not clear, however, exactly how the Russian saps were intended to be used in the attack. Although Martin refers to emerging from the saps, the attackers were to launch from the parallels. The records contain no reference to opening the saps into the sunken road with charges, bored or otherwise, and it is not clear when or how the saps were opened. On the night of 23 September, engineers attempted to place explosive charges beneath the German wire, which the artillery had not sufficiently gapped. The Engineer Companies 3/1 and 3/1 bis were to place long charges (like Bangalore torpedoes), but the saps were not sufficiently advanced. Only five could be charged and only one fired successfully, blowing a breach of 7m. The failure of the others was attributed to the appalling weather, which was wet and stormy. The operation was postponed to the following night, when seventy-two charges were taken into the saps, pushed or carried by engineers described as crawling up the saps. Of these fifty blew sufficiently to allow the passage of troops through the wire.[5]

The preparatory bombardment began on 19 September, but as the saps progressed the French artillery was not able to fire on the German front line, owing to the danger to the men digging the saps. Martin described how the Germans took refuge in their front line from the bombardment on their rear and an anonymous officer of 28th Regiment told how from their own lines they could see shovelfuls of earth being thrown out as the Germans repaired their trenches at leisure. On 24 September, the front line and saps were evacuated in order to bombard the German front line briefly. On 25 September the parallels and open saps from which the attackers were to leave were packed with troops waiting to attack and flooded by heavy rain. The same officer says that there were so many men in the new positions that it was impossible that the Germans were not aware of them. Corporal Paul Andrillon of the 119th Regiment was optimistic, however:

> ...at about 1100 we occupy the saps, the spectacle is superb, on all the points of the plain our guns are raging, impossible to distinguish anything of the Boche's, there is only smoke, everyone has confidence in the outcome of the attack.[6]

Zero hour was 1235. Ten minutes before, the French discharged flame throwers from the front line about every 30m along the frontage of the attack. In places there were enormous flames and thick plumes of black smoke, but the fire was not spread everywhere. Paul Andrillon described the moment of attack:

> ...advance. No sooner got out, the Boche machine gunners in the front line spray us with a rain of bullets. I managed 10 metres on my feet and then collapsed knocked down like a sack of potatoes.[7]

The war diary of the 24th Regiment reported the fate of the first wave:

> All who left the saps and parallels were mown down... The wounded of the first, second and third waves fell into the heads of the saps and the parallels... The obstruction of the communication trenches is extreme; orders and information arrive only very slowly.[8]

The leading elements were stopped dead with heavy losses. Units then became completely mixed up, the following waves crammed into the saps and parallels were unable to advance.[9] Vincent Martin took refuge in a shell hole:

> The captain being wounded, it was impossible for us to try to get to our jumping off trench without getting killed, the enemy machine-guns and rifles are directed on anyone who raises his head. The other comrades lined up beside us, faces to the ground, are dead. The night comes, the able bodied combatants who had taken refuge in the shell holes crawled and dropped down into the sap heads which had been dug by each of us, but no sooner had I arrived but they were crammed full of dead and wounded. I spent the night on the corpse of a former comrade whom I turned over onto his

stomach so that I could sit on his pack which he still wore on his back. What horror! At day break our stretcher-bearers clear the dead and wounded and us the survivors, imprisoned in these cursed saps, under fifty centimetres of ground, we took again our place as soldiers in the jumping off trench where we are now also regrouped. We can then witness the horrible spectacle of death that there is in front of us: three successive lines of corpses in horizon blue, face down, weapon in their hands, facing the enemy that killed them! One could not dwell on this failure…[10]

The French attack, which had as its objective the summit of the Vimy Ridge, was repeated the following day, gaining the sunken road, and during the following two weeks pushed further up the slopes to the ridge. Vincent Martin condemned the attack:

After a 72-hour bombardment, where all the available artillery is used to destroy all Germans found in front of us, it is still us, the infantry: men, NCOs and officers up to colonel, who will be put to death for the glory of our generals, incompetent mass murderers, and so very ignorant of the situation.[11]

The Russian saps, and General Hache's 'new and very special process', had not contributed to the attack as hoped. He had used siege methods to attempt to create a broad breach in the German defences, but had launched the attack before the breach was formed and failure resulted. On the same day as the launch of the Third Battle of Artois, 25 September, the British also used Russian saps at the Battle of Loos as a means of pushing the front line closer to the Germans so that the assaulting troops would have a shorter distance to attack. On the 15th Division front this was reduced to less than 200yds and on the 9th Division front, opposite the Hohenzollern Redoubt, it was 150yds. During the night before the attack the heads of the saps were opened out and linked to form a new trench from which the attack could be launched.[12] These to some extent helped the troops, giving them a shorter distance to cross, although the attacks were only partially successful.

In May 1915, Colonel Ernest Swinton RE at GHQ formulated a plan with Norton Griffiths to use deep tunnels to smuggle troops past the German defences:

The idea was that we should arrange for the sudden intervention of a useful force behind the German front. This was to be done by means of galleries started well behind our own front, driven at depth in the clay far below that of the enemy mine system, and then inclined upwards to break ground at night behind his front in different woods, where the exits would be boarded over and concealed until the moment for action, which would be when we made an attack on the surface. Then, when the enemy was fully occupied on his front, British machine gunners and sappers would suddenly appear from out of the earth in his rear, 'shoot up' his heavy-gun detachments and cut his communications.[13]

Such a scheme, implausible as it may sound, came close to execution on the Gallipoli peninsula, where there was significant experimentation in the use of tunnels to cross no man's land. In the cramped positions around Anzac Cove, the development of a defensive mining system against shallow level mines was combined with underground sapping. At the Pimple, saps on either flank had been completed by the end of May and more were begun between them, with the intention of joining them with a transversal tunnel which would form a new front line when they were 90ft out. The first 14ft of the three new saps (later called B3, B5 and B6) were to be underground to pass beneath the built-up parapet of the Australian front line. The blowing of a Turkish mine at Quinn's Post on 29 May, which alerted the Australians to the danger of countermining, caused them to modify the sapping operations and continue sapping by shallow tunnels. These had an average of 18in of head cover and, largely driven without timber supports, were Russian saps in all but name.

By opening recesses from the transversal tunnels in which sentries could be stationed they became a means by which the Australians could push forward their positions and improve their observation over the Turks.[14]

As the tunnels lengthened ventilation holes were drilled about every 45ft:

This was generally accomplished by means of an old bayonet on the end of a rifle. Owing to the presence of so many dead Turks in the ground through which we were tunnelling, these holes were very necessary. They also served to keep the drives at one level. At night time, great care had to be taken that they were blocked with sacking or something to ensure that no light was

Drawing by Cyril Lawrence of B4, the second southernmost of the underground saps towards Lone Pine from the Pimple position. The leading company of the Australian 2nd Battalion attacked from these openings on 6 August 1915. From *The Gallipoli Diary of Sergeant Lawrence*.

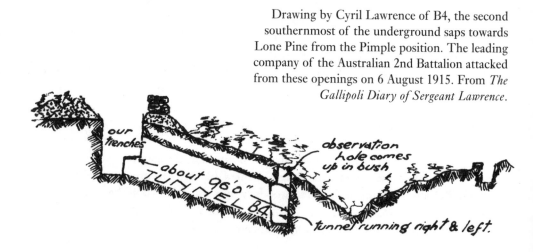

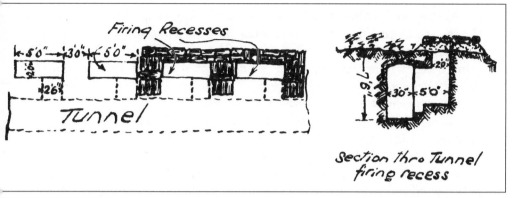

Drawing by Cyril Lawrence of the underground firing line planned in the C Group of tunnels opposite Johnston's Jolly, 1 July 1915. From *The Gallipoli Diary of Sergeant Lawrence*.

visible from above. (Lance Corporal Cyril Lawrence, 2nd Field Company, Australian Engineers)[15]

The method was safer than open sapping, although in due course the Turks became aware of the work through sound and by discovering the ventilation holes:

> About 11pm tonight a Turk shoved his hand down the air hole in the drive just opposite me. It scared the wits out of us all. We could hear them crawling around above us all night. The men in the firing line evidently shot one, as we could hear him groaning just above us. (Lance Corporal Cyril Lawrence, 2nd Field Company, Australian Engineers, 15 June 1915)[16]

In early June General Walker, temporarily commanding the 1st Australian Division, decided to make a new forward line underground along most of the right Central Sector of Anzac. Also in June, a semi-underground system to extend the front line was adopted for the right sector. At Tasmania Post on the southern part of the Anzac position, a number of short tunnels were driven forward at the request of Lieutenant Colonel Smith, commanding the 12th Battalion, in order to gain a view into the Valley of Despair, a steep gully in front of the position. These ended in 'bombing-holes', openings in which sentries were stationed and barbed wire put out. Two of the tunnels were continued towards the Turkish trench without encountering Turkish countermining. Smith suggested to Brigadier General MacLagan (commanding 3rd Australian Brigade) that the mines could be blown and the tunnels used as communication routes to aid an attack to take the Turkish trench on the edge of the valley. General Birdwood, commanding the Anzac Corps, took up the proposal, as the attack could serve as a feint to distract from the coming Suvla Bay landing. When the Turks extended their position opposite Tasmania Post north, the Australians lengthened two more of the bombing-hole tunnels towards their trench. MacLagan asked Birdwood for two days extra to complete the tunnels and an attack using these galleries was fixed for moonrise of 31 July 1915. In a carefully planned assault, four mines were to be fired from the tunnels and an assault made by the 11th Battalion, led by Captain Leane. The tunnels would then be opened up to allow reinforcement of the captured Turkish position.

The mines were to be fired at zero but, at the signal, only the two outer mines detonated. Leane nevertheless led his men forward and, as they reached the Turkish trench, the southern of the two central mines blew, burying small numbers of both Turks and Australians, and parties of men reached the Turkish trench with debris still raining on them. The fourth mine never exploded, but the Turkish troops left their trench on being attacked. While the trenches were assaulted the four mine tunnels were opened into the craters for communication use, with parties of infantry digging from both directions in the tunnels and the craters. The air in the tunnels was found to be sufficiently pure, the explosive gases having vented through the crater, and within an hour three were clear enough to allow some supplies to be passed through into the craters. It was not possible to get men through the tunnels until the early morning and during the night they crossed the open: by the small hours three were open for communication. The congestion in the tunnels, however, was apparently the reason that water stored ready in Tasmania Post was not taken forward. The captured position, named Leane's Trench, was held against Turkish counterattacks and the use of tunnels for communication, like the blowing of mines, had been a partial success.

Birdwood issued orders for another small attack against a post in front of Ryrie's Post, immediately south of Tasmania Post. The tunnels were regarded as sufficiently essential to the attack for it to be indefinitely postponed on 5 August on the objections of the OC 3rd Field Company, Major Clogstoun. Clogstoun reported that his tunnels were unlikely to reach the Turkish trenches by the date of the attack and that, unlike at Leane's Trench, the Turks were already mining in front of Ryrie's. If the position was captured it would be unlikely that full communication using tunnels would be established in less than eighteen hours and, as the area was swept by Turkish flanking fire, it was doubtful whether the attackers could hold out that long.

A more ambitious use of tunnels for the attack was already in hand at Lone Pine using the underground front line formed from the B Group tunnels as a diversion from the breakout attack being made north from Anzac. Seven saps were linked by a transversal to form the underground front line and two, B5 and B6, were extended to form galleries for offensive mining. The assault on Lone Pine on 6 August was to be a more ambitious version of that on Leane's Trench and troops were actually to assault from the tunnels. Three battalions were to attack and the leading company of each was to depart from the underground firing line just 40 to 60yds from the Turks.

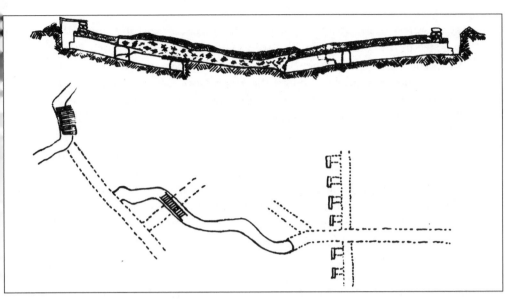

Drawing by Cyril Lawrence of the B5 tunnel showing six of the 5ft x 2ft openings from the underground firing line from which the leading company of the 3rd Battalion attacked Lone Pine on 6 August. The two remaining companies of the 1st also crossed no man's land by this tunnel later in the evening. The shaded portion shows the continuation of the tunnel dug the following day, which broke into Turkish mine tunnels and was connected to the old Turkish front line. From *The Gallipoli Diary of Sergeant Lawrence*.

The tunnels were widened and the space required by each battalion was carefully worked out. In its methodical timing the Lone Pine operation resembled a French sapping and mining assault of early 1915. The infantry were to assault at 5.30pm but, probably because of the complexity of the operation, the preparations were phased. The engineers began opening the exits the night before and completed the task three and a half hours before zero. At this time three mines were blown in no man's land in order to create some cover for the attackers.[17] The preparatory bombardment was carried out during the afternoon and was augmented one hour before zero by fire from heavy naval guns offshore.

The Australian official historian described the scene at the centre of the attack front, with the Brigade Major of the 1st Brigade at the tunnel entrance and the CO of the 3rd Battalion at the exits:

In the opening of the main tunnel – B5, leading forward from the old firing line to the new underground line – stood Major King, whistle in one hand, watch in the other. At the corresponding opening in the underground line was Major McConaghy of the 3rd, ready to repeat the signal for the attack – three blasts of the whistle. Watches had been twice compared and corrected, and while the officers gave a few last hints to their men they kept an eye on the minute-hand as though they were starting a boat-race. 'Five twenty-seven – get ready to go over the parapet,' said a young officer crouched in the corner of one fire-step, glancing at his wrist-watch. Almost immediately the order came: 'Pull down the top bags in that recess.' The men on the step dragged down the uppermost row of sandbags, thus rendering the exit easier. 'Prepare to jump out,' said the officer [Capt D.T. Moore], putting his whistle between his teeth... A whistle sounded and was repeated shrilly along the front. In a scatter of falling bags and earth the young officer and his men scrambled from the bay. Rifle-shots rang out from the enemy's trenches, gradually growing into a heavy fusillade. One of the men leaving that particular bay fell back, shot through the mouth. From every section of the Pimple, and from the holes of the forward line, troops were similarly scrambling; the sunny square of the Daisy Patch and the scrub south of it were full of figures running forward. (Charles Bean, War Correspondent)[18]

On reaching the Turkish trenches, in many places 'instead of a trench, they were confronted by a continuous sandy mound forming the roof of a covered gallery.'[19]. The Turks had roofed their trenches with heavy timbers, which were impossible to remove and were largely unbroken by the bombardment. In places New Zealand and British howitzer fire had smashed the timbers and nearly half of the garrison had additionally retreated into mine galleries; the Australians then reached their lines too swiftly for them to emerge and man the fire steps. The shelters and tunnels thus became death-traps for many of the front-line troops.

As the Turkish front line was fought over, the opening up of the tunnels to supply the attackers was only slowly achieved. Bean describes a slow stream of walking wounded from B5 tunnel. It was not practicable to bring reserve troops through the tunnel; the leading company had to be taken over the open. The two remaining companies were 'trickled slowly through' and then dashed the remaining distance to the old Turkish line. By sundown, through heavy fighting, the Lone Pine position was secured against counterattack. Problems were encountered by 2nd Field Company in all three tunnels which were supposed to provide access across no man's land to supply the captured position. In B5 tunnel 36 sappers, whose task it was to open up the tunnel for communication, had moved forward of the underground line prior to the attack to make way for the infantry. By 5pm, however, 30 were affected by gas from the mine blown from a branch gallery (B37). Struggling with the effects, they only managed to create a decent air hole at 8pm and could not open the end of the tunnel to the surface until 9pm. A sap dug from B5 tunnel to Lone Pine was not completed until 1am. Parties breaking through the other tunnels (B6 and B8) discovered the overhead cover to be 7ft 6in, much thicker than expected. B8 was opened by 4am but required deepening, while B6 was extended to meet a Turkish tunnel, which was accomplished by 8am.[20]

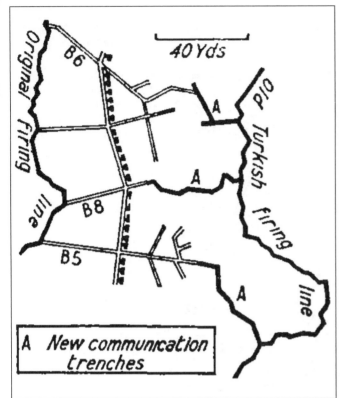

Communication from the Pimple to Leane's Trench after capture on 6 August 1915. From Bean, *The Story of Anzac*, Vol. 2.

Early the following day Cyril Lawrence was sent to complete the B5 tunnel into the Turkish lines and passed the place where the 3rd Battalion had attacked.

> What a different appearance the whole place has assumed since I saw it last. It is just torn to pieces, sandbags blown to smithereens and parapets just levelled. Anyhow, on down through the tunnels until we reach our old underground firing line. The daylight is coming in through the opened-up recesses, through which the first line hopped out, and lying all along it are the forms of fellows killed even before they had got out into the open... (Lance Corporal Cyril Lawrence, 7 August 1915)[21]

Shallow underground saps (again Russian saps in all but name), in places only 6in below the surface, had been quickly run out at the Nek in preparation for the attack of 7 August. Had the attack been a success they were to be converted into communication trenches.[22] The underground warfare at Lone Pine, while appearing to follow the conventions of siege warfare in the early blowing of the mines, was significant and innovative. The difficulties faced at Lone Pine were to be encountered by the British on 1 July 1916 when communication tunnels were attempted on a larger scale.

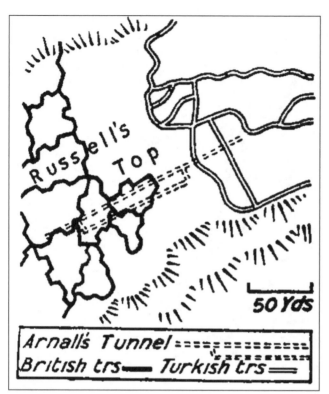

Arnall's Folly, the tunnels dug beneath the Nek through which troops were to pass to capture the Turkish position from the rear. From Bean, *The Story of Anzac*, Vol. 2.

In September, when Australian offensive activity was almost entirely moved underground, an ambitious project was put forward by Major General J.G. Legge, commanding the 2nd Australian Division, which echoed that discussed by Swinton and Norton Griffiths in France. Two deep-level galleries, wide enough for troops to move through two abreast, were to be driven beneath the Turkish rear trenches to emerge in the rear of the Nek position. The chief engineer of the Division opposed the scheme, but it was approved by Birdwood on 21 September. The work was carried out under Captain Harry Arnall, a Cornish-born New South Wales miner, with a party of miners from the infantry, and special efforts were made to keep it secret. When, in early December, Arnall's tunnels approached the Turkish lines, the engineers working on the 60ft deep-level mining system heard Arnall's miners working below them. Not having been told of the scheme, they assumed it to be a Turkish mine and began tunnelling to meet it. Despite the secrecy of the project, knowledge of the scheme became current in the 2nd Division: 'some critics, putting it down as a wild venture, gave the tunnel the nickname of "Arnall's Folly" by which it was generally known.'[23]

The tunnels were not complete before evacuation and it is not clear where or how the tunnel was intended to emerge behind the Turkish lines, or how the attackers would exit safely without being detected.

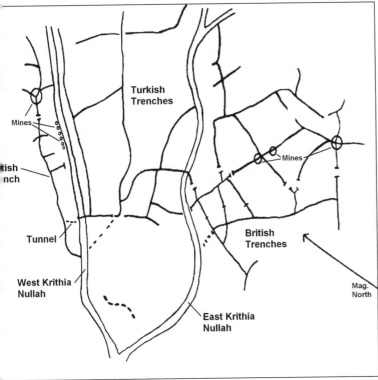

The area of the attack at Krithia Nullah on 19 December 1915 by the 5th Highland Light Infantry. Based on the map in *The Fifth Battalion Highland Light Infantry in the War.*

The problems that might have been encountered if Arnall's tunnels had been used are seen in an attack made on 19 December, one of three made on the Helles front to cover the withdrawal at Anzac. The 5th Highland Light Infantry attacked a Turkish trench between the west and east Krithia Nullahs which was overlooked on either side by cliffs about 40ft high. The trench was too heavily defended by a thick expanse of barbed wire to allow attack from the front. During the previous month a tunnel was driven inside the western cliff, through which troops were to emerge on the left flank of the Turkish position. In late November Joseph Murray was sent to complete the delicate work of tunnelling through the cliff:

I have been working to-day in what is known as Beri's Sap on the left of the Gully. It is a special job and we have been brought into this sector to put the finishing touches to it. Considerable work has already been done; a gallery has been driven down very close to the edge of the Gully and we now have to go forward parallel with the cliffs and keeping as near as possible to them. Measurements have to be taken almost continuously to prevent our breaking through prematurely. We have a long way to go – beyond the Turkish firing and support lines, getting beneath that part of the support line which is in the Gully. The Turkish firing line in the Gully is only a short trench but the redoubt and the mass of barbed wire have made the position unassailable... Some other way has to be found and this is our job. (Able Seaman Joseph Murray, 26 November 1915)[24]

The intention was to leave just a thin crust of earth, to be broken through immediately before the attack was launched. However, on 10 December, as the miners neared the edge of the cliff, Joseph Murray relates that they miscalculated and suddenly earth gave way to reveal a faint glimmer of daylight. They at once erected a barricade to prevent further falls of earth, but Murray was well aware of the danger of Turkish discovery of the tunnel.[25] In fact the premature opening of the tunnel was probably to have serious consequences for the planned attack. By 19 December, Murray recorded that they had nine charges in place, three of which would bring part of the cliff crashing down. The gallery running up to the cliff face had three short branches, which were to be rapidly opened out. The tunnel, however, presented problems. The attackers needed to reach the trench before the Turkish defenders, as a member of the Highland Light Infantry described:

The attack... was obviously handicapped in this race by the fact that it must be initiated from the mouth of a tunnel, entrance to which was difficult and from which it would be necessary to emerge into the nullah man by man. Time was bound to be lost in hastily assembling each party at the mouth of the tunnel and getting it started on its mission, while to rush men forward individually as they left the tunnel would inevitably result in confusion, disorganization and possible disaster.[26]

The troops were still emerging from the tunnel as the attack was in progress, and those equipped for consolidation with picks and shovels as well as rifles had great difficulty passing along it. Most seriously, the Turks appear to have detected the tunnel. This might have been after the premature partial break-in and possibly also because of a small 'man-hole' opening which had been used to reconnoitre the position at night. The attackers concluded afterwards that they had detected this or the noise of the tunnelling, for the Turks directed heavy fire on the opening of the tunnel from the start of the attack:

...whether he had heard mining operations being carried out on the cliff or not cannot be definitely stated, but this fire was responsible for a great number of the casualties which we suffered. (Anon. Officer, 5th Battalion, Highland Light Infantry).[27]

A portion of the Turkish trench was retained, but of those attacking from the tunnel one-third of the force, three officers and six other ranks, were killed. The survivors had mixed feelings about the value of the tunnel:

> It was a great piece of engineering work and in some ways proved very useful when the attack was ultimately carried out, although in others it probably accounted for a number of the casualties which the battalion suffered.[28]

It is a matter of speculation whether this experience contributed to caution in the use of Russian saps by VIII Corps when it reached the Western Front following evacuation from Gallipoli. The experiences of using tunnels for the assault on the peninsula highlighted the hazards of their use in the attack: emerging from a tunnel was highly dangerous as secrecy was very difficult to achieve if a tunnel was to be advanced close to the enemy positions. A rapid assault was also very difficult to achieve by men emerging from a small number of tunnel openings. On the Western Front the British developed the Russian sap as a means of reinforcing the position immediately after capture, rather than as a means of getting troops across no man's land for the initial assault. Instructions for preparations to be made before large-scale attacks, issued by GHQ in February 1916, instructed that:

> Saps must be pushed forward as far as possible to facilitate making communication trenches between the two opposing lines after the assault. The entrances to these saps should be dug under the front parapets and if time allows continued by making Russian saps instead of saps above ground.[29]

These were considered necessary because very soon after an attack was launched the Germans would render no man's land impassable with highly effective artillery barrages and British troops who might have gained the German front trench were cut off from reinforcement and supply. They were then highly vulnerable to counterattack, which would drive them from the captured positions. The Russian saps were designed to form a protected means of communication across no man's land, either as a covered tunnel or broken out to form a trench. Two Russian saps were dug before the Hohenzollern attack of 2 March 1916 to prepare communication trenches to the flanking craters, and these were broken open as the attack began.

An ambitious scheme of Russian saps was prepared for the Somme offensive of 1 July 1916. Saps driven across no man's land were to have mortar emplacements constructed in branches on either side and were to be opened out prior to zero hour. In the north 252 Tunnelling Company prepared twelve, requiring a large force of attached labour, and by April 1916 the Company had 1,900 infantry attached (see map, p210). As the saps neared the German lines, work was ceased at night to

Drawing by Col F.G. Guggisberg RE, showing experiments with extending saps by forcing jack, and also the method of including mortar positions in branches from tunnels. From 8th Division CRE War Diary, 7 June 1916.

prevent the Germans from detecting them, but patrols succeeded in locating the northernmost sap, from John Copse, and twice blew surface charges in an attempt to destroy it, killing nine men.[30] The Germans also directed shellfire at the saps, but despite detection the saps were completed on time.

The five tunnels on the 31st Division front were opened at 6.30am, one hour before zero, and at least one contained emplacements for Stokes mortars. The failure of the attack meant that the tunnels became blocked with wounded and never functioned as a link to the German line. On the northern flank John sap, 458ft long, was opened to form a communication trench called 'Russian Trench' into a mine crater in no man's land. Many of the 12th York & Lancaster sheltered in this trench when unable to cross no man's land.[31] From the southern tunnel in the 31st Division, Bleaneau, the mortars each opened fire with 150 rounds at 7.20am, but the rate of fire was so high with this weapon that their ammunition was expended within eight minutes. By 7.28 there was no fire on the German front line, and German survivors were manning their parapet ready to repel the attack. The opening of the sap attracted grenades and the mortar commander was killed. The tunnelling officer at the end of this sap, Captain Alexander Donald, believed that machine guns would have been more effective in these forward posts given that the German front line was still capable of resistance.[32]

In fact the 4th Division, next in line to the south, placed Lewis machine guns in its four sap heads instead of mortars. However, of four Lewis gun teams in the head of Cat Street and Beet Street tunnels, two were put out of action by a British shell during the final bombardment of the German front line shortly before zero. The remainder were all casualties by the early afternoon of 1 July, especially from German grenades, with the exception of one officer and three men.[33]

After hearing Donald's account, an assistant of Brigadier Harvey reported that the ends of these saps, which were very close to the German lines, should have been used to blow charges to deal with the resistance in the enemy front line: 'The failure to utilize the northern saps for blowing destructive & demoralising charges at the moment of attack appears to have been an error.'[34]

Prior to the attack the divisions attacking on the northern front had opposed firing mines from the ends of the saps as they believed that the artillery would have dealt with the resistance in the front line and they would not be necessary.[35]

On the 29th Division front, of three saps driven either side of the Hawthorn mine, two reached within 30yds of the German front line and contained Stokes mortar positions. The third, Sap 7, connected a sunken lane which ran across no man's land midway between the British and German lines. This was used to file the two leading companies of the 1st Lancashire Fusiliers and a mortar team into the cover of this lane prior to the attack. An official cameraman, Geoffrey Malins, also passed through Sap 7 to film the men waiting to attack:

The tunnel was no more than two feet six inches wide and five feet high. Men inside were passing ammunition from one to the other in an endless chain and disappearing into the bowels of the earth.

The shaft took a downward trend. It was only by squeezing past the munition bearers that we were able to proceed at all, and in some places it was impossible for more than one to crush through at a time. By the light of an electric torch, stuck in the mud, I was able to see the men. They were wet with perspiration, steaming, in fact; stripped to the waist; working like Trojans, each doing the work of six men.

The journey seemed endless. I could tell by the position that I was climbing. My guide was still in front, and letting me know of his whereabouts by shouting: 'Straight ahead, sir! Mind this hole!'

The latter part of the shaft seemed practically upright. I dragged my camera along by the strap attached to the case. It was impossible to carry it.

We were nearing daylight. I could see a gleam only a few feet away. At last we came to the exit. My guide was there.

'Keep down low, sir. This sap is only four feet deep. It's been done during the night, about fifty yards of it. We are in No Man's Land now, and if the Germans had any idea we were here, the place would soon be an inferno.'

'Go ahead,' I said. It was difficult to imagine we were midway between the Hun lines and our own. It was practically inconceivable. The shell-fire seemed just as bad as ever behind in the trenches, but here it was simply heavenly. The only thing one had to do was to keep as low as possible and wriggle along. The ground sloped downwards. The end of the sap came in sight. My guide was crouching there, and in front of him, about thirty feet away, running at right angles on both sides, was a roadway, overgrown with grass and pitted with shell-holes. The bank immediately in front was lined with the stumps of trees and a rough hedge, and there lined up, crouching as close to the bank as possible, were some of our men. They were the Lancashire Fusiliers, with bayonets fixed, and ready to spring forward.[36]

The Germans, having been warned by the detonation of the Hawthorn mine at 7.20am, were ready when the Lancashire Fusiliers attacked and opened heavy fire on them as they left the cover of the lane, completely stopping their attack.

The 29th Division wished to keep the tunnels clear for establishing secure signals communication with the captured position and supplying water and ordered before the attack: 'The tunnels will only be used for runners and for getting telephone wires and water pipes forward. They will not be used as communication trenches.'[37]

Sappers were stationed in the tunnels with a water pipeline ready to run into the captured German front line.[38] Pioneers were detailed to dig trenches to link the tunnels, named First Avenue and Mary, with the captured trenches, but found the British trenches congested with wounded and dead from the failed attack and the German barrage. They found the tunnels impossible to pass through as they were full of wounded, with signallers and orderlies trying to get through.[39]

Saps in front of Thiepval, Ovillers and La Boisselle were the task of 179 Tunnelling Company. On the 36th Ulster Division ten saps were run from the front line north-east of Thiepval Wood (see map, p212). The intention was for each of the ten tunnels to have two mortars, firing from T-headed emplacements. On 1 July, mortars fired from at least six of the saps at five minutes before zero and, under the cover of this fire, the Ulstermen left their trenches to lie down in no man's land about 100yds from the German lines. This fire and the British bombardment had a powerful effect on the German defenders and the forward waves of the 36th Division were able to take the front line and push deep into the German positions. During the day, however, the effects of the German counter-barrage and the failure of the units on either side of the division reduced the gains to the German front line only, where the attackers could not be resupplied. None of the ten tunnels approached close to the German front line and attempts to connect them with trenches across the remaining distance proved impossible owing to German fire. At 8.40am a company of the 16th Royal Irish Rifles Pioneers was sent to dig a trench from the end of Sap No.5, which was about 900ft from the German line (about 320ft north-west of the present day Connaught Cemetery). They made several attempts but were shot down each time they left the end of the tunnel, losing about twenty men before they could begin.[40] Following the attack, the Division recommended narrowing no man's land before an attack and using Russian saps running across no man's land:

The 36th Division successfully crossed a No Man's Land of 400 yards but found the passage of reinforcements and runners afterwards of the greatest difficulty. Parallels should therefore be pushed forward to 200 yards or even nearer and should be supplemented by Russian saps as far as possible across No Man's Land. These saps should be close below the surface so that the top can be thrown off; the roots of the grass serve as a useful guide. Deep underground tunnels of any length are not desirable.[41]

On the 32nd Divisional front, two medium trench mortar emplacements and two communication tunnels, Inverary and Sanda, were prepared. The attack was not a success, with troops in the Leipzig Salient again beleaguered in part of the front line, but in these circumstances the tunnel positions were found to be of value. The two mortar positions extended to within 111 and 115ft of the German line and contained emplacements for 2in trench mortars firing a 60lb 'toffee apple' projectile. The Division reported favourably on the value of the tunnelled positions despite some difficulties:

For two days the guns in these Saps fired without having any German shells near them. On the third and fourth day of firing they were heavily shelled. Our own gas, when liberated from the front line, slightly gassed two of the gun team waiting in the Saps and some time elapsed before these positions were again fit for use. … As battle positions they were undoubtedly a great success and enabled targets to be engaged 500 yards behind the German front line.[42]

After initial success, troops were forced back into the Leipzig Salient, which was packed with troops cut off from their own lines by the German fire in no man's land. Inverary and Sanda were driven to within 86 and 170ft of the German front line and the 17th Northumberland Fusiliers Pioneers were ordered to open them as soon as possible after the assault and dig a trench to link them to the German line. Such was the congestion of dead and wounded and the heavy fire in the British trenches that the platoon responsible for Sanda tunnel, under Lieutenant H. Shenton Cole, was unable to even reach it until about 4pm:

Cole found the sap choked with dead and wounded men of the assaulting battalions, who had crawled in there for safety from the incessant machine-gun and whiz-bang fire which swept the whole front. A few men were sent along the sap who, with great difficulty, crawled through among the dead and wounded and broke through at the far end, which had been blown in by a chance shell. Having thus ascertained the point from which the trench was going to start, Cole led out the rest of the platoon across the open, going warily from shell-hole to shell-hole under heavy fire, till he had men distributed in a rough line, four men in each shell-hole from the sap end to the enemy's front line opposite, which was now in our hands. The men worked towards each other, two each way, and thus, with the loss of only two or three men wounded, the trench was completed...[43]

The communication opened up through Sanda tunnel enabled water and supplies to be got into the Leipzig Redoubt and wounded men to be evacuated. Hance, commanding 179 Company, later claimed credit for the successful operation of Sanda tunnel in supplying the Leipzig Salient, which he had constructed double width, with a wooden partition down the middle to allow two-way passage:

> Sentries posted at each end controlled the traffic, and, whilst it might be inhuman to prevent a wounded man from sheltering in one of these tunnels, it is no great hardship to ask him to 'keep to the left'. At any rate the tunnel was an unqualified success, and elicited the highest commendation from the Brigadier... [Goring-Jones, commanding 146 Brigade]. Although it was of double width it only received one direct hit, which damage was repaired at night. (Major H.M. Hance)[44]

South of the 32nd Division, 8th Division faced the fortified village of Ovillers, flanked by the open expanses of Nab and Mash Valleys, which were swept by fire from the Leipzig Redoubt and La Boisselle. On the boundary of two Divisions, south of the Leipzig Redoubt, a tunnel was driven 50yds into no man's land from Mersey Street and emplacements constructed for four Vickers machine guns. These guns were to cover the attacking troops by firing up Nab (later known as Blighty) Valley, where no man's land was a quarter of a mile wide, to deal with positions and German machine guns where no attack was to be made. After the first line was taken the machine gunners were to break out of the tunnels to further assist the advance. Initial waves in the north had some success on 1 July, but at 10.55am the commander of the machine gun section in the Mersey Street tunnel reported to his company commander that:

> ...he fired from the tunnel position 6,000 rounds sweeping the German front line & up towards Farm De Mouquet. He had 5 men overcome and faint with cordite fumes. He then started breaking through the tunnel and experienced considerable difficulty. At about 9am he had broken out in two places. All this time the enemy trenches were difficult to see owing to the smoke & haze. He was under the impression that our advance had been a success. 2/Lt Hampton took two guns out & disappeared. It was afterwards found that he & practically all the gun teams of his two guns were killed or wounded 30yds from the tunnel. 2/Lt. Steel not knowing this ordered his teams out; the first 3 men were killed & the gun had to be left a few yards away in the open. He then stopped more men leaving & with his one remaining gun worked round to the Nab & learnt that we were not holding

the German front line. His men being exhausted he put them in a dugout &
reported to me for orders. (Captain J.F. Jessop Weiss, MGC)[45]

Facing Ovillers the 8th Division had two communication tunnels, each with four
Stokes mortar positions, prepared by 179 Tunnelling Company. Waltney, through
chalk, ran 520ft with its east end 380ft from the German line, while Rivington was
cut through clay and had been driven further, 600ft, and closer, 40ft, to the German
front line. Hance did not construct these double width as he had Sanda, but the
standard dimension of 5ft 6in in height and 3ft 6in wide at the floor and 2ft 6in wide
at the roof, a size that he felt was to narrow.[46] The ends of both were to be opened
directly the German front line had been taken by blowing explosive charges rather
than breaking out with picks, and it was thought that the crater opening would
resemble a shell hole and so not arouse suspicion. The mortars covered the
movement of the infantry into no man's land, as in the 36th Division. However, as
the troops rose to the attack at 7.30am, from Ovillers, La Boisselle and the German
second line, a terrific volume of machine-gun and rifle fire poured into the attackers
and, as they neared the German front line, the artillery barrage came down on no
man's land. A handful of the 2nd Lincolns, on whose front Waltney tunnel was
situated, got into the German front trench, but were forced out into no man's land.
Waltney was opened but seems to have played little or no part. Rivington, on the
front of the 2nd Royal Berkshires, was not opened as the infantry were unable to
reach the German front line. In the broad expanse of no man's land, where 8th and
34th Divisions advanced with very heavy losses up Mash Valley, no saps seem to have
been used, although Sappers of 207 Field Company reported working on them in
May between Argyll Street and Dorset Street trenches, and north of Keats Redan
they seem to have been given up.

Opposite La Boisselle one Russian sap was prepared, although without trench
mortar emplacements, which were instead constructed in the British lines (see map,
p122). The tunnel was started from Kerriemuir Street, aiming at the northern end
of the Schwaben Höhe (the Lochnagar mine was under the southern tip). It was
driven 410ft through chalk, reaching to within 120ft of the German line. The last
150ft were worked with the bayonet only and at night German patrols were heard
constantly overhead. Hance constructed it to the standard 3ft 6in width, with 12 to
14ft of overhead cover.

A platoon of the 18th Northumberland Fusiliers Pioneers under Lieutenant
Nixon was to open up the Kerriemuir Street tunnel and dig a communication trench
connecting it to the German front line. The tunnel end was about 470ft from the
Lochnagar mine charge: his orders were therefore to shelter twelve of his men in the
end of the tunnel nearest the British line until the mine had detonated and then,
after checking that the gas was safe, begin breaking open the remaining 2ft of head
cover. After the last wave of the 102nd Brigade attack had passed he was to call
forward the rest of his platoon, who were sheltering in a mine shaft, and construct

two ramps out of the tunnel. After the last wave of the 103rd Brigade had passed he was to begin digging the trench to the German front line. On arriving at the tunnel the night before the attack, however, Nixon was told by Hance that he would have to break through 12ft of cover rather than 2ft. Nixon therefore started work at midnight and by 8.30am had only broken through sufficiently for the signals cables to be passed through. In the meantime, the attacks by the two brigades had been made and had gained a foothold only around the Schwaben Höhe. By 10am men were able to pass through the tunnel, but the work was badly impeded by wounded coming back through the tunnel and stores being brought forward. The communication trench reached the German front line by 7pm. Hance witnessed the congestion in the tunnel:

> This tunnel was immediately used as a communication, I myself saw with what eagerness, by parties carrying bombs and other supplies up, & by wounded coming down. Consequently it was immediately blocked, and I am convinced, that such tunnels, though altogether admirable in conception, have been made too small, and, to be efficient, must have two roads for traffic both ways.[47]

The 9th Cheshires were sent to reinforce the troops which had gained possession of the Lochnagar crater and the remains of the Schwaben Höhe. The commander of D Company arrived at about this time:

> The mine tunnel (which had been opened out to the captured German line) and our front near to it, I found to be entirely blocked by wounded and unwounded. I had this trench and tunnel cleared and posted Sentries at both ends and at head of rear communication trench to regulate all traffic. (Lieutenant A. Vincent Ward, 9th Cheshires)[48]

The commanding officer of the Northumberlands Pioneers stated that the whole battalion passed through the tunnel. Although it was claimed in the official history that this tunnel connected into the Lochnagar crater, and included a map showing this, the tunnel and the communication trench reached the German line about 330ft north-west of the crater lip.[49] As at the Leipzig Redoubt, this tunnel served its original purpose in reinforcing the position at the critical period after it was first gained, although the battle had not gone at all to plan. The 34th Division orders for the attack contained no reference to the Kerriemuir tunnel, perhaps for the sake of secrecy, and the commander of the 15th Royal Scots later complained that the tunnels were never made known to them and had they been told of them they might have come into use sooner.[50] On the whole, Hance's view of the Russian saps that his Company had constructed was that they needed to be wider and partitioned to allow two-way traffic, otherwise:

...their utility was very limited. They were almost immediately blocked with wounded, and I saw fresh troops etc coming up passing over the bodies of their wounded comrades, which was certainly not good for morale.[51]

The 21st Division had two saps across no man's land. One, Dinnet Street, south of Sausage Valley, had been prepared during September and October 1915 on the orders of General Maxse in the expectation of a general advance following the Battle of Loos.[52] This was broken open and converted into a trench during the night before the attack and used by the leading attacking companies of 10th King's Own Yorkshire Light Infantry to get forward of the British wire five minutes before zero. This did not prove sufficient to overcome the German machine gunners, who emerged from their dugouts in time to bring heavy fire on the attackers.[53] The other sap, Purfleet, seems to have been of no use to the 4th Middlesex and 10th West Yorkshires.

In the southern part of the Somme, especially a wide front of Hickling's 183 Tunnelling Company, there was a very different outcome on 1 July. Along the fronts of the 7th, 18th and 30th Divisions were eighteen Russian saps, which were designed to be broken out for communication purposes, but many of which were also used to blow comparatively small charges. Nine or ten of the saps which ran through the surface clay were extended to the German front line by silently using an auger to cut out a wide diameter bore hole, which was charged with 200 to 500lbs of explosive in a method resembling the German sapping and mining attacks of the winter of 1914–15. The risk involved with this is illustrated by an encounter of the commanding officer of the 6th Royal Berkshires with one of Hickling's men prior to the attack:

> The officer responsible came to me very agitated running out of our end of the trench to say the whole show was given away as his augur head had pierced through into an officers' dug out & he could hear every word they were saying. He thought they must know and all was discovered. On enquiry I elicited from him the fact that there had been no interruption in their talk – no dead silence – no raised voices – so was able to assure him that according to human nature all was well!! I identified the spot later and it was quite true that he had just pierced through into an officers dug out! (Lieutenant Colonel B.G. Clay)[54]

The attacks of the 7th and especially the 18th and 30th Divisions and the French to their right were markedly successful with objectives quickly gained. The reasons for this success were broadly threefold: the positions to be assaulted were not so easily defended, the Germans had fewer troops in their front lines and the British learnt more sophisticated artillery and counter battery tactics from the French and benefitted from their gun batteries. The saps played a role in this success by bringing firepower to bear on the German front line in the first minutes of the attack. Four of Hickling's Russian sap galleries on the 18th Division housed forward machine-gun emplacements and two also contained very large flamethrowers, in the first British use of this weapon. Four flamethrowers were intended to be used on 1 July, but two galleries where installation was prepared, south-west of Mametz, at Kiel Trench, and between Carnoy and Casino Point, were damaged by shellfire. The two remaining were immediately to the left of the mine crater field at Carnoy and shot flame for a distance of 282 and 261ft in an attack which was effective, yet also localized.[55]

In contrast to the north, where the congestion caused by the failed attacks and heavy German barrages greatly hindered the opening and operation of the saps, Hickling was able to open his saps for traffic very quickly. On the 18th Division he blew the mines and charges at 7.27am and then rapidly opened the tunnels for traffic through 'manholes', in one case immediately afterwards, in three cases at 7.35 and the fifth at 7.45am. Hickling then had a larger exit made into the craters blown at the ends, the quickest of which opened at 7.55. Two others were delayed until 2pm, either owing to damage from German shellfire or the greater depth of the tunnel.[56] Even these delayed openings were much faster than the connections made at the Leipzig Salient and La Boisselle. Although Hickling's men were hampered by the German barrage, it was not as heavy as in the north and there were not the streams of wounded and men trying to get forward, as the waves had succeeded overland and had moved on to their objectives. Paradoxically, however, had the attack been held up at the German front line then the tunnels might have been more important to the attack. Hickling himself pointed out that the Russian saps had little role in the success:

> These saps in the event were very little used for communication, as intended, as the advance on the whole length of front prepared by 183 Company was successful. If the attack had been only partly successful as in other places, they would undoubtedly have been very valuable.[57]

On the front of the 30th Division at Maricourt, Hickling also tried using hydraulic forcing jacks or pipe pushers to drive tubes of explosive through the ground. This device, which had failed at St Eloi on 27 March, was also found unreliable where the flinty chalk of the Somme was close to the surface and was experimented with at Ovillers by the 8th Division until the commanding Royal Engineer had observed the pipe emerging from the ground in no man's land. Only one of Hickling's was found satisfactory on 1 July, blowing a long narrow crater 180ft long, 15ft wide and 7$\frac{1}{2}$ft deep. Another intended to be 220ft long only worked in the first and last 50ft, the other sections either failing to explode or only blowing a trench 5ft wide by 2ft deep.[58]

Soon after 1 July, Harvey's assistant, Stokes, visited the Somme Tunnelling Companies. Trower's 252 Company was, he reported: '…rather depressed now owing to the uselessness of its 10,000ft of galleries in assisting the attack and will naturally work now with poorer spirit.'[59]

Stokes concluded that the northern saps should have been used for a greater number of charges, as were Hickling's, rather than, as at Serre, trying to dig right up to the German trench. Whereas most of Hickling's charges had been small he felt that the charges should have been larger, that is, the size of the Hawthorn mine. The purpose of the charges was to deal with the German front line, to assist the infantry in getting across no man's land and to prevent the tunnel openings having grenades thrown into them:

> The comparatively long distance between the lines in this sector led to the failure of the infantry attack, although the guns & infantry did all that was possible against skilfully sheltered enemy. But this long distance was also the R.E. opportunity, owing to the surprise that was possible in carrying out gallery schemes. Under the methods followed, too much thought seems to have been given to facilities after occupation of enemy lines & too little to the means of getting infantry across 200 yards of good field for machine gun fire. Where lines are so far apart, it is naturally the front line that costs most. The failure to utilize the northern saps for blowing destructive & demoralising charges at the moment of attack appears to have been an error.[60]

Preedy reported on 9 July that the shallow galleries should be 'constructed wherever possible.' He specified the form that they should take, with entrances in the support trench rather than the front line, in pairs 50ft apart to avoid being damaged by the same shell, but linked for ventilation, and 10 to 15ft of overhead cover to make them safe from shell damage. He recommended following many of Hickling's practices, including using a borer from the end of the tunnel, 50ft from the German line in clay or 90ft in chalk. The charges blown would quickly complete the trench into the German line and destroy barbed wire and dugouts. Emplacements for Stokes mortars and machine guns should be built at 30ft on the flanks of the tunnels; machine guns were more useful than mortars. Manholes or exits for the troops were needed for use before the tunnels could be opened into the craters. Tunnels to cross 200yds of no man's land took two and a half to three and a half months to construct. They needed effective traffic control, ventilation and lighting.[61] Although many of Preedy's recommendations were to be taken up in 1917, an attempt to use four Russian saps, constructed by 174 Tunnelling Company, in an attack at Hamel on 3 September was unsuccessful. As on 1 July the fire on no man's land was too heavy for Pioneers to link the ends of the saps to the German front line and the 39th Division was forced out of the German front line.[62]

The Somme battle continued until November 1916, and the Battle of the Ancre, launched on 13th, was a major attempt to take the northern battlefield, where the attack had completely failed on 1 July. The front line at Serre and Beaumont Hamel had remained static until then and the saps dug for the 1 July and 3 September

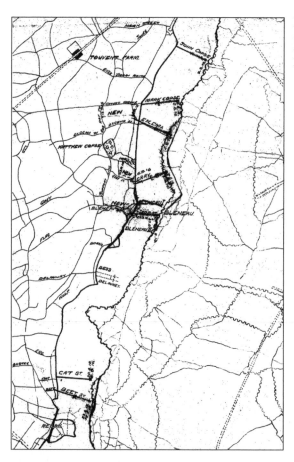

Russian saps between Serre and the Redan prepared for the 13 November 1916 attack. From NA WO153/905.

attacks were reused and improved. The problem with the Serre tunnels in particular was that the Germans now knew exactly where they were. The state of the trenches rendered four of the ten saps from Serre to the Redan completely inaccessible, but 252 Company had been maintaining the remainder since 22 July. The Germans went out at night into no man's land to destroy them and in August and September blew fifteen charges against Grey, Excema, John and Bleaneau. On 8 September they smashed the whole of Bleaneau except the first 120ft. On 18th they blew a charge against Grey and then heavily bombarded the trenches; when eleven infantry went into the tunnel to shelter they were all killed by the carbon monoxide from the explosive. Orders to prepare the tunnels for the offensive were given and cancelled several times and 252 Company was working constantly to repair the tunnels owing to the frequency of bombardments and the very bad state of the trenches. For the Serre attack, by 31st and 3rd Divisions, Trower was instructed on 30 September to reopen John, Mark, Excema and Grey, his war diary commenting: 'Very dangerous work & very short time given.' There is no reference to using the tunnels as mortar or machine-gun emplacements as they had been on 1 July. They began work on 1

October, but the Germans blew the next day between John and Mark without damage, although ten infantry were gassed sheltering in Excema, of whom nine died. The entrances to Grey were twice smashed by shellfire.

The battle began at 5.45am on 13 November in darkness and dripping fog. Opposite Serre, 252 Company had opened John, Mark, Excema and Grey tunnels at midnight and Lewis guns were positioned outside the exits, but the attack again failed. There was no role for the tunnels and they reclosed the exits. For the attack on Beaumont Hamel, by 2nd and 51st Divisions, 252 Company had loaded the ends of Russian saps with charges designed to blow communication trenches at zero. They had driven new saps from the sunken lane, which had been incorporated into the British line after 1 July. This had significantly narrowed no man's land facing the village and North Street and South Street, running from the sunken lane, served to further reduce it. First Avenue (formerly Sap 6) was directed at the salient south of Beaumont Hamel which contained Y Ravine. Mary was on the far south of the divisional front and its end was in the 63rd Division area.

They opened these in the last week of October, but on 7 November both entrances to First Avenue tunnel were smashed in and completely lost, entombing eighteen men who were all rescued. Two days later it was again smashed in by shellfire, trapping two infantrymen who were not released until the following day.

On 13 November a 1,000lb bore charge in the end of Cat tunnel was blown to create a communication trench on the extreme left of 5th Brigade (2nd Division). The 5th Brigade took the German front line, but the attack to the north at the Quadrilateral failed and the trench was not completed. The tunnel was temporarily closed, but was eventually connected to the German front line on Redan Ridge, although the work was much hampered by snipers until darkness. North Street tunnel was opened up 25 minutes after zero and the tunnel was reported to have been very useful. In the 51st Division, the ends of South Street, First Avenue and Mary were extended by Pioneers assembled in the tunnels the remaining 50yds to the German lines, partly with tubes of explosives and partly by digging. This was not to be carried out until the captured German lines were consolidated and in the case of South Street this was not done until the afternoon of the second day of the attack.[63]

For the Hamel attack by 63rd Division 252 Company started work on 17 October on four tunnels in front of Hamel, dug for the 3 September attack by 174 Company. On 27th they loaded No.2 tunnel with a small mine charge of 600lbs ammonal, which was to be blown against a German salient. Trower reported that it made a very good crater into the German lines. The remaining three were opened and used as communication trenches and one was used additionally as a battalion headquarters.[64] The Brigade Major of 188 Brigade recalled that one of the tunnels was blocked or caved in and was cleared by sappers detailed to open it after the leading infantry had moved forward, but he was still distrustful of it:

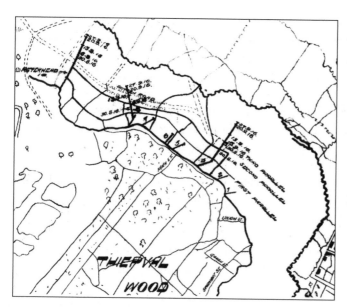

Russian saps dug at Thiepval up to 27 September 1916. Of ten saps dug for 1 July, saps 3, 8 and 10 (Peterhead) have been extended. The use of parallels linking the saps reflects siege warfare practice and the methods tried by the French in 1915. From NA WO153/905.

I believe the tunnel served its purpose in saving casualties amongst runners, reserves hurrying up etc. I was advised to use it myself during a forward recce but having inspected the entrance decided on the open route across the top.[65]

Harvey claimed in 1929 that one of the lessons of the Battle of the Somme was that 'Russian saps have solved the difficulty of crossing No Man's Land.'[66] This, however, was clearly not borne out by the experience of the Somme or of subsequent battles. GHQ reported on the value of the tunnels in the attack, giving recommendations as to their construction and reporting that their utility was greatest when the attack was temporarily held up:

The real use of these galleries is brought out when the infantry attack progresses very slowly. On the 13th November on that portion of the front at which the attack was successful, the advance was so rapid as to render these galleries unnecessary except in the case of the two tunnels, which were on the flank of the successful attack.

The reservations expressed by the Brigade Major of 188 Brigade were also addressed:

The infantry still appear to have a great prejudice against going down a tunnel and will only use it under strong provocation, but the utility of such tunnels has been proved and where they are prepared this disinclination on the part of the infantry should be overcome by preliminary explanation.[67]

A 5th Army letter, probably drafted by Preedy, in response to a request for more information by the 1st Army, denied that such a prejudice existed.[68] It had not been conceived on 1 July 1916 that men could use the tunnels to emerge one at a time from easily observed tunnel entrances, although plans for troops to emerge from tunnels behind enemy defences were put forward after the war by fiction writers. The practical difficulties, evidently understood more clearly during the war, prevented this method from being attempted.[69] The report by GHQ on Russian saps, however, led to the most important uses of subways, as they came to be called, for the offensives at Arras and Vimy Ridge in April 1917 to assist passage to and from the front line and also to mass troops safely and secretly for the attack.

Chapter 10

Underground Accommodation and Communications

In 1917 the Russian sap evolved into the infantry subway when the use of underground galleries to get men across no man's land gave way to the use of tunnels to allow safe movement up to the front line. This chapter will examine the use of tunnels for communication and of deep dugouts for accommodation. Underground accommodation became a major feature of trench warfare from 1915 when the Germans in particular began to excavate deep and extensive dugouts.

German dugouts as developed during 1915 with cover increased to 5m and double bunks for eight men, shown in relation to the fire and support trenches. From Seesselberg, *Der Stellungskrieg.*

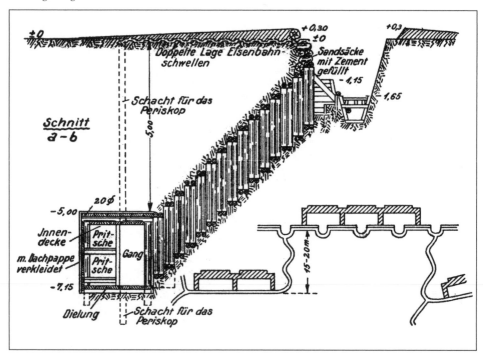

The aim was to accommodate men in or close to the front line so that a large number were available, protected from bombardment, to repel attacks by the enemy infantry. The German policy was to defend the front line at all costs and to accommodate as many troops as possible in the front line in underground bunkers. The French discovered these excavated in chalk at Vimy Ridge when they captured Carency, Ablain-Saint-Nazaire and Neuville-Saint-Vaast in May and June 1915 and studied them carefully. When Capitaine Thobie examined them he concluded that they completely prevented a surprise attack on the trenches:

> Thanks to this security, it was enough to leave sentries in the trench, and the majority of the men rested in the shell proof dugouts. Access to these German shelters was by either a staircase gallery or a shaft. They were very comfortable, measured ten metres in length, two metres in width and 1.80 metres height. They were cased with jointed beams of eight centimetres thickness and covered by five to six metres of earth. This type of dugout with these dimensions was not at that time unique and the form and the dimensions adopted by our enemies depended much on the configuration of the ground and the nature of the subsoil.[1]

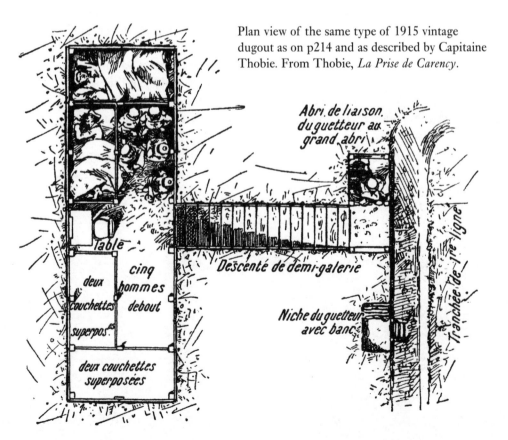

Plan view of the same type of 1915 vintage dugout as on p214 and as described by Capitaine Thobie. From Thobie, *La Prise de Carency*.

Abri. de liaison. du guetteur au grand abri

Descente de demi-galerie

Table

cinq hommes debout

deux couchettes superpos.

deux couchettes superposées

Niche du guetteur avec banc

Tranchée de 1re ligne

South of Arras, the German officer Ernst Jünger lived from the winter of 1915 until the summer of 1916 in a deep dugout at Monchy-au-Bois and described being able to pass at a depth of 6m underground from one flank of the position to the other, with a 60m gallery from his platoon headquarters to his company commander's dugout:[2]

What strongholds we used to have, with galleries as long and comfortable as a Dickens' novel, whence left and right there opened out living-rooms and sleeping-rooms and ammunition-chambers and exits and entrances and cross-communications, and where one could traverse one's whole front like a mole without once coming to the surface. At Monchy, besides a comfortable dugout for quiet times, where a wide shaft directed the light of day straight on to my writing table, I was master of an underground dwelling approached by forty steps hewn in the solid chalk, so that even the heaviest shells at this depth made no more than a pleasant rumble when we sat there over interminable games of cards. In one wall I had had a bed hewn out, immense as the box-beds of Westphalian cottages, where, protected from the slightest noise and encased in stout oaken boards, I slept in a casket of soft dry chalk. At its head hung an electric light so that I could read in comfort till I was sleepy. The walls were adorned with pictures in colour from *Jugend*, and the whole was shut off from the outer world by a dark-red curtain with rod and rings; it was displayed to visitors, with a running commentary of jest, as the last word in luxurious depravity. In those days, secured by wire fifty metres wide, one could venture to sleep in pyjamas, and the automatic that lay to hand beside the ash-tray was only used when it was desired to break the monotony by going on patrol. Those were splendid days.[3]

The chalk quarry beneath Monchy-au-Bois used for the defence of the village, discovered according to Jünger via the well (shown right) by a company cook of the 73rd Hanoverian Fusiliers. The dotted line shows an access gallery dug to a communication trench. From Seesselberg, *Der Stellungskrieg.*

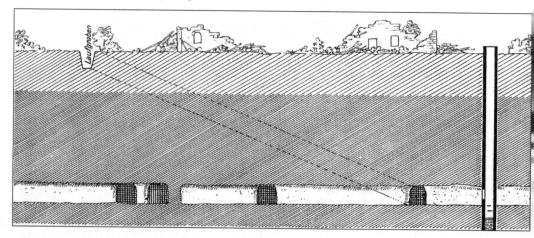

The Germans also made use of natural or man-made underground quarries and catacombs, which were particularly prevalent in chalk areas. Jünger described how such an excavation beneath Monchy-au-Bois was discovered in 1915:

There was a quarry out of which in times of peace limestone had been got for building, and this was an important part of the defences. It had been discovered only by chance. A company cook, whose bucket had fallen into a well of spring water, went down after it and discovered a hole that seemed to connect with a large cave. The matter was looked into, and a second entrance was broken through into a bomb-proof refuge that held a considerable body of men.[4]

Monchy-au-Bois was immediately behind the German front line and the catacombs were used for accommodation as well as safe movement to and from the front line. A German inventory produced in 1918 listed over 600 such underground spaces in northern France.[5]

During the offensives of September 1915, the Allies used prolonged bombardments to destroy the German defences prior to infantry attacks. The German 6th Corps lost positions to the British at Loos and the French at Souchez and afterwards issued instructions addressing the need to increase the size of dugouts:

The moral effect of almost three days of the most intense preparatory bombardment is naturally very great. The strain on the infantry under such conditions is quite terrific. In order to render officers and men capable of a supreme effort and to preserve their fighting energy through the exhaustive strain of days of continuous battle it is necessary to provide in the most careful and farseeing manner for the bodily comfort of the troops. It is also important that the men should not be accommodated in the dugouts in small parties of three or four, but in two or more groups under responsible leaders. This will enhance the prospects of a successful resistance.[6]

The French and British also managed to surprise the Germans before they could leave the shelter of their dugouts by using artillery fire which moved forward over the German positions and behind which, in theory, the attacking infantry advanced protected from German fire. The British adopted the French term 'barrage', meaning 'barrier', for this type of bombardment, which in 1915–16 was in the form of a 'lifting barrage', jumping from one line of trenches to the next. During 1916–17 the technique was refined into the 'creeping barrage', in which every part of the German defences was shelled. The shelling could not completely destroy the deep dugouts, but served to prevent the Germans from leaving their cover to fire on the advancing infantry. Success depended on the attackers staying as close as possible behind the moving wall of shells so that they arrived in the German trenches before the Germans could emerge from their dugouts. German 6th Corps instructions to address the danger of defenders being trapped in their dugouts included the posting of good lookouts, an efficient system of alarm bells and proper exits. The most important point was the speed with which the infantry left the safety of the dugouts to man the trench once the enemy barrage had lifted from their position:

> Above all… every group commander and individual man must know that the success or failure of the defence depends entirely on the timely manning of the parapet. All must be made to understand that the moment the enemy enters our trenches he begins bombing the dugouts. The great point, therefore, is not to lose a second but, even if the alarm is not given in time, to hurry to the firing line the moment the artillery fire lengthens.[7]

The German Second Army, holding the Somme front, reacted to the lessons of the September battles by continuing to build stronger deep dugouts:

> On the whole, mined dugouts about three metres below the surface have proved satisfactory. The losses from the intense bombardment were comparatively slight. The entrances to the dugouts were often destroyed or blocked. The frames of these must, therefore, be well braced and specially strong. Steep slopes above the entrances must be avoided. Very heavy shells (28 centimetre) penetrated into these dugouts.[8]

The Germans also used underground accommodation to shelter and conceal troops before their attack at Verdun on 21 February 1916. The French were aware of these excavations but took them to be defensive structures. Known as Stollen, or tunnels, the underground barracks, 30–45ft deep, had steps leading up to the communication or assault trenches and were constructed to house the first-line reserves rather than the initial waves. The 2nd Company of the 30th Pioneers built ten such dugouts accommodating 500 men in the second line in the forest position at Ville. Those in the woods of Consenvoye, less than 12,000yds from the French front line, had accommodation for 12,000 men.[9] The dangers of underground shelters where large numbers of men were confined in potentially highly dangerous conditions were shown by two incidents during the fighting at Verdun in 1916, when ammunition explosions killed 650 Germans in Fort Douaumont on 8 May and more than 500 French in the Tavannes railway tunnel, used for accommodation and communication, on 4 September.[10]

The German policy of deeper dugouts was highly successful in repelling the central and northern parts of the Franco-British attack on the Somme of 1 July 1916, where their use contributed to the spectacular British casualties of 57,000.

However, the commander of the British 4th Army, General Rawlinson, had anticipated the German tactic. When he was required by General Haig to capture not only the German front line, but also all of the defence lines behind, he extended the duration of the British bombardment so that the German positions could still be destroyed. He proposed this extension in an amended plan which he submitted to Haig on 19 April 1916:

> ...bearing in mind the existence of numerous dug-outs and cellars in the enemy's lines, I do not think that the moral effect of a six-hours' intense bombardment will be so great as that of one extended over several days. The effect on moral of a long, accurate bombardment, which will pulverize strong points one by one, gradually knock in communication trenches, prevent reliefs being carried out, and systematically beat down the enemy's defences, will, to my mind, be much greater, especially as with many new gun detachments we cannot expect very accurate shooting in a hurricane bombardment.
>
> A long bombardment gives the enemy no chance of sleep, food and ammunition are difficult to bring up, and the enemy is kept in a constant state of doubt as to when the infantry assault will take place. His troops in the front line must be relieved every 48 hours, or they will break down under the strain, and it will be our business so to regulate our fire as to inflict heavy losses, even at night, on any relieving detachments he may endeavour to bring forward.[11]

The bombardment was to last a week, extended one day owing to bad weather, which prevented the spotting of the fall of the shells. The experience of the defenders was described by a German junior medical officer:

> A few days before the awaited onset of the British offensive on the Somme, I was transferred to an infantry regiment. We had to strengthen the German lines south of Beaumont-Hamel. On June 24, 1916, the British gunners opened up and their fire increased in intensity, combined with fierce gas attacks. For seven days and seven nights the ground shook under the constant impact of light and heavy shells, and in between the bombardments gas alarms were sounded, and we could hardly breathe. Our dug-outs crumbled, tumbled on top of us, and our positions were razed to the ground. Again and again we had to dig ourselves and our comrades out of masses of blackened earth and splintered wooden beams. Often we found bodies crushed to pulp, or bunks full of suffocated soldiers. The 'drum-fire' never ceased. No food or water reached us. Down below, men became hysterical and their comrades had to knock them out, so as to prevent them from running away and exposing themselves to the deadly shell splinters. Even

the rats panicked and sought refuge in our flimsy shelters; they ran up the walls, and we had to kill them with our spades.

My first-aid post was in a hollow dell, and the sappers had taken the precaution to provide it with two exits. One of these received a direct hit, but we had the other left, and got busy clearing the first one—you never know! On the morning of July 1st the British gunners directed their fire on our rear position and their armies went over the top in solid formations. ...they did not expect any body on the other side to have survived the bombardment. But German machine-gunners and infantrymen crawled out of their holes, with inflamed and sunken eyes, their faces blackened by fire and their uniforms splashed with the blood of their wounded comrades. It was a kind of relief to be able to come out, even into air still filled with smoke and the smell of cordite. They started firing furiously, and the British had frightful losses. (Stefan Westmann, Reserve Infantry Regiment 119)[12]

The British artillery bombardment, although prolonged, was spread over too great a depth of front and the heavy shells were insufficient in quantity and reliability. The bombardment was inadequate in terms of sheer weight in destroying the German mined dugouts. The British also lacked skill and experience in using the barrage to keep the Germans trapped in their dugouts until the infantry had captured their trenches. Only on the southern Somme front did the attackers achieve success where the British 18th and 30th Divisions were assisted by French gunners and the French attacked south of the River Somme. Capitaine Thobie examined the dugouts captured in the French sector, which were of a variety of designs, ranging from a simple covered arch of corrugated iron to an elaborate complex built into the banks of the Somme Canal at Frize. The most common type was larger and deeper than those he had seen in 1915, 8m deep as opposed to 5–6m, and with multiple entrances. He described the difficulty of attacking ground beneath which extended networks of dugouts:

With such buried shelters, potential embryonic forts, casemates and redoubts, one sees that it is very difficult to destroy the main enemy defence works. They are almost always so well concealed as to be impossible to detect. One is thus obliged to make an area bombardment over the whole zone where reports from prisoners or aviators might indicate their existence. And, in spite of the incredible expenditure of ammunition which the bombardment requires, one still finds many shelters intact and groups of men who overcame the bombardment because they had remained concealed. They are complexes, true octopuses, which surface suddenly from the ocean of iron and fire which every artillery preparation now comprises. They quickly extend their tentacles to the surrounding trenches and create in a few moments all the small pockets of resistance which our infantrymen run up against. If these miniature fortresses do not fall in the fury from the first attack they must then be encircled and progress is seriously impeded. We have enormous material means however: special shells, asphyxiating gases, etc... The tank appears to give invaluable help in these cases. ...

The German soldier is taught that in combat his survival depends on his tools. The capacity for labour of our enemy and his tenacity in the execution of any work increases considerably the magnitude of the achievement of our valiant troops. In Herbécourt, in Frize, in Combles, powerful deeply buried timbered dugouts, formidable redoubts, were taken even though the artillery was unable to destroy them all beforehand. Some of these shelters whose importance impresses us are already known; yet what an arduous task, what a jump in the unknown, when the time comes to leap over the parapet![13]

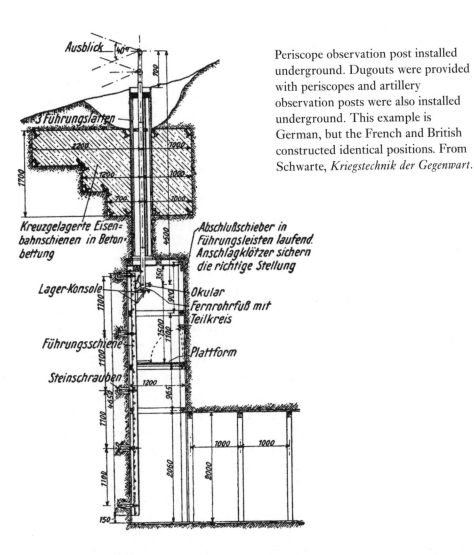

Periscope observation post installed underground. Dugouts were provided with periscopes and artillery observation posts were also installed underground. This example is German, but the French and British constructed identical positions. From Schwarte, *Kriegstechnik der Gegenwart.*

The Allied response in 1916 to the German dugouts was threefold. Firstly they increased the quantity of heavy artillery to destroy them. Secondly, the coordination between the creeping barrage of field artillery and the advancing infantry was to prove more decisive than the ability physically to destroy them with a direct hit from a heavy shell. Thus the aim was to trap the Germans in their dugouts until the attackers were in their trenches, at the top of the steps. Thirdly, the problem of German troops emerging from tunnels after the attackers had passed over their positions was dealt with by troops which the British termed 'Moppers Up', assigned to clear out the deep dugouts with explosive, incendiary and gas grenades. These tactics were introduced during the Somme fighting of 1916, but were not fully developed until 1917. The German response during the Battle of the Somme was, partly, to go deeper. To protect against heavier guns they increased the thickness of earth from a recommended 6m to 7–8m and more in the case of command posts and medical or signals bunkers. Dugouts were required to have two entrances and be connected by tunnels to form accommodation for a platoon.[14] This was to play into the Allies' hands, as they developed the means to tackle the deep dugouts. In August 1916 the replacement of the German Chief of Staff, General von Falkenhayn, by General von Hindenburg and his principal assistant Lieutenant General Ludendorff saw the reduction in the reliance placed on deep-tunnelled defences. This change in command was to have major repercussions for German defensive policy in 1917, but did not prevent a series of defensive disasters for the Germans.

The French and British regarded the trenches as jumping-off points for attacks rather than permanent homes for their infantry and this influenced their lack of use of deep dugouts in 1915 and 1916. In particular French defensive positions and accommodation in the front line were generally compared unfavourably with those of the Germans. However, despite a lack of manpower, following the increasing intensity of bombardments in 1915 they advocated the digging of deep shelters. From the end of 1915 they defined 'bombproof' as withstanding systematic and regular fire from 150mm shells and also individual 210mm mortar rounds. Experience showed the French that shelters constructed by the 'cut and cover' method and protected only with logs and earth were unable to resist these heavy shells fitted with delay fuses and only mined galleries or dugouts could provide sufficient protection. They therefore required all shelters to be tunnelled, except where water was found too close to the surface to permit their excavation. The minimum head cover was 6m of hard, compact chalk: where this was not available a bursting layer of logs or concrete was to be included.[15]

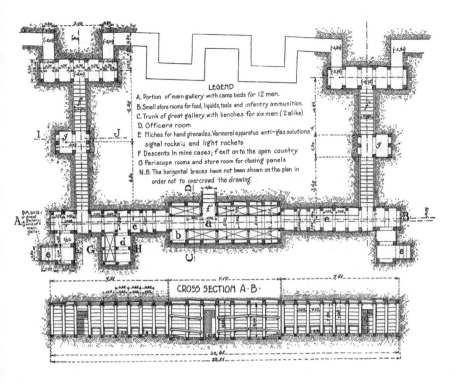

LEGEND
A. Portion of main gallery with camp beds for 12 men.
B. Small store rooms for food, liquids, tools and infantry ammunition.
C. Trunk of great gallery with benches for six men (2 alike)
D. Officers room
E. Niches for hand grenades, Vermorel apparatus anti-gas solutions signal rockets and light rockets
F Descents in mine cases; f exit on to the open country
G Periscope rooms and store room for closing panels
N.B. The horizontal braces have not been shown on the plan in order not to overcrowd the drawing.

CROSS SECTION A·B·

French design of deep gallery shelter with 6.7m head cover, as per instructions of January 1917. From an American translation, *Notes on the Construction of Deep Gallery Shelters.*

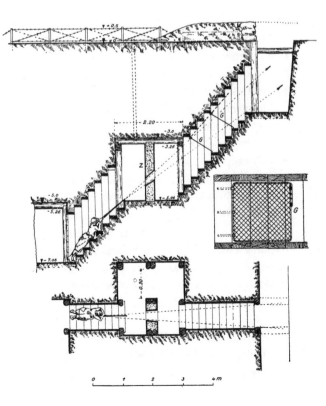

French method of defence of a deep gallery shelter, showing loophole for rifle fire and mesh gates to hinder entry and catch grenades being thrown down the stairs. The stairs and ventilation holes of dugouts were increasingly provided with bomb-traps to contain the explosions of grenades. From Seesselberg, *Der Stellungskrieg.*

The majority of British underground accommodation up to and during 1916 was of shallow cut and cover rather than deep tunnelled construction.[16] Where the British took over trenches from the French on the Somme in the autumn of 1915 they found very deep dugouts cut into the chalk. However, anticipating the German change in policy a year later, the British regarded them as highly vulnerable where they were close to the Germans. Those seen by the commander of the Tyneside Scottish Brigade at La Boisselle were up to 30ft deep and held as many as fifty men:

> There were numerous deep dugouts in our front trench, but it would have been impossible for the men to get out of them in time to repel a surprise raid; in fact, these dugouts would have proved mere traps, so their use was prohibited, and the entrances were closed up by a network of barbed wire. The deep dugouts in the supports and reserve trenches were, however, found most useful not only for the shelter of the garrisons of the trenches, but for use as advanced dressing stations, company and Battalion Headquarters, and signallers' dugouts, and for R.E. and ammunition dumps. (Brigadier General Trevor Ternan, commanding 102nd Infantry Brigade).[17]

The Somme saw a major expansion of the use of such underground accommodation behind the front line to support attacks. For the assault on La Boisselle a significant portion of the Tyneside Irish Brigade was housed in a series of around forty-five dugouts in the reverse slopes of the Tara and Usna hills 1000yds (900m) behind the British front line either side of the Albert–Bapaume road. These were at about 20ft depth and linked by underground passages, although the labour available from miners in the Tyneside units made them the exception rather than the rule.[18]

Following the Somme, the British used extensive dugouts for both headquarters and troop accommodation for the 1917 offensives at Vimy, Arras, Messines and Ypres.

As the work of offensive mining declined, many tunnelling companies became wholly employed on this work in the run up to attacks. For the Messines operation they built twenty-four shell-proof battle headquarters for brigade staffs and twenty-eight battalion headquarters and dugout shelters for 200 officers and 10,000 men. For the Third Battle of Ypres the tunnellers constructed twenty-three brigade headquarters, sixty-two battalion headquarters, seven artillery, seven dressing stations, twenty-three observation posts and fourteen tunnelled dugout systems incorporating troop accommodation.[19] Such a system beneath the ruins of the village of Wieltje, which housed the headquarters of the 107th Brigade in August 1917, was recalled by a staff officer, Captain Cyril Falls:

> Wieltje dug-outs! Who that saw it will forget that abominable mine, with its 'town major,' its thirteen entrances, the water that flowed down its main passages and poured down its walls, its electric light gleaming dully through

steam-coated lamps, its sickly atmosphere, its smells, its huge population of men – and of rats? From behind sack-curtained doorways the coughing and groaning of men in uneasy slumber mingled with the click of typewriters. In the corridor one would fall over a runner, slimy from head to foot with mud, resting while he waited for a return message to the front line. One advantage only it had: it was safe within.[20]

Communication tunnels were used immediately behind the front line to provide safe passage and many were dug in the Ypres Salient by both sides, although the wet sand made the construction of shallow inclined entrances difficult: in most places they were almost vertical. For the Messines operation these were constructed in four places to a total of 15,000ft length.[21] Where the geology was more favourable in the chalk areas they were used even more extensively and the attack on Vimy Ridge on 9 April 1917 benefited more from such tunnels than from mines. The letter sent on 5 December by GHQ to Army commanders concerning the use of communication tunnels for the final attacks on the Somme was received as 1st and 3rd Armies were preparing for the Arras and Vimy Ridge attacks. Such tunnels were to be a major feature of the battles, but in many ways were quite different from the Russian saps used on the Somme. They were termed 'subways' and were not intended to extend far across no man's land. Rather they were used to enable the infantry to get to their assembly trenches safely and secretly from the support trenches or from farther back. In particular the exposed Zouave Valley west of Vimy Ridge was identified as a vulnerable area as the Germans laid a barrage into the valley at the first suggestion of an attack. Six of the subways were tunnelled into the eastern slope of the valley, from 300 to 1,537yds. Mulqueen's Company was responsible for four which, he recalled, were commenced before the arrival of the Canadians at Vimy Ridge. Blue Bull, Vincent, Cavalier and Tottenham Road were:

> ...named after the nearby communication trenches and a great deal of planning with the Division and Brigades preceded their construction. The 9th (Scottish) Division was in the line when Tottenham Road was started and it is probable that its location was fixed with an eye to its use if and when an attack were launched against the Ridge. Certainly before this and the other three tunnels were completed, their importance in the proposed attack became paramount.

Two of the longest were dug by Mulqueen's former Company, 172, on what was to become the 3rd Canadian Division front: the Goodman was 1,883yds and the Grange 1,343yds (of which part is open to the public in the Vimy Memorial Park). Twelve subways in all were used for the Canadian Corps attack, measuring in total six miles. They were constructed 6ft 6in in height and were wide enough for two laden men to pass. Most had electric lighting and some were equipped with tramways used especially for bringing forward ammunition for connected heavy mortar positions. The subways were also used to provide accommodation for battalion and brigade headquarters, cookhouses and latrines. They had their own water supply, piped from two large underground reservoirs each holding 50,000 gallons, and electrical power from generators. They also provided a secure conduit for signals cables and housed signals stations. The dressing stations in the subways were 34ft by 9ft and were dry and well-lit.

Very careful attention was paid to traffic control in the light of the experiences on the Somme when the tunnels were so congested by wounded as to be unusable. The 4th Division scheme allocated military police to each subway with an officer at the eastern end and a sergeant at the western end and a telephone to keep them in communication. A plan of the subways was placed at each entrance and mid-way along, with direction boards at each junction. At the western entrance a large signboard guided troops coming across the Zouave Valley to the subway so that they could go directly to it. The officer had complete control over the tunnel traffic from nine hours before the attack. A system of traffic lights was used: when the assaulting troops were moving forward to the assembly positions only up traffic was permitted, the only exceptions being individual officers, medical personnel and runners. A red light at the tunnel entrance indicated that it was to be used for up traffic only and military police at each entrance enforced this. Thus the tunnel would be kept clear for the successive waves of the attack troops to get forward rapidly. Through one subway alone it was estimated that the traffic amounted to 9,700 men between 5 and 11 April.[22]

The ends of some of the subways were used to create bored trenches using the Wombat borer. In five of the subways blown trenches were prepared using the borer, 6in diameter bores of about 200ft charged with ammonal cartridges. Three of these were actually blown at thirty seconds after zero, the longest being 195ft long and 14ft deep at the Chassery craters, where the 2nd Canadian Mounted Rifles assaulted, although it is unlikely that these blown trenches were used owing to the rapid success of the attack. The troops did not depart directly to attack from the subways, but the first waves used them to reach the assembly trenches about two hours before zero. The succeeding waves then used them where necessary. The capture of the ridge was a dramatic success for the Canadian Corps and the British Tunnelling Companies. An officer of 185 Company, whose unit had dug the Douai, Bentata and Zivy subways, wrote home enthusiastically to his father four days after the attack:

Our work had been intimately connected with the early stages of the advance, and it is satisfactory to know from G.H.Q. that its purpose (the subways) was successful. We were attached to the Canadians and all the officers with whom we came in contact were enthusiastic about the results, and undoubtedly we were responsible for saving innumerable casualties in the initial stages and I dare say more will be heard of it later on.

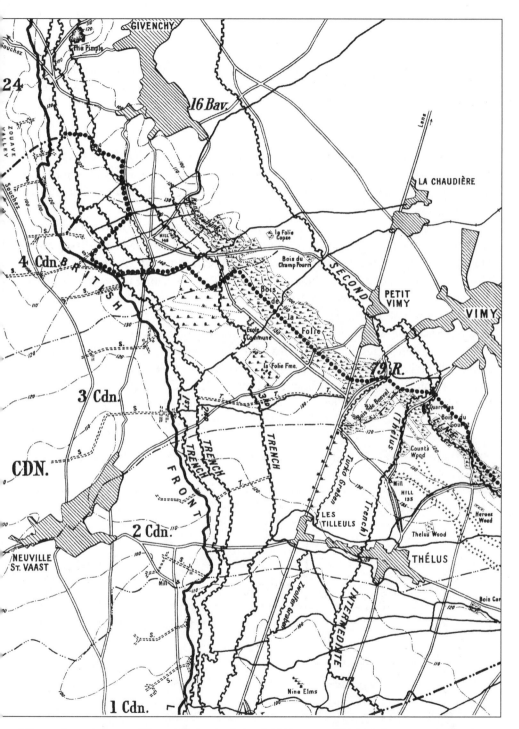

The twelve subways at Vimy dug for the 9 April 1917 attack. British subways are marked 'S', the German Schwaben and Volker tunnels marked 'T'. From *Military Operations, France and Belgium, 1917*, Vol. 1.

However, he later revised his view:

> It transpired a few months afterwards that except in a few cases the uses to which these subways were put were somewhat exaggerated, whilst the monetary cost was high. It is also noteworthy that the tunnels were not made for battle purposes of this kind again.[23]

Like the Russian saps on the Somme, the subways were little used where the attack successfully secured the front line and where German mortar and artillery fire was prevented from interfering with the troops coming forward for the next phase of the attack.

The tunnelling work planned for the Battle of Arras east of the town resembled more that of the later stages of the Somme offensive, with Russian saps driven across no man's land with machine-gun positions or bored mines at the ends. The major difference was the opportunity to incorporate extensive existing underground spaces discovered in Arras and immediately behind the British lines and link these with the Russian saps. The British initially explored the Arras sewers. The sewers at Ypres had been used by the RE Signal Service as a protected means of running telephone cable where they were too small to admit a full-grown man, and a small Belgian boy was paid to take the line through. These sewers, however, were later destroyed by the German bombardment with 430mm howitzers.[24] The Crinchon sewer in Arras by contrast was 'a beautifully bricked tunnel' 8ft high and 6ft wide, with footpaths on

Sketches of details of the Vimy the subways. From the War Diary of the Canadian Corps Chief Engineer.

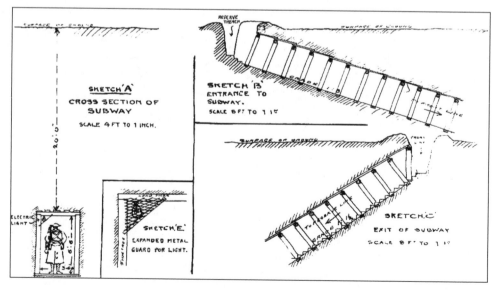

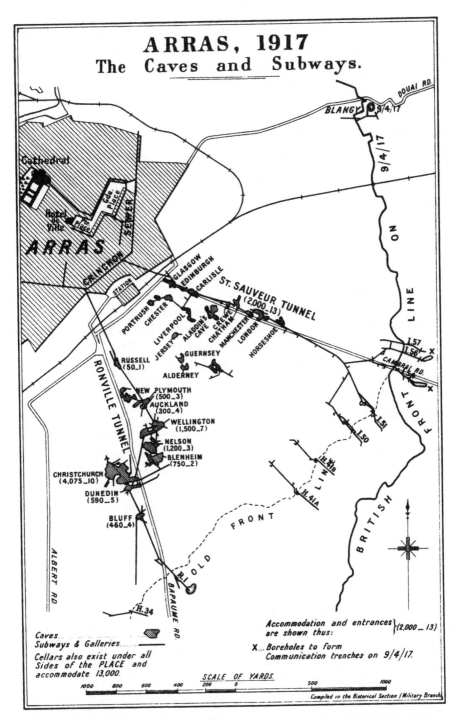

ARRAS, 1917
The Caves and Subways.

Caves and subways prepared for the Battle of Arras, April 1917. The British line before the German withdrawal is shown dotted and indicates the six subways extending into no man's land, which were rendered redundant before the British attack. From Falls, *Military Operations, France and Belgium, 1917*, Vol. 1.

either side of the water course.[25] It ran along the course of the old fortifications like a ring road on the eastern side of the old town and the British drove several inclined entrances from the cellars in the Grande Place and other locations in the town to this sewer. Arras was built on hard chalk, and many of the seventeenth-century houses were provided with deep cellars, which were found useful for accommodating troops. Some 13,000 British troops were housed. In addition, in October 1916, the British discovered the first of a series of large disused underground chalk quarries on the eastern and south-eastern outskirts. The New Zealand Tunnelling Company was withdrawn from front line mining to exploit these for a future attack:

> These cellars and underground quarries formed the basis of the scheme on which the company now embarked. They were to be connected, opened up, and made habitable for troops, so that when the day for attack came the men could issue from them safe, warm and dry, and utterly unsuspected by the enemy. Two series of these caves and underground quarries were discovered stretching towards the enemy lines, one under the suburb of Ronville and one under St. Saveur and the Arras-Cambrai Road.
>
> The Ronville caves were by far the larger, some of them immense caverns hundreds of feet in diameter and twenty to forty feet high. Pillars of chalk had been left at regular intervals to support the roof, but in the centuries that had elapsed since their abandonment, falls had gradually formed them into inverted cones springing away to the domed roof between, so high that it was barely discernable in the candle light.
>
> To make these caverns safe and habitable was no easy matter, for as soon as they were opened to the cold wet winter air the chalk commenced to swell and crack, and slabs weighing many tons would come crashing down without an instant's warning. To timber up to the heights of these roofs was out of the question, so instead the floor was raised by dumping therein the chalk cut from the galleries and dugouts until the roof was close enough for clear observation and support. (Lieutenant J.C. Neill, New Zealand Tunnelling Company)[26]

These caves were to accommodate 11,500 troops and the largest, Christchurch, held 4,000. The caves were provided with water and electricity and protected by gas-proof doors. They carried telephone cables, exchanges and line testing-points. A tramline ran from the sewer to the St Saveur caves. Just over half a mile from the front line a cave was equipped as a main dressing station, as it was anticipated by VI Corps that the congestion in Arras during the attack would prevent the evacuation of wounded for treatment, so advanced dressing stations were equipped and manned to perform the functions of a main dressing station. These were established in caves, cellars and the basements of buildings. The chief was close to the 3rd Division trenches, two sloped entrances allowed stretchers to be carried direct from the communication trenches, while an approach at the back allowed motor ambulances to collect casualties. Named Thompson's Cave after the Corps Director of Medical Services, it was able to accommodate 700 casualties on stretchers fitted in two tiers. It also contained dressing and operating rooms, kitchens and latrines. The accommodation close behind the front line enabled it to act as a corps dressing station for severely wounded requiring urgent attention. The cave was used for the first two days of the offensive until a large shell exploding on the top of the cave burst a water main, which caused the roof to collapse in two places.[27]

The New Zealanders also constructed two long tunnels towards the front line, one linking the St Saveur cave system and the other the Ronville caves so that men

PLAN OF "THOMPSON'S CAVE".
BATTLE OF ARRAS, APRIL 1917.

Entrance from Iceland St.

RUE DU TEMPLE

A
B
D
C
D
E
F
G
E
E
G
H
J
K
L
N

Entrance from Hunter St.

WAITING WARD FOR ICELAND
DRESSING ROOM CASES.
RESERVE STRETCHERS.
ICELAND DRESSING ROOM.
HUNTER WAITING WARD.
MEDICAL & QUARTER MASTERS STRS
R.A.M.C. OFFICERS QUARTERS
QUARTERS FOR R.A.M.C. PERSONNEL
HUNTER DRESSING ROOM.
OPERATING THEATRE (SURGICAL SPECIALIST.)
COOKHOUSE.
QUARTERS FOR RESERVE OR RESTING BEARERS.
MORTUARY.
OFFICERS WARD.

DYNAMO & WATER STAND PIPE.
EXIT LOBBY.
DEEP TRENCH LATRINES.

PASSAGES AND SPACES UNMARKED WERE USED AS WARDS.

0 10   50   100
SCALE OF FEET.

Well fitted Cottage pump.

O.

P

RUE ST QUENTIN.

Exit to Rue St Quentin

Sweep for cars.

Plan of the main dressing station established in Thompson's Cave for the Battle of Arras in April 1917. Thompson's cave is shown in the illustration on p229 just below Guernsey. From *Medical Services General History*, Vol. 3.

could if necessary get all the way to the front line through the caves and tunnels and avoid especially the heavily shelled area of the railway station. The St Saveur tunnel ended in five exits from Russian saps in no man's land and the Ronville with one, although others were probably under preparation. About seven miles of tunnels and subways were constructed in just over four months.[28]

> Along the brightly lighted gallery a constant stream of traffic went safely from the heart of Arras to the front line – ammunition, rations and engineers' supplies were no longer carried painfully by fatigue parties along the wet and much strafed communication trenches, but went easily forward on trucks dry and safe.[29]

By January 1917 the Russian saps were being driven across no man's land but, as at the Somme, progress was hampered by the saps being blown in. However, the most frequent cause was British shell fire, and on occasion trench mortar 'toffee apple' bombs when cutting the British wire fell short, trapping parties of tunnellers at the ends of collapsed tunnels. On one occasion a 50ft tunnel that had to be driven to rescue them was dug in a record time of nine hours. The saps were cut quietly through clay using push-picks and to avoid alerting the Germans the men wrapped their boots in sacking and speaking above a whisper was forbidden. When one of the saps holed into a German gallery it was carefully closed and charged with 2,200lbs of ammonal (this appears to have been the only mine blown on the Arras front on 9 April).[30]

As this work was progressing, however, the Germans made a dramatic move which seriously dislocated the tunnellers' preparations for the Arras offensive. In February they withdrew from the Somme battlefield up to 30 miles to the prepared positions of the Hindenburg line. These positions were described by a British staff officer as:

> …two great lines, from five hundred to two thousand yards apart, each consisting of front and support trenches. The system constituted in all probability the most formidable fortification constructed in the course of the war. The Germans had sited and dug it at their ease, to a great extent with gangs of Russian prisoners and forced civilian labour. The trenches were wide, deep, and well revetted. The mined dug-outs were all designed to a pattern; the stairways, supports, and all timber used in them having been turned out by the sawmills in replica by the thousand pieces. They represented the first successful application of mass production to the construction of dug-outs.[31]

These new positions were to provide formidable obstacles for the Allies to assault in 1917 and 1918. Between 17 and 28 March the Germans withdrew additionally from the line south-east of Arras up to a point just south of the Cambrai road. The immediate consequence at Arras was that, after the British had moved forward to locate the new German line, the end of the Ronville tunnel was left 1,000yds behind the new British front line. Of nine Russian saps extended beyond the British front line only three, from the St Saveur tunnel either side of the Cambrai Road, were still actually in no man's land. There was no time to lengthen the remainder and so on the day of the attack only some units of the 12th Division were able to pass underground all the way to their own front line or beyond. By the time of the attack the description in a War Diary was applicable only to that Division: 'Now it is possible to get from the crypt of the Cathedral to under the German wire without braving one shell in the open.'[32]

Equally, it was only the 12th Division that was to derive potential benefit from the three remaining Russian saps. Wombat bores were driven from two (I.54 and I.56) to form communication trenches linking them with the front line. From the other machine-gun emplacements were prepared which were to be broken out immediately before zero on 9 April. The bores were blown at zero, 5.30am, and soon afterwards were connected with the old German front line. Neill was stationed in the northernmost of the three saps (I.57), which was about 25yds from the German front line trench and from which machine guns were supposed to fire from forward emplacements to sweep the German parapet. Before zero, however, the plan went badly wrong:

Our orders were to remove this cover just before Zero and to open the end of the gallery itself into No-man's land, continuing it as an open trench into the German front line, immediately the battle opened.

At 10 p.m. a concentrated bombardment with gas shells fired from trench mortars was opened on the enemy positions, continuing for more than an hour. Many of these shells fell short and landed about our gallery, through the much broken roof of which the gas percolated, filling the gallery.

A gas curtain was hastily rigged just behind the first opening – an incline up to the front trench – and efforts were made by a fire to draw the gas from the gallery, but in vain.

There was nothing for it but to go forward and open up the end so that a natural current of air would clear the gas out. These forward galleries were not electrically lit so it meant groping by dim candle light, through a hundred and fifty yards of narrow winding gallery with eyes streaming and smarting from the tear gas that got in under the box respirators. Arrived at the end desperate efforts were made to remove the cover to the open air, but to work effectively in a box respirator, almost blinded and after coming through the ordeal of the gallery, was a physical impossibility and constant relays of fresh men were necessary before at last the work was done and it was possible to tear off the suffocating gas masks and breathe the clear night air.

A machine-gun section was waiting back behind the gas curtain to man the forward positions but not being miners they could not be induced to face the still gas filled gallery and so arrived at their battle positions too late, though so successful was the attack that their guns were not required. A wonderful battle picture was the reward of the solitary watcher who remained on guard at one of these openings.

As the watch hands crept towards the fateful half-past five the first faint streaks of the wintery dawn began to colour the sky so that the dim outlines of the German parapet close at hand and the shattered stakes and wires of his entanglements all round could be faintly seen.

An ominous stillness had fallen along the whole battle line, almost terrifying after the infernal racket of the last few days.

Suddenly three tremendous reports in quick succession – the company's mines – a pause of a fraction of a second and then the enemy parapet disappeared in a spouting wall of flame, the opening barrage.

The watcher turned back to look towards our own lines and saw wave after wave of dim figures advancing steadily at a leisurely walk – Jocks and Tommies – as steady and unconcerned as at a field day at the base.

They waved and shouted cheerily to the Tunnellers as they passed and some of the wounded were glad to be helped to the shelter of the gallery.

All was hustle therein now and it was not long before our part was finished and the complete communication made to the German trench. (J. C. Neil, New Zealand Tunnelling Company)[33]

The failure of the advanced machine-gun position did not result in the failure of the attack along the Cambrai road. The Russian saps were quickly connected to the captured German front line, but because of the success of the attack were not needed. As at Vimy, the attackers at Arras made dramatic advances during the first few days of the battle and the whole of the German front line was quickly taken, despite the loss of the benefits of the Russian saps. The initial success, however, at Vimy and Arras did not last and the bitter frustration felt by the tunnellers was expressed by Neil:

...to those on the spot the high hopes based on the tremendous success of the first day were quickly dashed to earth when it was realized that no fresh troops were available to relieve and carry on the work so splendidly commenced by the few divisions which made the attack.[34]

Graham of 185 Company recalled that the offensive marked the end of mining on the Arras–Vimy front, but was not a decisive victory and brought instead a change of the role of the tunnellers to dugout construction:

> We were bitterly disappointed that all the huge preparations had come to this, as we were dead sick of trenches and the smell of dug-outs. True, we had got all the high ground and a vastly superior position for observation, but we had had high hopes that the offensive would bring in its wake some open fighting and perhaps the beginning of the end... We did not anticipate another phase of mining as the lines settled down at an almost prohibitive distance apart and I think we were all content to help the infantry and gunners by making them comfortable dug-out accommodation. As a unit we grew less important from a front line point of view, although our efficiency was always felt. At mining we were omnipotent and our own masters; at dug-outs we were 'nobody's children'. Still, mining was a dirty game in more senses than one.[35]

During the Vimy-Arras offensive German defensive tactics were undergoing a radical change, which had begun on the Somme following the appointment of von Hindenburg. The German policy of strong defence of the front line, and immediate counterattack to regain it if lost, had caused losses during the Somme almost as high as the British attackers, even though they should have held an advantage. General Ludendorff revised German defensive policy to replace the rigid defence of the front line at all costs with a more intelligent and flexible system. The increased Allied use of heavy artillery, and in particular as the attackers learned to coordinate artillery with the infantry, caused the deep dugouts to become a liability. During the Somme fighting from July to November 1916, the Germans took to abandoning their prepared defences, targeted by a devastating weight of artillery, and crawled into shell holes in no man's land. Instructions issued in November and December emphasized weaker garrisons on the front line, which could change position to avoid bombardment. This was developed into a system of elastic, in-depth defence, in which lightly-held outposts would screen main defences and force the attackers to advance beyond the support of their field artillery and fall victim to counterattack troops.[36]

The German command was becoming conscious of the danger that deep dugouts were beginning to present, but it was not until after the Allied offensives of April and May 1917 that the Germans prohibited them in the front line. For their attacks in April, May and June 1917 the French and British used very heavy bombardments to attempt to destroy underground defensive positions, and also coordinated the forward movement of a creeping artillery barrage with their infantry advance. Communication and accommodation tunnels repeatedly proved disastrous for the Germans when used defensively in 1917. The new German tactics were not thoroughly applied by army commanders and usually the Allies were able to achieve success on the first day of operations before inertia gripped the advance. On Vimy Ridge a programme of replacing deep dugouts with concrete bunkers had been delayed by winter weather and shortage of labour. The Canadian attackers were aware of the extensive German dugouts, especially on the rear slope protecting the reserve companies, which had to be reached before the barrage moved off to prevent the Germans counterattacking. Machine-gun barrage fire in particular was used to keep the Germans trapped in these dugouts and two communication tunnels until the infantry reached them. The Schwaben tunnel on Vimy Ridge ran about 1,350m from the German second trench almost to the second line. The Volker tunnel ran about 520m, linking the German first, second and third line trenches. The Canadians learnt of these several months before the attack and specially targeted them on 9 April 1917 by assaulting infantry as well as parties of tunnellers with demolition charges. The officer leading the tunnellers was shot rushing the Schwaben tunnel, but the forward part was quickly taken and the 2nd Canadian Mounted Rifles captured over 150 Germans, many of whom were still half-dressed. German communication along this tunnel broke down on the morning of the attack. The Germans were captured at the forward end at 6am, but no news reached the battalion headquarters near Bois de Bonval until an hour later when a wounded man who happened to pass the entrance informed them that the English (i.e. the Canadians) were in the battalion position and already held the third trench.[37]

The best-known of the German communication tunnels were on the west bank of

Bavarian miners of the 4th Field Pioneer Company at work on a communication tunnel, sketched by Pioneer Götz. From Lehmann, *Bayerische Pioniere im Weltkriege*.

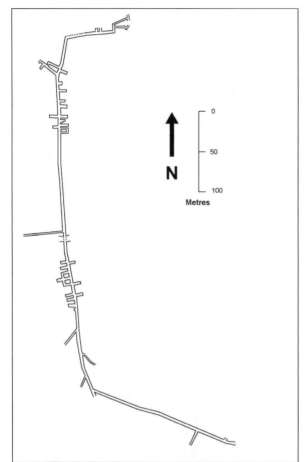

The 740m German Gallwitz communication tunnel on the Mort Homme. Based on *Topographische Strukturfragmente auf der Höhe Mort Homme.*

the Meuse, where they lacked cover or concrete shelters on the exposed slopes of Hill 265 and Hill 295 (Mort Homme). Towards the end of 1916 they began the excavation of the Gallwitz, Kronprinz and Runkel (or Bismarck) tunnels, which were opened at the beginning of May 1917. The 3rd Company of the 7th Westphalian Pioneers was assigned to work on the Runkel tunnel at three points on 4 April using large timber frames 120 x 180cm and in the hard rock only three or four were required for support each day. The tunnel ran just under 1km from Hill 265 south-east to Hill 295, allowing access and also accommodating reserves.[38] No sooner were these tunnels in use than there occurred an event in the Champagne sector which demonstrated the danger of German over-reliance on tunnels and the failure to adopt the system of defence in depth. Mont Cornillet, a 207m high German-held hill, was a powerful artillery observation post which dominated the surrounding area and formed one of the bastions of the R1 Stellung. French attempts to capture Mont Cornillet during the Third Battle of Champagne failed on 17 April and 4 May 1917 and the French learned from a prisoner that the Germans were using a system of tunnels with three exits on the German side of the hill to protect a large number of reserves, who were able to carry out strong counterattacks.

The tunnels, apparently originally chalk quarries, consisted of three timbered galleries, about 3m wide and 2.3m high, between 120m and 143m in length and joined by a single transverse corridor of 154m. The tunnels ran into the side of the hill with up to 18m of cover, but a series of shafts provided light and ventilation. The maximum capacity was three battalions, one in each gallery, which included battalion headquarters, field kitchens, an aid post and ten days supply of water, food and ammunition. Resupply took place at night by carrying parties. The German front line was on the forward slope of the hill and on the rear slope between the summit and the tunnel entrances there was a line of shelters. The Germans were resolved to hold the hill and placed almost all their manpower within 500m of the front line. Thus two battalions of the 173rd Regiment (223 Division) were deployed in the tunnel or the shelters with the third battalion in reserve.[39]

The scene of the disaster of Mont Cornillet showing the situation on the morning of 20 May 1917, with collapses caused by French direct hits and the spread of carbon monoxide. In the three galleries driven beneath the hill the remains of 321 German soldiers were found sixty years later. From Knies, *Das Württembergische Pionier=Bataillon Nr. 13.*

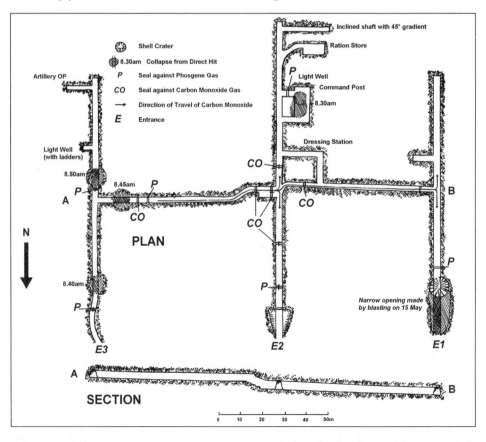

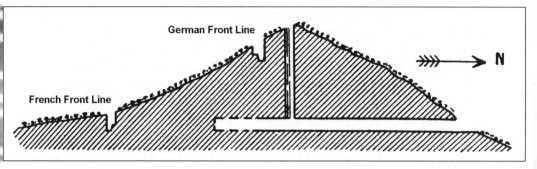

Diagram of the Cornillet tunnel, showing the entrances on the German side and the ventilation shaft opening just behind the German front line, which was on the forward slope of the south side of the hill. The French front line was on the lower slopes. From Seesselberg, *Der Stellungskrieg*.

When the French attacked the position on 17 April they managed to destroy the German surface positions facing them on the southern slope of the Cornillet, but those hidden on the northern slope were still intact. The French did not manage to take the summit and only got into the southern part of the circular trench around the hill. The tunnel entrances were damaged, but were repaired, and the Germans were able to launch effective counterattacks from the tunnel and the smaller Voss and Bremen shelters nearby. When the French attempted another attack on 4 May the two German battalions could again leave the tunnel and immediately counterattack. The French struggled to reach the summit of the Cornillet and failed to destroy the tunnel or its entrances. On 17 May the 173rd Regiment was relieved by the 476th (242 Division). By this time there was no surface trench system left, just connected shell holes which were occupied during the day by small groups while the rest remained in the tunnel. The French positions were only 25-100m away. The tunnel seemed to hold a mythical strength to the French, expressed in a report:

> Our positions lie threateningly opposite the Cornillet hill, on which the Germans have built a well-known and dreaded position... The hill resembles a huge dragon stretched lazily out but ready at any time to be roused with a terrible anger, hurl fire, death and ruin on those who dare to come too close. The deep position appears unapproachable, impenetrable; protected and covered by the huge seams of chalk, one above the other, which form the hill. Inside life flows through three wide spacious main arteries with many galleries and entrances. By means of cleverly placed air shafts, fresh air gets into this underground world. And so it lay before us on 17th May; our commanders knew its strength, they were aware how dangerous and deadly these positions were for our attacking troops. The monster had to be slain at all costs.[40]

The French bombardments had deforested the slopes, leaving the ground a white desert of chalk. They now rendered the shelters on the north slope, between the summit and the tunnel entrances, uninhabitable and identified the tunnel entrances from aerial photographs. The 476th Regiment was concerned that the tunnel was vulnerable to poison gas and altered the deployment so that the first and second battalions, minus a company, sheltered in the tunnel. The five remaining companies were in reserve in shelters. The tunnel housed the commanders of the 1st and 2nd Battalions, of which Major Wintterlin was senior, with headquarters, six companies of infantry (60 to 100 men in each), elements of two machine-gun companies, two platoons of regimental pioneers (80 men) and two platoons of the 376th Pioneer Company (80 men), plus artillery officers and medical personnel. On 17th the Germans repulsed some strong probing attacks. The French then turned an increasingly powerful fire on the tunnel and entrances, and the garrison expected an attack at any moment. Collapses and blockages to the ventilation shafts were cleared by the Pioneers on 17 and 18 May, but inside the tunnels were so airless that candles and cigarettes burned with a dim light. At daybreak on 18th the French bombardment reached its peak, with heavy calibre guns guided by low-flying aircraft with such accuracy that the central and eastern entrances were partly buried. After several hours work the pioneers managed to clear them and also used explosives to blow open the third entrance. The night of the 18–19 May was an ordeal with many casualties. As morning approached the French fire seemed to die down, but in the afternoon increased again to the strength of the day before. The German artillery was, however, still able to repulse the French infantry and they now prepared for an attack by using a much heavier destructive fire. To prevent repair to the damage they targeted the entrances with a large number of gas shells from midnight until 4.30am, which filled the tunnels with phosgene. The German gas masks proved adequate, however, and they managed to clear the tunnels of gas using ventilation units. The Pioneers erected partitions to try to keep the phosgene from penetrating into the whole system. That night the French barrage reached:

> …an extraordinary ferocity. Heaviest calibre weapons, gas shells and incendiary attacks raged on the hill and rear positions, until with the coming of the morning a slight drop was noticed. But the calm of this beautiful Sunday morning was short and deceptive.[41]

On 20 May morale remained good in the tunnels: 'with real comradeship officers and men together shared the dangers of the fighting.' Early in the morning the French fire died down and most men were asleep in the tunnel. They had managed to maintain communication with the hill and regimental headquarters by runners and messenger dogs even under the most severe fire. After two hours lull, at about 7.30am heavy French fire began again and included 400mm shells, again directed extremely accurately by aircraft. One of the dogs was wounded and the other, arriving at the tunnel entrance with its report, searched confusedly for its handler, who had been buried under rubble. At 8am, Major Wintterlin sent word back that his food supply was still adequate but he urgently requested German aircraft to drive away the French spotter aeroplanes. The French appear to have been attempting to pitch heavy shells down the ventilation shafts.

What occurred in the tunnel during 20 May can be partially pieced together from the accounts of those who managed to escape and a description of the aftermath by two French doctors. The entrances became blocked and the exploding shells produced carbon monoxide, against which the gas masks gave no protection. The Pioneers tried to seal parts of the tunnels to prevent the spread of the carbon monoxide, but 'the gas crept through the seals and into all of the tunnels and had its sinister effect',[42] and parts of the tunnel fell silent as men succumbed and collapsed. At about 8.30am a shell came down a shaft near to the command post occupied by Wintterlin and the commander of the other battalion, Captain Count von Rambaldi, collapsing part of the tunnel. Wintterlin managed to escape but Rambaldi was buried beneath debris and desperate efforts began to free him. Wintterlin gathered his officers to discuss the situation near to one of the entrances when, about ten minutes afterwards, a second shell collapsed the tunnel at this point, killing and burying all fifteen officers. According to the chief medical officer, Dr Nagel, almost the whole destruction of the gallery occurred in a few minutes. The eastern tunnel, where the 1st Battalion was housed, was completely lost when both the entrance and the linking corridor collapsed:

> Those who were in the gallery succumbed in a few seconds to the carbon monoxide that the bursting shells at this point spread with great force. They underwent a gentle death, without pain, without suspecting that their sleep was to be for an eternity. Only one man, who was close to the ventilation shaft, was able to escape to the surface; when he shouted back down below there already reigned a deathly quiet and no reply came.[43]

In the western tunnel the entrance was not destroyed but the situation was little better. Nagel found everyone rendered unconscious by carbon monoxide. His assistant medical officer Köbel found his way to the aid post but collapsed in Nagel's arms. Another officer, Lieutenant Dauer, was seized with a terrible delirium. The large central gallery had remained intact and they moved into this area and erected screens to try to prevent the carbon monoxide from spreading. Those gassed who still showed signs of life were carried to the aid post and given oxygen. The hardest work was the attempt to rescue Captain Rambaldi, whose legs were trapped under a mass of chalk. After six hours of work he was freed and Nagel was astonished and relieved to see that his legs were not broken. Despite the efforts to isolate it, the carbon monoxide spread into the central gallery and by 2pm all the sleeping men had succumbed. Nagel had fifty oxygen breathing sets but they were inadequate for the men still in the tunnel:

> It was not a cheerful scene in the aid post, oxygen ran short, the gas victims suffered a great deal, groaned, coughed, were contorted in all directions, crawled on all fours to beg to be given oxygen to relieve them, it was terrible to be able to help only by administering morphine. Slowly a heavy tiredness started to invade me and I sought a corner to sleep. I could not lie on top of my dead comrades, not that, my conscience would not allow me. And so the comings and goings and the horror kept me awake and this saved me; those who fell asleep were lost.[44]

At around 3pm Captain Süss, the senior surviving officer, sent back a report that the carbon monoxide was worsening and again requested cover against the spotter aircraft. An officer trying to reach the tunnel from regimental headquarters was wounded en route. By 4pm Captain Süss and Reserve-Lieutenant Killguss of the Pioneers were convinced that further occupation of the tunnels was futile and ordered their evacuation. Those infantry able to move were ordered into the shell holes and a trench running northwest from Cornillet. Only those engaged in rescue were to stay. The French gun fire on the entrances was so heavy that it prevented most from leaving. Nagel attempted to evacuate Rambaldi, but he declined to be carried through the bombardment and, despite urgings, he asked to be left in the tunnel. Nagel and the surviving medical personnel left the tunnel.

The French launched their attack at 4.25pm and by 5.30pm had overrun almost all of the Cornillet position above ground, encountering some German resistance only in a small area west of Cornillet. The few Germans above ground in shell holes to the south of the summit were shattered by the violence and duration of the bombardment. They saw the attack launched and released yellow rockets to warn the observation posts and the tunnel garrison. However, the Germans were not able to launch a counterattack from the tunnel as before. An officer who was taken prisoner was astonished to see no one leaving the tunnel and shouted in vain down the ventilation shafts. He found the entrances either collapsed or blocked with bodies, with no signs of life from the garrison. At about 5pm Süss reported by messenger dog that all three entrances were blocked and his situation was critical. An order from regimental headquarters to evacuate the tunnel and word that a company was on its way never reached him, '...nothing more was heard or seen from Captain Süss and the rest of the men.'[45] The French attackers swept over the tunnels, arriving at the entrances almost at the same time as the last shells of their barrage. They did not attempt to enter but threw in grenades and incendiary bombs and waited while the poison gas continued to take effect. During the night some of the garrison were able to escape via an airshaft and were immediately taken prisoner.

Eventually two French doctors managed to enter the tunnels through the remains of one entrance, but inside they found no signs of life. After 30m they came across a heap of bodies, tangled one on top of the other. A little further on was a recess with a signal station, next to which were four bodies face down on the ground. Another was seated on a stool wearing a gas mask and still holding the telephone receiver in his hand. Some way on, where the main and transverse galleries crossed, the path was completely blocked by the fallen roof. The shell which came down the shaft and smashed the command post had sent carbon monoxide into the deepest corners of the tunnels. The corpses that they found in this passage had badly swollen faces with ruptured blood vessels from the explosion. From their appearance they did not appear to have suffered. The exit from the central gallery was completely blocked by a heap of bodies where men had tried to escape the tunnel and been torn apart at the entrance by French shells. There were perhaps one hundred men at this point, almost all young, lying in about five layers, wearing gas masks, some with fixed bayonets and carrying bags of grenades and filled water bottles. Others were still standing where they had suffocated. They noticed an officer lying on a stretcher, his legs in a plaster cast. A little further on were two machine guns, on one of which lay a German soldier, stretched out, his arms hanging lifeless. Ammunition and empty cartridge cases were scattered on the floor. In the tunnel commander's dugout Wintterlin's jacket, bearing his Iron Cross First Class, still hung on a hook. Large stocks of water, food and ammunition remained in the storage chambers. In the Aid Post wounded lay on the ground on mattresses and stretchers and alongside them the asphyxiated medical orderlies. Around a shaft and a large hand-operated ventilator a number of men were gathered who had tried to get fresh air but had succumbed to phosgene gas from the shelling around the shaft. At this point the French had to turn back because the air was still bad:

> One has to exit the tunnel as one entered, by climbing over the mountain of corpses, which reaches to the ceiling. Over the lifeless bodies, one comes out in the open at last, in the bright sunlight.[46]

Some attempts to recover the bodies were made in 1933, but work was stopped by the danger of poison gas and the international situation. In 1973 workmen penetrated 12m into a tunnel and discovered human remains and during 1974–75 German Pioneers with French Army assistance recovered the bones of 321 soldiers.[47] The German tragedy of the Cornillet tunnel demonstrated again the danger of reliance on underground defences once the attacker had developed tactics to deal with them and almost no soldier in the two battalions participated in the battle. The French demonstrated the ability to overcome such positions using highly accurate bombardment with gas and extremely heavy artillery and a very precisely timed barrage. The French captured the German Mort Homme tunnels on 20 August 1917 without their having been fully completed and again they formed a trap for the defenders. The French Moroccan Division took the ground above the Kronprinz Tunnel and guarded the entrances. The following day the garrison surrendered, comprising, it seems, 1,100 men, including a colonel and three battalion commanders.[48]

The Cornillet disaster confirmed the need for the radical change in defensive tactics that the German Command was attempting to impose on commanders. After the British breakthrough at Arras, Ludendorff appointed Colonel von Lossberg as Chief of Staff to the German 6th Army to enforce the new methods, which contributed to the slowing of the British Arras offensive. The Cornillet Tunnel, however, was just one example of the vulnerability of tunnels and deep dugouts to these tactics.

In June 1917 the General Staff issued a series of instructions based on the experience of the Allied spring offensives to emphasize again the new principles, which were not universally observed and which did not appear to be fully understood. Those issued on 10 June, based on the spring offensives rather than Messines, were emphatic about the danger of deep dugouts:

> Deep-mined dugouts in the front line and large tunnels have again proved to be mantraps. Any deep dugouts which may still exist in the foremost line should therefore be destroyed (at the beginning of the battle, at the latest), and large tunnels should be reduced in size by blowing up portions of them.[49]

At the end of June instructions 'The Construction of Defensive Positions' were issued by German headquarters which were informed by the Messines battle.[50] Again commanders were not fully following the new doctrine: instructions were more explicit and prescriptive. Dugouts in the old trenches, especially the first and also the second lines, had proved to be mantraps and strict limits were placed on the numbers of men accommodated in the forward zone. As the destructive fire of the enemy increased the mass of the infantry were to be moved from the forward trenches and dugouts and distributed in depth in the open before the enemy infantry attacked. During the battle continuous, linear trenches were no longer insisted on. Instead a pattern of shell holes was to be the basis of the defences, which would not be easily identifiable as defended positions and would be held by groups and single machine guns. The shell holes were to be linked by tunnels lined with mining frames and the spoil concealed by being thrown into nearby holes or scattered over the ground. The first line was to contain small dugouts for only one-sixth of the garrison. These were little more than shelters and prefabricated galvanized corrugated iron sheets were introduced for this purpose, known as Schützenhöhlen or Siegfried shelters. Deep dugouts were only to be constructed in the second and third lines. In the second line, these were to accommodate a third of the trench garrison and beyond that half of the garrison was to be in dugouts. Where it was possible to construct mined dugouts they were to be covered by 8–10m of earth. There were to be at least two exits, wide and high enough to allow rapid exiting by the garrison, supported by strong timbers and well protected. The use of old trench lines was warned against owing to the prevalence of dugouts in the front line: 'The majority of the dugouts are in the first trench. This leads to crowding in the forward line with disastrous consequences.'[51]

Where the defence line was in the back areas, the first trench was to be abandoned and a new one dug in front. In the Flanders the presence of ground water dictated whether dugouts could be constructed and the German defences depended especially on concrete bunkers, which were shellproof and could be rapidly evacuated to meet an attack. Instructions in October 1917 limited the size of dugouts to accommodate no more than two NCOs and sixteen men.[52]

German defence of shell holes, showing the positioning of the entrance to avoid the fall of flat trajectory shells and anti-grenade mesh which could be rolled down to protect it. Although this accommodation might be in the area of the front line, the small dugout would house a few men only in line with German regulations. From Seesselberg, *Der Stellungskrieg.*

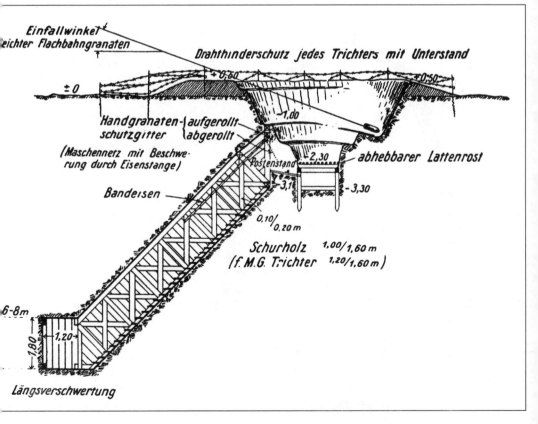

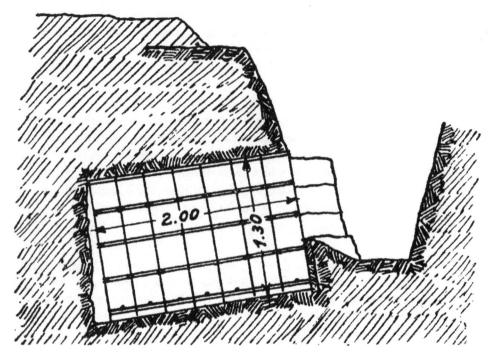

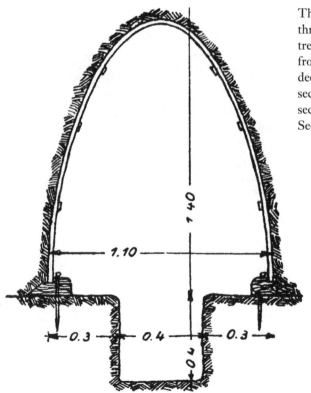

The use of Siegfried shelters, a three-man shelter in a front line trench, designed to prevent men from being trapped by attackers in deep dugouts. The prefabricated sections were also used to make secure dugout entrances. From Seesselberg, *Der Stellungskrieg*.

These restrictions severely limited the comfort and protection afforded to soldiers in the front line and caused Ernst Jünger to look back in the middle of 1918 with nostalgia at his accommodation at Monchy two years before, but also to reflect on the dangers of the deep dugouts:

> Little can be said for the dugouts... They are what are called Siegfried dugouts, that is to say, semicircular holes, penetrating the wall of the trench to a distance of three metres and protected from above with a covering of earth, at the most two metres deep. The frame consists of thin circular sheets of corrugated iron that scarcely support the weight of the earth heaped on them and give only just room enough for two men to lie at length. ... those who bivouac in them and who in their moments of rest keep their eyes fixed on the zinc roof, the mouse-trap that must infallibly crush them at the first direct hit. ... Compared with earlier days, then, when we dug ourselves ten metres and more into the earth, there has been a serious decline in security. ... The war has become more mobile and such works of construction no longer pay. And then it must be admitted that with the attack on Verdun the series of great onslaughts of material made the contrast between the safety of these gigantic strongholds and the front-line trenches, swept with flame and shattered with shell, far too great. But apart even from the moral factor, the occupants of these caverns, in the event of an attack, had as far to go before they could reach the trench as if they had to climb the stairs of a four-storeyed house. Thus it often happened that they had a warm reception half-way up from bombs and burning phosphorus without being able to strike a blow, particularly when the men on guard in the trench had long since given their lives in its defence without any one below being any the wiser.
>
> Hence, after a particularly tragic disaster on Vimy Ridge, an order appeared one day that no dugout in the front line was to be more than two metres deep, and that all those already in existence were to be blown up.
>
> What this iron order meant can be understood only by those who know the mass of stuff that, often without a break for weeks together, was flung on the trenches. To have to crouch under fire without cover, belaboured without a pause by shells of a calibre sufficient each one to lay a fair-sized village in ruins, without any distraction beyond counting the hits mechanically in a half-dazed condition, is an experience that almost passes the limits of human endurance. For this reason the men who issued the order, and threw hundreds of thousands naked and defenceless into the fire, took on themselves one of the heaviest responsibilities the mind can conceive. And yet, even though I may be one of the victims, I can but admit they were right.[53]

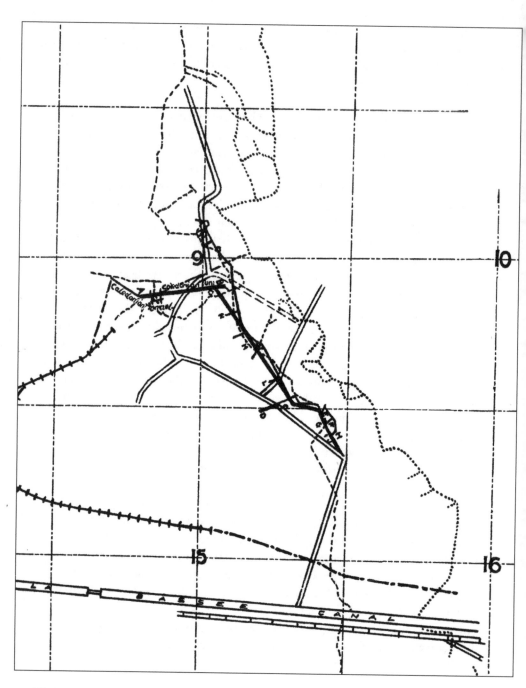

The northern section of the Givenchy–Hulluch subways, showing the transversal converted into an infantry communication tunnel and the extension, Caledonian or Bunny Hutch tunnel. From Ball, 'The Work of the Miner on the Western Front'.

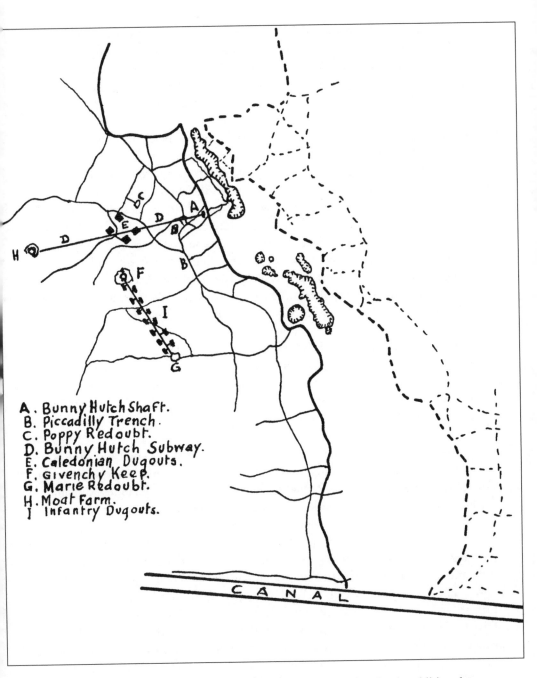

A. Bunny Hutch Shaft.
B. Piccadilly Trench.
C. Poppy Redoubt.
D. Bunny Hutch Subway.
E. Caledonian Dugouts.
F. Givenchy Keep.
G. Marie Redoubt.
H. Moat Farm.
I. Infantry Dugouts.

The infantry dugouts and defensive tunnels, in the same area, showing in addition the tunnel linking Givenchy Keep with Marie Redoubt. From Grieve and Newman, *Tunnellers.*

In contrast to the Germans, the British expanded underground accommodation in parts of their front line although, like the Germans, they made lavish use of dugouts and tunnels for support and counterattack troops. On the 1st Army front north of Vimy Ridge, where the opposing mine systems reached an impasse in the summer of 1916, the British enlarged their transversal tunnel, which ran beneath or in front of their front line into a communication subway in which it was possible to walk underground almost continuously for four miles.[54] The northernmost portion of this line was at Givenchy-lès-la-Bassée and here, during the German attacks in April 1918, the British underground defences were put to a severe test. At Givenchy the subway ran for about 720yds beneath the British front line up to the northernmost point at Bunny Hutch shaft head where it ran back at a right angle to Moat Farm in the support lines. This tunnel, called Bunny Hutch or Caledonian tunnel, was dug by 251 Tunnelling Company to provide an additional access to the mine system in case the Germans should have gained occupation of the British front line and they had to blow the shaft head. The underground defences in Givenchy had been conceived in the summer of 1916 by the 1st Army Controller of Mines, Lt Col G.C. Williams, and the scheme, described by the commander of 251 Company, Major H.J. Humphrys, was:

> ...that the front line should consist of a number of detached posts, strongly fortified, access to which should be obtained by interconnected underground tunnels, well lighted and connected to dug-outs and forward headquarters, all of which should be constructed by the tunnelling companies.[55]

Off Bunny Hutch tunnel was a complex of dugouts housing troops for counterattack. A separate tunnel linked two key strong points in the support line, Givenchy Keep and Marie Redoubt, 300yds apart, and included dugouts to accommodate two battalions with 40ft of cover and numerous exits. In March 1918, the 55th West Lancashire Division practised daily evacuation of the tunnels and dugouts to man the Givenchy positions as rapidly as possible.[56] This sector was recognized as of key significance owing to the coalfields in the area and the proximity to the Flanders battlefield, which was the main line protecting the channel ports. The German attack of 9 April, the opening of the Battle of the Lys, fell primarily on a Portuguese division, which gave way, but to the south the 55th Division halted the German advance. On the morning of the attack the Germans penetrated 300yds into the village as far as the church, but isolated posts in the front line held out and strong points in the rear halted the attackers. During the morning British counterattack platoons drove the Germans out of the Givenchy positions. The attack failed because the Germans did not follow the tactics required to deal with underground defences: they did not keep up with their barrage to catch the defenders underground and did not mop up the British in the posts that they bypassed when penetrating.

In a subsequent attack on 18 April the Germans showed more preparation for overcoming the underground defences. The British 1st Division, which had relieved the 55th thirty-six hours previously, was not practised in the defence of the sector and in particular in making a rapid exit from the dugouts and tunnels in the event of attack. The attackers this time kept very close to their barrage (aided apparently by heavy guns firing short) and rushed the front line from just 40yds at the moment that their barrage moved forward. The tunnel exits, probably identified during the previous attack, were targeted by the Germans with gas shells and fire was particularly heavy around the Moat Farm and Givenchy Keep dugouts. The two right companies of the 1st Black Watch were caught before they could emerge from their dugouts and possibly also the enlarged transversal tunnel. Despite the strong points suffering direct hits by heavy shells on both shaft heads they nevertheless resisted the fire. All troops except for a few lookouts remained below and the Adjutant of 251 Tunnelling Company, Captain E.J. Ritchie, described the precautions taken by the miners:

> Following the procedure which had been agreed upon, parties of one N.C.O. and a few sappers were detailed to remain at the bottom of each stairway or entrance, with orders to effect any necessary repairs and to blow the stairway or entrance should the enemy gain possession of the trenches.[57]

The left of the Black Watch held out at Givenchy Keep and was reinforced via the tunnel by Loyal North Lancashires from Marie Redoubt. The Moat Farm position, used as a dressing station, was filled with wounded and, Ritchie recounted, the British were caught in Bunny Hutch tunnel:

> Unfortunately, at one time the enemy gained a strong footing in the trenches at the dug-out entrances and as they had commenced throwing gas bombs down, the position had to be surrendered on humane grounds, for the sake of the wounded below.[58]

The survivors were ordered out by the Germans, the NCOs first, followed by the other ranks. A wounded tunnelling officer was carried out on a stretcher by his men.[59] Before dark, however, a British counterattack retook their trenches. Ritchie was in no doubt that the underground defences were the key to repelling the attack:

> This battle justified the Controller of Mines policy of deep dug-outs, as without the deep dugouts, there is no infantry in the world that could have held Givenchy Ridge that day, because the intense bombardment in the early morning would have wiped them out, whereas our casualties through shell fire were comparatively light up to the time of the general attack.[60]

However, the battle again showed the vulnerability of deep dugouts and tunnels if troops were not well-trained in rapid evacuation the moment the barrage passed over, and the danger if the attacker gained control of all entrances. It also showed the Germans adopting the methods which the Allies had developed for overcoming deep shelters.

Deep dugouts, caves and subways offered great advantages both to defenders and attackers. In particular the British disaster of 1 July 1916 stands as the most successful use of underground shelters in withstanding prolonged artillery bombardment and enabling the infantry garrison to repel an infantry attack. The Germans used deep underground shelters to great advantage in their defensive battles of 1915 to 1916. In late 1916 the Allied experience in dealing with them caused the Germans to radically alter their defensive theory and abandon their use in the front line. The dissemination of the new doctrine throughout the German army took time, however. The Allies' lack of experience of the defensive battle was exposed by the German attacks of spring 1918, but the example of Givenchy shows the successful British use of underground defences and the shortfalls of German attack tactics in dealing with linked centres of resistance of the type that they had invented and used so effectively in 1916. Subways and underground accommodation aided attackers at Verdun and Vimy, but could not solve the problem of crossing no man's land. Caves and subways offered great advantages to attacking infantry in concealment, shelter and rest in the days before an attack during their own bombardment and the increased enemy shelling that it attracted. Such refuges meant that troops were able to advance to the attack direct from their places of rest without an exhausting and dangerous approach march into battle. The use of subways at Arras and Vimy was part of greater British and Canadian experience in running and coordinating operations. Their use in 1917 reduced many of the dangers and difficulties faced by the British at the Somme in 1916 when their trenches were heavily shelled and become congested by wounded men. Accommodation and communication tunnels, however, were highly vulnerable to any kind of fluidity returning to operations. Enemy withdrawal rendered the work useless, while rapid advance placed the garrisons at great risk. By the summer of 1917 deep underground shelters in the front line were largely rendered obsolete by more effective methods of attack.

Chapter 11

Conclusion

Siege warfare reached its highest level of development during 1914 to 1918 in a war which was not a siege. Although Germany had rejected military mining by 1914, it was nevertheless able quickly to revive its capability through the availability of fortress troops which could be attached to its field army. There seemed no alternative but to mine on the Western Front as a means of breaking the strong field defences. Germany dominated mining during 1914 to 1915 and continued to maintain supremacy against France throughout the war. The British mining success was the result of the willingness to divert considerable manpower resources and the ability to recruit and integrate civilian specialists into the BEF. If ever there was an example of an individual making a difference it was Sir John Norton Griffiths who, through his force of personality and influence, ensured that full use was made of available technical expertise. Norton Griffiths also pushed for mining to be used on a large scale, which required the reforms carried out in early 1916 whereby control of mining was vested in the General Staff and at Army level in the BEF. This ensured that the potential advantage which the BEF gained from mining was directed towards the largest possible tactical goal. However, having assembled the means to carry out mining operations, the BEF had difficulty in making effective use of it and in 1916 lacked the skill and experience to conduct complex operations. Symptomatic of this were both the superior ability of the Germans to take mine craters compared to the British, and the tragedy of 1 July 1916.

German control of mining remained at divisional level and the British success at Messines in June 1917 can be ascribed in part to the British adoption of the tactical control of mining at Army level, with an Inspector of Mines at GHQ. The German failure to do so allowed local considerations to prevail over mining policy, and the failure to enforce in-depth defence where this would have negated much of the British mining effort. The German failure also stemmed from inability to create units which were as effective as the British by channelling the right manpower into the units, to provide them with as good equipment, to give mining priority and to allow the tunnelling companies to run themselves effectively. There seemed no need for the German pioneers to relinquish control of units which were carrying out a long-established activity which they knew well how to do. Among the British there was both a more serious knowledge vacuum and also a tradition of amateur soldiering, which allowed in particular the civilian middle classes and skilled workers a foothold into the military caste. For this reason it is impossible to imagine a Norton Griffiths figure being tolerated in the German army.

The nineteen mines undoubtedly contributed to the victory of Messines and this was rightly regarded by the miners as their greatest success, where their efforts were properly used and integrated into the heart of the attack plan. The Germans were not, as has been claimed, intending to withdraw from the ridge. However, by mid-1917 the effectiveness of mining was becoming diminished by the use of in-depth defence by the Germans. Messines was a bite and hold battle, albeit on a large scale, which was a prelude to further operations in which mining could play no part. It was part of a process of wearing down the Germans and of convincing them that, no matter how they changed their tactics, the British had the will and the means to overcome their defences. The key to the operations which followed Messines, however, was the integration of artillery with infantry, tanks and aircraft – in short the all-arms battle – which restored a degree of mobility and momentum to operations. The invention of this type of battle was the military revolution which occurred during 1914–18. Military mining was expanded by mass mobilisation and technology to a scale and intensity which was without precedent but, at the moment of its zenith, it had become obsolete. The scaling down of mining in 1917 by Germany and France, and subsequently also Britain, indicates that it did not have a role in future operations. The integrated battle was the key to breaking the deadlock of the Western Front, but mining served a purpose in rendering vulnerable powerful linear defence lines. In retrospect some may say that it was not worth the effort, but at the time there seemed no alternative.

The wasted British effort of Russian saps during the Somme was also largely due to lack of experience of operations. Open and closed sapping was tried and rejected by the French during 1915 and employed with mixed results at Gallipoli. The lack of use to which the Russian saps were put on the Somme has led to assertions about their missed potential. The idea of troops disgorging from tunnels which had been driven across no man's land undetected by the enemy remains a fantasy of fiction writers. That they were not attempted as a means of crossing no man's land after 1916 suggests that no one at the time seriously believed that such a method was feasible. To understand what might have been on the Somme we should look at the Battles of Vimy and Arras, where tunnels were used as a means of concealing and protecting troops prior to the attack immediately behind the jumping-off positions. At Arras most of the tunnels driven up to the front line and into no man's land were rendered useless by the German withdrawal. Trench warfare, after all, involved highly developed field defences and not the permanent fortresses against which mining had been traditionally used.

The most extensive role for underground warfare in the inter-war period was in the French Maginot line defences, which were carefully prepared against mining attack and incorporated countermines with seismomicrophones. The British re-formed Tunnelling Companies in 1939, resurrecting the same numbers as had been used in 1915–18, but they never regained their role. Some retained their tunnelling function in Gibraltar, while others were used in bomb disposal where shaft-sinking was required. The German Atlantic Wall defences incorporated tunnelled accommodation but relied principally on concrete for resistance to bombardment. The most important use during the Second World War of underground defences was for civilian protection against air raids, and this continued in the Cold War era with defence against nuclear attack. In 1953 a plan was conceived to drive a half-mile tunnel from the American to the Russian sectors of Berlin in order to tap cables carrying signals traffic between the HQ of Soviet Forces in Berlin and Moscow. The Americans drove the tunnel and the British task was to tunnel upwards and install a tap chamber adjacent to the cables. No.1 Specialist Team RE was formed with the purpose and relearnt the technique of spiling from the 1920s military mining manual in order to work silently through the sandy soil. The chamber was created without detection and the tap operated for almost a year until betrayed by a double agent.[1] In Vietnam the North Vietnamese famously used tunnels for refuge and to infiltrate American defences, and it required the formation of special US and Australian units to combat them. Perhaps the closest to the defences based on the underground quarries in France is the Tora Bora complex of tunnels, bunkers and fortified caves in Afghanistan. Originally constructed with funds from the US Central Intelligence Agency to aid Mujahedeen resistance to Soviet invaders, this reputedly became a refuge for Osama bin Laden and 1,000 Taliban fighters. In siege situations, tunnels continue to be used not by the attackers but by the besieged, as at Sarajevo in 1993 or Gaza in 2009. British military mining in Gibraltar, which had begun in 1782 with the initiative of Sergeant Major Ince proposing tunnelling through the rock to create gun batteries in the cliff face, ended with the disbandment of the Specialist Team RE in the mid-1990s.

In 1915 the military mistrusted miners and in particular their reputation for industrial militancy. Miners are physically tough and will disregard personal danger but look after their mates, on whom they are wholly reliant. They have their own codes of behaviour and are mistrustful of outsiders, and are in turn liable to be feared by the rest of society. Those soldiers who allowed them freedom to work as they wished discovered that they had much in common, and reaped the rewards.

Notes

Chapter 1

1. Kenneth Wiggins, *Siege Mines and Underground Warfare*, (Shire, Princes Risborough, 2003), pp. 10–11.
2. Wiggins, ibid., pp. 18–19.
3. R. Ernest Dupuy and Trevor N. Dupuy, *The Encyclopedia of Military History*, (Jane's Publishing Company, London, 1980), pp. 524–5.
4. Captain Genez, *Histoire de la Guerre Souterraine*, (Librairie Militaire Berger Levrault, Paris, 1914) (translated in *Royal Engineers Journal*, Vol. XX, 1914), p. 321.
5. Bruno Zschokke, *Handbuch der militärischen Sprengtechnik für Offiziere aller Waffen*, (Verlag von Veit & Comp., Leipzig, 1911), p. 162.
6. Mark Grimsley 'Siege of Petersburg' in John Whiteclay Chambers II (Ed.), *Oxford Companion to American Military History*, (Oxford University Press, Oxford, 1999), p. 546; 'V L', 'The Engineers in Grant's Campaigns of 1864–5', *Royal Engineers Journal*, Sept. 1938, p. 131.
7. Zschokke op. cit., p247–249.
8. Dupuy op. cit.
9. *Extracts from the old mining regulations Issued by the General of Pioneers, Army Headquarters, Laon, April 1915*. SS461 General Staff 1916.
10. Zschokke, op. cit., p. 163; [anon.] *Instruction allemand sur le service du pionier dans la guerre de siège (1913)*, (Ministère de la Guerre Paris 1915); [anon.] *Sprengvorschrift von 1911*, (Georg Bath, Berlin, 1918).
11. Col. G.H. Addison, 'The German Engineer and Pioneer Corps,' *The Royal Engineers Journal*, Vol. LVI Dec. 1942, p. 313.
12. Toepfer (Captain), 'Technics in the Russo-Japanese War', (from the *Kriegstechnische Zeitschrift*, 1906), *Professional Memoirs. Corps of Engineers, United States Army and Engineer Department at Large*. Vol. II, No.6 (1910) pp. 192–3; 201.
13. Anon., 'German regulations for field fortifications and conclusions reached in Russia from the battles in defensive positions in Manchuria' [Translation from *The Militär Wochenblatt*], *Professional Memoirs. Corps of Engineers, United States Army and Engineer Department at Large*, Vol. II, No.7 (1910), pp. 365, 369.
14. Major De Pardieu, *A Critical Study of German Tactics and of the New German Regulations*, (trans. Captain Charles F. Martin), (United States Cavalry Association, Kansas, 1912), p. 117.
15. *Écoles du Génie, Instruction Pratique, École de Mines, Livre de l'Officier (approbation ministérielle du 25 Juillet 1908)*, (Imprimerie Nationale, Paris, 1916); *Écoles du Génie, École de Mines, approbation ministérielle du 16 Juillet 1901, Édition mis à jour jusqu'au 30 avril 1909*, (Imprimerie Nationale Paris 1918).

16. *La Butte Meurtrie Vauquois La guerre des mines 1914–1918*, (Les Amis de Vauquois et de sa Région, 2004), p. 180.
17. *Report of the Siege Operations held at Chatham July and August 1907*, (Chatham: School of Military Engineering, 1907), p. 7.
18. Ibid., p. 27.
19. Ibid., p. 31.
20. Ibid., p. 45.
21. Ibid.
22. Ibid., p. 30.
23. Mining in France 1914–1917 by Major-General R.N. Harvey, late Inspector of Mines, p. 1, National Archives (NA), WO106/387.
24. *First Report of the committee on Siege and Fortress Warfare, 1908*, p. 3, NA, WO33/2986.
25. Major G.R. Pridham, RE, *Siege Operations carried out by the 20th and 42nd Companies, Royal Engineers, June, 1913*, p. 11, NA WO279/50.
26. Op. cit., p. 12.
27. Op. cit., p. 11.
28. Interim Report of Major-General Hickman's Siege Committee, November 1914, NA, WO33/699; Report of the Committee on Siege Artillery Material, December 1914, NA, WO33/701.
29. *Military Engineering (Part II.) Attack and Defence of Fortresses*, General Staff, War Office, 1910. (London: HMSO 1910), p. 5.
30. Major General H.L. Pritchard RE (Ed.), *History of the Corps of Royal Engineers*, Vol. V., (Chatham, The Institution of Royal Engineers, 1952), p. 454.
31. Genez, op. cit., p. 394.
32. Lt Col R.N. Harvey, 'Obstacles. Their tactical use, construction, and methods of destruction or surmounting them,' *The Royal Engineers Journal*, Vol. XX, No. 4, October 1914, p. 217.
33. Harvey, Mining in France, op. cit., pp. 1–2.
34. Colonel Toepfer, 'Minenkämpfe' in M. Schwarte (Ed.) *Die Militärischen Lehren des Großen Krieges*, (Ernst Siegfried Mittler und Sohn, Berlin, 1920), p. 211.
35. Op. cit., p. 212.

Chapter 2

1. [Anon.], *1er et 21e Régiments du Génie Historique*, (Judas & Machard, n.d.), p. 67.
2. Ministère de la Guerre, État-Major de l'Armée – Service Historique, *Les Armées françaises dans la grande guerre*, Vol. II, (Imp. Nationale, Paris, 1931), App. 427.
3. Report of article by Col. Baills in *Revue du Génie Militaire*, June 1929, *RE Journal* December 1929 Vol. XLIII, p.189; August Lehmann, *Das K. B. [Königliches Bayerisches] Pionier=Regiment* (Max Schick, Munich, 1927), pp. 97, 99.
4. General Staff, *Handbook of the German Army at War, April, 1918*, reprinted as *German Army Handbook April 1918*, (Arms and Armour Press, London, 1977), pp.97–100.
5. Karl Witte, *3. Rheinisches Pionier=Bataillon Nr. 30* (Gerhard Stalling, Berlin, 1928), pp. 39–40.
6. Ernst Schmidt, *Argonnen*, (Gerhard Stalling, Berlin, 1927), p.120.
7. [Anon.], *1er et 21e Régiments du Génie Historique*, op. cit., p.45.
8. Witte, op. cit., pp. 41–42, 52–53.

9. Quoted in Henry de Varigny, *Mines et Tranchées*, (Berger-Levrault, Paris, 1915), pp.64–65.

10. *Les Armées françaises dans la grande guerre*, Vol. II, op. cit., p.114.

11. Captain W. Grant Grieve and Bernard Newman, *Tunnellers*, (Herbert Jenkins, London, 1936), pp. 25–26.

12. A German VII Corps report quoted by Grieve and Newman (ibid.) states all ten mines fired, but this is contradicted by the History of the 7th Pioneers which states that the charge in Sap 6 could not be used. W. Buhr, *Die Geschichte des I. Westf. Pionier=Bataillons Nr. 7 und seiner Kriegsverbände im Weltkriege 1914/18*, (Gerhard Stalling, Oldenburg, 1938), pp. 119–122.

13. Buhr, ibid.

14. VII Corps report, Grieve and Newman op. cit., p. 29.

15. Brigadier General J.E. Edmonds, *Military Operations, France and Belgium, 1915*, Vol. 1, (MacMillan and Co. Ltd, London, 1927), pp. 20–22.

16. *Les Armées françaises*, op. cit., Vol.2, p. 212.

17. Ibid., Appendix 510, Letter to armies 30/12/14.

18. G.H. Addison, *The Work of the Royal Engineers in the European War, 1914–1918 Miscellaneous* (Institution of Royal Engineers, Chatham 1927), p. 7.

19. Mining in France 1914–1917 by Major-General R.N. Harvey, late Inspector of Mines, p. 1, NA, WO106/387.

20. Interview with F.G. Hyland, Barrie Papers, Royal Engineers Museum (REM).

21. Mining in France, op. cit., pp. 2–3, Harvey states that the GOC IV Corps wrote to GHQ on or about 3 December 1914 asking for a battalion of sappers and miners; *Military Operations* 1915 Vol. 1, op. cit., p. 33 and *Tunnellers*, op. cit., p. 25 probably following Harvey also date this letter to 3 December 1914; *Tunnellers* p. 25 also states that Rawlinson wrote to 'Army headquarters' and that his proposal was received 'with approval, and forwarded to G.H.Q., with a strong recommendation that it should be adopted', however, armies were not created in the BEF until 26 December 1914; [Anon.], *The Work of the Royal Engineers in the European War, 1914–19. Military Mining* (Institution of Royal Engineers, Chatham, 1922), p. 1 states that the demand came from IV Corps at the end of December and that it was 'warmly supported' by the GOC 1st Army (i.e. Gen. Haig).

22. *Military Operations*, 1915, Vol. 1, op. cit., p. 33, no date is given for the instruction but it is presumed to have come after 26 December.

23. Tunnellers' Old Comrades Association (TOCA) *Bulletin* No.2, 1927, p. 18.

24. Sir John Norton Griffiths, 'Memorandum on Moles', TOCA *Bulletin* No.3, 1928, p. 58.

25. Mining in France, op. cit.

26. TOCA *Bulletin* No.2, 1927, p. 18–19. Norton Griffiths's memory of the sequence of events was not perfect as the mining attack suffered by the 16th Lancers near Hill 60 took place on 21 February 1915.

27. Friedrich Seesselberg, *Der Stellungskrieg 1914–1918*, (E.S. Mittler and Son, Berlin, 1926), p. 296.

28. Hartenstein, *Das Ruhrhessische Pionier=Bataillon Nr. 11 im Weltkriege 1914–1918*, (Bernhard Sporn, Zeulenroda, 1936), p.128.

29. Paul Heinrici [Ed.], *Das Ehrenbuch der Deutschen Pioniere*, (Verlag Tradition Wilhelm Rolf, Berlin [1931], p. 146.

30. Quoted in Heinrici, op. cit.
31. Seesselberg, op. cit., p. 309.
32. Commandant R. de Feriet, *La Crête des Éparges 1914–1918*, (Payot, Paris, 1939), pp. 69–86.
33. Maurice Genevoix, *Les Éparges*, (Pierre de Tartas, 1974), p. 99.
34. Feriet, op. cit.

Chapter 3

1. Capitaine [Hippolyte-Michel] Thobie, *La Prise de Carency par le Pic et Par la Mine*, (Berger-Levrault, Paris 1918), p. 142. Thobie commanded the 20/11 Engineer Company and this section is largely based on his detailed account of the assault on Carency.
2. Ibid., p. 148.
3. Ibid., p. 194.
4. War Diary, French 70th Infantry Division, [SHAT].
5. Thobie, op. cit., p. 229.
6. Major General Belin, Note au sujet des travaux de mines, GQG, État-Major, 3e Bureau, No. 820 3/3/15, Annexe 1055, Ministère de la Guerre, État-Major de l'Armée – Service Historique, *Les Armées françaises dans la grande guerre*, Vol. II, (Imp. Nationale, Paris, 1931).
7. This section is drawn from the detailed recent study by Jean-Jacques Gorlet, *La Guerre de Mines dans l'Oise 1914–1917 en secteur calme*, (Société Archéologique Historique et Scientifique de Noyon, 2005).
8. Gorlet, op. cit., p. 173.
9. Gorlet, op. cit., p. 167.
10. Gorlet, op. cit., p. 172.
11. Commandant R. de Feriet, *La Crête des Éparges 1914–1918*, (Payot, Paris, 1939), pp. 173, 178.
12. Ibid., p. 179.
13. Ministère de la Guerre, État-Major de l'Armée – Service Historique, *Les Armées françaises dans la grande guerre*, Vol. III, (Imp. Nationale, Paris, 1931), p. 634.
14. Nivelle, 'Note pour le 2 C.A.', 14/5/1916, annex 311, Ministère de la Guerre, État-Major de l'Armée – Service Historique, *Les Armées françaises dans la grande guerre*, Vol. IV, (Imp. Nationale, Paris, 1933).
15. André Pézard, *Nous autres, à Vauquois 1915–1916*, (Paris, La Renaissance du Livre, 1918), p. 282.
16. The section on Vauquois is based largely on the study by les Amis de Vauquois, *La Butte Meurtrie Vauquois La guerre des mines 1914–1918*, (Les Amis de Vauquois et de sa Région, 2004).
17. Pézard, op. cit., pp. 236–237.
18. Amis de Vauquois, op. cit., p. 240; Karl Witte, *3. Rheinisches Pionier=Bataillon Nr.30* (Gerhard Stalling, Berlin 1928), pp. 63–64.
19. Adolf Buchner, *Der Minenkrieg auf Vauquois*, (W. Goertz, Karlsfeld, 1982), p. 57.
20. Pézard, op. cit., p. 276.
21. Buchner, op. cit., p. 54.
22. Report of Captain Durant 20/12/1917 Service Historique de la Défense, Département de l'armée de Terre (SHAT) – 2 V 221, quoted in Amis de Vauquois, op. cit., p. 279.

23. Buchner, op. cit., p. 62. Feikert states that they entered the gallery and took a French prisoner which is not confirmed by the account in Amis de Vauquois, op. cit., p. 280.

24. Buchner, op. cit., p. 61.

Chapter 4

1. Captain W. Grant Grieve and Bernard Newman, *Tunnellers*, (Herbert Jenkins, London, 1936), pp. 37.

2. TOCA Bulletin No. 2, 1927, pp. 18–19.

3. Grieve & Newman, op. cit., pp. 39, 46. Brigadier General J. E. Edmonds, *Military Operations, France and Belgium, 1915*, (MacMillan and Co. Ltd, London, 1927). Vol. 1, p. 29.

4. Grieve & Newman, op. cit., pp. 53–54.

5. Diary of Sir John Norton Griffiths, 10/4/1915, NA WO158/129.

6. Edmonds, *Military Operations* 1915 Vol. 1, op. cit., p. 168; [Anon.], *The Work of the Royal Engineers in the European War, 1914–19. Military Mining*, (Institution of Royal Engineers, Chatham, 1922), pp. 20–22.

7. Norton Griffiths diary, op. cit., 19/4/1915.

8. Edmonds, *Military Operations* 1915 Vol. 1, op. cit., p. 167.

9. Held, [et al] *Das Königlich Preussische Garde=Pionier=Bataillon und seine Kriegsverbände 1914/18*, Vol. 1, (Carl Fr. Berg, Berlin, 1932), p. 264.

10. Grieve & Newman, op. cit., p. 46; Edmonds, *Military Operations* 1915 Vol. 1, op. cit., p. 31.

11. *Military Mining*, op. cit., p. 23; 'W.G.' [Walter Gard'ner], *One Mole Rampant*, [privately published, c.1921], p. 151–2.

12. *Who's Who in Wales*, 1926, quoted by L. Hughes and J. Dixon, *"Surrender Be Damned" A History of the 1/1st Battalion the Monmouthshire Regiment, 1914–18*, (CWM Press, Caerphilly, 1995), p. 298.

13. Letter of 12/7/1915, Gard'ner, *One Mole Rampant*, op. cit., pp. 213–215.

14. For a detailed account of the Hooge mine see Peter Barton, Peter Doyle & Johan Vandewalle, *Beneath Flanders Fields, the Tunnellers' War 1914–1918*, Spellmount, Staplehurst, 2004), pp. 155–157.

15. Hepburn states in an interview with Barrie in 1960 that he went from 20ft to 60ft depth in July 1915 but he is probably confusing this with later shafts, Barrie papers, Royal Engineers Museum (REM); Norton Griffiths diary, op. cit., 18/6/1915 & 11/7/1915 gives depths for these shafts as 21ft but on 2/11/1915 refers to the 'old level' as 30ft; Mulqueen, *Memoirs of Major F.J. Mulqueen, DSO MC*, Royal Engineers Library (REL), states 'about 35ft'.

16. Gard'ner, *One Mole Rampant*, op. cit., p. 217.

17. Barton, et. al., *Beneath Flanders Fields*, op. cit., p. 152.

18. Geoffrey Cassels, the officer responsible for this mine, provided a detailed account to Barrie in 1960, Barrie papers, op. cit., Barrie used this in his own book, Alexander Barrie, *War Underground*, (Star Books, London, 1981, originally Frederick Muller, London, 1962) and also forms part of a detailed description in Barton, et. al., *Beneath Flanders Fields*, op. cit., pp. 148-154.

19. Plan Pl. VII Craters on Cuinchy Front in *Military Mining*, op. cit. shows the centre of the mine blown from No. 2 tunnel as 80ft NW of H brickstack. These blows were

reported to have buried a complete platoon of the 14th Westphalian Division, W. Buhr, *Die Geschichte des I. Westf. Pionier=Bataillons Nr. 7 und seiner Kriegsverbände im Weltkriege 1914/18* (Gerhard Stalling, Oldenburg, 1938), p. 134.

20. Quoted by Edmonds, *Military Operations* 1915 Vol. 2, op. cit., p. 31.
21. Buhr, *Geschichte des I. Westf. Pionier=Bataillons Nr. 7*, op. cit., p. 135.
22. Ibid., pp. 134–137.
23. Grieve & Newman, op. cit., p. 68; *Supplement to the London Gazette*, 2/10/1915.
24. Norton Griffiths diary, op. cit., 14/6/1915.
25. Edmonds, *Military Operations* 1915 Vol. 2, op. cit., p. 94; War Diary 176 Tunnelling Company, RE, NA, WO95/244.
26. Edmonds, *Military Operations* 1915 Vol. 2, op. cit., pp. 263–264.
27. Ibid., p. 252.
28. Ibid., pp. 253 & 255.
29. Ibid., p. 257.
30. Grieve & Newman, op. cit., p. 70–71.
31. Geoffrey Sparrow & J.N. MacBean, *On Four Fronts with the Royal Naval Division*, (Hodder & Stoughton, London, 1918), p. 88.
32. J. Murray, *Gallipoli As I Saw It*, (William Kimber, London, 1965), pp. 116-118.
33. R. East, (Ed.), *The Gallipoli Diary of Sergeant Lawrence of the Australian Engineers – 1st A.I.F. 1915* (Melbourne University Press, Melbourne, 1981), p. 24.
34. C.E.W. Bean, *The Story of Anzac* [Vol. 2] *from 4 May, 1915, to the Evacuation of the Gallipoli Peninsula*, (Angus and Robertson Ltd, Australia, 1941) p. 815.
35. East, *Lawrence diary*, op. cit., p. 87.
36. Bean, *The Story of Anzac*, op. cit., p. 817.
37. Ibid., p. 820.
38. Ibid., p. 861.
39. Table based on ibid., p. 879.
40. Grieve & Newman, op. cit., p. 86 state it was more than twenty mines.
41. Murray, *Gallipoli As I Saw It*, op. cit., p. 188.
42. Major General H.L. Pritchard, RE, (Ed.), *History of the Corps of Royal Engineers, Vol. VI, Gallipoli, Macedonia, Egypt and Palestine 1914–18*, (The Institution of Royal Engineers, Chatham, 1952), p. 93.
43. Maj Gen R. Napier Harvey, 'Notes on Mining from the G.H.Q. Viewpoint', TOCA *Bulletin*, No. 4, 1929, p. 29.
44. Letter to Alexander Barrie 7/2/1960, Barrie papers, REM. Cropper later felt that Norton Griffiths and Harvey had taken the credit for his idea to go under the ridge using the blue clay layer, partial interview transcript, Barrie papers REM; Barrie, *War Underground*, op. cit., pp. 193–194.
45. Norton Griffiths diary, op. cit., 20/12/1915.
46. Harvey, Mining in France, op. cit., p. 7.
47. R. N. Harvey, 'Military Mining in the Great War, A Lecture delivered at the S.M.E., Chatham, on November 14th, 1929', *Royal Engineers Journal*, XLIII Dec. 1929, p. 538.
48. Maj. Gen G.H. Fowke, Chief Engineer, to GS, GHQ, 3/3/1915, notes from War Office records, Barrie Papers, REM.

Chapter 5

1. Maj Gen R.N. Harvey, 'Military Mining in the Great War, A Lecture delivered at the S.M.E., Chatham, on November 14th, 1929', *Royal Engineers Journal*, XLIII Dec. 1929, p. 539.
2. Notes from War Office records, Barrie papers, REM; Harvey, Military Mining in the Great War, op. cit., p. 539.
3. Norton Griffiths diary, op. cit., 12/12/1915.
4. Speech by Norton Griffiths, 'Tunnellers' Old Comrades Association Annual Dinner, 1927', TOCA *Bulletin*, No. 2, 1927, p. 21.
5. Norton Griffiths diary, op. cit., 24/10/1915, 11/12/1915.
6. Details of charges from 170 Tunnelling Company War Diary, noted in Barrie papers, REM; Brigadier General J. E. Edmonds, *Military Operations, France and Belgium, 1916*, [Vol. 1], (Imperial War Museum, London, nd, originally published 1932), p. 175 records the charges incorrectly.
7. Edmonds, *Military Operations, France and Belgium, 1916*, [Vol. 1], op. cit., pp. 174–175; Barrie, *War Underground*, op. cit., includes details about this attack in Chapter 10 probably derived from an interview with William Morgan of 170 Tunnelling Company which has not survived amongst the interview transcripts in the Barrie papers in REM.
8. *Military Operations, France and Belgium, 1916*, [Vol. 1] Appendices, (Macmillan and Co. Ltd, London, 1932), p. 49 Appendix 7, 36th Infantry Brigade Order No. 79, 1/3/1916.
9. Ibid.
10. Edmonds, *Military Operations, France and Belgium, 1916*, [Vol. 1], op. cit., pp. 176–177.
11. [Anon.], *The Work of the Royal Engineers in the European War, 1914-19. Work in the field under the Engineer-in-Chief, B.E.F., Geological Work on the Western Front*, (Institution of Royal Engineers, Chatham, 1922), Fig. 10, Section C.
12. Mulqueen Memoirs, op. cit., p. 41.
13. Ibid., pp. 41–42.
14. Lt Gen R. Fanshawe GOC 5th Corps to 2nd Army, 9/11/1915, 'War Diaries - St. Eloi Operations', Library and Archives Canada (LAC).
15. Edmonds, *Military Operations, France and Belgium, 1916*, [Vol. 1], op. cit., p. 178.
16. Norton Griffiths diary, op. cit., 7/12/1915.
17. War Diary, 172 Tunnelling Company, NA WO95/244.
18. Edmonds, *Military Operations, France and Belgium, 1916*, [Vol. 1], op. cit., p. 178.
19. War Diary, 172 Tunnelling Company, op. cit., 18/2/1916.
20. Norton Griffiths diary, op. cit., 18/2/1916.
21. Letter J.A. Douglas to Alexander Barrie 3/2/1960, Barrie papers, REM.
22. Norton Griffiths diary, op. cit., 3/3/1916.
23. Letter J.A. Douglas op. cit.
24. Edmonds, *Military Operations, France and Belgium, 1916*, [Vol. 1], op. cit., p. 179.
25. Ibid.
26. Ibid.
27. 9th Infantry Brigade Operation Order No. 25 by Brig Gen H.C. Potter 25/3/1915, 'War Diaries - St. Eloi Operations', LAC.
28. Harvey, Mining in France, op. cit., p. 9.
29. Edmonds, *Military Operations, France and Belgium, 1916*, [Vol. 1], op. cit., p. 182;

Francis Buckley, *Q. 6. A And Other Places Recollections of 1916, 1917, 1918*, (London, Spottiswoode, Ballantyne & Co. Ltd, 1920), p. 39.

30. Lt Col W. Wilde 31/3/1916 'Report by CO 1/NF Report on Operations at St Eloi on 27th/28th March 1916', 'War Diaries - St. Eloi Operations', LAC.
31. Report by Lt Col G.G. Ottley CO 4RF 31/3/16, 'War Diaries - St. Eloi Operations', LAC. He believed that mine no. 6 had failed to explode.
32. Ibid.
33. Edmonds, *Military Operations, France and Belgium, 1916*, [Vol. 1], op. cit., p. 187.
34. Edmonds, *Military Operations, France and Belgium, 1916*, [Vol. 1], op. cit., p. 189.
35. Letter J.A. Douglas to Alexander Barrie 14/9/1960, Barrie papers, REM.
36. Haldane, 'Operations at St Eloi from March 26th to 29th 1916', 'War Diaries - St. Eloi Operations', LAC.
37. Brig Gen H.C. Potter, 'Lessons to be learnt from the Operations at St Eloi March 27th 1916', 'War Diaries - St. Eloi Operations', LAC.
38. Haldane, 'Points regarding the Operations of March 27th, 1916', 'War Diaries - St. Eloi Operations', LAC.
39. Haldane Report re operations 27 March – 3 April 1916, 'War Diaries - St. Eloi Operations', LAC.
40. 'Extracts from Report of 2nd Army to GHQ on the St Eloi operations', 'War Diaries - St. Eloi Operations', LAC.
41. Ibid.
42. *SS112 Consolidation of Trenches and Localities after Assault and Capture*, p. 1.
43. Diary of Major R.S.G Stokes, 11-13/5/1916, 18/5/1916, 20/8/1916, NA, WO158/137.
44. Brigadier General J. E. Edmonds, *Military Operations, France and Belgium, 1917*, Vol. II, 7th June – 10th November Messines and Third Ypres (Passchendaele), (HMSO, London, 1927), p. 5.
45. [Anon.], *The Work of the Royal Engineers in the European War, 1914–19. Military Mining*, (Institution of Royal Engineers, Chatham, 1922), p. 18.

Chapter 6

1. War Diary 252 Tunnelling Company, 30/4/1916, NA, WO95/406.
2. Op. cit., 20/5/1916.
3. In addition, on the 29th Division front, half of the 18-pdr guns firing a shrapnel barrage were to lift three minutes before zero. Edmonds, *Military Operations, France and Belgium, 1916*, [Vol. 1], op. cit., p. 430–431. Apparently the heavy artillery was lifted on the whole corps front to keep the successive advance on the main German rearward defences in step. R. Prior and T. Wilson, *The Somme*, (Yale University Press, New Haven and London, 2005), p. 72.
4. Lt Geoffrey Malins OBE, *How I Filmed the War*, (Herbert Jenkins Limited, London, 1920), pp. 162–163.
5. Quoted in Edmonds, *Military Operations, France and Belgium, 1916*, [Vol. 1], op. cit., p. 431.
6. Letter to J.E. Edmonds, 21/1/1930, NA CAB45/138.
7. fn. Letter to J.E. Edmonds, nd, October 1929, NA CAB45/189; the Official History states that this was four hours before zero rather than 6pm the night before. Edmonds, *Military Operations, France and Belgium, 1916*, [Vol. 1], op. cit., p. 429.

8. Letter Hunter-Weston to Edmonds, 12/12/1929, NA CAB45/138.

9. Letter Ruthven to Edmonds, 30/10/29, NA CAB45/137; Letter de Lisle to Edmonds 12/11/1929, NA CAB45/189.

10. Letter Fuller to Edmonds, 24/1/1930, NA CAB45/188.

11. Letter Harvey to Edmonds, nd, February 1930, NA CAB45/189.

12. Letter Trower to Harvey 14/2/1930 NA CAB45/189.

13. Letter Harvey to Edmonds, 27/2/1930, NA CAB45/189.

14. Letter Preedy to Harvey 22/3/1930, NA CAB45/189.

15. Letter de Lisle to Edmonds 12/11/1929, NA CAB45/189.

16. Edmonds, *Military Operations, France and Belgium, 1916*, [Vol. 1], op. cit., p. 430.

17. Letter de Lisle to Edmonds, op. cit.

18. Letter to J.E. Edmonds, nd, October 1929, NA CAB45/189.

19. Interview transcript, Barrie papers, REM.

20. H.M. Hance 'Notes on the German Mining System at La Boisselle', 179 Tunnelling Company WD, NA WO95/244.

21. Letter H.M. Hance to Edmonds, June 1930, NA CAB45/134.

22. 103 Brigade Op Order No 24, 21/6/1916, 103 Brigade WD, NA WO95/2464; 101 Brigade Op Order No 34, 23/6/1916, 101 Brigade WD, NA WO95/2455.

23. Letter H.M. Hance to Edmonds, op. cit.

24. Edmonds, *Military Operations, France and Belgium, 1916*, [Vol. 1], op. cit., p. 382.

25. Mining Report by H.M. Hance, 5/7/1916, WD 34 Division GS, NA WO95/2432.

26. Letter Harvey to Edmonds, nd, February 1930, NA CAB45/189.

27. The Brigade Commander states that they delayed their advance two minutes for the mine but also states incorrectly that the mines were blown at 7.30am. Brig Gen Trevor Ternan, *The Story of the Tyneside Scottish*, (The Northumberland Press, Newcastle-Upon-Tyne, 1919), p. 104.

28. Mining Report by H.M. Hance, 5/7/1916, op. cit.

29. Letter A.G.B.Urmston (former CO 15th Royal Scots) to Edmonds, 11/6/1930, NA CAB45/191. Urmston states that his battalion's advance was delayed five minutes owing to the mine and this is repeated in the official history. However, I cannot find this in any orders and it may refer to the effect of the mine rather than an order.

30. Letter Maxse to Mary Maxse, 5/9/1915, West Sussex Record Office, (154).

31. Norton Griffiths diary, op. cit., 8/10/1915.

32. Untitled report, Appendix XIII, 55th Infantry Brigade War Diary, NA WO95/2046.

33. *German Mining Officer's Diary Captured at Fricourt, July 1916*, General Staff SS465 1916, pp. 4–5.

34. Description of German workings at Fricourt from Mining Note No. 46 'Further Notes on Enemy Mining Methods', NA WO158/130.

35. Grieve and Newman, *Tunnellers*, op. cit., p. 125; Edmonds, *Military Operations, France and Belgium, 1916*, [Vol. 1], op. cit., p. 348 states incorrectly that all three of the Tambour mines detonated.

36. Edmonds, *Military Operations, France and Belgium, 1916*, [Vol. 1], op. cit., p. 357.

37. Letter H.C.B. Hickling to Edmonds, nd, NA CAB45/134.

38. Grieve & Newman, *Tunnellers*, op. cit., p. 123; Letter H.C.B. Hickling to Edmonds, op. cit.; Edmonds, *Military Operations, France and Belgium, 1916*, [Vol. 1], op. cit., p. 349 states incorrectly that the mine 'completely destroyed' Bulgar Point.

39. Weekly Mine Report 183 Tunnelling Company RE, War Diary 18 Division GS, NA WO95/ 2015.
40. Experimental Craters & Galleries, NA WO153/1254.
41. Grieve & Newman, *Tunnellers*, op. cit., p. 131.
42. 252 Tunnelling Company WD, NA WO95/406; Edmonds, *Military Operations, France and Belgium, 1916,* [Vol. 2], op. cit., p. 492.

Chapter 7
1. Frederick J. Mulqueen, *Memoirs of Major F J Mulqueen, DSO MC,* REL, p. 81.
2. Mulqueen, op. cit., p. 84.
3. Canadian Corps Scheme of Operations 19/3/1917, NA WO158/424.
4. Lt Col G.P.G. Robinson RE, *The Durand Mine and First World War Tunnel System in the Grange Area of the Canadian Memorial Park, Vimy* (School of Military Engineering, Chatham, 1989) unpublished report, RE Library, p. 3; Harvey, 'Mining in France', op. cit., p. 15.
5. Quoted Nigel Cave, *Battleground Europe Arras Vimy Ridge,* (Leo Cooper, London, 1996), p. 167 (presumed source Report by 1st Army Inspector of Mines on Operation of 9 April 1917 National Archives WO158/138).
6. [Anon.], *The Work of the Royal Engineers in the European War, 1914–19. Work in the field under the Engineer-in-Chief, B.E.F., Geological Work on the Western Front,* (Institution of Royal Engineers, Chatham, 1922), p. 28–29.
7. J.C. Neill (Ed.), *The New Zealand Tunnelling Company, 1915–1919,* (Whitcombe & Tombs, Auckland, 1922), pp. 80–81; Jonathon Nicholls, *Cheerful Sacrifice,* (Leo Cooper, London, 1990), p. 107.
8. Otto Füsslein, 'Der Minenkrieg in Flandern' in Paul Heinrici [Ed.], *Das Ehrenbuch der Deutschen Pioniere,* (Verlag Tradition Wilhelm Rolf, Berlin, 1931), p. 543, hereafter '*Ehrenbuch*'.
9. *Oberkommando des Heeres, Der Weltkrieg 1914 bis 1918, Die Kriegführung im Frühjahr 1917,* Vol. 12, (E.S. Mittler & Sohn, Berlin, 1939), p. 428, hereafter *German Official History.*
10. Genealogical data on Otto Füsslein, http://www.holger-fuesslein.de/Fuesslein/n_2.htm#6.
11. Colonel Töpfer 'Minenkämpfe' in M. Schwarte (Ed.) *Die Militärischen Lehren des Großen Krieges,* (Ernst Siegfried Mittler und Sohn, Berlin, 1920), p. 212.
12. Hermann Cron, *Imperial German Army 1914–18: Organisation, Structure, Orders of Battle,* (Helion and Company, Solihull, 2006) originally published as *Geschichte des Deutschen Heeres im Weltkriege 1914–1918,* (Berlin, Militarverlag Karl Siegismund, 1937), p. 157.
13. Günther Rückbeil, *Das 1. Rheinische Pionier=Bataillon Nr. 8 und seine Kriegsverbände im Weltkriege 1914/18,* (Gerhard Stalling, Berlin, 1926), p. 113.
14. [Anon.], *Vorschriften für den Stellungskrieg für alle Waffen. Teil 2. Minenkrieg,* (Kriegsministerium, Berlin, 1916), p. 10.
15. Füsslein, *Ehrenbuch,* op. cit., p. 543.
16. Held, [et. al.] *Das Königlich Preussische Garde=Pionier=Bataillon und seine Kriegsverbände 1914/18* (2 Vols.), (Carl Fr. Berg, Berlin, 1932), p. 269.
17. Füsslein, *Ehrenbuch,* op. cit., p. 543.

18. Hackett's words are here as given by Grieve & Newman and are taken to be more plausible than those in the *London Gazette*, Captain W. Grant Grieve and Bernard Newman, *Tunnellers*, (Herbert Jenkins, London, 1936), pp. 163–168; *Supplement to the London Gazette*, 5 August, 1916, p. 744; J.C. Dunn, *The War the Infantry Knew*, [1938], p. 217.
19. Füsslein, *Ehrenbuch*, op. cit., p. 543.
20. Füsslein, *Ehrenbuch*, op. cit., p. 542.
21. Füsslein, *Ehrenbuch*, op. cit., p. 543.
22. Füsslein: 'richtige Wasserfänger', Füsslein, *Ehrenbuch*, op. cit., p. 543.
23. Füsslein, *Ehrenbuch*, op. cit., p. 544.
24. Ibid.
25. Ibid.
26. *Tunnellers*, op. cit., pp. 209–214; Füsslein, *Ehrenbuch*, op. cit., p. 543.
27. *Tunnellers*, op. cit., pp. 214–216; Brigadier General J. E. Edmonds, *Military Operations, France and Belgium, 1917*, Vol. II, 7th June – 10th November Messines and Third Ypres (Passchendaele), (HMSO, London, 1927), p. 60.
28. Füsslein, *Ehrenbuch*, op. cit., p. 544.
29. Map NA WO158/285, reproduced in Peter Barton, Peter Doyle & Johan Vandewalle, *Beneath Flanders Fields, the Tunnellers' War 1914–1918*, (Spellmount, Staplehurst, 2004), p. 180.
30. Map NA WO153/449 reproduced in *Beneath Flanders Fields*, op. cit., p. 167.
31. *Tunnellers*, op. cit., pp. 216–218; [Anon.], *The Work of the Royal Engineers in the European War, 1914–19. Military Mining*, (Institution of Royal Engineers, Chatham, 1922), p. 40.
32. Grieve & Newman state that Bedson served in the White Haven collieries but his service record states Cadeby. *Tunnellers*, op. cit., pp. 218–223; Service record of William Henry Bedson, NA.
33. *Tunnellers*, op. cit., pp. 223–224.
34. *Tunnellers*, op. cit., pp. 225–227.
35. Edmonds, *Military Operations, France and Belgium, 1917*, Vol. II, p. 57.
36. *Tunnellers*, op. cit., pp. 230–231.
37. *Geological Work*, op. cit., p. 30; *Tunnellers*, op. cit., pp. 231–232; Füsslein, *Ehrenbuch*, op. cit., p. 545.
38. *Tunnellers*, op. cit., pp. 232–235; Alexander Barrie, *War Underground*, (Star Books, London, 1981, originally Frederick Muller, London, 1962), pp. 243–244.
39. Mining plan, NA WO153/909.
40. *Tunnellers*, op. cit., pp. 235–236; Bryan Frayling 'Tunnellers', *Royal Engineers Journal*, August 1988, p. 172.
41. Mining plans NA WO153/909.
42. Füsslein, *Ehrenbuch*, op. cit., p. 547.
43. *German Official History*, op. cit., pp. 430–431, translated in [Anon.], 'The Messines Ridge Mines, 7th June, 1917. German Accounts', *Royal Engineers Journal*, Vol. LIV, 1940, p. 349.
44. *German Official History*, op. cit., p. 437 and Messines Ridge Mines, op. cit., p. 350.
45. *German Official History*, op. cit., pp. 441–442 and Messines Ridge Mines, op. cit., p. 350–351.

46. Brig R.N. Harvey, State of offensive mines on Second Army front intended for use during the operations, 16/4/1917, 'Messines – Wytschaete', NA, WO158/215.
47. C.E.W. Bean, *The Official History of Australia in the War of 1914 – 1918 Volume IV The Australian Imperial Force in France: 1917* (Australia: Angus and Robertson Ltd 1933), p. 577. Hereafter *Australian Official History*.
48. Brig Gen J. H. Davidson for Lt Gen, Chief of the General Staff to Second Army, 24/5/1917, 'Messines – Wytschaete', NA, WO158/215.
49. Letter Lt Gen L. E. Kiggell to Plumer, 29/5/1917; Summary of Proceedings of a Conference held at Pernes at 11am, 30th May, 1917, Lt Gen Kiggell, 31/5/1917. 'Messines – Wytschaete', NA, WO158/215.
50. Interview with Hudspeth, Barrie papers, REM.
51. Harvey, 'Mining in France', op. cit., pp. 19–20.
52. Letter H. R. Kerr to Barrie, 8/3/1962, Barrie Papers, REM.
53. Ralph G. Hamilton, *The War Diary of the Master of Belhaven* (London 1924), p. 304.
54. Translation of the history of the 204 (German) Division in Australian War Memorial 26/6/190/1, quoted in R. Prior and T. Wilson, *Passchendaele: The Untold Story*, (Yale, London, 1996), p. 61.
55. *Australian Official History*, op. cit., p. 959.
56. Edmonds, *Military Operations, France and Belgium, 1917*, Vol. II, pp. 59-60.
57. Quoted in Myles Dungan, *Irish Voices from the Great War*, (Irish Academic Press, Dublin, 1995), p. 159.
58. Frayling *Tunnellers*, op. cit.
59. Cyril Falls, *The History of the 36th (Ulster) Division*, (M'Caw, Stevenson & Orr, Limited, Belfast, 1922), p. 92.
60. Frayling *Tunnellers*, op. cit.
61. Gen Sir Charles Harington, *Plumer of Messines*, (John Murray, London, 1935), p. 104. This arrangement of corpses seems likely to have been a macabre soldiers' prank.
62. *Tunnellers*, op. cit., p. 244.
63. *Australian Official History*, op. cit., p. 602.
64. *Australian Official History*, op. cit., p. 549.
65. Harvey, 'Mining in France', op. cit., p. 21.
66. Ibid.
67. Füsslein, *Ehrenbuch*, op. cit., p. 548.
68. Ibid.
69. Major Soffner, 'Oblt. Sonne, führer der 3./Pi. 25' in Paul Heinrici [Ed.], *Das Ehrenbuch der Deutschen Pioniere*, (Verlag Tradition Wilhelm Rolf, Berlin, 1931), p. 304. *Military Mining*, op. cit., p. 18.

Chapter 8

1. [Anon.] *Extracts from the old mining regulations Issued by the General of Pioneers, Army Headquarters, Laon, April 1915.* [SS461 General Staff 1916].
2. Quoted by Friedrich Seesselberg, *Der Stellungskrieg 1914–1918*, (E.S. Mittler and Son, Berlin, 1926), pp. 304–305.
3. *Military Engineering (Vol. IV) Demolitions and Mining*, (HMSO, London, 1923), p. 137.
4. J. C. Neill (Ed.), *The New Zealand Tunnelling Company, 1915–1919*, (Whitcombe & Tombs, Auckland, 1922), p. 38.

5. Tunneller, 'Messines', TOCA *Bulletin*, No. 5, 1930, pp. 17–18.
6. Seesselberg, op. cit., p. 305.
7. Tunneller, 'Messines', op. cit., p. 18.
8. *Military Engineering (Vol. IV) Demolitions and Mining, 1923* op. cit., p. 103.
9. Report CO 12th West Yorkshire Regiment, 30/3/1916, 3rd (British) Division reports, 'War Diaries – St. Eloi Operations', Library and Archives Canada (LAC).
10. Held [et. al.], *Das Königlich Preussische Garde=Pionier=Bataillon und seine Kriegsverbände 1914/18* [Vol. 1] Potsdam, 1932, Carl Fr. Berg, Berlin, p. 264.
11. Op. cit. p. 265.
12. Alexander Barrie, *War Underground*, (Star Books, London, 1981, originally Frederick Muller, London, 1962), pp. 196–203.
13. Peter Barton, Peter Doyle & Johan Vandewalle, *Beneath Flanders Fields, the Tunnellers' War 1914–1918*, Spellmount, Staplehurst, 2004), pp. 180–181.
14. Walter Kranz, quoted in Barton, et. al., *Beneath Flanders Fields*, op. cit., pp. 74–75.
15. [Anon.], *The Work of the Royal Engineers in the European War, 1914–19. Work in the field under the Engineer-in-Chief, B.E.F., Geological Work on the Western Front*, (Institution of Royal Engineers, Chatham, 1922), pp. 23–28; for a detailed account of this important subject, see Peter Doyle's chapter 5 in Barton, et. al., *Beneath Flanders Fields*, op. cit.
16. Capitaine [Hippolyte-Michel] Thobie, *La Prise de Carency par le Pic et Par la Mine*, (Berger-Levrault, Paris, 1918), p. 167–168.
17. [Anon.], *Notice sur les Travaux Scientifiques de M. Jean Perrin*, (Édouard Privat, Toulouse, 1923), pp. 64–65.
18. Johan Somers, *Imperial German Uniforms and Equipment 1907–1918*, [Vol. 1.], (Schiffer Military History, Atglen, PA, 2005), pp. 162–163.
19. *Military Engineering (Vol. IV) Demolitions and Mining, 1923* op. cit., p. 171.
20. H. Standish Ball, 'The Work of the Miner on the Western Front, 1915–1918', *Transactions of the Institution of Mining and Metallurgy*, Vol. XXVIII, 1919, p. 206.
21. Lieutenant von Klingspor quoted in Seesselberg, op. cit., p. 305.
22. [Anon.], *The Work of the Royal Engineers in the European War, 1914–19. Military Mining*, (Institution of Royal Engineers, Chatham, 1922), pp. 29–31.
23. Maj Gen Sir W. G. MacPherson (et. al., Eds.), *Medical Services Diseases of the War*, Vol. II, (HMSO, London, 1923), p. 573 (Chapters XIX to XXI by D. Dale Logan).
24. Oberstleutnant a. D. Bok, 'Eine Episode aus dem Minenkrieg württembergischer Pioniere', Paul Heinrici [Ed.], *Das Ehrenbuch der Deutschen Pioniere*, (Verlag Tradition Wilhelm Rolf, Berlin, 1931), pp. 528–530 (from a translation by Peter Lane).
25. G. F. F. Eagar, 'The training of officers and men of the tunnelling companies of the Royal Engineers in mine-rescue work on active service in France', *Transactions of the Institute of Mining Engineers*, 1919–20, Vol. LVIII, pp. 304–324; comments by Eagar following papers by David Dale Logan, 'The difficulties and dangers of mine-rescue work on the Western Front; and mining operations carried out by men wearing rescue-apparatus' and 'Accidents due to structural defects of apparatus or injury to apparatus; and the future of the Proto apparatus', *Transactions of the Institute of Mining Engineers* 1918–19, Vol. LVII, pp. 242–243.
26. Frederick J. Mulqueen, *Memoirs of Major F. J. Mulqueen, DSO MC*, REL, p. 39.
27. R. C. Smart, *Recent Practice in Self-Contained Breathing Apparatus*, (Charles Griffin & Co. Ltd, 1921), pp. 222–231; Simon Jones, 'A Mine Rescue Officer on the Western

Front', *The Royal Engineers Journal*, Vol. 109, 1995, pp. 250–255; MacPherson, *Medical Services Diseases of the War*, Vol. II, op. cit., pp. 602–604.

28. Simon Jones, *World War I Gas Warfare Tactics and Equipment*, (Osprey, Oxford, 2007), pp. 40–41; account by D. Dale Logan in MacPherson, *Medical Services Diseases of the War*, Vol. II, op. cit., pp. 547–550.

Chapter 9

1. Captain A. Gay, 'Sapping Operations, Especially for Infantry: From a lecture to cadets at Saint Maixant, France by Capt A. Gay, French Army', *Professional Memoirs*. Corps of Engineers, United States Army and Engineer Department at Large. Vol.10 (1918), p. 206.
2. Ministère de la Guerre, État-Major de l'Armée – Service Historique, *Les Armées françaises dans la grande guerre*, Vol. III, (Imp. Nationale, Paris 1931), p. 256; Appendix 1113, 6/8/1915, Note relative à l'attaque projetée du 3e C.A.
3. Op. cit., Appendix 1127 Hache GOC 3rd Corps to Urbal GOC X Army, 8/8/1915.
4. 'Le Journal de Vincent Martin' (apparently a memoir rather than a diary), http://pagesperso-orange.fr/119RI/journalmartin.html.
5. War diaries of French 36th, 39th & 74th Infantry Regt's, Engineer Company 3/1 and 5th Infantry Division, Service Historique de la Défense, Département de l'armée de Terre (SHAT).
6. 'Journal de Paul Andrillon Caporal à la 12e Cie 119e RI', http://pagesperso-orange.fr/119RI/journalandrillon.html.
7. Ibid.
8. War diary 28th Infantry Regt., (SHAT).
9. War diary 12th Infantry Bde., (SHAT).
10. Martin, op. cit.
11. Ibid.
12. Brigadier General J. E. Edmonds, *Military Operations, France and Belgium, 1915*, (MacMillan and Co. Ltd, London, 1927) Vol. 2, p. 194; 236–7.
13. Major-General Sir Ernest D. Swinton, *Eyewitness*, London, Hodder and Stoughton, 1932, p. 118.
14. C. E. W. Bean, *The Story of Anzac from 4 May, 1915, to the Evacuation of the Gallipoli Peninsula*, (Angus and Robertson Ltd, Australia, 1941), Vol. 2, p. 259.
15. R. East, (Ed.), *The Gallipoli Diary of Sergeant Lawrence of the Australian Engineers – 1st A.I.F. 1915* (Melbourne University Press, Melbourne, 1981), p. 154.
16. *Gallipoli Diary of Sergeant Lawrence*, op. cit., p. 31.
17. The British Official History of the Gallipoli campaign claims that three mines were used to open up a gallery and that a long narrow crater formed was converted into a communication trench. This statement does not correspond to the location of the mines and is not borne out by the accounts in Bean (op. cit.) or the War Diary of 2nd Field Company. C. F. Aspinall-Oglander, *Military Operations Gallipoli, Vol. II, May 1915 to the Evacuation*, (William Heinemann, London, 1932), p. 181.
18. Bean, *The Story of Anzac*, Vol. 2, op. cit., pp. 502–503.
19. Ibid., p. 505.
20. War Diary 2nd Field Company Australian engineers, www.awm.gov.au.
21. *Gallipoli Diary of Sergeant Lawrence*, op. cit., p. 66.
22. Bean, *The Story of Anzac*, Vol. 2, op. cit., p. 817.

23. Bean, *The Story of Anzac*, Vol. 2, op. cit., p. 813.

24. J. Murray, *Gallipoli As I Saw It*, (William Kimber, London, 1965), p. 168.

25. Murray, op. cit., p. 174.

26. [Anon.], *The Fifth Battalion Highland Light Infantry in the War 1914–1918*, (MacLehose, Jackson and Co., Glasgow, 1921), p. 64.

27. Op. cit., p. 67.

28. Op. cit., p. 61.

29. GHQ Instruction OB1207, 2/2/1916, in Brigadier General J. E. Edmonds, *Military Operations, France and Belgium, 1916*, [Vol. 1] Appendices, (Macmillan and Co. Ltd, London, 1932), Appendix 16, pp. 91–124.

30. Captain W. Grant Grieve and Bernard Newman, *Tunnellers*, (Herbert Jenkins, London, 1936), pp. 116–7.

31. Brigadier General J. E. Edmonds, *Military Operations, France and Belgium, 1916*, [Vol. 1], (Imperial War Museum, London, nd, originally published 1932), pp. 429, 444.

32. Diary of R. S. G. Stokes, Assistant Inspector of Mines, 4/7/1916, NA WO158/137.

33. Letter G. A. Robson MC, late Lt 1st Bn Rifle Brigade, to J. E. Edmonds, nd, NA CAB45/137.

34. Stokes diary, op. cit., 4/7/1916.

35. Ibid.

36. Lt. Geoffrey Malins OBE, *How I Filmed the War*, (Herbert Jenkins Limited, London, 1920), pp. 156–157.

37. 29 Division Order No 36, 14/6/16 transcript in 'First Avenue' DVD produced by the Durand Group.

38. Letter of Colonel A. F. G. Ruston, 1/3rd Kent Field Company, RE, to J. E. Edmonds, NA CAB45/137.

39. War Diary 1/2 Monmouthshire Regiment, transcript in 'First Avenue' DVD produced by the Durand Group.

40. War Diary 16 Royal Irish Rifles, NA, WO95/2498.

41. Report c.16/8/16, 10 Corps GS War Diary, NA WO95/851.

42. 32 Division GS War Diary, 1/7/16, NA WO95/2368.

43. Lt. Col. J. Shakespear, *A Record of the 17th and 32nd Service Battalions Northumberland Fusiliers (N.E.R.) Pioneers 1914–1919*, (Northumberland Press Limited, Newcastle upon Tyne, 1926), p. 34.

44. Letter H. M. Hance to J. E. Edmonds, June 1930, NA CAB45/134.

45. Report on action of 70th Company Machine Gun Corps on July 1st 1916, War Diary 70 Infantry Brigade, National Archives, WO95/2185.

46. Hance letter, op. cit.

47. Report Major H. M. Hance to Chief Engineer 3rd Corps, 27/7/1916, RE Library.

48. 9th Bn The Cheshire Regiment War Diary, NA WO95/2090.

49. *Military Operations, France and Belgium, 1916*, [Vol. 1] Map Volume, (MacMillan and Co. Ltd, London, 1932), Map 8.

50. Letter Lt Col A. G. B. Urmston to J. E. Edmonds, 11/6/1930, NA CAB45/191.

51. Hance letter, op. cit.

52. War Diary 179 Tunnelling Company, RE, NA WO95/244.

53. Edmonds, *Military Operations, France and Belgium, 1916*, Vol. 1, op. cit., p. 359.

54. Letter B. G. Clay to J. E. Edmonds, 3/12/1929, NA CAB45/132.

55. Maj. Gen. C. H. Foulkes, "Gas!" The Story of the Special Brigade, (William Blackwood & Sons Ltd, Edinburgh & London, 1934), pp. 162–163; War Diary Special Section, RE, NA WO95/122; Peter Barton, *The Somme*, (Constable, London, 2006), contains an illustrated reconstruction of the Livens flame projector.
56. Weekly Mine Report 183 Tunnelling Company, RE, 18 Division GS, War Diary, NA WO95/2015.
57. Letter H. C. B. Hickling to J. E. Edmonds, nd, NA CAB45/189.
58. Weekly Mine Report 183 Tunnelling Company, op. cit.
59. Stokes diary, op. cit., 4/7/1916.
60. Ibid.
61. Report by Lt Col F. Preedy, Controller of Mines, 4th Army, NA WO158/335.
62. Brigadier General J. E. Edmonds, *Military Operations, France and Belgium, 1916*, (Vol. 2), (Imperial War Museum, London, nd, originally published 1932), p. 281; War Diary 174 Tunnelling Company WD, NA WO95/404.
63. Edmonds, *Military Operations, France and Belgium, 1916*, Vol. 2, op. cit., p. 502.
64. Major R. G. Trower, Summary of Operations of 252nd Company Royal Engineers during attack of November 13th 1916, National Archives WO158/335.
65. Letter C. E. G. Shearman to J. E. Edmonds, 20/1/1937, NA CAB45/137.
66. R. N. Harvey, 'Military Mining in the Great War, A Lecture delivered at the S.M.E., Chatham, on November 14th, 1929', *Royal Engineers Journal*, XLIII Dec. 1929, p. 542.
67. Chief of the General Staff, GHQ, to Armies, 5/12/1916, NA WO158/335.
68. 5th Army to 1st Army, 15/12/1916, NA WO158/335.
69. *Tunnellers*, op. cit., p. 129; Graham Seton Hutchison, *The W Plan*, (Thornton Butterworth, London, 1929).

Chapter 10

1. Capitaine Thobie, *La Prise de Carency par le Pic et Par la Mine*, (Berger-Levrault, Paris 1918), pp. 38–39.
2. Ernst Jünger, *The Storm of Steel* (trans. Basil Creighton), (Constable, London, 1994) (1929), pp. 59–60.
3. Ernst Jünger (trans. Basil Creighton), *Copse 125 A Chronicle from the Trench Warfare of 1918*, (Zimmerman & Zimmerman, 1985), p. 17.
4. Jünger, *Storm of Steel* op. cit., p. 35.
5. *Unterirdische Anlagen (Katakomben) in Nordfrankreich*, Herausgegeben im Auftrag des AOK2, [February 1918].
6. [Anon.], 'Experience Gained from the September (1915) Offensives on the Fronts of the Sixth and Third Armies', *German and Austrian Tactical Studies Translations of Captured German and Austrian Documents and Information Obtained From German and Austrian Prisoners from the British, French and Italian Staffs*, (Government Printing Office, Washington, 1918), p. 13.
7. Ibid., p. 17.
8. Ibid., p. 22.
9. Witte, Karl, *3. Rheinisches Pionier=Bataillon Nr.30* (Gerhard Stalling, Berlin 1928), p. 97; Georges Blond, *Verdun*, (MacMillan, New York, 1964), pp. 14–15.
10. Alistair Horne, *The Price of Glory Verdun 1916*, (Penguin Books, London, 1964), pp. 216, 303–306.

11. Brigadier General J. E. Edmonds, *Military Operations, France and Belgium, 1916*, [Vol. 1] Appendices, (MacMillan and Co. Ltd, London, 1932), App. 10, 'Amended Plan submitted by the Fourth Army to GHQ 19th April 1916,' p. 80.
12. Stephen Westman, *Surgeon with the Kaiser's Army*, (William Kimber, London, 1968), pp. 94–95.
13. Thobie, op. cit., p. 82.
14. 'Lessons Drawn from the Battle of the Somme,' *German and Austrian Tactical Studies*, op. cit., p. 87.
15. [Anon.], *Deep Gallery Shelters, Translated at the Army War College from a French Study*, July 1917, (Washington, Government Printing Office, 1917), p. 5; [Anon.], *Notes on the Construction of Deep Gallery Shelters, Translated and edited at Army War College*, October 1917, (Washington, Government Printing Office, 1917), p. 7; [Anon.], *Notes on the Construction and Equipment of Trenches, Compiled from the latest sources*, Army War College April 1917 (Washington, Government Printing Office, 1917).
16. Brigadier General J. E. Edmonds, *Military Operations, France and Belgium, 1916*, (Vol. 1), (Imperial War Museum, London, nd, 1932), p. 284.
17. Brig Gen Trevor Ternan, *The Story of the Tyneside Scottish*, (The Northumberland Press, Newcastle-Upon-Tyne, 1919), p. 82.
18. GOC 103 Brigade to 34 Division, 11/6/1916, WD, 103 Infantry Brigade, NA WO95/2464; Lt. Col. J. Shakespear, *The Thirty-Fourth Division 1915–1919*, (H. F. & G. Witherby, London, 1921), pp. 28–29.
19. 'Mining in France 1914–1917' by Major-General R. N. Harvey, late Inspector of Mines, National Archives, WO106/387, pp. 19, 23.
20. Cyril Falls, *The History of the 36th (Ulster) Division*, (M'Caw, Stevenson & Orr Ltd, Belfast, 1922), pp. 112–113.
21. Harvey, Mining in France, op. cit., p. 19.
22. First Army Administrative Report on the Vimy Ridge Operations, NA WO158/900.
23. H. W. Graham, *The Life of a Tunnelling Company*, (J. Catherall & Co. Ltd, Hexham, 1927), p. 74.
24. R. E. Priestley, *The Signal Service in the European War of 1914 to 1918 (France)*, (Institution of Royal Engineers, Chatham, 1921), pp. 118–119.
25. J. C. Neill (Ed.), *The New Zealand Tunnelling Company, 1915-1919*, (Whitcombe & Tombs, Auckland, 1922), p. 63.
26. Neill, op. cit., pp. 63–64.
27. Maj. Gen. Sir W. G. MacPherson, *Medical Services General History* Vol. III, (HMSO, London, 1924), p. 74–76.
28. Captain W. Grant Grieve and Bernard Newman, *Tunnellers*, (Herbert Jenkins, London, 1936), p. 159.
29. Neill, op. cit., p. 65.
30. Neill, op. cit., pp. 72–74.
31. Falls, *History of the 36th (Ulster) Division*, op. cit., p. 127.
32. Captain Cyril Falls, *Military Operations, France and Belgium, 1917*, [Vol. I], *The German Retreat to the Hindenburg Line and the Battle of Arras*, (Imperial War Museum, London, nd) (1940), pp. 217–218.
33. Neill, op. cit., pp. 77–80.
34. Neill, op. cit., p. 81.

35. Graham, op. cit., pp. 182–183.
36. Timothy T. Lupfer, *The Dynamics of Doctrine: the changes in German tactical doctrine during the First World War*, (Combat Studies Institute, Fort Leavenworth, Kansas, 1981), pp. 13–15.
37. Falls, *Military Operations, France and Belgium, 1917*, Vol. 1, op. cit., pp. 323–325, Map 10; Jonathon Nicholls, *Cheerful Sacrifice*, (Leo Cooper, London, 1990), p. 84.
38. W. Buhr, *Die Geschichte des I. Westf. Pionier=Bataillons Nr. 7 und seiner Kriegsverbände im Weltkriege 1914/18* (Gerhard Stalling, Oldenburg 1938), p. 160.
39. '3. Inf.-Regt. 476. Die Katastrophe im Cornillet-Tunnel (20. Mai 1917)', in Generalleutant Otto v. Moser, *Die Württemberger im Weltkriege*, (Chr. Belser A G, Stuttgart, 1927), pp. 537–541; Oberstleutnant L. Knies, *Das Württembergische Pionier=Bataillon Nr. 13 im Weltkrieg 1914-1918*, (Chr. Belser A. G., Stuttgart, 1927), pp. 114–117 (my thanks to John Lane for German translations); Ministère de la Guerre, État-Major de l'Armée – Service Historique, *Les Armées françaises dans la grande guerre*, Tome V, 2nd Vol., Annexes 1st Volume, (Imp. Nationale, Paris 1937), Annexe No 351; Extrait d'un rapport émis par le médecin allemand du bataillon, médecin en chef, le Docteur Nagel 11/476, http://pagesperso-orange.fr/champagne1418/recit/recit9.htm# cornillet; 'Note on Mont Cornillet Tunnel,' [Anon.], *Notes on Recent Operations* No. 2, Edited at the Army War College from French and British Sources, July, 1917, Washington, Government Printing Office.
40. Die Katastrophe im Cornillet-Tunnel, op. cit., pp. 537–538.
41. Ibid., p. 539.
42. Knies, op. cit., p. 115.
43. Nagel report, op. cit.
44. Nagel report, op. cit.
45. Die Katastrophe im Cornillet-Tunnel, op. cit., p. 540.
46. Ibid., p. 541.
47. A. Girod, http://www.lced.org/div_04.php.
48. [Anon.], *Verdun An Illustrated Historical Guide*, (Éditions Lorraines Frémont, Verdun, nd), pp. 40, 106.
49. 'The Experience Gained During the English-French Offensive in the Spring of 1917, 10th June, 1917, Issued by the Chief of the General Staff of the Field Army', *German and Austrian Tactical Studies*, op. cit. pp. 181–182.
50. 'Extracts from The Construction Of Defensive Positions, Translation of a German document, dated German Army Headquarters, June 30, 1917', *German and Austrian Tactical Studies*, op. cit. pp. 127–132.
51. Op. cit., p. 132.
52. Lt Col von Thaer, CGS, 'The Construction of Positions for the Coming Winter', (Translation of a German document captured by the British), Headquarters American Expeditionary Forces, General Staff, Intelligence Section (A), October 19, 1917, *German and Austrian Tactical Studies*, op. cit. pp. 139–142.
53. Jünger, *Copse 125*, op. cit., pp. 17–20.
54. [Anon.], *The Work of the Royal Engineers in the European War, 1914–19. Military Mining*, (Institution of Royal Engineers, Chatham, 1922), p. 18.
55. H. J. Humphrys, letter to J. E. Edmonds, 16/7/1931, private papers of descendant of writer.

56. Brig Gen J. E. Edmonds, *Military Operations, France and Belgium, 1918*, [Vol. II], *March–April: continuation of the German offensives*, (MacMillan and Co., Ltd., London, 1937), p. 160.
57. Capt E. J. Ritchie, 'The Fight for Givenchy Ridge, April 1918 and the Part Played by the 251st (T) Coy. R.E.,' TOCA *Bulletin*, No. 13, 1938, p. 64.
58. Ibid.
59. Grieve & Newman, *Tunnellers*, op. cit., p. 283.
60. Ritchie, op. cit., p. 65.

Chapter 11

1. Brigadier R. M. Merrell, 'The Berlin Spy Tunnel – a Memoir', *The Royal Engineers Journal*, Vol. 116, 2002, pp. 105–107.

Bibliography

Only works actually consulted are included.

Unpublished Documents
Detailed references for archival sources are given in the chapter notes.

National Archives, Kew
War Diaries.
Diary of Sir John Norton Griffiths.
Diary of Maj. R.S.G. Stokes.
Maj. Gen. R. N. Harvey, 'Mining in France 1914–1917'.
Mining Plans.

Royal Engineers Museum, Chatham
Alexander Barrie papers.
Just a Small One (magazine of 172 Tunnelling Company) 1915, 1916

Royal Engineers Library, Chatham
F.J. Mulqueen, *Memoirs of Major F. J. Mulqueen, DSO MC,* (unpublished typescript).

Library and Archives Canada
http://www.collectionscanada.gc.ca/archivianet/020152_e.html
Canadian Army War Diaries.
British Army War Diaries concerning St Eloi operation.

Service Historique de la Défense, Département de l'armée de Terre
http://www.memoiredeshommes.sga.defense.gouv.fr/jmo/cdc.html
French Army War Diaries.

West Sussex Record Office
Sir Ivor Maxse papers.

Published sources
Books

G.H. Addison, *The Work of the Royal Engineers in the European War, 1914–1918 Miscellaneous* (Institution of Royal Engineers, Chatham, 1927).
Amis de Vauquois, *La Butte Meurtrie Vauquois La guerre des mines 1914–1918*, (Les Amis de Vauquois et de sa Région, 2004).

[Anon.], *Consolidation of Trenches and Localities after Assault and Capture*, General Staff, SS112, 1916.

[Anon.], *Deep Gallery Shelters, Translated at the Army War College from a French Study*, July 1917, (Government Printing Office, Washington, 1917).

[Anon.], *Écoles du Génie, École de Mines, approbation ministérielle du 16 Juillet 1901, Édition mis à jour jusqu'au 30 avril 1909*, (Imprimerie Nationale, Paris, 1918).

[Anon.], *Écoles du Génie, École de Mines et d'Explosifs*, (Imprimerie Nationale, Paris, 1925).

[Anon.], *Écoles du Génie, École de Mines Supplément au Livre de l'Officier (approbation ministérielle du 22 Janvier 1917)*, (Imprimerie Nationale, Paris, 1917).

[Anon.], *Écoles du Génie, Instruction Pratique, École de Mines, Livre de l'Officier (approbation ministérielle du 25 Juillet 1908)*, (Imprimerie Nationale, Paris, 1916).

[Anon.], *Extracts from the old mining regulations Issued by the General of Pioneers, Army Headquarters, Laon, April 1915*, General Staff SS461, 1916.

[Anon.], *Feld=Anweisung Heeres=Sauerstoff=Schutzgerät*, [War Ministry, Berlin], 1917.

[Anon.], *The Fifth Battalion Highland Light Infantry in the War 1914–1918*, (MacLehose, Jackson and Co., Glasgow, 1921).

[Anon.], *First Report of the Committee on Siege and Fortress Warfare*, (War Office, 1908).

[Anon.], *German Army Handbook, April 1918*, (Arms and Armour Press, London, 1977).

[Anon.], *German and Austrian Tactical Studies Translations of Captured German and Austrian Documents and Information Obtained From German and Austrian Prisoners from the British, French and Italian Staffs*, (Government Printing Office, Washington, 1918).

[Anon.], *German Mining Officer's Diary Captured at Fricourt, July 1916*, General Staff, SS465, 1916.

[Anon.], *Instruction Allemand sur le Service du Pionier dans la Guerre de Siège (1913), Traduction du text allemand faite à la Section Technique Genie*, (Imprimerie Nationale, Paris, 1915).

[Anon.], *Interim Report of Major-General Hickman's Siege Committee, November 1914*, (War Office, 1914).

[Anon.], *Military Engineering (Part II) Attack and Defence of Fortresses*, (HMSO, London, 1910).

[Anon.], *Military Engineering (Part IV) Mining and Demolitions*, (HMSO, London, 1910).

[Anon.], *Military Engineering (Vol. IV) Demolitions and Mining*, (HMSO, London, 1923).

[Anon.], *Notes on Recent Operations* No. 2, Edited at the Army War College from French and British Sources, July, 1917, (Government Printing Office, Washington, 1917).

[Anon.], *Notes on the Construction and Equipment of Trenches, Compiled from the latest sources* Army War College April 1917 (Government Printing Office, Washington, 1917).

[Anon.], *Notes on Trench Warfare for Infantry Officers, Revised Diagrams. Issued by the General Staff, December 1916*, (HMSO, London, 1917).

[Anon.], *Notes on the Construction of Deep Gallery Shelters, Translated and edited at Army War College*, October 1917, (Government Printing Office, Washington, 1917).

[Anon.], *Notice sur les Travaux Scientifiques de M. Jean Perrin*, (Édouard Privat, Toulouse, 1923).

[Anon.], *Report of the Committee on Siege Artillery Material, December 1914*, (War Office, 1914).

[Anon.], *Report of the Siege Operations held at Chatham July and August 1907*, (School of Military Engineering, Chatham, 1907).

[Anon.], *Sprengvorschrift von 1911*, (Georg Bath, Berlin, 1918).

[Anon.], 'Tunnellers' Old Comrades Association Annual Dinner, 1927', Tunnellers' Old Comrades Association *Bulletin*, No. 2, 1927, pp. 13–24.

[Anon.], *Verdun An Illustrated Historical Guide*, (Éditions Lorraines Frémont, Verdun, nd).

[Anon.], *Vorschriften für den Stellungskrieg für alle Waffen. Teil 2. Minenkrieg*, (Kriegsministerium, Berlin 1916).

[Anon.], *The Work of the Royal Engineers in the European War, 1914–19, Military Mining*, (Institution of Royal Engineers, Chatham, 1922).

[Anon.], *The Work of the Royal Engineers in the European War, 1914–19, Work in the field under the Engineer-in-Chief, B.E.F., Geological Work on the Western Front*, (Institution of Royal Engineers, Chatham, 1922).

Alexander Barrie, *War Underground*, (Star Books, London, 1981, originally Frederick Muller, London, 1962).

Peter Barton, Peter Doyle & Johan Vandewalle, *Beneath Flanders Fields, the Tunnellers' War 1914–1918*, (Spellmount, Staplehurst, 2004).

Georges Blond, *Verdun*, (MacMillan, New York, 1964).

Adolf Buchner, *Der Minenkrieg auf Vauquois*, (W. Goertz, Karlsfeld, 1982).

Francis Buckley, *Q. 6. A And Other Places Recollections of 1916, 1917, 1918*, (London, Spottiswoode, Ballantyne & Co. Ltd, 1920).

W. Buhr, *Die Geschichte des I. Westf. Pionier=Bataillons Nr. 7 und seiner Kriegsverbände im Weltkriege 1914/18*, (Gerhard Stalling, Oldenburg, 1938).

C.E.W. Bean, *The Story of Anzac from 4 May, 1915, to the Evacuation of the Gallipoli Peninsula*, (2 Vols.), (Angus and Robertson Ltd, Australia, 1941).

C.E.W. Bean, *The Official History of Australia in the War of 1914 - 1918 Volume IV The Australian Imperial Force in France: 1917*, (Angus and Robertson Ltd, Australia, 1933).

Nigel Cave, *Battleground Europe Arras Vimy Ridge*, (Leo Cooper, London, 1996).

John Whiteclay Chambers II (ed.), *Oxford Companion to American Military History*, (Oxford University Press, Oxford, 1999).

Hermann Cron, *Imperial German Army 1914–18: Organisation, Structure, Orders of Battle*, (Helion and Company, Solihull, 2006) originally published as *Geschichte des Deutschen Heeres im Weltkriege 1914-1918*, (Berlin, Militarverlag Karl Siegismund, 1937).

Myles Dungan, *Irish Voices from the Great War*, (Irish Academic Press, Dublin, 1995).

R. East, (ed.), *The Gallipoli Diary of Sergeant Lawrence of the Australian Engineers – 1st A.I.F. 1915*, (Melbourne University Press, Melbourne, 1981).

Brigadier General J. E. Edmonds, *Military Operations, France and Belgium, 1915*, (2 Vols.), (MacMillan and Co. Ltd, London, 1927).

Brigadier General J. E. Edmonds, *Military Operations, France and Belgium, 1916*, (2 Vols.), (Imperial War Museum, London, nd) (1932).

Brigadier General J. E. Edmonds, *Military Operations, France and Belgium, 1916*, [Vol. I] Appendices, (MacMillan and Co. Ltd, London, 1932).

Brigadier General J. E. Edmonds, *Military Operations, France and Belgium, 1917*, [Vol. II], *7th June – 10th November Messines and Third Ypres (Passchendaele)*, (HMSO, London, 1927).

Brigadier General J. E. Edmonds, *Military Operations, France and Belgium, 1918*, [Vol. II], *March–April: continuation of the German offensives*, (MacMillan and Co. Ltd, London, 1937).

Cyril Falls, *The History of the 36th (Ulster) Division*, (M'Caw, Stevenson & Orr Ltd, Belfast, 1922).

Captain Cyril Falls, *Military Operations, France and Belgium, 1917*, [Vol. I], *The German Retreat to the Hindenburg Line and the Battle of Arras*, (Imperial War Museum, London, nd) (1940).

Commandant R. de Feriet, *La Crête des Éparges 1914–1918*, (Payot, Paris, 1939).

'W.G.' [Walter Gard'ner], *One Mole Rampant*, [Privately published, c.1921].

Captain Genez, *Histoire de la Guerre Souterraine*, (Librairie Militaire Berger Levrault Paris 1914) (translated in *Royal Engineers Journal*, Vol. XX, 1914).

Jean-Jacques Gorlet, *La Guerre de Mines dans l'Oise 1914–1917 en secteur calme*, (Société Archéologique Historique et Scientifique de Noyon, 2005).

H. W. Graham, *The Life of a Tunnelling Company*, (J. Catherall & Co. Ltd., Hexham, 1927).

Captain W. Grant Grieve and Bernard Newman, *Tunnellers*, (Herbert Jenkins, London, 1936).

Ralph G. Hamilton, *The War Diary of the Master of Belhaven*, (London, 1924).

Gen Sir Charles Harington, *Plumer of Messines*, (John Murray, London, 1935).

Hartenstein, *Das Ruhrhessische Pionier=Bataillon Nr. 11 im Weltkriege 1914–1918*, (Bernhard Sporn, Zeulenroda, 1936).

Paul Heinrici (Ed.), *Das Ehrenbuch der Deutschen Pioniere*, (Verlag Tradition Wilhelm Rolf, Berlin, 1931).

Held, (et. al.), *Das Königlich Preussische Garde=Pionier=Bataillon und seine Kriegsverbände 1914/18* (2 Vols.), (Carl Fr. Berg, Berlin, 1932).

L. Hughes and J. Dixon, *"Surrender Be Damned" A History of the 1/1st Battalion the Monmouthshire Regiment, 1914–18*, (CWM Press, Caerphilly, 1995).

Simon Jones, *World War I Gas Warfare Tactics and Equipment*, (Osprey, Oxford, 2007).

Ernst Jünger (trans. Basil Creighton), *The Storm of Steel*, (Constable, London, 1994) (1929).

Ernst Jünger (trans. Basil Creighton), *Copse 125 A Chronicle from the Trench Warfare of 1918*, (Zimmerman & Zimmerman, 1985) (1929).

George L. Kerr, *Practical coal mining: a manual for managers, under-managers, colliery engineers, and others*, (Charles Griffin & Co. Ltd, 1905).

Oberstleutnant L. Knies, *Das württembergische Pionier=Bataillon Nr. 13 im Weltkrieg 1914–1918*, (Chr. Belser A G, Stuttgart, 1927).

August Lehmann, *Das K. B. [Königliches Bayerisches] Pionier=Regiment* (Max Schick, Munich, 1927).

Karl Lehmann, *Bayerische Pioniere im Weltkriege*, (R. Piper & Co. Verlag, Munich., 1918).

Timothy T. Lupfer, *The Dynamics of Doctrine: the changes in German tactical doctrine during the First World War*, (Combat Studies Institute, Fort Leavenworth, Kansas, 1981).

Maj. Gen. Sir W.G. MacPherson (et. al., Eds.), *Medical Services Diseases of the War*, Vol. II, (HMSO, London, 1923).

Maj. Gen. Sir W.G. MacPherson, *Medical Services General History*, Vol. III, (HMSO, London, 1924).

Lt. Geoffrey Malins OBE, *How I Filmed the War*, (Herbert Jenkins Limited, London, 1920).

Ministère de la Guerre, État-Major de l'Armée – Service Historique, *Les Armées françaises dans la grande guerre*, Vol. II, (Imp. Nationale, Paris 1931).

Ministère de la Guerre, État-Major de l'Armée – Service Historique, *Les Armées françaises dans la grande guerre*, Vol. III, (Imp. Nationale, Paris, 1931).

Ministère de la Guerre, État-Major de l'Armée – Service Historique, *Les Armées françaises dans la grande guerre*, Tome IV, Vols. 1–3 , (Imp. Nationale, Paris, 1927–1936).

Ministère de la Guerre, État-Major de l'Armée – Service Historique, *Les Armées françaises dans la grande guerre*, Tome V, 2nd Vol., Annexes 1st Volume, (Imp. Nationale, Paris, 1937).

Generalleutant Otto v. Moser, *Die Württemberger im Weltkriege*, (Chr. Belser A. G. Stuttgart, 1927).

J. C. Neill (Ed.), *The New Zealand Tunnelling Company, 1915–1919*, (Whitcombe & Tombs, Auckland, 1922).

Jonathon Nicholls, *Cheerful Sacrifice*, (Leo Cooper, London, 1990).

Oberkommando des Heeres, *Der Weltkrieg 1914 bis 1918, Die Kriegführung im Frühjahr 1917*, Vol. 12, (E. S. Mittler & Sohn, Berlin, 1939).

C.F. Aspinall-Oglander, *Military Operations Gallipoli, Vol. II, May 1915 to the Evacuation*, (William Heinemann, London, 1932).

Maj. De Pardieu, *A Critical Study of German Tactics and of the New German Regulations*, (trans. Capt. Charles F. Martin), (United States Cavalry Association, Kansas 1912).

André Pézard, *Nous autres, à Vauquois 1915–1916*, (Paris, La Renaissance du Livre, 1918).

Maj. G. R. Pridham, RE, *Siege Operations carried out by the 20th and 42nd Companies, Royal Engineers, June, 1913*, (War Office, 1913), p. 11.

R. E. Priestley, *The Signal Service in the European War of 1914 to 1918 (France)*, (Institution of Royal Engineers, Chatham, 1921).

R. Prior and T. Wilson, *The Somme*, (Yale University Press, New Haven and London, 2005).

R. Prior and T. Wilson, *Passchendaele: The Untold Story*, (Yale, London, 1996).

Maj. Gen. H. L. Pritchard, RE, (Ed.), *History of the Corps of Royal Engineers, Vol. V, The Home Front, France, Flanders and Italy in the First World War*, (Institution of Royal Engineers, Chatham, 1952).

Maj. Gen. H.L. Pritchard, RE, (Ed.), *History of the Corps of Royal Engineers, Vol. VI, Gallipoli, Macedonia, Egypt and Palestine 1914–18*, (Institution of Royal Engineers, Chatham, 1952)

Lt. Col. G.P.G. Robinson, RE, *The Durand Mine and First World War Tunnel System in the Grange Area of the Canadian Memorial Park, Vimy* (School of Military Engineering, Chatham, 1989)

Günther Rückbeil, *Das 1. Rheinische Pionier=Bataillon Nr. 8 und seine Kriegsverbände im Weltkriege 1914/18*, (Gerhard Stalling, Berlin, 1926).

Ernst Schmidt, *Argonnen*, (Gerhard Stalling, Berlin, 1927).

M. Schwarte (Ed.) *Die Militärischen Lehren des Großen Krieges*, (E. S. Mittler & Sohn, Berlin, 1920).

M. Schwarte, *Kriegstechnik der Gegenwart*, (E. S. Mittler & Sohn, Berlin, 1927).

Friedrich Seesselberg, *Der Stellungskrieg 1914–1918*, (E. S. Mittler & Sohn, Berlin, 1926).

Lt. Col. J. Shakespear, *A Record of the 17th and 32nd Service Battalions Northumberland Fusiliers (N.E.R.) Pioneers 1914–1919*, (Northumberland Press Limited, Newcastle upon Tyne, 1926).

Lt. Col. J. Shakespear, *The Thirty-Fourth Division 1915-1919*, (H. F. & G. Witherby, London, 1921).

Johan Somers, *Imperial German Uniforms and Equipment 1907–1918*, [Vol. 1.], (Schiffer Military History, Atglen, PA, 2005).

Geoffrey Sparrow & J. N. MacBean, *On Four Fronts with the Royal Naval Division*, (Hodder & Stoughton, London, 1918).

R. C. Smart, *Recent Practice in Self-Contained Breathing Apparatus*, (Charles Griffin & Co. Ltd, 1921).

Maj. Gen. Sir Ernest D. Swinton, *Eyewitness*, London, Hodder and Stoughton, 1932.

Brig. Gen. Trevor Ternan, *The Story of the Tyneside Scottish*, (The Northumberland Press, Newcastle-Upon-Tyne, 1919).

Capt. [Hippolyte-Michel] Thobie, *La Prise de Carency par le Pic et Par la Mine*, (Berger-Levrault, Paris, 1918).

Capt. H. D. Trounce, *Notes on Military Mining*, (Engineer School, Washington DC, 1918).

Henry de Varigny, *Mines et Tranchées*, (Berger-Levrault, Paris, 1915).

Stephen Westman, *Surgeon with the Kaiser's Army*, (William Kimber, London, 1968).

Kenneth Wiggins, *Siege Mines and Underground Warfare*, (Shire, Princes Risborough, 2003).

Karl Witte, *3. Rheinisches Pionier=Bataillon Nr. 30* (Gerhard Stalling, Berlin, 1928).

Bruno Zschokke, *Handbuch der militärischen Sprengtechnik für Offiziere aller Waffen*, (Verlag von Veit & Comp., Leipzig, 1911).

Articles

Col. G. H. Addison, 'The German Engineer and Pioneer Corps,' *The Royal Engineers Journal*, Vol. LVI Dec. 1942, pp. 307–328.

[Anon.], 'German regulations for field fortifications and conclusions reached in Russia from the battles in defensive positions in Manchuria' [Translation from *The Militär Wochenblatt*], *Professional Memoirs. Corps of Engineers, United States Army and Engineer Department at Large*, Vol. II, No.7 (1910), pp. 347–369.

[Anon.], 'The Messines Ridge Mines, 7th June, 1917. German Accounts', *Royal Engineers Journal*, Vol. LIV, 1940, pp. 345–353.

H. Standish Ball, 'The Work of the Miner on the Western Front, 1915–1918', *Transactions of the Institution of Mining and Metallurgy*, Vol. XXVIII, 1919, pp. 189–248.

Bryan Frayling 'Tunnellers', *Royal Engineers Journal*, August 1988, pp. 170–176.

Capt. A. Gay, 'Sapping Operations, Especially for Infantry: From a lecture to cadets at Saint Maixant, France by Capt A. Gay, French Army', *Professional Memoirs. Corps of Engineers, United States Army and Engineer Department at Large*. Vol.10 (1918).

Harvey, R. N. Lt Col, 'Obstacles. Their tactical use, construction, and methods of destruction or surmounting them,' *The Royal Engineers Journal*, Vol. XX, No. 4, October 1914, pp. 217–222.

Bryn Hammond, 'Professionals and specialists: military mining on the Western Front', *Imperial War Museum Review*, No. 6 (Trustees of the Imperial War Museum, London, n d).

Maj. Gen. R. N. Harvey, 'Military Mining in the Great War, A Lecture delivered at the S.M.E., Chatham, on November 14th, 1929', *Royal Engineers Journal*, XLIII December 1929.

Maj. Gen. R. N. Harvey, 'Notes on Mining from the G.H.Q. Viewpoint', Tunnellers' Old Comrades Association *Bulletin*, No. 4, 1929.

Alistair Horne, *The Price of Glory Verdun 1916*, (Penguin Books, London, 1964).

Simon Jones, 'A Mine Rescue Officer on the Western Front', *Royal Engineers Journal*, Vol. 109, 1995, pp. 250-255.

W. Kranz, 'Minierkampf und Kriegsgeologie im Wytschaetebogen', *Vierteljahreshefte für Pioniere*, 1935.

'V. L', 'The Engineers in Grant's Campaigns of 1864-5', *Royal Engineers Journal*, Vol. LII, 1938, pp. 452–454.

David Dale Logan, 'The difficulties and dangers of mine-rescue work on the Western Front; and mining operations carried out by men wearing rescue-apparatus' and 'Accidents due to structural defects of apparatus or injury to apparatus; and the future of the Proto apparatus', *Transactions of the Institute of Mining Engineers*, Vol. LVII, 1918–19, pp. 197–259.

Brig. R. M. Merrell, 'The Berlin Spy Tunnel – a Memoir', *Royal Engineers Journal*, Vol. 116, 2002, pp. 105–107.

H. Tatham, 'Tunnelling in the Sand Dunes of the Belgian Coast', *Transactions of the Institution of Mining and Metallurgy*, Vol. XXVIII, 1919, pp. 249–260.

Capt. Töpfer, 'Technics in the Russo-Japanese War', (from the *Kriegstechnische Zeitschrift*, 1906), *Professional Memoirs. Corps of Engineers, United States Army and Engineer Department at Large*. Vol. II, No.6 (1910), pp. 174–201.

O. H. Woodward, 'Notes on the Work of an Australian Tunnelling Company in France', *Australasian Institute of Mining & Metallurgy, Proceedings*, No. 37, 1920, pp. 1–53.

Published digital media

Durand Group, *First Avenue Operation Beaumont Hamel 2002* (CD-ROM), (Durand Group, 2002).

Unpublished Dissertation

Ritchie Wood, *The Contribution of the British Mining Effort on the Western Front to the Allied Victory*, (Masters Degree, Birmingham University, 2008).

Internet sources

A. Girod, 'Les exhumations du Mont Cornillet', (2005), http://www.lced.org/div_04.php

Nagel, 'Extrait d'un rapport émis par le médecin allemand du bataillon, médecin en chef, le Docteur Nagel 11/476', http://pagesperso-orange.fr/champagne1418/recit/recit9.htm#cornillet

[Anon.], 'Topographische Srukturfragmente auf der Höhe Mort Homme', (Historischer Studienkreis Hamburg / Berlin), http://www.archivaria.de/morthomme.html

Index